SYNONYMS OF
THE OLD TESTAMENT

SYNONYMS OF
THE OLD TESTAMENT

THEIR BEARING ON CHRISTIAN DOCTRINE

BY THE

REV. ROBERT BAKER GIRDLESTONE, M.A.

HON. CANON OF CHRIST CHURCH, LATE PRINCIPAL OF
WYCLIFFE HALL, OXFORD

AUTHOR OF "DEUTEROGRAPHS," "FOUNDATIONS OF THE BIBLE,"
"DOCTOR DOCTORUM," ETC.

WM. B. EERDMANS PUBLISHING COMPANY
GRAND RAPIDS   MICHIGAN

This is a reproduction of the second edition,
which appeared in 1897

ISBN 0-8028 1548-0

'WHOSO is armed with the Text, the same is a right Pastor, and my
best advice and counsel is, that we draw water out cf the true Fountain ; that is, diligently to read in the Bible.   He is a learned Divine
that is well grounded in the Text ; for one text and sentence out of
the Bible is of far more esteem and value than many writings and
glosses, which neither are strong, sound, nor armour of proof.'

MARTIN LUTHER.

Reprinted, November 1983

PHOTOLITHOPRINTED BY EERDMANS PRINTING COMPANY
GRAND RAPIDS, MICHIGAN, UNITED STATES OF AMERICA

EXTRACT FROM PREFACE
TO THE FIRST EDITION

IN selecting subjects, it was hard to know where to stop; but
the leading topics of religious thought have been the same in all
ages of the Church; and the writer's aim has been to investigate
the usage of the terms in which these subjects were originally
brought before the human mind by the Great Author of our being.
Whilst admitting the importance of studying the writings of the
Early Fathers, and the works of English and foreign divines of
various schools, the writer holds that the pious, diligent, and
accurate study of the Sacred Text is the appointed means of obtaining a wise and practical understanding of the Truth, both as it
regards the character and work of God and the duty and hopes
of man.

To be unbiassed is impossible; but the writer has never wittingly evaded any text or any consideration which seemed to mili-
tate against a previously formed impression. He has endeavoured
to work as a student, not as a controversialist; and the various
chapters have been worked out independently, not as parts of a
system, although as a matter of fact they have thrown much light
on each other. Some readers will object that too many controverted
points are introduced; whilst others will complain that the writer's
views on doctrinal subjects are not sufficiently pronounced. Believing that sound theology ought to be based on accurate Biblical criticism, the writer could not discuss sacred words without touching
upon their doctrinal import. On the other hand, having put
together the materials which could best aid in the formation of a
judgment on the chief doctrines of the Bible, it seemed both un-
wise and unnecessary, even if there had been time and space for
the undertaking, to work out the details of a theological system.

A secondary aim has not been overlooked in preparing the following pages, namely, to illustrate the importance of the study of Hebrew. The difficulties at the outset are considerable, but when they are once overcome, every hour spent on the Hebrew Bible amply repays the student.

The English translations of texts do not always follow the A.V., nor has elegance been aimed at in translation, the object being the greatest possible clearness. Sometimes an alternative rendering or a paraphrase has been incorporated into the text, in order to bring out the sense more clearly.

The spelling of Hebrew words in Roman characters has often been a source of perplexity, owing to the variety of forms which they assume, and the different sounds which Hebrew letters take under different circumstances. The writer fears he has not been altogether successful or consistent in this matter, but he has generally followed Ewald's system, especially in putting TH for the Hebrew ט, the sound of which is neither T nor TH, but something between the two.

The chief books which have been used in the course of the preparation of the work are the Bible in various languages, Wilson's 'English-Hebrew Concordance' (Macmillan), a most valuable work; Fürst's 'Hebrew Concordance,' the 'Englishman's Hebrew Concordance' (Longman), and the Greek Concordances of Kircher, Trommius, and Bruder. Buxtorf's Rabbinical Dictionary has also been referred to, in order to ascertain the (comparatively) modern usage of Hebrew terms; but Rabbinical studies, whilst deeply interesting, do not contribute so much to the understanding of the Scriptures as might be supposed.

In conclusion, the author earnestly desires that readers of this book may gain—as *he* has gained in writing it—a deepened conviction of the truth, the unity, and the authority of the Scriptures, and that it may influence members of various parties and denominations to enter upon a critical and systematic study of the Sacred Records in their original languages. They will thus be drawn nearer to one another, and will be stimulated to live 'in unity of spirit, in the bond of peace, and in righteousness of life,' awaiting the Master's return to reward all who have laboured in His spirit and on His side;—'and then shall every man have praise of God.'

PREFACE

TO THE SECOND EDITION

DURING the quarter of a century which has passed away since this book was published, theological studies have made a considerable advance, both at the Universities and throughout the country. The issue of the Revised English Bible has done much for the ordinary student, and many of the points adverted to in the following pages have been dealt with in it, though not all. In some respects the Revisers might have gone much further, both in the choice and uniformity of renderings, and in the use of the hyphen.

I have dealt with the Scriptures not as a collection of Jewish literature, but as trustworthy and authoritative documents which are Divine in their origin, though Human in their expression. Having to do solely with the meaning and usage of words, I have avoided all reference to modern critical theories of the O. T. In preparing the work for the press in this revised form, I have kept before me, first, the needs of busy people who have not time to learn Hebrew, and secondly, the requirements of beginners in Hebrew, who need more encouragement than they sometimes get, my object being to help them to study Christian doctrine in the light of O. T. terminology.

I must add, in closing, an expression of thanks to my friend Prof. Sayce, who has kindly added references to the corresponding Assyrian words throughout.

HAMPSTEAD,
January 1897.

vii

CONTENTS

CHAPTER I.

ON THE TRANSLATION AND INTERPRETATION OF BIBLICAL TERMS.

CHAPTER II.

THE NAMES OF GOD.

CHAPTER III.

THE NAMES OF MAN.

CHAPTER IV.

THE SOUL AND THE SPIRIT.

Contents

Contents

CHAPTER XI.

REDEMPTION AND SALVATION.

CHAPTER XII.

ATONEMENT, FORGIVENESS, ACCEPTANCE.

CHAPTER XIII.

PURIFICATION, BAPTISM.

CHAPTER XIV.

JUSTIFICATION.

CHAPTER XV.

SANCTIFICATION, ANOINTING.

CHAPTER XVI.

OFFERINGS, ALTAR.

CHAPTER XVII.

WORD, LAW, COVENANT.

CHAPTER XVIII.

WORSHIP, PRAISE, PREACH.

CHAPTER XIX.

TEMPLE, TABERNACLE, CONGREGATION, CHURCH.

CHAPTER XX.

PROPHET, PRIEST, ELDER, MINISTER.

CHAPTER XXI.

KING, JUDGE, PUNISH.

CHAPTER XXII.

NATION, PEOPLE.

PAGES

CHAPTER XXIII.

EARTH, WORLD, HEAVEN.

CHAPTER XXIV.

DESTRUCTION, DEATH, HELL.

CHAPTER XXV.

SATAN, TEMPTER.

CHAPTER XXVI.

WITCHCRAFT, DIVINATION, SOOTHSAYING.

CHAPTER XXVII.

IDOL, GROVE, HIGH PLACE.

CHAPTER XXVIII.

ETERNAL, AGE TO COME.

SYNONYMS

OF THE

OLD TESTAMENT

CHAPTER I.

ON THE TRANSLATION AND INTERPRETATION OF BIBLICAL TERMS.

§ 1. *Need of Accuracy in the Translation and Interpretation of Scripture.*

THE controversies which exist in the Christian Church are a source of trouble and perplexity to every thoughtful mind. It might naturally be supposed that those who profess to follow one and the same Master, to venerate one and the same Book as the final court of appeal in matters pertaining to religion, would agree on all questions of faith and ecclesiastical order; but this is far from being the case. Roman Catholic theologians have sometimes asserted that Protestantism is the real source of religious dissensions, inasmuch as it exposes the Scripture to the private judgment of the individual; and they tell us that there would be no differences of opinion among Christians if all were to abide by the teaching of the Papal Church. There are many reasons, however, which may fairly lead us to doubt the propriety of such a solution. In the first place, controversy did not spring up with the Reformation. There were nearly a hundred shades of opinion, more or less erroneous, which had to be contended against in the earliest ages of the Church; and there were as hot discussions on theological questions in the Middle Ages as there are now. Secondly, there are far greater divergences of thought in religious matters among

A

the adherents of the Papacy than the world generally suspects.[1]
Thirdly, it is to be observed, that though the modern Church of
Rome has laid down in the decrees of the Council of Trent a scheme
or basis of doctrine according to which all Scripture is to be interpreted, yet she has never ventured to publish an infallible commentary which should explain all the hard passages of Scripture.
Thus even under Roman rule the door of controversy is practically
left open.   There were expositors of the Scripture in the Church
long before Christians were divided into Roman Catholics, Greek
Church, and Protestants.   Which of them shall we follow?   Shall
it be Origen or Chrysostom? Jerome or Augustine?   The answer
which the Church of Rome, in common with all other Churches,
has to give is, that no interpretations of Scripture by an individual,
however learned, are to be regarded as infallible; all that can be
done by the authorised leaders of the Church is to indicate a certain
line of faith, ecclesiastical order, and practice, according to which
the Bible ought to be interpreted, and by which all commentators
ought to be guided and tested.

In accordance with this view, one of the most learned of Roman
Catholic divines, Cardinal Cajetan, says, that if a new sense be discovered for a text, though it is opposed to the interpretation of a
whole torrent of sacred doctors, it may be accepted, provided it be
in accordance with the rest of Scripture, and with the teaching of
the Church.[2]   To Scripture alone, he adds, do we reserve this
authority, that we believe a thing *to be so* because it is *written so*.
The conclusion is, that the more thoroughly we study the Bible in
a right spirit and on just principles of interpretation, so much the
more closely shall we draw near to one another in faith and life.

---

[1] Jeremy Taylor, in his *Liberty of Prophesying*, gives an almost interminable
list of the differences of opinion which have existed in the Church of Rome.

[2] Cajetan, *Præf. in Pent.*   The original passage is as follows:—'Si quando
occurrerit novus sensus Textui consonus, nec a Sacra Scriptura nec ab Ecclesiæ
doctrina dissonus, quamvis a torrente Doctorum sacrorum alienus, æquos se præ-
beant censores.   Meminerint jus suum unicuique.   Solis Scripturæ Sacræ autori-
bus reservata est hæc autoritas, ut ideo credamus sic esse, quia ipsi ita scripserunt:
alios autem, inquit Augustinus, ita lego, ut quantalibet sanctitate doctrinaque præ-
polleant, non ideo credam sic esse, quia ipsi ita scripserunt.   Nullus itaque detes-
tatur novum Scripturæ sensum, ex hoc quod dissonat a priscis Doctoribus; sed
scrutetur perspicacius Textum ac contextum Scripturæ; et si quadrare invenerit,
laudet Deum, qui non alligavit expositionem Scripturarum Sacrarum priscorum
Doctorum sensibus, sed Scripturæ integræ sub Catholicæ Ecclesiæ censura.'
Cardinal Pallavicini (*Hist. Conc. Trid.* vi. 18) discusses the view thus boldly
enunciated by his brother Cardinal—a view by no means generally approved of—

The Bible is to be regarded in two aspects. It has its use for the unlearned, and its use for the teacher. The O. T. tells the story of God's dealings with man in language which is plain to the most unlettered. The N. T. likewise unfolds the truth concerning the Lord Jesus in terms which come home to every heart. The little child and the untaught man will find many hard words, many puzzling arguments, many allusions to Eastern customs and to points of contemporary history of which they know nothing; but they will also find certain solid facts which they can grasp, and they will meet with living words which will arrest their attention and cause them to regard God in a new light. The simple student may thus become a theologian in the true old sense of the word, though ignorant of what modern writers sometimes call theology : he may attain that loving and reverential disposition towards his Maker and Redeemer which is described as 'the beginning of wisdom,' though knowing nothing of the Early Fathers or of the German School of Thought.

It has been held in all ages of the Church that the humble and devout reading of the Scriptures is one of the most profitable sources of growth in godliness ; and nothing but the exigencies of controversy can have led the authorities of the Church of Rome to discourage the study of the Bible by the laity.[1]

Jerome, the prince of translators, and a 'churchman' of the highest order, speaks soundly on this point. So does Augustine ; and so do Chrysostom, Ambrose, Basil, and the leading Fathers of the Early Church. They knew that 'as the body is made lean by hunger and want of food, so is the soul which neglects to fortify itself by the Word of God rendered weak and incapable of every good work.'[2]

and says that it is not contrary to the decrees of the Council of Trent, as they simply declare heretical any doctrine or exposition which is opposed to the universal teaching of Fathers, Popes, and Councils.

[1] No translation of the Bible can be circulated with the sanction of the Papacy unless it be made from the Latin Vulgate, and be accompanied with notes taken from the 'Catholic doctors ; ' and even then no layman is (theoretically) permitted to read it unless he have a licence from his priest. The practical consequence of these steps has been that the Bible is almost an unknown book among the Roman Catholic laity.

[2] Augustine. Compare the words of Ambrose, '*Omnes ædificat scriptura divina.*' The acrimony with which the circulation of the Scriptures has been opposed by the Popes and their subordinates since the days of the Reformation presents a painful contrast with the earnest exhortations of such men as Jerome and Augustine.

It may, however, be said that the reading of the Bible should at any rate be confined to those who are previously instructed in Christianity. But there is nothing in its pages which calls for such restriction. Practically also it is found that the Scriptures in the mother tongue have penetrated further than the living voice of the missionary, and in hundreds—nay, probably thousands—of instances they have been the means of leading men to the knowledge of God. 'Missionaries and others,' says Sir Bartle Frere in his essay on Missions, 'are frequently startled by discovering persons, and even communities, who have hardly ever seen, and perhaps never heard, an ordained missionary, and who have nevertheless made considerable progress in Christian knowledge, obtained through the medium of an almost haphazard circulation of tracts and portions of Scripture.' The Reports of the British and Foreign Bible Society and the records of the various Missionary Societies abundantly testify to this point.

But the Bible is also the text-book for the theological teacher, and the final court of appeal on all religious questions. Even the Church of Rome, though putting her ecclesiastical traditions on a level with the Scripture, generally seeks to obtain the sanction of God's Word for her teaching, and never professedly holds any doctrine which, according to her interpretation, is positively opposed to the Bible. To this Book, then, all churches and denominations turn for support; and whatever our view of inspiration may be, we practically take its words as the basis of our teaching and as the standard of our orthodoxy.

§ 2. *Text and Linguistic Peculiarities of the Hebrew O. T.*

It would be quite beside the present purpose to discuss theories of inspiration, to attempt a solution of the various questions which relate to the Canon, or to weigh the authority of different texts, MSS., and readings. Suffice it to say that, with regard to the O. T., the text as now received, with the punctuation and accentuation [1]

---

[1] By *punctuation* is here signified, not the marking of pauses in the sense, but the determination of the vowel sounds. Supposing that in some old English inscription we met with the abbreviated word BRD, we might have to determine whether it stood for BREAD, BIRD, BARD, BEARD or BOARD. This we could usually do by means of the context; but there might be doubtful cases, and if such existed we should be glad to know how the word had been understood by others in past times. Thus tradition would come in to aid our reasoning powers, though, after all, tradition itself might sometimes be at fault. This just illus-

which represent the traditional way of reading it in early times, may be taken as substantially the same as that which existed when our Lord gave the weight of His authority to 'the Scriptures.' Several hundred Hebrew MSS. have been brought to light in modern times, and by their aid the Received text might be considerably amended;[1] but the changes thus introduced, though very numerous, and often of the deepest interest, would not affect the body of the book. The same is true in the case of the N. T., in which we have substantially (whether in the Received or the Revised Text) the writings which were regarded as authoritative in the early church.

The more closely we study the Hebrew Bible, the more we shall be struck with the uniform precision with which doctrinal terms are used throughout its pages. However we may choose to account for this fact, its practical bearing is manifest. If the Hebrew Scriptures use theological terms with marked exactitude, translations made from them are plainly missing something of Divine truth unless they do the same.[2]

There are some 1860 Hebrew roots in the O. T., many of which represent theological, moral, and ceremonial ideas, and our first busi-

---

trates the case of the Hebrew points. They were added to MSS. somewhere about the fifth century after Christ, in order to perpetuate the traditional mode in which the Hebrew words of the Bible used to be pronounced. Generally speaking, they are undoubtedly right ; but they are not infallible, and sometimes they are capable of correction by means of MSS. and early versions. The case of the word *bed* for *staff*, in Gen. **47**. 31, is the most familiar sample of the existence of two traditional modes of giving vowel sounds for a word whose consonants are the same.

The *accents* mark the tones, the emphasis, and the pauses in Hebrew, and thus they too at times affect the sense and even the division of the verses.

[1] Kennicott's two Dissertations, his Introduction to the Hebrew Bible which he edited, and the posthumous volume of his criticisms, illustrate what may be done in this direction. He may have been led to speak too strongly against what he conceives to be the wilful corruption of the text by the Masoretic Jews, but he has conferred a benefit by his labours upon both Jew and Christian, which, alas ! neither the one nor the other has yet learned to appreciate. Döderlein and Meisner's Critical Hebrew Bible contains the most convenient collection of readings from Kennicott's and De Rossi's MSS. Reference may here be made to *Deuterographs* (published by the Oxford Press), where the parallel texts of Kings and Chronicles and other books are so printed that the textual variations may be seen at a glance.

[2] The rule that each word of the original shall always have the same rendering is not to be pressed too far, but in argumentative and doctrinal passages it is very important. It would be easy to name a hundred passages, even in our Revised Version, which have seriously suffered through the neglect of this principle.

ness must be to find out their exact meaning. The opinion formerly held by some scholars, that all Hebrew words are equivocal, is now generally regarded as an exaggeration; and, although there are differences of opinion as to the meaning of some words, the dictionaries of such men as Gesenius and Fürst, being the embodiment of Jewish tradition confirmed and checked by investigations into cognate languages, give us a fair general idea of the meaning of the roots. This, however, is not enough. The Bible being regarded as a statute-book among Christians, the exact shade of meaning to be given to each Hebrew word ought, if possible, to be ascertained; and this can only be effected by an induction of instances leading to a definite conception of the sacred usage in each case.[1] When this has been discovered, the student is naturally led to inquire how far the sense thus arrived at has been, or can be, represented in other languages.

In making a translation of the Bible, it is impossible at first to find adequate words for some of the ideas which it contains; and there must always be a risk of considerable misunderstanding for a time. It is only gradually that the Biblical usage of a word becomes engrafted into a national language; and it has been noticed that the more fixed a language is at the time the translation is made into it, the greater is the difficulty of diverting words from their general use to the sacred purposes of the Bible.[2] The Hebrew language, though poor in some respects, *e.g.* in tenses, is rich in others; and probably no better language could have been selected for the purpose of preparing the way for Christ. Its variations of Voice give shades of meaning which cannot be found in the Indo-European languages. Its definite article, the way in which genders are marked in the verb as well as in the noun, its mode of marking emphasis and comparison, the gravity and solemnity of its structure, the massive dignity of its style, the picturesqueness of its idiom—

---

[1] The Founder of Inductive Science has not neglected to remind us that its principles are applicable to the study of the Bible. He urges an inquiry into 'the true limits and use of reason in spiritual things,' which would 'open men's eyes to see that many controversies do merely pertain to that which is either not revealed or positive, and that many others do grow upon weak and obscure inferences or derivations;' he calls men to investigate the Scriptures themselves instead of resting in Scholastic Divinity, because 'the more you recede from the Scriptures by inferences and consequences, the more weak and dilute are your positions;' and he extols 'positive divinity, collected upon particular texts of Scriptures.'—Bacon's *Advancement of Learning,* last chapter.

[2] See Rhenius on the principles of translating the Bible.

these make it peculiarly fitting for the expression of sacred truth.
Indeed, it is often a lesson in moral philosophy to take a Hebrew
dictionary and trace the gradual growth of meaning in certain words
as their signification advances from things which are seen and temporal to those which are not seen and eternal. Persons who have
made this point a study can well sympathise with the saying of
Luther, that he would not part with his knowledge of Hebrew for
untold gold.[1]

But how is it possible that a translation (unless it be in a cognate
language such as Arabic) should bring out all the shades of thought
which are to be found in the Hebrew Bible ? Thus the play upon
words,[2] which is so frequent in the original, as in the naming of
Jacob's sons or in the blessing pronounced upon them by their father,
can rarely be reproduced in another language. Such distinctions
as exist between the rest which means cessation and that which
signifies quietness, or between the fear which signifies terror
and that which marks respect, are often left unnoticed by translators. Again, who would have supposed that three Hebrew words
are rendered window in the account of the Deluge, three rendered
sack in the story of Joseph's brethren in Egypt, three rendered
leaven in the account of the Passover, three rendered ship in the
first chapter of Jonah, and five rendered lion in two consecutive
verses of Job (4. 10, 11) ? There are many other curiosities in
Hebrew which cannot be reproduced, such as the strange fact that
the same word is sometimes used not only in different senses, but
even with flatly contradictory meanings. For example, one word
signifies both to bless and to curse ; the same is the case with

---

[1] 'Hac quantulacunque cognitione infinitis millibus aureorum carere nolim'
(*Prol.* in Ps. **45**). Mr. Craik, in his little work on the Hebrew language
(Bagster), gives a few apt illustrations of the original meanings of its words.
'It has been well observed,' he says, 'that the original notions inherent in the
Hebrew words serve to picture forth with remarkable distinctness the mental
qualities which they designate. Thus, for instance, the usual term for "meek"
is derived from a root which signifies to afflict. The usual term for "wicked"
comes from a root that expresses the notion of restlessness. A "sinner" is
one who misses the mark. To "delight" in anything is literally to bend
down towards it. The "law" is that which indicates the mind of God
"Righteousness" is that which is perfectly straight. "Truth" is that
which is firm. "Vanity" that which is empty. "Anger" is derived from
a root meaning to breathe, quick breathing being a sign of irritated feeling.
To "trust" is to take shelter under, or to lean upon, or to cast oneself
upon. To "judge" is radically to smooth or make equal.'

[2] A large number of instances of *paronomasia* will be found at the end of
Canon Wilson's *Hebrew Concordance* (Macmillan).

words signifying to redeem and to pollute; to join and to separate; to afflict and to honour; to know and to be strange; to lend and to borrow; to sin and to purge; to desire and to abhor; to hurt and to heal.[1] Again, how much significance lies in the circumstance that a common word for buying and selling also means corn, that a name for money also means a lamb, that the general word for cattle is adopted to signify possession, and that the common name for a merchant was Canaanite.

As an illustration of the richness and variety of the Hebrew language, it may be mentioned that seven different words are rendered black in the A. V.; there are eight words for an axe, for an archer, for a hook; nine are rendered wine; twelve words stand for beauty, and the same number for body; thirteen for light, for bough, and for hand; fourteen are rendered dark; sixteen are rendered anger and chief; eighteen are rendered fear; twenty are rendered bind and cry. The words afraid or affrighted stand for twenty-one Hebrew words; branch for twenty-two; deliver for twenty-five; cover for twenty-six; gather for thirty-five; cut for forty-two; come for forty-seven; destroy for fifty-five; break for sixty; cast for sixty-one; bring for sixty-six; go for sixty-eight; and take for seventy-four.

§ 3. *The LXX a Connecting Link between the Hebrew O. T. and the Greek N. T.*

We now pass from the Hebrew original to the ancient Greek version, commonly called the Septuagint (LXX); and we may take as our starting-point the remark of a late scholar,[2] that the Christian revelation must be regarded as *Hebrew thought in Greek clothing*. No human language is capable of setting forth adequately the truth about the Divine Being; but it is a great help that the Scripture is written in *two* languages, one of a Semitic type and the other Aryan, the latter being not mere ordinary Greek, such as might be found in Plato or Demosthenes, but Greek of a peculiar kind, the leading words of which conveyed to the *Jewish* mind ideas which the Hebrew O. T. had originated.

Very different estimates have been formed respecting the value

---

[1] The Voice, however, is not always the same in these cases.

[2] Professor Duncan. Cappellus expressed the same sentiment in almost the same words.

of the LXX by various writers. In the early days of Christianity both Jews and Christians were inclined to regard it as a work of inspiration; and most of the early versions of the O. T. were made from it. But when the Jews found that it was so freely quoted and so much used by Christians, they took refuge in the assertion that it was not a faithful translation; and on this account the Greek versions of Theodotion, Aquila, and Symmachus were made. It was too late, however, to disparage a version which had been prepared before the days of controversy between Jew and Christian had begun; and the charges made against it were really the means of confirming its value, for Jerome was led to make his version from the Hebrew, partly at least that Christians might see that both Hebrew and Greek practically taught the same truth.

Modern critics have sometimes run to extremes in dealing with the LXX. Isaac Voss held that it was inspired; Cappellus, Munster, and Buxtorf attached but little value to it; Morinus respected it highly, but was inclined to correct it by the Latin Vulgate. Perhaps the fairest estimate of its value is to be found in the work of Hody on early versions, and in the criticisms of Kennicott.

This early Greek translation is, indeed, of the greatest value to the Biblical student, partly because it contains certain readings of importance which are not to be found in the existing Hebrew Bibles; partly also, because its renderings, though often free and paraphrastic, and sometimes even illiterate and unintelligible, frequently represent the traditional sense attached to the sacred text among the Alexandrian Jews. But, after all, the main value of the LXX lies in this, that it represents in a great measure the Greek religious language of many of the Jews of our Lord's time, and by its pages the Greek of the N. T. may be illustrated at every turn. Those who have access to Grinfield's Hellenistic Greek Testament, or any similar book, are aware that there is hardly a verse in the N. T. the phraseology of which may not be illustrated, and to some extent explained, by reference to the LXX. This fact, which is allowed by all students, has, nevertheless, hardly received that full attention from translators which it deserves. The idea that the LXX is often an indifferent authority from a literary and critical point of view, has caused them to neglect its study,[1]

---

[1] Certainly, if the Hebrew original were lost and our translation were made from the LXX, each word being rendered according to classical usage, whilst the substance of the O. T. would remain the same, we should have a very different (and a very mistaken) idea of many of its details.

whereas it ought to be regarded as a sort of dictionary in which
every N. T. word and phrase ought to be looked out, in order that
its usage in Judæo-Greek might be ascertained. Philo is good,
Josephus is good, but the LXX is best of all; both because of its
subject-matter, and because of the influence which it has exercised
over Christian theology.

It has often been remarked how much the English language
now owes to the Authorised Version of the Bible. Many English
words and phrases used in tracts and sermons, and other religious
writings, can only be understood by reference to the Bible. The
words themselves may sometimes be found in the works of authors
who lived before our version was prepared, and also in the writings
of many whose acquaintance with religious topics is very limited ;
but it is to the Bible that we turn for an explanation of such
words as *edify, justify, atonement, faith,* and *grace*. These and
many other words have been taken out of their ordinary secular
usage, and have been adopted for Christian purposes. Little by
little the new sense has eclipsed and obscured the old, so that in
some cases the latter has vanished altogether. As generations
succeed one another, if religious instruction and conversation continues, and if our Bible is not materially altered, Biblical language
may become still more naturalised amongst us.

What is true in the case of the English language has also been
perceived in many other languages ;—wherever, in fact, the Bible
is much studied. It often happens that missionaries gather their
knowledge of a new language, not from native literature, for
perhaps there is none, but from a translation of the Scriptures.
This forms the basis of their vocabulary, and the standard of their
idiom. Mr. Medhurst, in one of his works on China, notices that
this was the case in Malacca, where 'the style of preaching and
writing became in consequence very stiff and unidiomatic, and so
a new and barbarous dialect sprang up among the professors of
Christianity, which was in many instances barely intelligible to
the Mahometan population who speak the regular Malayan tongue.'

To take one other illustration of the mode in which a religious
language is formed, the reader may be reminded of the vocabulary
at the end of Dean Nowell's Catechism. It contains a list of
Latin words and modes of expression peculiar to Christians, and
differing from the ordinary classical usage.[1] We find among them

---

[1] Vocabula nostratia, et loquendi formæ Christianorum propriæ, in quibus a
communi more verborum Latinorum discessum est.

the words for angel, apostle, flesh, believe, create, crucify, demon, devil, elect, gospel, Gentile, idol, justify, sanctify, mediator, minister, mortify, repentance, resurrection, sacrament, scripture, temptation, tradition, and Trinity.

Applying these remarks to the influence of the LXX on Judæo-Greek, we may cite the opinion of Father Simon, who points out [1] that the versions made by the Jews have been servile renderings, and that style has never been considered in them. 'The words employed in these versions are not used in the ordinary style; rather the Jews, in their desire to give a verbal rendering to the words of the Hebrew text, have formed a certain strange language, which one might call the language of the synagogue. The Greek of the Septuagint version, and even that of the N. T., is of this nature. . . . It is this which has led certain learned critics to call it Hellenistic, so as to distinguish it from ordinary Greek.'

The late Dr. Campbell, of Aberdeen, ought to be named as having forcibly expounded the same view in his 'Preliminary Dissertations.'

The LXX may thus be regarded as a linguistic bridge spanning the gulf which separated Moses from Christ. Thus, to take a single short book, in the Epistle of St. James we meet with certain Greek words rendered *dispersion, temptation, trial, doubting, first-fruits, respect of persons, Lord of Sabaoth, in the last days, stablish your hearts, justify, double-minded, long-suffering, of tender mercy, faith, spirit, wisdom, the judge.* A Jew trained in the use of the LXX would naturally give to these words a peculiar richness and fulness of meaning from their usage in the Law and the Prophets when they appear as the rendering of certain Hebrew words and phrases.

The same would be the case with such expressions as 'son of perdition,' 'children of wrath,' 'if they shall enter into

---

[1] *Critique V. T.* 2. 3. Similar remarks are made by this acute writer in the very interesting preface to his French translation of the N. T. This work, including the Preface, was translated into English by William Webster, Curate of St. Dunstan's-in-the-West, and printed by Charles Rivington, in St. Paul's Churchyard, in 1730. Simon's rendering of the Greek would be generally regarded as too free, though not so paraphrastic as the version made by De Sacy. Whilst aiming at 'expressing the pure word of God with all possible exactness,' he was the very opposite of a *servile* translator. His remarks on the Greek particles and prepositions, viewed in relation to the Hebrew, are very instructive.

my rest,' 'by the hand of a mediator,' 'go in peace,' 'living waters.' [1]

It may be objected, however, that the use of the LXX was confined to a small portion of the Jews, that most of them spoke Aramaic, or (as it is called in the N. T.) Hebrew, and that therefore we must not press the resemblances between the Greek Testament and the LXX too far. The popular belief certainly is that our Lord and His disciples spoke in Aramaic,[2] an idea which is usually based on the fact that three or four words of this dialect are found amidst the Greek of the N. T. When Diodati propounded his view that our Lord was in the habit of speaking in Greek, it met with general contempt. De Rossi, no mean critic, controverted this novel view (as it was considered) in a treatise of some learning, though of short compass.[3] Dr. Roberts, in his 'Discussions on the Gospels,' has taken up the subject again, and has upheld the views of Diodati with much skill; but his arguments do not altogether carry conviction. It is strange that there should be any uncertainty about a point of such deep interest. There is probably more to be said on each side than has yet been said. The fact is, that a large number of the Jews in our Lord's time were bilingual: they talked both Aramaic and Judæo-Greek. We know that St. Paul's speech in Acts 22. was delivered in Hebrew, whilst that given in Acts 24. must have been delivered in Greek. Whilst, therefore, some of the discourses contained in the Greek Gospels must be considered as translations, others may possibly give us the *ipsissima verba* of Him who spake as never yet man spake. One thing is certain, that if the Greek Gospels do not give our Lord's original discourses, it is in vain to look to any other source for them. If *they* are not originals, we have no originals. The Syriac version of the N. T. bears evident traces of having been made from the Greek; so does the early Latin; so do all the other early versions; nor is there

---

[1] Mr. Webster rightly states, in his *Grammar of New Testament Greek*, that the influence of Hebrew on the Greek Testament is lexical rather than grammatical, but he somewhat underrates the bearing of the Hebrew voices, tenses, particles, and prepositions on N. T. Greek. Dr. Delitzsch, in the learned introduction to his translation of the Epistle to the Romans into Hebrew (Leipsig, 1870), has some interesting remarks on this subject.

[2] A compound of Aramaic and perhaps Arabic dialects, of which there were two or three forms, *e.g.* the Galilean, which was ruder than that spoken in Jerusalem. See Walton's *Prolegomena* on this subject; also De Rossi's work, referred to below; and compare Neubauer in *Studia Biblica*.

[3] *Dissertazioni della lingua propria di Cristo*, Milan, 1842.

any other practical conclusion to be arrived at than this, that the Greek Gospels are to be taken as accurate accounts of the words and deeds of the Saviour, written in a tongue which was intelligible to most Jews, to all Greeks, to many Romans, and to the great bulk of people whom the Gospel could reach in the course of the first century.

The LXX had certainly received a quasi-authorisation by age and custom in our Lord's time. Father Simon considers that it may have obtained its name from the fact that it was sanctioned by the Sanhedrim, which consisted of seventy members. He remarks that the Synagogue was used not only for a place of religious service, but as a school. And whereas the Talmud prohibited the reading of the law in any language but Hebrew during divine service, the LXX and also the Chaldee Targums were the main basis of teaching during school hours. Thus the Hebrew sacred books constituted the canon, whilst the LXX, so far as its rendering of those sacred books is concerned, became what we may call the Authorised Version in daily use in the school, and to a certain extent in the family; and the style of the N. T. would naturally be accommodated to it.[1]

---

[1] NOTE ON ST. MATTHEW'S GOSPEL.—A possible solution of a long-standing difficulty may be here presented for the consideration of the learned. The old tradition is that St. Matthew wrote his Gospel in Hebrew, and there is no reason to doubt it ; but the opinion of some modern scholars who have subjected the matter to the severest criticism is that it was written in Greek. But, even if their view is correct, some copies may have been specially prepared *in Hebrew characters* for those Jews who talked Greek but did not read it. In the present day we find Greek, Spanish, German, Polish, Persian, and Arabic works (especially Bibles) written and printed in the Hebrew character. Occasionally in the time of Origen, the Hebrew Scriptures were written in Greek letters. Why, then, should not the Greek Scriptures have been written in Hebrew characters for the benefit of a portion of the Jewish people who would otherwise have been debarred from access to them ? Transliteration is very common now. Arabic Scriptures are printed in Syriac characters, Turkish in Armenian, Turkish in Greek, Kurdish in Armenian, Indian languages in Arabic, Malay and even Chinese in Roman. The version which the Caraite Jews especially esteem is a Greek Pentateuch, printed at Constantinople in Hebrew characters. According to the opinion of most scholars, the whole Hebrew Scriptures have been transliterated from Samaritan characters, whilst the Samaritans still retain a text of the Pentateuch in their own character. There would, therefore, be nothing novel or extraordinary in the plan which is here conjectured to have been adopted by St. Matthew or some of his followers, namely, to make copies of the Gospel in Hebrew characters. Any person not versed in the study of Hebrew would naturally suppose, on seeing such a copy, that it was written in the Hebrew language. It is true that such scholars as Origen and Jerome would not be so imposed upon ; but there is no proof that either of these learned men had ever held the book in their hand.

The whole Bible may be regarded as written 'for the Jew first;'[1] and its words and idioms ought to be rendered according to Hebrew usage. The shades of meaning represented in the Hebrew Voices ought to be borne in mind by the translator, the *Piel* or intensive being peculiarly a technical or ceremonial Voice. Where critics or theologians differ as to the sense conveyed by the original, the translator must content himself by adhering to the most literal or the most natural rendering of the text. The great danger is the tendency to paraphrase. This may be illustrated by Martin Luther's translation of δικαιοσύνη θεοῦ 'the righteousness which is valid before God.'[2] The phrase certainly needs exposition, as many similar condensed expressions do, but the translator must leave this task to the expositor.

§ 4. *Our Lord's Method of Interpreting the O. T.*

There are about 600 quotations from the O. T. into the N. T. The great proportion of these are in accordance both with the Hebrew original and with the LXX, and where they vary it is frequently owing to textual corruption. They present us, when taken together, with a systematic key to the interpretation of the O. T. But it is curious to observe the great variety of deductions that have been made from examining the mode of citation. Father Simon, in his 'Critique' on the O. T. (lib. i. chap. 17), tells us that our Lord followed the method of interpreting the Scriptures which was adopted by the Pharisees, whilst He condemned their abuse of those traditions which had no solid foundation. 'St. Paul,' he continues, 'whilst he was one of the sect of the Pharisees, had interpreted Scripture in the light of tradition ; and the Church apparently from the beginning preferred this mode of elucidating the Bible to that adopted by modern grammarians who stick to the words. Thus neither our Lord nor His apostles appear to have taken pains to cite passages of Scripture word for word ; they have had more regard for the sense than for the letter of the text.' 'Their citations were made after the method of the Pharisees, who took no exact account of the words of the text when they cited it, being persuaded that religion depended more on the preconceived

---

[1] It may be objected that some portions at least of the N. T. were intended for Gentile readers ; this *may* have been the case, but they were written by Jews, and consequently more or less in the Judæo-Greek diction.

[2] *Die Gerechtigkeit, die vor Gott gilt.*

opinions (*préjugés*) obtained by tradition than on the simple words of Scripture which were capable of diverse explanations.' This bold statement, which if true would be very convenient for the Church to which Father Simon belonged, requires considerable modification. There were two schools among the Jews of our Lord's day who tampered with the letter of Scripture.   There were the Pharisees, who so overlaid Scripture with legal niceties of man's invention, that the Word of God was practically made void by their traditions.   And there were the Cabbalists, who applied a mystical interpretation to the very letters of which the words of Scripture were composed, and thus lost the plain sense which lay on the surface.   In opposition to these two schools, our Lord generally adopted the plan of interpreting the Scripture with its context, and with a due regard both to the claims of grammar and the harmony of the Divine plan of revelation.   In this respect, as in others, He left us an example that we should follow in His steps.

§ 5. *Illustrations of the Use of the LXX in Translating the N. T.*

A few instances may be given, in conclusion, to illustrate the bearing which the language and idiom of the LXX has upon the meaning of the N. T.

(*a*) In 2 Thess. 3. 5, we read, 'The Lord direct your hearts into the love of God and into the patient waiting for Christ.' The latter words are more literally rendered in the margin and in the R. V. 'the patience of Christ.' This expression would not convey much sense to the reader, unless he took it to signify ' the patience which Christ exhibited when he suffered,' or 'the patience which Christ bestows upon his people.'   Were our translators right in departing from the literal rendering, and in giving a clear and definite meaning to the Apostle's words, and one which is in strict conformity with the context? Yes; they have doubtless hit the sense; and their view of the passage is confirmed by the Greek rendering of Ps. 39. 7, which literally runs thus, 'And now what is my patience? is it not the Lord?' This answers to the rendering of the A. V. and R. V., 'And now, Lord, what wait I for? My hope is in thee.' It may well be supposed that if this passage from the LXX was not in the Apostle's mind as he wrote, yet the phraseology of it, which was so familiar to him, gave form to his thought.

(*b*) In a Greek Testament which is in the hand of every student, it is said in a note on 2 Thess. 1. 11 (on the words 'fulfil all the good pleasure of his goodness') that 'ἀγαθωσύνη will not refer with any propriety to God, of whom the word is *never* used.'[1] Accordingly, it is altered in the R. V. But the usage of the LXX should be considered before the question be thus summarily decided. Accordingly, on turning to that book, we find that the word ἀγαθωσύνη is used of God in at least three passages.

(c) Readers of the English Bible must have experienced some surprise at meeting twice over with the singular expression, 'thy holy child Jesus' in Acts 4. 27 and 30 (see also, Acts 3. 13, 26). The Greek word παῖς may certainly be rendered child, though the diminutive παιδίον is more usually adopted in the N. T. for this purpose. But why should the Christians make such special mention of 'the holy child'? The usage of the N. T. may first be consulted. The word occurs at most twenty-five times. In seven or eight of these passages it is rendered 'servant,' whilst in others it is rendered 'child.' It is first applied to our Lord in Matt. 12. 18, where the prophecy of Isaiah (42. 1) is referred to. Our translators here wisely allowed themselves to be guided by the Hebrew word, of which παῖς is the rendering, and to translate 'Behold my servant whom I have chosen.' In accordance with this passage the Virgin Mary sings of God, 'He hath holpen his servant (παῖς) Israel' (Luke 1. 54); and Zacharias praises God for raising up a horn of salvation (*i.e.* a mighty Saviour) in the house or family of His servant (παῖς) David. It is natural to suppose that the Christians referred to in Acts 4. 27, 30, did not mean to speak of Christ as God's child, but as His servant. This view is borne out by the fact that they had in the very same prayer in which the words occur used the same expression with reference to David's saying, 'Lord, thou art God . . . who by the mouth of thy servant (παῖς) David hast said, why did the heathen rage.' For these reasons it would be well to translate παῖς servant in the four passages in the Acts in which it is used of the Lord.

An examination of other passages in which David is called God's servant will greatly tend to confirm the rendering given above. See Jer. 33. 15; Ezek. 34. 23, 24; 37. 24, 25.

These samples, perhaps, are sufficient to illustrate the way in which the LXX forms a connecting link between the O. T. and the N. T. Many more will be brought to light in the course of the following pages, in which the leading Hebrew terms relating to the

---

[1] *Vide* Alford in loco.

nature of God and man, the work of redemption, the ministrations under the law of Moses, together with other important topics, are discussed. If all difficult passages in the N. T. were dealt with in accordance with the principles thus illustrated, it does not seem too much to say that many obscurities would be removed, and the perplexities in which the plain English reader often finds himself involved would be considerably reduced.

Before closing this chapter a word must be added concerning the language in which the earliest pages of the Bible were written. It is, to say the least, possible that the records of the events which happened before Abraham's time are themselves pre-Abrahamic. If so, they may have been written in a language or dialect very different from Biblical Hebrew. The same hypothesis would hold good in a measure with reference to the records of the period between Abraham and Moses. All that we can do, however, is to take the Book of Genesis as it stands, and to discuss its words as if they were the original, or at any rate as if they fairly represented it, just as we take the Greek of the Gospels as an adequate representation of the language in which our Lord usually spoke.

CHAPTER II.

THE NAMES OF GOD.

A TRANSLATOR of the Bible into the languages of heathendom finds his work beset with difficulties at every step. He has to feel about for bare words, and this not merely in such matters as weights, measures, animals, and trees, but in others of far greater importance. He constantly has to pause and consider whether he had better use a native word which but indifferently represents the original, or whether it be preferable to transfer or transliterate a word from the Hebrew, Greek, or some other language. In the one case he is in danger of creating a misunderstanding in the mind of his readers; in the other he is certain to convey no sense at all until by oral teaching, or otherwise, the newly-grafted word has become familiar. He wants to speak of the flesh, and can only find a word which signifies meat; he has to speak of angels, and must choose between messengers and genii; he wants to write of the kingdom of heaven, and finds that such a thing as a kingdom is unknown; he has to speak concerning the soul and the spirit to those who are apparently without a conception of anything beyond the body, as was the case with the Bechuana tribes.[1] Thus a version of the Scripture must needs be full of anomalies and obscurities at first, and though the substantial facts contained therein may be plainly set down, a clear understanding of its details will only be arrived at after much study on the part of native readers.

The difficulty of the translator usually begins with the name of God. To us English people this is so much a thing of the past that we cannot understand it; but, as a matter of fact, it has caused perplexity, if not dissension, in the case of many new translations. In China the missionaries of the various Christian bodies are not to this day agreed as to the right word to be adopted, and consequently they will not all consent to use the same editions of the Bible.

---

[1] See Moffat's *South African Sketches*. Things are very different among the Bechuanas now.

Some approve of the name *Tien-Chu,* a title which signifies 'the Lord of heaven,' which has been adopted for three centuries by the Roman Catholics; some adopt *Shang-ti,* the Confucian name for 'the Supreme Ruler;' others are in favour of *Shin,* which is generally supposed to mean 'spirit.' The controversy between the upholders of these various opinions has been very warm and earnest, and has called forth several deeply interesting essays. The arguments have usually gathered round one question,—Ought we to choose a *generic* name for God, *i.e.* a name which represents to the heathen mind a *class* of beings, or ought we to choose what may be called a *proper* name, even though that name may present a most unworthy notion of the Deity?

§ 1. *The Name* ELOHIM.

The general Hebrew name for God is **Elohim** (אלהים). Sometimes it is used with a definite article, sometimes without. Altogether it occurs 2555 times. In 2310 of these instances it is used as the name of the living and true God, but in 245 passages it appears to be adopted in lower senses.

Although plural in form,[1] the name is generally used with a singular verb when it refers to the true God.[2]

This name properly represented One only Being, who revealed Himself to man as Creator, Ruler, and Lord. It was His own peculiar title, and ought to have been confined to Him. Accordingly we read, 'in the beginning God (**Elohim** in the plural) created (in the singular) the heavens and the earth.'

The first hint at the possibility that the title **Elohim** might be shared by others besides the Creator is to be found in the serpent's suggestion, 'Ye shall be as **Elohim,** knowing good and evil' (Gen. 3. 5). The translators of the A. V. render the word 'gods,' but our first parents only knew of one **Elohim**; they heard His voice from time to time, and perhaps they saw His form; they addressed Him in the singular number; and the idea of any other being to be called **Elohim** but this One could not have entered their imagination

---

[1] This is indicated by the termination *-im,* as in such words as Cherub-im and Seraph-im. Dr. Sayce tells me that in the Tel el Amarna tablets Pharaoh is addressed as gods.

[2] The exceptions are Gen. 20. 13, 35. 7; 2 Sam. 7. 23 (but see 1 Chron. 17. 12). The Samaritan Pentateuch has altered those in Genesis to the singular Sometimes the adjective which agrees with Elohim is plural, as in Jos. 24. 19; sometimes singular, as in 2 Kings 19. 4.

until the Tempter said to them, 'Ye shall be as God, knowing good and evil' (see R. V.).

In after ages the worship of the Creator as **Elohim** began to be corrupted. The Name, indeed, was retained, but the nature of Him who bore it was well-nigh forgotten. When men were divided into different nations, and spoke various dialects and languages, they must have carried with them those notions of **Elohim** which they had inherited from their fathers, but the worship which was due to Him alone was in the lapse of ages transferred to the souls of the departed, to the sun, moon, and stars, and even to idols made by men's hands.

It has been supposed that some sanction is given to the theory that the name **Elohim** is generic by the fact that idols are called by this name in Scripture. Some instances of this usage may therefore be cited for examination.

In Gen. 35. 1, 2, 4, we read as follows : 'And **Elohim** said unto Jacob, Arise, go up to Beth-el and dwell there, and build there an altar, unto the **El** that appeared to thee when thou fleddest from before thy brother Esau. Then Jacob said to his house and to all that were with him, Put away the strange **Elohim** that are among you . . . and they gave unto Jacob all the strange **Elohim** that were in their hands, and their earrings which were in their ears, and Jacob hid them under the oak which was by Shechem.' The **Elohim** in this case seem to have been images, perhaps charms worn on the person, similar to those which the ancient Egyptians used to wear, and which have been exhumed or manufactured by hundreds in modern days. The word **nacar** (נכר), here rendered stran ge, is used in Scripture in two opposite senses, for *to know*, and *not to know;* it here probably means foreign or alien, in which sense it is frequently applied to idolatrous worship in Scripture.

In Gen. 31. 19, we read that Rachel had stolen her father's images (**teraphim**[1]), but Laban calls them his **Elohim** (verse 30), and Jacob, adopting the word, says, 'with whomsoever thou findest thine **Elohim**, let him not live.' Laban, then, worshipped **teraphim** as **Elohim**, though he ought to have known better, for he knew the name of **Jehovah** (Gen. 30. 27, 31. 49), and he was not ignorant of the real **Elohim**, whom his own father had worshipped (Gen. 31. 29, 50, 53).

We also read of 'the **Elohim** of Egypt' (Exod. 12. 12, A.V. gods ; the margin has princes, but see Num. 33. 4) ; of molten **Elohim**

---

[1] For further remarks on the nature of the *Teraphim*, see chap. xxvii. § 7.

(Lev. **19**. 4); of 'the **Elohim** of the heathen' (Exod. **23**. 24); also of Chemosh, Dagon, Milcom, and other idols which were designated as **Elohim**. When the Israelites made the molten calf out of their golden earrings (Exod. **32**. 3, 4), they said of it, 'These be thy **Elohim**, O Israel,' by which they practically meant 'this is thy God,' for they regarded the image as a representation of **Jehovah** (verse 5).[1]

Jethro, the father-in-law of Moses, draws a distinction between the true and the false **Elohim** when he says, 'Now know I that **Jehovah** is greater than all the **Elohim**, for in the matter wherein they dealt proudly he was above them' (Exod. **18**. 11); yet this very confession is so worded as to imply not only that the priest of Midian had hitherto been in the dark on the subject, but also that he still had a lingering belief in the existence of inferior **Elohim**. The same ignorance and superstition was to be found amongst the children of Israel; and the primary lesson which the Lord sought to teach them during their journeyings in the wilderness was that they were to restore the name **Elohim** to its original and sole owner. 'Thou shalt have no other **Elohim** before me'[2] (Exod. **20**. 3). 'Make no mention of the name of other **Elohim**, neither let it be heard out of thy mouth' (Exod. **23**. 13). '**Jehovah** he is **Elohim** in heaven above and upon the earth beneath; there is none else' (Deut. **4**. 39). So in the Song of Moses (Deut. **32**. 37, 39) we read concerning the heathen, 'Where are their **Elohim**, the rock on which they leaned? . . . I even I am he, and there is no **Elohim** with me.' Once more, the utter anomaly of using the word **Elohim** for others than the true God is clearly indicated in the prayer of Hezekiah (2 Kings **19**. 18), 'Of a truth, **Jehovah**, the kings of Assyria have destroyed the nations and their lands, and have cast their **Elohim** into the fire : for they were no **Elohim** but the work of men's hands, wood and stone.'

---

[1] David Mill, in one of his *Dissertationes Selectæ*, discusses the symbolical meaning of the golden calf, and comes to the conclusion that it represented, not Apis, but Typhon (*i.e.* Set), to whom the Egyptians attributed all evil. The people of Israel knew full well that their God had looked with no favouring eye upon Egypt, and it is therefore not improbable that in choosing a symbol to represent Him they would select that which the Egyptians regarded as their evil genius.

[2] Literally, 'in addition to my face.' Some Hebrew students regard this expression not merely as a Hebrew idiom, but as setting forth that the Face or Manifestation of God is God. They have hence argued for the Deity of Christ; but the argument in the form in which it is sometimes advanced is rather perilous, because it is inapplicable to other passages, *e.g.* Exod. **33**. 20 : 'Thou canst not see my face, for there shall no man see me and live.' It is nevertheless true that we do behold 'the glory of God in the face or person of Jesus Christ' (2 Cor. **4**. 6).

§ 2. *The Name* Elohim *and the Trinity.*

It is clear that the fact of the word **Elohim** being plural in form does not at all sanction polytheism ; but we have now to consider whether it may fairly be taken as a testimony to the plurality of Persons in the Godhead. It is certainly marvellously consistent with this doctrine, and must remove a great stumbling-block out of the path of those who feel difficulties with regard to the acknowledgment of the Trinity in Unity. Great names are to be cited for taking a step further, and for adducing, as a proof of the Trinity, the words, '**Elohim** said, Let *us* make man in *our* image after *our* likeness' (Gen. **1.** 26). Father Simon notes that Peter Lombard (1150) was the first to lay stress upon this point ; though probably the argument was not really new in his time. Many critics, however, of unimpeachable orthodoxy, think it wiser to rest where such divines as Cajetan in the Church of Rome and Calvin among Protestants were content to stand, and to take the plural form as a *plural of majesty*, and as indicating the greatness, the infinity, and the incomprehensibleness of the Deity. Perhaps the idea unfolded in the plural form **Elohim** may be expressed more accurately by the word Godhead or Deity than by the word God ; and there is certainly nothing unreasonable in the supposition that the name of the Deity was given to man in this form, so as to prepare him for the truth that in the unity of the Godhead there are Three Persons.

As long as the passage above quoted stands on the first page of the Bible, the believer in the Trinity has a right to turn to it as a proof that Plurality in the Godhead is a very different thing from Polytheism, and as an indication that the frequent assertions of the Divine Unity are not inconsistent with the belief that the Father is God, the Son is God, and the Holy Ghost is God. It is well known that the Hebrews often expressed a word in the plural, so as to give it a special or technical meaning, as in the case of the words Blood, Water, Wisdom, Salvation, Righteousness, Life ; and this is in favour of what has just been advanced. The use of the plural in the language of majesty and authority tends to the same conclusion. In these cases it is implied that the word in the singular number is not large enough to set forth all that is intended ; and so in the case of the Divine Name the plural form expresses the truth that the finite word conveys an inadequate idea of the Being Whom it represents.

Other names of God will be found to be in the plural also ; and it is worthy of notice that in the well-known passage in Ecclesiastes (12. 1) the Hebrew runs thus, 'Remember now thy Creators in the days of thy youth.'

§ 3. *Secondary Uses of the Name* ELOHIM.

Another use of the word **Elohim** has now to be noticed. We read in Exod. 4. 16, that God said to Moses, with reference to his brother Aaron, 'thou shalt be to him in the place of **Elohim**.' From these words it would appear that Moses was to be regarded by Aaron as standing in immediate relation to God,—not, however, as on a level with Him, for God did not say 'thou shalt be *as* (כ) **Elohim**,' but '*for* (ל) **Elohim**.'[1] Moses was instructed to convey the Divine message to Aaron, who, in his turn, was to announce it to Pharaoh. Similarly in chap. 7. 1, the Lord says to His servant, 'Behold I have appointed thee **Elohim** to Pharaoh, and Aaron shall be thy prophet.' It is evident that the name of God was here given to His human representative, as such. The LXX has τὰ πρὸς τὸν θεόν.

The usage of the word in these passages may be illustrated by a reference to our Lord's teaching. When accused by the Jews of making Himself God, He answered, 'Is it not written in your law, I said, Ye are gods? If he called them gods, unto whom the word of God came,—and the Scripture cannot be broken,—say ye of him, whom the Father hath sanctified, and sent into the world, Thou blasphemest; because I said, I am the Son of God?' (John 10. 34–36.) The passage which our Lord here refers to is in Psalm 82, and begins thus: 'Elohim taketh his stand (נצב) in the gathering of El; in the midst of **Elohim** he doeth judgment.' The Psalmist proceeds to rebuke this gathering of **Elohim**, who were evidently judges, and who were responsible for judging in accordance with the word of the Lord: 'How long will ye administer perverted justice, and favour wicked men? Deal justly with the poor and fatherless: acquit the afflicted and needy. Deliver the poor and

---

[1] The R. V. is in error here. In chap. 6. 7, we have the same expression (לאלהים) rendered in the A. V., 'I will be to you a *God.*' It might be best, therefore, to consider the emphatic verb *to be* in the above passage as signifying (in conjunction with the preposition) *to represent*—'Thou shalt represent **Elohim** to him.' In Zech. 12. 8, there is a more remarkable expression; it is said that 'the House of David shall be as God and as the Angel of the Lord before them.' Here we have not representation but equality; and the passage has its fulfilment in Christ.

needy : rescue them from the hand of wicked men.' Yet the rebuke was unheeded. Alas! 'They know not, neither do they perceive; they go on walking in darkness : all the foundations of the land (*i.e.* its judges) are moved from their course.' Then comes the retribution following on their neglect of these august privileges and duties. 'It is I myself[1] that said ye are **Elohim** ; and all of you children of the Highest. Yet after all ye shall die as Adam, and as one of the princes shall ye fall.' The Psalmist concludes with the prophetic aspiration, 'Arise, thou **Elohim**, administer just judgment in the land : for it is thou that hast all the nations for thine inheritance.' Our Lord, by referring to this Psalm, evidently meant His hearers to understand that if earthly judges were called 'gods ' in Scripture because they were to regulate their decisions by the Word of God, it could be no blasphemy in Him whom the Father hath sent into the world to call Himself Gods Son. If *they* represented God, how much more did *He*.

In accordance with the words of the Psalm just referred to, we read in Exod. 22. 8, 9, 'If the thief be not found, then the master of the house shall be brought unto the judges (**ha-Elohim**), to decide whether he hath put his hand unto his neighbour's goods. The cause of both parties shall come before the judges (**ha-Elohim**), and whom the judges (**Elohim**) condemn, he shall pay double to his neighbour.' In the twenty-eighth verse, where our translators have somewhat unfortunately put 'thou shalt not revile the gods,' we read **Elohim** again, and consistently with the previous passages we should render it, 'thou shalt not revile judges, nor speak evil of a leader among thy people.' See R. V., margin. This passage was referred to with a latent shade of irony by St. Paul when he was called to account for speaking sharply to Ananias, who professed to judge him after the law whilst causing him to be smitten contrary to the law (Acts 23. 5).

The judges are also called **Elohim** in Exod. 21. 6, where the account is given of the master boring his servant's ear in the presence of the magistrates. It is possible that the witch of Endor, when she said, 'I see **Elohim** ascending from the earth,' used the word in this sense, that we might render the passage, 'I see judges ascending

---

[1] It is only in some such way as this that one can express the force of the emphatic Hebrew personal pronoun. Our translators have not often adopted this plan, but in other versions (*e.g.* the French of Ostervald) the distinction between the expressed and the unexpressed pronoun has been marked in this way. The R. V. fails here.

from the earth.' Both the noun and the participle are in the plural number in this passage.[1] The R. V. has noted this point.

In all these passages the word **Elohim** indicates not beings who are to be worshipped, but a body of responsible magistrates who are called by this name because they represent the only true **Elohim**, who is God of gods and Lord of lords. Accordingly we read that 'the men between whom there is a controversy shall stand before **Jehovah**, before the priests and the judges' (Deut. **19**. 17).

§ 4. *The Application of the Name* ELOHIM *to Angels.*

There is yet another use of the word **Elohim** which must not be passed over. The Samaritan Version and also the LXX have adopted the word angels to represent it in several places, and the English translators, partly guided by the teaching of the N. T., have occasionally followed their example.

Some critics have been inclined to render the words in Gen. **3**. 5, 'Ye shall be as angels'; but there is no ground for such an interpretation. In Job **38**. 7, 'the sons of God' who shouted for joy are designated angels by the LXX, but this is by way of commentary rather than translation. Compare Ps. **138**. 1.

In Heb. **1**. 6, we read, 'when he bringeth the first-begotten into the world, he saith, And let all the angels of God worship him.' The writer here cites words which are to be found in some copies of the LXX in the Song of Moses (Deut. **32**. 43), but there is no Hebrew equivalent for them in our existing text. The verses which follow carry the reader on from the day of Moses to a time yet to come when God 'will avenge the blood of his servants, and will render vengeance to his adversaries, and will be merciful to his land and to his people.' This will be at the time of the restitution of all things which have been spoken of by all the holy prophets from old time (Acts **3**. 21). Whilst the writer of the Epistle to the Hebrews probably had the Song of Moses in his mind when he quoted the words of the LXX, there may be a secondary reference to Psalm **97**. 7, where we read, 'worship him all ye gods (**Elohim**),' but where the LXX has rendered, 'worship him all ye his angels.'

In the 8th Psalm the A. V. runs thus, 'What is man, that thou art mindful of him? and the son of man, that thou visitest him? For thou hast made him a little lower than the angels, and hast

---

[1] See chap. xxvi. § 3, for a further reference to the scene here noticed.

crowned him with glory and honour. Thou madest him to have dominion over the works of thy hands.' Here the Hebrew has **Elohim**; and were it not for the sanction given to the LXX interpretation in Heb. 2. 7, our translators would probably have given a literal rendering, as the R. V. has done.

Gesenius, Hengstenberg, and other critics, understood the Psalmist to mean that the Son of Man should be but little below the glory of God. So Calvin, 'parum abesse eum jussisti a divino et cœlesti statu.' We might, perhaps, paraphrase the words, 'thou hast bereft [1] him for a little while of the divine glory.' Compare Phil. 2. 7. In giving this interpretation of the words, though we do not adopt the exact rendering of the LXX, we arrive at a substantial agreement with its teaching. The fact announced in the Hebrew text with regard to man generally, is fulfilled with regard to Christ in such a mode as the LXX describes, and as the writer of the Epistle to the Hebrews sanctions.

§ 5. *Difficulties in Translating the Name* Eloнıм.

We have seen that the name **Elohim** is properly a title belonging to one Being, who is the Creator of heaven and earth, and the Sustainer of all existence. The question now returns, how is the word to be dealt with in translation? Three possible courses present themselves. The Hebrew word might be transliterated, as is sometimes done with the name Jeнovah; or the name of some native object of worship might be substituted for it; or the original meaning of the word might be reproduced by a translation.

To deal with the last proposal first, there could be no valid objection to such a course, if no better plan presented itself. It is agreed by almost all scholars that the name **Elohim** signifies the putter forth of power. He is the Being to whom all power belongs. The lowest of heathen tribes are compelled to acknowledge that there is a Power in existence greater than their own, and the missionary constantly has to take this acknowledgment as a basis on which he may plant a more complete theology.

The proposal that the Hebrew name for the Divine Being should be transliterated, and used alone or in combination with those of native deities, has been received with greater favour by some missionaries. They have looked upon it as a means of avoiding the

---

[1] The word is so rendered in Eccles. 4. 8.

danger in which every translator is manifestly involved, of giving a seeming sanction to false religion by the adoption of a name which conveys false ideas. But, after all, whilst seeking to escape one evil, the transliterator runs into another, for he would be laying himself open to the charge that he was setting forth strange gods.

The other plan is to single out that name which is, on the whole, the best representative of a personal and powerful Being, leaving it for the general teaching of Scripture and for the oral instruction of the missionary to lift up men's minds to higher ideas of this Being than they had before.

If all the names of God were to be rejected which had ever been used for idolatrous purposes, it is hard to know what would be left. **Elohim** itself was so used; the same is the case with the Arabic form *Allah*, with the Greek *Theos*, the Ethiopic *Amlak* (cf. *Moloch*), the Egyptian *Nout*, the Hungarian *Isten*, the Albanian *Pernti*, the Tartar *Tengri*, and many others, which are sanctioned in time-honoured versions. Nay, what would happen to the Georgian *Ghut*, the Persian *Khuda*, the German *Gott*, and the English *God?* Fortunately our idea of God comes not from the etymology of the word, nor from its use in the days of our heathendom, but from the truths which we have been taught about Him from our childhood. This is exactly the point to be borne in mind. The truth about God is gathered not so much from the Name as from what is taught concerning Him who bears it. The knowledge of the nature and character of God is gradually acquired through the study of the Scriptures.

The American Bishop Boone, in his contribution to the Chinese discussions, says that we should render the name of God by the highest generic word which represents an object of worship. If this theory were to be carried out, then the first verse of the Bible would practically run thus : ' In the beginning an object of worship created the heavens and the earth.' This, however, would be an inversion of the right order of thought. God is to be worshipped because He is Creator. His works constitute, in great measure, His claim to worship. The same writer also quotes Lactantius and Origen in favour of a generic name for God. These learned men wrote centuries after the matter had been practically settled, so far as regards the Greek language, by the usage of the LXX, and when it would have been too late, even if it had been good for any reason, to substitute *Zeus* for *Theos*. Dr. Malan, indeed, has shown, in his work on the Names of God,[1] that *Zeus* and *Theos* were originally, in all probability, the same word.   But we have a greater witness than Dr. Malan, even that of the Apostle of the Gentiles, who, after quoting two heathen hymns written in honour of *Zeus*, argues from them in favour of the spiritual nature of *Theos*, who made the world.

The passage in the Acts (chap. 17.) here referred to deserves special notice.   When St. Paul reached Athens he found that it was wholly given to idolatry (κατείδωλον), an expression which falls in all too well with the Roman satirist's remark that it was easier to find a god than a man in that city.   Accordingly, the Apostle held constant discussions (διελέγετο), not only with the Jews and proselytes whom he found in the synagogue,[2] but also with anybody whom he could meet with in the Agora.   Here certain of the Epicureans, who were Atheists, and of the Stoics, who were Pantheists, fell in with him from day to day;[3] and while some spoke of him with utter scorn—his Gospel being 'foolishness' to them—others came to the conclusion that he was setting forth certain *demons* (A. V. 'gods') which were foreign to their city.   By 'demons' these philosophers meant very much the same as the Mahommedans mean by their *genii;* their ideas about them would be very vague.   Sometimes they seem to have been regarded as the souls of the departed, sometimes as guardian angels, sometimes as evil influences, sometimes as what we call *demi-gods.*[4]

Here, then, St. Paul found himself confronted with idolatry and demon-worship, the two substitutes for the worship of the living God which are to be found amongst almost all the nations of the earth.   Even the *fetish* of the African rain-maker is connected with a mysterious unseen power, which is supposed to work upon a man's life and possessions.   The acknowledgment of such hidden influence harmonises all too readily with Pantheism, and is not inconsistent even with Atheism.   A man may be a Positivist

---

[1] *Who is God in China?*—a powerful argument in favour of *Shang-ti.*

[2] The A. V. runs thus: 'Therefore disputed he in the synagogue with the Jews, and with the devout persons ;' but there ought to be no comma after the word Jews.   The σεβόμενοι, or devout proselytes, went to the synagogue, where Paul doubtless discoursed in Greek.   The R. V. is correct.

[3] The imperfect tense is used throughout.

[4] No distinction can be drawn between δαίμων and δαιμόνιον ; both were applied to the deity, to fortune, to the souls of the departed, and to genii or demigods, beings part mortal part divine (μεταξὺ θεοῦ τε καὶ θνητοῦ) as Plato calls them (*Symp.* p. 202 *d.*).

and yet a Spiritualist. He may, in profession at least, deny that
there is a personal *causa causarum*, and yet may give way to a
superstitious respect for certain shadowy powers, which are to him
realities, and which exercise an appreciable influence on his thoughts
and ways. This arises from the necessity of his nature. His
consciousness announces to him the reality of unseen and immaterial entities, though he does not care to proclaim the fact to the
world. If he is highly civilised and scientific, he may dismiss these
phantoms as creations of the imagination ; but if he is a member of
a barbarous and uncultivated tribe, from which the true idea of God
has apparently died out, he will become the prey of the rain-maker,
the conjurer, or the witch, by whose arts his superstition will be
systematically developed. The *fetish* or object which he regards
with awe, whether it be merely a bit of rag or a bundle of feathers,
becomes to him an embodiment of the dark and terrible side of his
spiritual feelings. As long as the sun shines and the rain descends
and the fruits of the earth abound,—as long as a man has health,
and strength, and prosperity,—he cares little about fetish or demon,
and still less about God ; but when trouble comes he will follow the
example of Jonah's mariners, who 'cried every man unto his god,'
and will seek by magic or superstitious arts to avert the misfortunes which have befallen him, and to propitiate the evil spirit
whom he has unwittingly offended. This sad story of human superstition is well known to every missionary who has laboured among
rude tribes of idolaters ; and it may help us to understand the state
of things which Christianity has had to displace ever since its
earliest promulgation.

But to return to St. Paul's speech at Athens. ' He seemeth,'
said the sage, ' to be a setter forth of strange (*i.e.* foreign)
demons.'[1] Accordingly, impelled by curiosity, they gather round
the Apostle, and lead him out of the bustling Agora up the rock-
cut steps by which we still mount to the Areopagus. There to his
male and female audience, half-cynical, half-interested, the Apostle
of the Gentiles delivered a model missionary address, and conferred
a lustre on Athens which neither the oratory of Demosthenes, the
statesmanship of Pericles, the philosophy of Plato, nor the art of
Phidias can surpass. ' Athenians !' he seems to say, ' ye appear
to me to be far too much given to demon-fearing already; it
is a mistake therefore to suppose that I have come to set forth
more demons for your acceptance. My mission is a very different

---

[1] The very charge made against Socrates (Xen. *Mem.* 1. 1. 2 ; Plato, *Ap.* 24 *b.*).

one; for whilst coming through your city, and inspecting the objects which you regard with reverence, I met with an altar on which was written, "To GOD THE UNKNOWN." Besides the demons whom you fear, then, there is evidently a being called GOD, whom you regard with reverence, even though you are ignorant about His true nature. *This* is the Being whom I am setting forth to you.'[1]

Having thus awakened the attention of his hearers, he concentrated their mind on the word GOD. 'The God who made the *cosmos* and all that is in it, He, being possessor and ruler of heaven and earth, cannot have His Presence confined within the minute space which human hands are able to compass round with walls (and here no doubt the speaker pointed to the buildings that lay at his feet), neither can He be ministered to (θεραπεύεται) by hands of mortal men, as if He had any necessities which they could relieve—seeing that it is He that is the giver of life in all its aspects to all men. The nations which dwell on the face of the whole earth have sprung from one source, and have been distributed through many ages, and among various countries, by His will and agency. And it is for them to seek God,[2] if haply they may feel Him[3] and find Him. And, after all, He is not far off from any single person among us, for it is through union with Him that we have life, movement, and even bare existence; as some of your own poets[4] have said, "For we are His offspring." Seeing, then, that there is such a relationship existing between God and man, we ought to know better than to suppose that the Deity (τὸ θεῖον) can be really like a cleverly carved piece of stone or metal. If these things do not represent the real life of man, how can they possibly represent Him from whom that life flows?'

St. Paul's argument rested not on the name of God, but on the Divine operations and attributes. He knew full well that the word *Theos* did not convey the whole truth about the Divine Being to the mind of his hearers, and that *Zeus* was still further from being a fair representative of **Elohim**; but he confirmed what he

---

[1] Καταγγέλλω; compare the ξένων δαιμονίων καταγγελεὺς of v. 18.

[2] Not 'the Lord,' as A. V.

[3] The point is somewhat obscured in the A. V. and R. V., which read, 'feel *after* him.' The verb ψηλαφάω means to 'handle' (1 John 1. 1); hence, to feel an object in the dark. The nations were intended to have an *impression* of God's existence, though they were in darkness as to His real nature.

[4] The hymns to Jupiter which he quotes were written by Cleanthes the Stoic, of Assos (300 B.C.), and by Aratus of Soli, near Tarsus (270 B.C.).

had to say about the *Theos* who made the heaven and the earth by reference to two hymns dedicated to *Zeus*, who was also described as maker of all things. He thus worked round to the original idea of **Elohim**, and laid the foundations of sound Gospel teaching on one of the noblest products of natural theology.

§ 6. *Other Names for God.*

Although the plural **Elohim** is ordinarily used for God, the singular form **Eloah** is found in fifty-seven passages, most of which are in the Book of Job. Only six times is **Eloah** applied to any but the true God.

The Aramaic form **Elah** is found thirty-seven times in Ezra, once in Jeremiah, and forty-six times in Daniel. Of the eighty-four passages where it occurs, seventy-two refer to the True God. The Assyrian form is **Ilu**.

The more simple and elementary form **El**, which is frequently adopted either alone or in dependence on another substantive, to express power or might, is used of the True God in 204 passages, and of others in eighteen passages. It is found especially in Job, the Psalms, and Isaiah.

The names **El**, **Elah**, **Eloah**, and **Elohim** seem to express the same idea, even if they are not all connected etymologically,—though it may prove that they are. All occur, together with **Jehovah**, in Deut. 32. 15–19.

The plural of **El** is **Elim**, which is supposed to be used of false gods in Exod. 15. 11; Ps. 29. 1, 89. 6; and Dan. 11. 36; in each of which passages, however, the word may be rendered 'mighty ones.' **Elim** is never used of the true God.

El is sometimes used in compound names, as **El-Shaddai**, rendered in the A. V. 'Almighty God,' **Beth-el**, 'the house of God;' and in other cases it is used apparently to add force and sublimity to an idea, as when we read of 'mountains of **El**,' *i.e.* 'mighty mountains.'

The titles of the Messiah contained in Isa. 9. 6, have been subjected to a good deal of criticism from Jewish and Gentile pens, partly, no doubt, because the name **El** occurs in the expression which our translators have rendered 'the mighty God.' In this passage we read, 'His name shall be called Wonderful, Counsellor.' These words may, perhaps, be taken in their connection with one another as a parallel to Isa. 28. 29, where the same words in rather different forms are rendered, 'wonderful in counsel,'

and applied to the Lord of Hosts.[1]   Again, 'His name shall be called
the Mighty God.'   In the LXX, Luther's, and other versions, we
find this title broken up into two, and translated ' Mighty, Hero,'
or 'Mighty, Powerful'; but the order of the Hebrew words is in
favour of A. V., which is consistent with Isa. 10. 21, and Jer. 32. 18,
where the expression reappears.   The remaining title, The Everlasting Father, has been rendered in some recensions of the LXX
and in the Vulgate the Father of the Coming Age, and in
other versions the Father of Eternity; the last, which is the
best rendering, when read in the light of the N. T., would signify
that the Messiah was to be the Father, Spring, or Source of Everlasting Life to all the world.   Lastly, as He was to be the Father of
Eternity, so was He to be called the Prince of Peace, one whose
dominion should establish a holy peace (in all the fulness of meaning
of that word) throughout the world.

§ 7. *The Almighty.*

The name **Shaddai** (שַׁדַּי) is always rendered Almighty.

The LXX renders it by the word θεός, κύριος, and παντοκράτωρ,
God, Lord, and Almighty.   In five passages we find ἱκανός,
which we might translate All-sufficient.   Jerome adopted the
word *Omnipotens*, Almighty, and other versions have followed in
his track.

The title **Shaddai** really indicates the fulness and riches of
God's grace, and would remind the Hebrew reader that from God
cometh every good and perfect gift,—that He is never weary of
pouring forth His mercies upon His people, and that He is more
ready to give than they are to receive.   The word is connected with
a root which signifies a breast, and hence the idea is similar to that
contained in our word exuberance.   Perhaps the expressive word
bountiful would convey the sense most exactly.[2]   This rendering
will be illustrated and confirmed by a reference to some of the
passages in which **Shaddai** occurs, as they will be found specially to
designate God as a Bountiful Giver.   The first passage in which the

---

[1] The word for *wonderful* is literally *a wonder* (see Isa. 29. 14).   The verb
related with it is constantly used of God's *wonderful* works.   Sometimes it signifies
that which is *hidden*, or *difficult*, as in Gen. 18. 14, ' is anything too *hard* for the
Lord ;' Jud. 13. 18, ' Why askest thou my name, seeing it is *secret ?* '   Perhaps
wonderful would be a better rendering here, as the cognate verb occurs in the next
verse, where we read that the angel did *wondrously*.

[2] Compare the rendering *allgenugsame* in the Berlenburger Bible.

word is found is Gen. **17.** 1, where we read that 'Jehovah appeared to Abram, and said, I am **El-Shaddai**; walk before me, and be thou perfect: And I will make my covenant between me and thee, and will multiply thee exceedingly . . . and thou shalt be a father of a multitude of nations. Neither shall thy name any more be called Abram, but thy name shall be Abraham; for a father of a multitude of nations have I made thee. And I will make thee exceedingly fruitful, and I will make nations of thee, and kings shall come out of thee.'

The title is next found in Gen. **28.** 3, where Isaac says to Jacob, '**El-Shaddai** bless thee, and make thee fruitful, and multiply thee, that thou mayest be an assemblage of peoples.'

The third passage is Gen. **35.** 11, where God says unto Jacob, 'I am **El-Shaddai**: be fruitful and multiply; a nation and an assemblage of nations shall be of thee, and kings shall come out of thy loins' (compare Gen. **48.** 3).

The fourth passage is Gen. **43.** 14, where Jacob, in the intensity of his anxiety on behalf of his youngest son whom he is about to send into Egypt, throws himself upon the tender compassion of the All-Bountiful God, and says, '**El-Shaddai** give you tender mercy before the man, that he may send away your other brother and Benjamin.'

There is only one other place in Genesis in which this name is found, namely, Gen. **49.** 25, where Jacob is blessing his son Joseph, and says, 'From the **El** of thy father, there shall be help to thee; and with **Shaddai**, there shall be blessings to thee, blessings of heaven above, blessings of the deep that lieth under, blessings of the breasts (here the word **shad** is used in its original sense), and blessings of the womb.'

These passages appear to establish the fact that whilst the name **El** sets forth the Might[1] of God, the title **Shaddai** points to the inexhaustible stores of His Bounty.

Passing by the reference to this name in Exod. **6.** 3, which will be discussed in a later section, it may be noticed that **Shaddai** is only once again used in composition with **El**, namely, in Ezek. **10.** 5; without **El** it is used twice by Balaam (Num. **24.** 4, 16), twice by

---

[1] When we read of the Mighty One of Israel, or the Mighty God of Jacob or Israel, the word for Mighty is usually *Abir* or *Avir* (אָבִיר), a word marking strength and excellence. Sometimes *gadôl* (גָּדוֹל), great, is used, *e.g.* in Deut. **7.** 21; and in one or two cases the Hebrew name for a Rock is used to set forth the firmness of the Divine power: see for examples, Isa. **30.** 29. The 50th Psalm begins with the three names **El, Elohim, Jehovah** (A. V. The Mighty God, even the LORD).

Naomi (Ruth **1**. 20, 21), twice in the Psalms (**68**. 14, 91. 1), and three times by the prophets (Isa. **13**. 6 ; Ezek. **1**. 24 ; Joel **1**. 15). These are the only places in which it is to be found in the Bible except in the Book of Job, in which we meet with it thirty-one times.

§ 8. *The Lord.*

The word usually rendered 'Lord,' or 'my Lord,' is **Adonai** (אדני). This is a special form of **Adon**, a word which signifies Master, and which exactly answers to the Greek Κύριος. **Adon** is sometimes rendered Sir in the A. V., as in Gen. **43**. 20 ; Owner, as in 1 Kings **16**. 24 ; but generally Master, as in Gen. **24**. 9. The plural form **Adonim** and its plural construct form **Adonei** are used in the same sense ; but when the word is applied to God, the form **Adonai** is adopted. The termination of the word, as in the case of **Shaddai**, may mark an ancient plural form, but this is uncertain. In the A. V., as in other versions, **Adonai** is frequently rendered 'my Lord.' The title indicates the truth that God is the owner of each member of the human family, and that He consequently claims the unrestricted obedience of all. It is first used of God in Gen. **15**. 2, 8, and -18. 3, &c. It is rare in the Pentateuch and historical Books, but frequent in the Psalms, Isaiah, Jeremiah, Ezekiel, Daniel, and Amos.

The words which we read in the 110th Psalm and the first verse, if literally translated, would run thus :—'**Jehovah** said unto my **Master**[1] sit thou on my right hand until I make thine enemies thy footstool ;' and our Saviour's comment might be rendered, 'If David call him **Master**, how is he his Son ? '

The expression 'the Lord God,' which first occurs in Gen. **15**. 2, and is frequently found in the O. T., especially in the prophetical Books, is literally 'my Lord Jehovah.'

When we meet with the title 'Lord of Lords,' as in Deut. **10**. 17, the words are literally '**master of masters**,' *i.e.* Divine master of all those who possess or obtain authority.

In the Psalms and elsewhere there is found that significant title which the apostle Thomas gave to the Lord Jesus when he had optical and sensible demonstration that He was risen from the dead. Thus in Ps. **35**. 23, the sacred writer uses the double title

---

[1] According to the present Masoretic punctuation the word is in the singular —**Adoni**, not **Adonai**.

Elohai and **Adonai**, 'my God and my Lord;' and in Ps. 38. 15, we find **Adonai Elohai**, 'my Lord, my God.'

The claim upon man's service which is set forth in the title **Adonai** is well illustrated by Mal. 1. 6, where Jehovah says, 'A son honoureth his father, and a servant his master (or masters); if, then, I be a father, where is mine honour? and if I be a master (**Adonim** [1]), where is my reverential fear?'

§ 9. *The Most High.*

The Hebrew title rendered 'Most High' is **'Elion** (עֶלְיוֹן), for which the LXX usually has the reading ὁ ὕψιστος, the Highest. The word **'Elion**, however, is not confined to this sacred use. It is found in Gen. 40. 17; 1 Kings 9. 8; 2 Chron. 7. 21; 2 Kings 18. 17; 2 Chron. 23. 20, 32. 30; Neh. 3. 25; Jer. 20. 2, and 36. 10.

This title is first applied to God in the account of Melchizedek (Gen. 14. 18–22); it is used by Balaam, who 'knew the knowledge of the Most High' (Num. 24. 16); and Moses adopts it when he speaks of the Most High dividing the earth among the nations (Deut. 32. 8; compare Acts 17. 26). It occurs also several times in the Psalms, *e.g.* Ps. 18. 13, 'The Highest gave his voice;' Ps. 78. 35, 'They remembered that God was their Rock, and the High God their Redeemer.' In Ps. 89. 27, this title is applied to the Messiah :—'I will make him my firstborn, higher than the kings of the earth.'

When we read of the Most High God in Micah 6. 6, the Hebrew **Marom** (מָרוֹם), exalted, is used ; compare Ps. 99. 2, 113. 4, 138. 6 ; and Isa. 57. 15, where a simpler form of the same word is rendered High, and applied to God.

§ 10. *Jehovah.*

All the titles by which the living and true God was made known to Israel have now been brought under consideration with the exception of one, namely, **Jehovah** (יְהוָה), which occurs about 5500 times in the O. T. This name has been preserved by our translators in a few passages, but the word LORD, spelt in small capitals, has usually been substituted for it. The LXX set a

---

[1] Some MSS. here read **Adonai.**

precedent for this course by almost invariably adopting the word Κύριος, Lord, as a rendering, the only exception being Prov. 29. 26, where δεσπότης, Ruler or Master, is found.

The shorter form, **Jah**, occurs in Exod. 15. 6, and 17. 16, in each of which passages our translators have rendered it Lord; it is also found a few times in Isaiah, and in thirty-five passages in the Psalms, the earliest instances being Ps. 77. 11, and 89. 8. We are familiar with it in the expression Hallelujah, *i.e.* Praise Jah, also in compound names such as Elijah and Jehoshua.

It is a strange fact, with respect to the word **Jehovah**, that critics should differ as to its pronunciation, its origin, and its meaning. The first difficulty has arisen from the mystery with which the Jews have always surrounded this sacred and (as they hold) incommunicable name; but we may rest content with the traditional pronunciation of the word until there is stronger reason than appears at present for the substitution of **Jahveh**, or of some other form. The Assyrians represent it in Israelitish names by the forms *Yahu* and *Yahava* (Sayce). The doubt about the signification of the name is owing probably rather to the finiteness of the human understanding than to any uncertainty as to the revelation of **Jehovah** contained in Scripture.[1]

Whatever may be the opinion about **Elohim**, it is generally agreed that **Jehovah** is not a generic or class name, but a personal or proper name. Maimonides says that all the names of God which occur in Scripture are derived from his works except one, and that is Jehovah; and this is called 'the plain name,' because it teaches plainly and unequivocally of the substance of God. A Scotch divine has said, 'In the name Jehovah the Personality of the Supreme is distinctly expressed. It is everywhere a proper name, denoting the Person of God, and Him only; whence Elohim partakes more of the character of a common noun, denoting usually, indeed, but not necessarily or uniformly, the Supreme. The Hebrew may say *the* **Elohim**, the true God, in opposition to all false Gods; but he never says *the* **Jehovah**, for Jehovah is the name of the true God only. He says again and again *my God*, but never *my* **Jehovah**, for when he says "my God" he means Jehovah. He speaks of *the God of Israel*, but never of *the* **Jehovah**

---

[1] In some foreign translations of the Bible the name Jehovah is rendered *The Eternal*. Perhaps there is no word which, on the whole, conveys the meaning of the name so well; but, after all, the truth which it represents is too many-sided to be rendered by any one word.

of Israel, for there is no other Jehovah. He speaks of *the living God*, but never of *the living* **Jehovah**, for he cannot conceive of Jehovah as other than living.' [1]

The meaning, and, in all probability, the etymology [2] of this name, is to be looked for in Exod. 3. 14, where, in answer to the question of Moses as to the name of the Elohim who was addressing him, the Lord said to Moses, 'I AM THAT I AM.' [3]—'Thus shalt thou say unto the children of Israel, I AM hath sent me unto you . . . **Jehovah**, the **Elohim** of your fathers—of Abraham, and of Isaac, and of Jacob, hath sent me unto you; this is my Name for ever, and this is my Memorial [4] unto all generations.' Again, in the sixth chapter (verses 2, 3), we read, 'I am **Jehovah**, and I appeared unto Abraham, and unto Isaac, and unto Jacob, by (the name of) **El-Shaddai**, and, as regards my name **Jehovah**, I was not fully known by them; yet, verily, I have established (or rather, taking the tense as a prophetic future,—I will establish) my covenant with them to give them the land of Canaan.' These two passages taken together elucidate the following points: first, that though the name **Jehovah** was in frequent use as the title of the **Elohim** of the Patriarchs, yet its full significance was not revealed to them; secondly, that it was to be viewed in connection with the fulfilment of God's covenant and promise that now, after the lapse of some hundred years, the true import of the name was to be unfolded by the manifestation of a personal living Being, working in behalf of Israel, so as to fulfil the promises made to the Fathers. Thus the

[1] See Fairbairn's *Dict. of the Bible*, art. *Jehovah*.

[2] There has been much difference of opinion as to the formation of the word; but it may be noted that the *v* introduced into the name may be illustrated by the *v* in the name of *Eve*.

[3] The words above rendered 'I AM THAT I AM' are almost unapproachable, after all. Owing to the vagueness of the Hebrew tense (which is the same in both parts of the sentence) we might render them in various ways, but none are better than our own, denoting as they do a Personal, Continuous, Absolute, Self-determining Existence. It ought to be observed that the Hebrew word rendered I AM occurs in several important prophetic passages, in which it has generally been rendered '*I will be*.' Thus, in this same chapter of Exodus, and the 12th verse, we read, 'Certainly *I will be* with thee;' so in Gen. 26. 3, '*I will be* with thee and will bless thee;' and in Gen. 31. 3, '*I will be* with thee.' In these and similar passages we might render the words 'I AM with thee.' They mark an eternal, unchanging Presence. Compare the identical words used by the Lord (Jesus Christ?) in Acts 18. 10, 'I AM with thee, and no man shall set on thee to hurt thee;' also John 8. 58, 'Before Abraham came into being I AM.'

[4] Compare Hos. 12. 5, '**Jehovah** is his memorial,' *i.e.* the name by which His attributes were always to be brought to mind.

sublime idea of an unchanging, ever-living God, remaining faithful to His word through many generations, began to dawn upon the mind of Israel, and that which was hoped for, and sealed up in the Name during the Patriarchal age, began to work itself out into a substantial reality. God's personal existence, the continuity of His dealings with man, the unchangeableness of His promises, and the whole revelation of His redeeming mercy, gather round the name **Jehovah**. 'Thus saith **Jehovah**,' not 'thus saith **Elohim**,' is the general introduction to the prophetic messages. It is as **Jehovah** that God became the Saviour of Israel, and as **Jehovah** He saves the world; and this is the truth embodied in the name of **Jesus**, which is literally **Jehovah**-Saviour.

It is supposed by some critics that the contributors to the early Books of the Bible were of different schools of thought, some believing in **Elohim**, some in **Jehovah**, and some in both. This is no place for discussing such a theory. Undoubtedly some writers preferred to use one name and some another. This is demonstrated by a comparison of parallel texts in Kings and Chronicles.[1] Taking the Books as they stand, the important point to notice is that the various names of God are used by the sacred writers advisedly, so as to bring out the various aspects of His character and dealings. Thus, the first chapter of Genesis sets forth Creation as an act of power; hence **Elohim** is always used. The second chapter, which properly begins at the fourth verse, brings **Elohim** into communion with man; hence He is called **Jehovah Elohim**. In the third chapter it may be observed that the Serpent avoids the use of the name **Jehovah**. In the fourth chapter the offerings of Cain and Abel are made to **Jehovah**, and this is the case with the whole sacrificial system, both under the Patriarchal and the Levitical dispensation. In many cases the offerings to **Jehovah** are accompanied by the calling on His name (see Gen. 12. 8, 13. 4); and probably from the earliest days the Name of **Jehovah** was taken as the embodiment of that hope for the human race which found its expression in sacrifice and in prayer (see Gen. 4. 26).

Although man had fallen, **Jehovah** had not forsaken him; His Spirit still strove with man (Gen. 6. 3), but the judicial aspect of His nature had to be exercised in punishment, as we see from the history of the Deluge, the confusion of tongues, and the destruction of Sodom and Gomorrha. In Gen. 9. 26, **Jehovah** is called the

---

[1] See *Deuterographs*.

God of Shem; and in **14**. 22, He is identified by Abram with **El-'Elion**, 'the Most High God,' who is 'the Possessor of heaven and earth.'

In Gen. **15**. 1, we are introduced to the expression which afterwards became so familiar, 'the Word of **Jehovah**;' and throughout that remarkable chapter the name **Elohim** does not occur, because it is the name **Jehovah** which God adopts when making His communications and covenants with man. In chap. **16**. 'the angel of **Jehovah**' is spoken of for the first time, and appears to be identical with **Jehovah** Himself; He is also described by Abraham as 'the Judge of all the earth' (chap. **18**. 25).

The Patriarchs are frequently represented as worshipping and holding spiritual communication with **Jehovah**, who seems to have revealed Himself in a human form to these privileged children of Adam, whether through visions or otherwise (see Gen. **18**. 1, 2; **28**. 13–17; **32**. 24–30).

In Exod. **24**. 10, we are told of the Elders that 'they saw the God of Israel . . . and did eat and drink.' What a marvellous sight, and what a mysterious feast is here recorded! But this God of Israel must have been **Jehovah**, whom Jacob or Israel worshipped, and who was now revealing Himself to fulfil the promises made to the fathers.[1]

Jehovah is represented as in constant communication with Moses; and when He threatened that He would not go up to the land of Canaan with the people because of their idolatry, the lawgiver took the sacred tent which already existed (for there must have been worship from the beginning), and pitched it without the camp, and 'the cloudy pillar descended, and stood at the door of the tabernacle, and talked with Moses. And **Jehovah** spake unto Moses face to face, as a man speaketh unto his friend' (Exod. **33**. 9–11). Then it was that Moses besought this august Being to show him His glory, and His merciful answer was given and the revelation made: '**Jehovah**, the merciful and gracious **El**, longsuffering, and abounding in lovingkindness and truth. Keeping lovingkindness for thousands, pardoning iniquity and transgression and sin, and that will by no means hold men guiltless; visiting the iniquity of the fathers upon the children, and upon the children's children, unto the third and fourth generation' (Exod. **34**. 6, 7).

Here, then, we have the full meaning of the name **Jehovah**, and

---

[1] The LXX had not the courage to translate this literally, but rendered it, 'They saw the place where the God of Israel stood.'

we find that it sums up both the merciful and the judicial aspects of
the Divine character, so that while the title **Elohim** sets forth God's
creative and sustaining Power, **Shaddai** His Bounty, and 'Elion
His Sublimity, the name **Jehovah** sets forth His essential and
unswerving principles of mercy and judgment, and presents Him
as a Father, a Friend, and a Moral Governor.

§ 11. *The Lord of Hosts.*

The title **Jehovah** is often found embodied in the expression
'the Lord of Hosts' and 'the Lord of Sabaoth,' the former of
which is a translation of the latter.[1] This title first appears in
1 Sam. 1. 3. The LXX sometimes retains Σαβαώθ (compare Rom.
9. 29; James 5. 4), and sometimes renders it ὁ Κύριος τῶν δυναμεων,
and sometimes παντοκράτωρ, Almighty. Occasionally the name
Elohim is substituted for **Jehovah** in this connection, as in Ps. 80
7, 14, 19; Amos 5. 27.

In Exod. 12. 41, the Israelites are called 'the Hosts of the
Lord,' and hence it has been supposed that the title above mentioned signifies the captain or defender of the hosts of Israel.
Others regard the expression as referring to God's governments
of the 'host of heaven,' *i.e.* the stars; whilst others connect it
with the fact that God is attended by hosts of angels who are ever
ready to do His pleasure.

This title is often used in the minor prophets, and with especial
reference to God's majesty, sometimes also with reference to His
care for Israel, as, for example, in 2 Sam. 7. 26; Ps. 46. 7, 48. 8;
Zech. 2. 9. Probably the name would indicate to a Jew that God
was a Being who had many material and spiritual agencies at His
command, and that the universe of matter and the world of mind
were not only created, but also ordered and marshalled,[2] by Him;
who 'telleth the number of the stars, and calleth them all by their
names' (Ps. 147. 4; compare Isa. 40. 26).

---

[1] The French translation (Ostervald) has *l'Éternel des armées;* hence, no
doubt, is derived the questionable title 'the God of battles.' Luther has *Herr
Zebaoth.* Where we read of 'the God of Forces,' in Dan. 11. 38, a different
word is used, which literally means *strength.* Dr. Sayce compares the Assyrian
title *Bil Kissati,* 'lord of legions.'

[2] The *collocation,* as distinct from the *creation,* of the heavenly bodies, is
dwelt upon with great force by Dr. Chalmers in his Bridgewater Treatise.

§ 12. *The Angel of the Lord.*

The name **Jehovah**, again, is always used in the familiar expression, 'the angel of the Lord.' This title, in the opinion of some scholars, specially belongs to the Messiah. The late Dr. McCaul, in his Notes on Kimchi's Commentary on Zechariah, briefly states the reasons which led him to this conclusion. First, as to the word **Malac** (מלאך), he reminds us that it simply signifies a messenger,[1] leaving the rank and nature of the person so designated out of the question. Thus in Gen. 32. 1, 3, the word is applied first to God's angels, and, secondly, to Jacob's messengers. Then, as to the full expression **Malac Jehovah**, he opposes the opinion occasionally advanced, that it should be rendered 'the Angel Jehovah.' Again, he opposes the translation adopted by modern Jews, 'an angel of the Lord,' though it is occasionally sanctioned by the A. V., as in Jud. 2. 1. The absence of the article is no guide here, because the word angel is *in regimen, i.e.* is limited or defined by the word which follows it; and though the second word under such circumstances generally has a definite article, yet this would be impossible in the present instance, owing to the fact that יהוה (Jehovah) never receives one. Dr. McCaul thus reaches the conclusion that 'the angel of the Lord' is the right rendering, and he affirms that one and the same person is always designated thereby, as the expression is never used in the plural number. He then proceeds to show that 'the angel of God' occasionally spoken of in the singular number is the same person as 'the angel of the Lord.' This he does by citing Jud. 6. 20, 21, and also Jud. 13. 3, 9. In Gen. 16. 7–13, 'the angel of the Lord' is identified with 'the Lord' (*i.e.* **Jehovah**) and with **El**. The same is the case in Jud. 6. 11–16, and in Josh. 6. 2. A still more remarkable identification is found in Zech. 3. 2, when the angel of **Jehovah** is not only spoken of as Jehovah Himself, but is also represented as saying, 'Jehovah rebuke thee.'

But the writer proceeds to discuss Gen. 31. 13, where 'the angel of **Jehovah**' says of Himself, 'I am the God of Bethel, where thou anointedst the pillar, and vowedst the vow unto me.' On referring to the vision at Bethel, we read that this Being said, 'I am **Jehovah**, the God of Abraham thy father, and the God of Isaac.' Dr. McCaul

---

[1] More literally, an agent or worker. The word is found in another form in Gen. 2. 1, of God's works; there is, therefore, nothing unbecoming in applying the title to a Divine Being. Dr. Sayce points out that in some Assyrian inscriptions Nebo is called the *Sukkul*, or messenger of Bel Merodach.

justly adds, 'Where the law of Moses sets before us a Being who says of Himself that He is the God of Bethel, and that He is the object of Jacob's worship, what else can we conclude but that He is Very God, especially as the great object of this law throughout is to enforce the unity of God?' A similar inference may be gathered from Exod. 3. 4–6.

The above arguments prove that in *some*[1] cases there is a remarkable identification between **Jehovah** and the Agent who carries into effect the Divine purposes. When our Lord said, 'My Father worketh hitherto, and I work,' this great truth appears to have been in His mind; and it almost dawned upon the minds of His hearers, for we read that 'the Jews sought the more to kill him, because he said that God was his Father, making himself equal with God' (John 5. 17, 18). The whole mission of Christ was regarded and set forth by Him as the doing the Works of God, so that He was practically, what the O. T. indicates that He was to be, the Angel or Agent of **Jehovah**, giving effect and embodiment to the will of His Father. Moreover, as the Priest was the agent (A. V. messenger) of the Lord of Hosts under the old covenant (Mal. 2. 7), so Christ became the True Priest or Agent who should bring about a more spiritual system of worship, and a more close union between God and man.

§ 13. *How Translators deal with the Name Jehovah.*

It has been urged with some force, that the name **Jehovah** ought to have been adopted more generally in translations of the Bible, whereas it is confined to a very few.[2] Putting aside the difficulty as to the right spelling of the word, it may be observed that the

[1] The importance of making this qualification will be seen at once by pursuing the subject into the N. T. The 'Angel of the Lord,' in Matt. 2. 13, cannot well be identified with 'the young child' in the same verse. It may be noticed, however, that here (as in ver. 19, chap. 28. 2, 5, and elsewhere) the word Angel has no definite article. In the O. T. we must look to the context to find out whether *an* angel is meant, or whether *the* Angel or Agent of the Divine Will is referred to. In Zech. 1. 12, there is evidently a distinction of persons between the Angel of the Lord and the Lord of Hosts; the former intercedes with the latter in behalf of Israel. See also Jude 13.

[2] The Spanish translator De Reyna preserved **Jehovah** throughout the O. T., and his successor, Valera, though his version has since been altered, did the same. De Reyna defends the adoption of this course in his Preface at some length. Calvin also uses the word **Jehovah** in his Latin translation, and many modern translators have done the same.

LXX had set an example before our Lord's time which it would not be easy to depart from now. If that version had retained the word, or had even used one Greek word for **Jehovah** and another for **Adonai**, such usage would doubtless have been retained in the discourses and arguments of the N. T. Thus our Lord, in quoting the 110th Psalm, instead of saying, 'The Lord said unto my Lord,' might have said, '**Jehovah** said unto **Adoni**.' How such a course would have affected theological questions it is not easy to surmise ; nor is it needful to attempt any conjectures on the subject, as the stubborn fact remains before us that **Adonai** and **Jehovah** are alike rendered Lord in the Septuagint, and that the LXX usage has led to the adoption of the same word in the N. T. It is certainly a misfortune, and cannot easily be rectified without making a gulf between the O. T. and the N. T. How can it be got over?

Supposing a Christian scholar were engaged in translating the Greek Testament into Hebrew, he would have to consider, each time the word Κύριος occurred, whether there was anything in the context to indicate its true Hebrew representative ; and this is the difficulty which would arise in translating the N. T. into all languages if the title **Jehovah** had been allowed to stand in the O. T. The Hebrew Scriptures would be a guide in many passages : thus, wherever the expression 'the angel of the Lord' occurs, we know that the word Lord represents **Jehovah** ; a similar conclusion as to the expression 'the word of the Lord' would be arrived at, if the precedent set by the O. T. were followed ; so also in the case of the title 'the Lord of Hosts.' Wherever, on the contrary, the expression 'My Lord' or 'Our Lord' occurs, we should know that the word **Jehovah** would be inadmissible, and **Adonai** or **Adoni** would have to be used. But many passages would remain for which no rules could be framed.

It is to be noticed, in connection with this subject, that there are several passages in the O. T. referring to **Jehovah** which are adopted in the N. T. as fulfilled in the Lord Jesus Christ. Thus, in Joel 2. 32, we read, ' Whosoever shall call on the name of **Jehovah** shall be saved ;' but these words are applied to Jesus Christ in Rom. **10**. **13**. St. John (chap. **12**. 41), after quoting a certain passage from Isaiah, which there refers to **Jehovah**, affirms that it was a vision of the Glory of Christ (see Isa. **6**. 9, 10). In Isa. **40**. 3, the preparation of the way of **Jehovah** is spoken of, but John the Baptist adopts the passage as referring to the preparation of the way of the Messiah. In Mal. **3**. 1, there seems to be a very important identification of **Jehovah** with the Messiah, for we read, '**Jehovah**, whom ye (profess to) seek, shall suddenly come to his temple, **even** the angel of the covenant[1] whom ye (profess to) delight in.' In Rom. **9**. 33, and 1 Pet. **2**. 6–8, Christ is described as 'a stone of stumbling and a rock of offence,' titles which appear to be given to **Jehovah** in Isa. **8**. 13, 14. Again, in Isa. **45**. 23–25. Jehovah says, 'Unto me every knee shall bow . . . in **Jehovah** shall all the seed of Israel be justified.' But in Phil. **2**. 9, we read that God 'hath highly exalted Christ Jesus, and hath given him the name which is above every name, that in the name of Jesus every knee should bow, and every tongue confess that Jesus Christ is LORD (surely **Jehovah**), to the glory of God the Father.'

It would be deeply interesting to show how each of the names of God finds its embodiment in Him who is 'the Word of the Father.' Thus, as **Elohim**, Christ exercised Divine power, and also communicated supernatural powers to others. As **Shaddai**, Christ was all-sufficient, possessed of unsearchable riches, and always ready to pour forth His benefits on man. As '**Elion**, Christ was exalted in moral and spiritual nature, and also, as to position, made higher than the heavens. Lastly, as **Jehovah**, Christ is 'the same yesterday, to-day, and for ever,' ready to save to the uttermost, in close communion with His people, fulfilling all the Divine promises, and appointed to be 'Judge of all the earth.' 'I am Alpha and Omega, the beginning and the end, saith the Lord, which is, and which was, and which is to come, the Almighty' (Rev. **1**. 8).

---

[1] There is some difficulty about this passage. It would seem that the Old Covenant is spoken of. Who, then, was its Angel? Possibly there is a reference to Exod. **23**. 20–23, 'Behold, I send an angel before thee to keep thee in the way, and to bring thee into the place which I have prepared. Regard him (*not* beware of him, A. V.), and obey his voice, provoke him not; for he will not pardon your transgressions: for My Name is in him.' The coming of the Messiah was evidently to be the manifestation of One who had for a long time been in charge of the People of Israel. See Matt. **23**. 37.

CHAPTER III.

THE NAMES OF MAN.

IF it is strange that man, gifted though he is with great intelligence, should need a special revelation of the nature and character of his Maker, still more surprising is it that he should have to learn from the pages of Scripture the story of his own origin and destiny. Human nature, as portrayed in the Bible, is full of incongruities which illustrate at once the greatness and the littleness of man, his nearness to God, and his fellowship with the dust. The very names of man used by the Hebrew writers indicate the anomalies of his condition, for the principal words which are used represent him in four apparently inconsistent aspects :—as **Adam**, he is of the earth, earthy ; as **Ish**, he is endued with immaterial and personal existence; as **Enosh**, he is weak or incurable ; and as **Gever**, he is mighty and noble.

§ 1. *The Name Adam.*

The root of the word **Adam** (אדם) signifies to be red or ruddy, and is the ordinary word used for that purpose. It designates Esau's red lentil pottage, and gives him his name, **Edom** (Gen. 25. 30). It is used of the rams' skins dyed red in Exod. 25. 5, *al.* It marks the colour of the red heifer in Num. 19. 2, and of the red horses in Zech. 1. 8. It is the word used of the sardius stone or ruby in Exod. 28. 17, and Ezek. 28. 13 ; and of the ruddy tint of the flesh of the human being in Gen. 25. 25 ; 1 Sam. 16. 12 ; and Cant. 5. 10. In 2 Kings 3. 22, it is applied to the water which was as red as blood; and in Isa. 63. 2, to the red garments which He wore who came from **Edom**. Nor should we omit to notice that the ordinary Hebrew word for blood (**Dam**) is possibly connected with the same root.[1]

---

[1] See Gen. **9**. 6, where the two words are found together. Prof. Sayce points out a possible relationship in Assyrian between **Adamu**, man, and **Adman**, sanctuary.

Another form which the word takes is **Adamah**, the earth or soil, which may have received its name from its reddish tint. We here see why the first man was called **Adam**, and why the human race is generally called by the same name in the Hebrew Scriptures, *Homo ex humo*. Accordingly we read in Gen. 2. 7, that 'the Lord God formed man (**Adam**) of the dust of the ground (**Adamah**).'[1]

The word **Adam** is used in the O. T. for a human being in about 460 places. It is usually rendered in the LXX ἄνθρωπος, a human being, which occurs as its substitute in 411 passages; ἀνήρ, a man, is found only eighteen times, of which fifteen are in the Book of Proverbs; in Prov. 20. 24, θνητός, mortal, is used; in the Book of Job, βροτός, mortal, is adopted four times; and in Jer. 32. 20, we find γηγενής, earth-born, which is the closest translation of any.

The word is generally used throughout the O. T. to signify human nature or the human race generally, as contrasted with God above, or with the brute creation below. Thus it is used with great fitness in Exod. 33. 20, 'There shall no man see me and live,' and in Mal. 3. 8, 'Will a man rob God?' It is the word ordinarily used in the expression 'children of men' (*e.g.* in Gen. 11. 5). It is also found in the title 'son of man,' which occurs fifty-seven times in Ezekiel and once in Daniel (8. 17); compare also Ps. 8. 4; Job 25. 6, 35. 8, *al.* In all such passages special stress is laid upon the fact that the person thus designated is a child of Adam by descent, one of the great family of man, with a body framed of earthy material. The Lord Jesus frequently used this title with respect to Himself in order to teach His disciples that though He 'came down from heaven,' and was 'sent from God,' yet He was in very deed and truth a man.[2]

A few passages in which the word **Adam** is used for man

---

[1] It may also perhaps be inferred that primeval man was of a ruddy colour. Lanci's translation of the word **Adam** was *Il Rossicante*.

It is not always easy to determine when the word **Adam** should be regarded as a proper name, and when as a generic title. In Job 31. 33, we read of a man hiding his transgression *as* **Adam**, a remarkable reference to the story of the fall; but in Hos. 6. 7, where the same form is found, our translators have put into the text 'they *like men* have transgressed the covenant,' and have banished the name Adam to the margin. But see R. V.

[2] It is sometimes asked, How can a Person be at the same time God and the Son of God? The answer partly lies in the parallel question, How can a Person be at the same time Man and the Son of Man? Christ was not the son of any individual man, but was a partaker of human nature; and this was what He signified by the title 'Son of Man.' Similarly, by the title 'Son of God' He taught that He was a partaker of Deity.

deserve special notice.　In Dan. **10**. 16, 18, we read of 'one like the similitude or appearance of a man '—*like* an **Adam**, and yet not an **Adam**, because not yet incarnate.　In Ezek. **1**. 5, 8, 10, and **10**. 8, 14, we meet with a description of living creatures with 'the likeness of a man,' with 'the hands of a man,' and with 'the face of a man ;' and 'upon the likeness of the throne was the likeness as of the appearance of a man above upon it ;' and this, we are told, was 'the appearance of the likeness of the glory of the LORD ' (Ezek. **1**. 26, 28 ; see also chaps. **3**. 23, and **10**. 4).　It may be inferred that the Being whom Ezekiel thus saw in his vision was represented in human form but clothed with Divine attributes—not yet 'a son of **Adam**,' but 'One *like* a son of **Adam**.'

These remarkable passages indicate that human nature is intended to occupy a very high position in the scale of Creation, and that human nature was originally so constituted as to be capable of becoming the dwelling-place of the Most High.　They also prepared the mind for the truth set forth by St. John, who thus wrote of the Lord Jesus :—'The Word was made flesh, and dwelt (or *tabernacled*) among us (and we beheld his glory, the glory as of the only begotten of the Father), full of grace and truth.'　What Ezekiel saw in vision John saw in reality ; his eyes looked upon and his hands handled the Word of Life.

Two other passages have often attracted the attention of students.　In 2 Sam. **7**. there is recorded, first, the promise of God to keep an unfailing covenant with the seed of David, whose throne should be established for ever ; and secondly, David's expression of thankfulness on account of this promise.　In the opening of his song of praise (vv. 18, 19) he says, 'Who am I, O Lord God ? and what is my house, that thou hast brought me hitherto ?　And this was yet a small thing in thy sight, O Lord God ; but thou hast spoken also of thy servant's house for a great while to come.　And is this the manner of man, O Lord God ?'　The parallel passage (1 Chron. **17**. 17) runs thus : 'For thou hast also spoken of thy servant's house for a great while to come, and hast regarded me according to the estate of a man of high degree.'　The word translated **manner** in the one passage and **estate** in the other, is **torah**,[1] which is generally rendered 'law.'　The first passage might be rendered, 'And this is **the law** (or **order**) of **the man**,' and the second, 'Thou hast regarded me according to **the law** (or **order**) of **the man from on high**.'

---

[1] The word in Chronicles is spelt **Tor**, and occurs in this form nowhere else.

Some versions have rendered these passages so as to bring out more distinctly a reference to the Messiah. Thus, in Luther's version of 2 Sam. 7. 19, we read, 'That is a way of a man, who is God the Lord;'[1] whilst his rendering of 1 Chron. 17. 17, is, 'Thou hast looked upon me after the order (or form) of a man who is the Lord God on High.'[2] The words are grammatically capable of this rendering; but it is more in accordance with the context, and also with the structure of the passage, to regard the name of the Lord God as in the vocative case, in accordance with the rendering given by our translators. (See R. V. on Samuel.)

§ 2. *The Word Ish.*

The second name for man which is to be considered is **Ish** (אִישׁ). The original meaning of this word is doubtful. It is often supposed to be connected with **Enosh** (on which see below); and this theory receives a certain amount of confirmation from the fact that the plural of the latter word has almost always been used instead of the proper plural of **Ish**. Others incline to the supposition that the word may bear some relationship to the verb —if it may be called a verb—**Yesh** (יֵשׁ),—a root similar to the Latin *esse*, and to the English *is*. Others, again, connect it with the word **Ashash**, to found or make firm; or with the kindred form, **Ashah**. These words may all spring from a common source.

The first passage in which **Ish** occurs is Gen. 2. 23, where Adam said, 'This is now bone from my bone, and flesh from my flesh; she shall be called woman (**Ishah**), because she was taken out of man (**Ish**).[3] Although great names may be cited to the contrary, there seems to be no valid reason for departing from the implied derivation of **Ishah** from **Ish**.[3] The word **Ish**, being first used by man of himself in contradistinction to a second being of his own kind and springing from him, must represent some personal feeling of a kind to which Adam had hitherto been a stranger. Instead of being isolated and without a fellow, having God far above him, and the beasts of the earth below him, Adam found that he had a companion of a nature congenial to his own, 'a

---

[1] Das ist eine Weise eines Menschen, der Gott der Herr ist.

[2] Du hast angesehen mich als in der Gestalt eines Menschen, der in der Höhe Gott der Herr ist.

[3] The Vulgate keeps up the relationship between **Ish** and **Ishah** by rendering them **Vir** and **Virago**.

help,' as Scripture says, 'meet for him;' there was an *I* and a *Thou*, a personal relationship between two *selves* or *existences*, an **Ish** and an **Ishah**, the one springing from the other, and reflecting the other's nature—the same, yet distinct.

But whatever may be the origin of the word **Ish**, its usage is very plain, and is illustrated by the fact that the LXX renders it by ἀνήρ in about 1083 passages, and by ἄνθρωπος only 450 times. **Ish** is rightly translated a man as contrasted with a woman; a husband[1] as contrasted with a wife; a master as contrasted with a servant; a great and mighty man as contrasted with a poor and lowly one.

Ish is often used with qualifying nouns, as in Exod. **4.** 10, 'a man of words.' It sometimes implies greatness or eminence, and is thrown into contrast with **Adam**. Thus, in Ps. **49.** 2, the words 'low and high' are literally 'children of **Adam** and children of **Ish**;' Ps. **62.** 9, 'men of low degree (children of **Adam**) are vanity, and men of high degree (children of **Ish**) are a lie;' so also in Isa. **2.** 9, **5.** 15, and **31.** 8.

The word is often used in the sense of each or every one, *e.g.* Joel **2.** 7, 'They shall march every one on his ways.' It is used in the Hebrew idiom 'a man to his brother,' which signifies 'one to another,' as it is rendered in Exod. **25.** 20; Ezek. **1.** 11, &c., where reference is made to the wings of the living creature touching each other. The feminine form, **Ishah**, is used in exactly the same way. Thus we read in Exod. **26.** 3, 'The five curtains shall be coupled together, one to another;' literally, 'a *woman* to her *sister*.' Probably the much disputed passage, Lev. **18.** 18, which is so frequently discussed in relation to the marriage with a deceased wife's sister, ought to be rendered in accordance with this idiomatic form of expression.

The word is constantly used in such compound expressions as 'Man of Israel,' 'Man of God,' 'Man of understanding,' and 'Man of Sorrows.'

Where we read in Exod. **15.** 3, that 'the Lord is a man of war,' the word **Ish** is used. The passage does not mean that He is a human being—*this* would have involved the use of the word **Adam**. Again, when the sacred writer tells us in Josh. **5.** 13, that 'a man stood over against' Joshua, he does not use the word **Adam**, but **Ish**, which both here and elsewhere can be rendered Person or

---

[1] The word itself appears in Hos. **2.** 16, 'Thou shalt call me **Ishi**,' that is, My Husband.

Being. Compare also Dan. **9**. 21, **10**. 5, **12**. 6, 7 ; Zech. **1**. 8, &c., where the word is applied to Beings, who presented themselves in vision to the eye of the prophet, without necessarily being partakers of human nature.

There is a diminutive formed from the word **Ish**, namely, **Ishon** (אישון), which signifies the apple or pupil of the eye, literally the 'little man' which any one may see reflected in another person's eye.[1] It occurs also in Deut. **32**. 10, and in Prov. **7**. 2.[2] In Lam. **2**. 18, the figure is slightly different, the expression being literally 'the daughter of the eye;' and in Ps. **17**. 8, the two are combined, so that the literal rendering would be 'keep me as the little man, the daughter of the eye.' In Zech. **2**. 8, a different word is used for the pupil, representing the hole or gate of the eye rather than that which is reflected on it.

A verb has been derived from the word **Ish**, and is used in the expression 'shew yourselves men' (Isa. **46**. 8), answering well to the Greek ἀνδρίζεσθε. Compare the English phrase 'to be unmanned.'

§ 3. *The Word Enosh.*

The third word for Man is **Enosh** (אנוש), which occurs very frequently in the O. T., and is generally considered to point to man's *insignificance* or *inferiority*.[3] This word, like **Ish**, depends, in some measure, on its surroundings for its meaning, and often answers to our English word 'person,' by which it has been rendered in the A. V. in Judges **9**. 4, and Zeph. **3**. 4. Its plural form generally does duty for the plural of **Ish** as well. See, *e.g.*, Gen. **18**. 2, 16, 22, where the 'men' were angelic Beings.

In poetry **Enosh** occurs as a parallel to **Adam**. Thus, 'I will make a man (**Enosh**) more precious than fine gold; even a man (**Adam**) than the golden wedge of Ophir' (Isa. **13**. 12). It is occasionally introduced as a parallel with **Ben-Adam**, the son of man; thus, 'How much less man (**Enosh**) that is a worm, and the son of man (**Ben-Adam**) which is a worm' (Job **25**. 6); 'What is man (**Enosh**), that thou art mindful of him? and the son of man (**Ben-Adam**), that thou visitest him?' (Ps. **8**. 4); 'What is man (**Enosh**),

---

[1] This figure has found its way into other languages. See Gesenius' *Thesaurus* on the word.

[2] In the 9th verse of the same chapter it is rendered black (the idea being borrowed from the darkness of the pupil) and applied to night.

[3] The Assyrian *niou* for *eniou* is taken by Dr. Sayce as answering to **Enosh**.

that thou takest knowledge of him ? or the son of man (**Ben-Adam**), that thou makest account of him ?' (Ps. **144**. 3) ; ' Thou turnest man (**Enosh**) to destruction ; and sayest, Return, ye children of men ' (**Benai-Adam**, Ps. **90**. 3). In these passages it will be noted that the *insignificance* of man is especially in the writer's mind. In Job **4**. 17, our translators have rendered it mortal man : 'Shall mortal man (**Enosh**) be more just than God ? Shall a man (**Gever**)[1] be more pure than his maker ?' Here the word **Gever** must be used with a tinge of irony, as in Job **10**. 5, ' Are thy days as the days of man (**Enosh**)? are thy years as man's (**Gever**) days ? '

There are other passages where the insignificance of man is specially brought out by the use of **Enosh**, *e.g.* Job **7**. 17, ' What is man, that thou shouldest magnify him ? and that thou shouldest set thine heart upon him ?' Job **9**. 2, ' How should man be just before God ?' See also Job **15**. 14, **25**. 4 ; Ps. **9**. 20, **103**. 15 ; Dan. **2**. 43.

Enosh is sometimes used where man is brought into direct contrast with his Maker. Thus we read in Job **10**. 4, ' Hast thou (O God) eyes of flesh ? or seest thou as man seeth ?' Job **33**. 12, ' I will answer thee, that God is greater than man ;' Isa. **7**. 13, ' Is it a small thing for you to weary men, but will ye weary my God also ?' See also Isa. **29**. 13, and **51**. 7, 12.

In Ezek. **24**. 17, the prophet is forbidden to mourn or to eat 'the bread of men.' Here the Rabbinical commentators incline to take the word men as signifying other men, according to an ordinary Hebrew idiom, and they refer to the custom of the food of the mourner being supplied by a neighbour. Others read it 'the bread of husbands,' *i.e.* of widowed husbands, and the usage of the word in Ruth **1**. 11, and perhaps in Jer. **29**. 6 (in each of which passages **Enosh** occurs) gives some slight ground for this view. Others, again, consider the word here signifies mortal men.

The A. V. rendering of the word in 1 Sam. **2**. 33, ' in the flower of their age,' is hardly justified by other passages, and might well be replaced by a more literal translation without departing from English idiom ; it has the sanction, however, of the Vulgate and of Luther (see R. V.).

When we come to inquire into the etymology and original meaning of the word, we find it connected with the Hebrew root **anash**. This word occurs (usually in the form **anush**) in the follow-

---

[1] See below, § 4.

ing passages only :—2 Sam. **12.** 15, David's child was 'very sick;' Job **34.** 6, 'My wound is incurable;' Psalm **69.** 20, 'I am full of heaviness;' Isa. **17.** 11, 'Desperate sorrow;' Jer. **15.** 18, 'Why is my pain perpetual, and my wound incurable, which refuseth to be healed?' Jer. **17.** 9, The heart is 'desperately wicked;' Jer. **17.** 16, 'Neither have I desired the woeful day' (LXX, 'the day of man'); Jer. **30.** 12, 'Thy bruise is incurable and thy wound is grievous;' Jer. **30.** 15, 'Thy sorrow is incurable for the multitude of thine iniquity;' Micah **1.** 9, 'Her wound is incurable.'

These passages fix the meaning of the word. But it may be asked why a word which signifies incurable should be used to denote man. Perhaps the answer may be found in Gen. **4.** 26. Seth had been 'appointed' in the place of Abel, but man remained unchanged and unredeemed; so Seth's son was called **Enosh.** 'Then began men to call upon the name of Jehovah.' The race was 'incurable,' but the Lord was its hope. Thus, Seth's son may have been named **Enosh,** that is to say 'incurable,' because he was utterly unable to redeem himself from the bondage of corruption. This view of the matter is taken by Cocceius, who says that, 'as **Adam** was the name given to all who sprang from the dust of earth, so **Enosh** became the title of all those who are heirs of corruption.'

The Messiah was never designated by the name **Enosh,** because, though appointed to become a descendant of Adam, and destined to be made 'in the likeness of sinful flesh,' yet in Him there was to be no sin. But it is a remarkable thing that when the glorious coming of the Messiah to rule the nations is unfolded in Dan. **7.** 13, the Lord is described as 'one like a son of **Enosh.**' Compare the description in Rev. **5.** 6, 'A Lamb as it had been slain,' which indicates that the marks of His humiliation will accompany His glory.

§ 4. *The Word Gever.*

The last name for man which has to be noticed is **Gever** (גבר), which is used more than sixty times in the O. T., and represents man as a **mighty being.** This title is at first sight inconsistent with the name **Enosh;** but no one can weigh well the facts which human nature daily presents to his observation without coming to the conclusion that man is a marvellous compound of strength and weakness, and that while he is rightly called **Enosh** by reason of the corruption of his nature, he may also lay claim to the title of

Gever by virtue of the mighty energies which are capable of being exhibited in his life and character.

The Greek translators have rendered **Gever** by ἀνήρ in the majority of places where it occurs, but in fourteen passages they have been content with the more general word ἄνθρωπος. In the English Bible it is usually rendered Man, but in some places the original sense of the word has been adhered to, and it has been translated mighty.

The earliest passages where the word is found, with the exception of Gen. 6. 4, are: Exod. 10. 11, 'Go now ye that are men;' and Exod. 12. 37, 'About six hundred thousand on foot that were men, beside women and children.' Balaam uses this word when he designates himself 'the man whose eyes are open' (Num. 24. 3, 15). It is used of the male sex as opposed to the female in Deut. 22. 5, and is rendered 'man by man' where individuals are distinguished from tribes in Josh. 7. 14, and 1 Chron. 23. 3. It is twice applied to David with a significant reference to its real meaning, namely, in 1 Sam. 16. 18, 'A mighty valiant man' (lit. 'a mighty man of strength'), and 2 Sam. 23. 1, 'The man who was raised up on high.' See also 1 Chron. 12. 8, 28. 1 ; 2 Chron. 13. 3 ; Ezra 4. 21 ; 5. 4, 10 ; 6. 8.

The above-named passages plainly show the original meaning and the general usage of **Gever**, but in the poetical Books, in which this word occurs with greater frequency, there is not always the same marked clearness of signification. In the Book of Job there appears to be a slight irony in its use. Thus:—'Shall a man (mighty though he be in his own estimation) be more pure than his Maker?' (4. 17); '(mighty) man dieth and wasteth away' (14. 10); 'If a (mighty) man die, shall he live again?' (ver. 14); 'Can a (mighty) man be profitable unto God?' (22. 2); 'That he may hide pride from (mighty) man' (33. 17). See also 33. 29, 38. 3, 40. 7.

The word is used in Ps. 34. 8, 'Blessed is the man that trusteth in him,' where it points to the fact that however great a man may be, yet he is not to trust in his own strength, but in the living God. The same explanation may be given of its use in Ps. 37. 23, 'The steps of a man (A. V. 'of a good man') are ordered (or established) by the Lord.' Compare Ps. 40. 4, 52. 7, 94. 12, and 128. 4. In Ps. 88. 4, we read, 'I am as a (mighty) man that hath no strength;' the contrast here indicated between the name and the condition is very striking. The Psalmist says again (89. 48), 'What man is he that liveth and shall not see death?' The point of this question comes out far more clearly when the use of the word **Gever** is noticed, and the sentiment might be thus expressed, ' Is there any living man so mighty as to be able to avoid death ?'

Neither Isaiah nor Ezekiel use the word **Gever** at all, but we meet with it eight times in the prophecy of Jeremiah, and four times in the Book of Lamentations. The following are the most interesting examples:—Jer. **17.** 5, 7, 'Cursed is the (mighty) man (**Gever**) that trusteth in man (**Adam**, the earthy).' . . . 'Blessed is the (mighty) man that trusteth in the Lord.' Jer. **23.** 9, 'I am like a (mighty) man whom wine hath overcome.' With what force is the power of strong drink here delineated ! **Gever** is also found in Jer. **31.** 22, where the Lord says to the 'Virgin of Israel,' that He was about to create a new thing—'A woman shall compass a man.'[1]

Several words are related to **Gever**. There is the verb **gavar**, which is found in twenty-three places, and is usually rendered **prevail**; in Ps. **103.** 11, and **117.** 2, it is used of the moral efficacy and prevailing power of God's mercy. **Gevir** is used for 'lord' in Isaac's blessing (Gen. **27.** 29, 37). **Gevirah** is sometimes used for a Queen ; **Gevereth** for a mistress (rendered *lady* in Isa. **47.** 5, 7). **Gevurah** is rendered **force**, **mastery**, **might**, **power**, **strength**. **Gibbor** signifies **mighty**, and is frequently used both of God and man ; it is found three times in the expression 'the Mighty God,' namely, in Isa. **9.** 6, **10.** 21, and Jer. **32.** 18, passages which are deeply interesting in relation to the Deity of the Messiah.

The LXX has sometimes rendered **Gibbor** by γίγας, **giant**, as in Gen. **6.** 4, **10.** 8, 9 ; 1 Chron. **1.** 10 ; Isa. **3.** 2, **13.** 3 ; Ezek. **32.** 21: The general Hebrew name for a *giant* is not **gibbor**, which refers to might rather than stature, but **Rephaim**, Rephaites or sons of Raphah. The word used in Gen. **6.** 4, and also in Num. **13.** 33, is **Nephilim**, which is derived from the Hiphil or causative form of **Naphal**, to fall, and hence signifies *tyrants*, or those who make use of their power to cast down others. In the former of these passages the Vulgate has *giants*, and Luther *tyrants* ; in the latter the Vulgate has *monsters*, and Luther *giants (Riesen)*.

The word **methim** (מתים) is translated **men** in a few passages, chiefly in Job, Psalms, and Isaiah, also in Deut. **2.** 34. It perhaps means ' mortal,' but this is doubtful.

---

[1] Literally, 'a female shall compass (or enclose) a Mighty One.'

CHAPTER IV.

THE SOUL AND THE SPIRIT.

WHEN the writer of the Epistle to the Hebrews says that the word of God pierces 'to the dividing asunder of soul and spirit' (Heb. 4. 12), and when St. Paul prays that the 'spirit, soul, and body' of his converts may be preserved blameless (1 Thess. 5. 23), a psychological division of the immaterial part of human nature is drawn which is exactly similar to what we find running through the whole O. T. The Bible proceeds upon the supposition that there are two spheres of existence, which may be called *mind* and *matter;* it tells us that the key to the mystery of the universe is to be found, not in the material substance of which it is composed, nor in the agencies or influences which cause the phenomena of nature to follow one another in regular sequence, but to a Master-mind, who plans all things by His wisdom, and sustains them by His power. The Scriptures bring the immaterial world very close to every one of us; and whilst we are all only too conscious of our relation to things fleeting and physical, the Sacred Record reminds us on every page that we are the offspring of the absolute and unchanging Source of all existence. A man is sometimes tempted to say, 'I will believe only what I see;' but the first puff of wind or the first shock of electricity tells him that he must enlarge his creed. If he still stops short by asserting his faith only in the forces which affect matter, he will find himself confronted by the fact that the matter which composes the human frame becomes by that very circumstance subject to forces and influences to which all other matter is a stranger. He finds a world within as well as a world without, and he is compelled to acknowledge that his physical frame is the tenement of a super-physical being which he calls *self*, and which is on the one hand a recipient of knowledge and feeling obtained through the instrumentality of the body, and on the other hand an agent originating or generating a force which tells upon the outer world.

It is in respect to this inner life and its workings that man is the child of God. His structure is of soil, earth-born, allied with all physical existence, and subjected to the laws of light, heat, electricity, gravitation, and such like, as much as if it were so many atoms of vegetable or mineral matter. But the immaterial exist-ence which permeates that structure, investing it with consciousness, flooding it with sensibilities, illuminating it with understanding, enabling it to plan, to forecast, to will, to rule, to make laws, to sympathise, to love—this *ego*, this pulse of existence, this nucleus of feeling and thought and action, is a denizen of an immaterial sphere of being, though ordained by God its Father to live and grow and be developed within the tabernacle of flesh.

§ 1. *The Soul.*

The Hebrew equivalent for the word 'soul' in almost every passage in the O. T. is **Nephesh** (נפש), which answers to ψυχή in the Greek. The cognate verb **Naphash**, to re fresh, is found in Exod. 23. 12, 31. 17, and 2 Sam. 16. 14.[1] The word **Nephesh** has various shades of meaning and of rendering, which must be gathered as far as possible under one or two heads. The soul is, properly speaking, the animating principle of the body, and is the common property of man and beast. Thus, in Lev. 24. 18, we read, 'He that killeth a beast shall make it good ; beast for beast ;' this is literally, 'He that smiteth the soul of a beast shall recompense it ; soul for soul.' It is also used with respect to the lower animals in Gen. 1. 21, 24 ; 2. 19 ; Lev. 11. 46, *al.*, in which passages it has been rendered creature.

In some passages **nephesh** has been rendered 'anyone ;' the word is thus used in an indefinite sense, the soul representing the person, as when we speak of a city containing so many thousand 'souls.' Thus, we read in Lev. 2. 1, 'When any (lit. 'a soul') will offer a meat offering ;' Lev. 24. 17, 'He that killeth any man,' lit. 'that smiteth any soul of man'—the soul representing the life ; Num. 19. 11, 'He that toucheth the dead body of any man shall be unclean seven days,' lit. 'he that toucheth the dead (part) of any soul of a man shall be unclean seven days ;' also verse 13, 31. 19, and Num. 35. 11, 15, 30. In these passages a dead body is regarded as that which ought properly to be animated by the soul, but owing to the law whereby man has to return to the dust, the spectacle is

---

[1] In Assyrian, *napistu*, which means 'life,' is connected with *napâsu*, to ' expand,' and hence to ' breathe ' (Sayce).

seen of a soulless body, which is to be regarded as ceremonially unclean. Compare Lev. **21**. 11 ; Num. **5**. 2 ; **6**. 6, 11 ; **9**. 6. 7, 10.

In Ps. **17**. 9, 'deadly enemies' are literally 'enemies of my soul or life.' In Job **11**. 20, 'the giving up of the ghost' is 'the puffing forth of the soul.' So also in Jer. **15**. 9, the literal rendering is 'she hath puffed forth the soul.'

The soul is thus the source of animation to the body ; in other words, it is the life, whether of man or beast. Accordingly, **Nephesh** is rendered 'life' in Gen. **19**. 17, 19, where we read of Lot's life being saved ; Gen. **32**. 30, 'I have seen God face to face, and my life is preserved ; ' Gen. **44**. 30, 'His life is bound up in the lad's life ; ' Exod. **21**. 23, 'Thou shalt give life for life ; ' verse 30, 'He shall give for the ransom of his life whatsoever is laid upon him.'

In Deut. **24**. 7, we read, 'If a man be found stealing any (lit. 'a soul') of his brethren,' &c.; so in Ezek. **27**. 13, 'They traded the persons (lit. 'the souls') of men.' By the use of the word **Nephesh** here the wickedness of treating men as goods and chattels to be bought and sold is practically reprobated. This doubtless is the crime referred to in Rev. **18**. 13. Perhaps the word 'person' in the sense in which we speak of an offence against a man's person, or of a personal injury, is the best rendering in such passages. It is adopted in Gen. **14**. 21 ; Lev. **27**. 2 (where both men and beasts are referred to) ; Num. **5**. 6, **19**. 18, and Ezek. **16**. 5. A similar rendering is self, which is found in Lev. **11**. 43, 1 Kings **19**. 4, and Isa. **5**. 14.

In some passages the word soul is added to give emphasis, as in Gen. **27**. 31, &c., 'that thy soul may bless me.' Compare Matt. **26**. 38.

In Hebrew, as in most other languages, the shedding of a man's blood was a phrase used to represent the taking of his life, for 'the blood is the life.' In this oft-repeated phrase (*e.g.* Lev. **17**. 11, 14) we see that the blood is (*i.e.* represents) 'the soul ; ' and if the one flows out from the body, the other passes away too. In Prov. **28**. 17, we read literally, 'The man that doeth violence to the blood of a soul shall flee into the pit ; ' so in Ezek. **33**. 6, 'If the sword come and take away a soul (A. V. 'person') from among them . . . his blood will I require at the watchman's hands ; ' Jonah **1**. 14, 'Let us not perish for this man's life, and lay not upon us innocent blood.'

This mystical identification of the blood and the life is of great interest as bearing upon the atoning work of Christ. We are told that He poured out His soul unto death, and that He shed His blood for the remission of sins. Evidently the shedding of the blood was the outward and visible sign of the severance of the soul from the body in death; and this severance is regarded as a voluntary sacrifice offered by the Divine Son, in accordance with His Father's will, as the means of putting away sin.

But the **Nephesh** or soul is something more than the bare animating principle of the body; at least, if it is regarded in this light, a large view must be taken of that mysterious organisation which we call the body, and it must include the bodily appetites and desires. The word is rendered 'appetite' in Prov. 23. 2, and Eccles. 6. 7. Compare the words of Israel, 'our soul loatheth this light food' (Num. 21. 5). Other passages in which a similar idea is presented are Eccles. 6. 9, *al.* (desire); Isa. 56. 11 (greedy); Exod. 15. 9, *al.* (lust); Ps. 105. 22, *al.* (pleasure); Deut. 21. 14, *al.* (will).

Nephesh is also rendered mind and heart in several places where these words are used in the sense of desire and inclination, *e.g.* Gen. 23. 8; 2 Kings 9. 15.

Thus the soul, according to the O. T., is the personal centre of desire, inclination, and appetite, and its normal condition is to be operating in or through means of a physical organisation, whether human or otherwise. Hence, when we read that man or Adam became a living soul (Gen. 2. 7), we are to understand that the structure which had been moulded from the dust became the habitation and, to a certain extent, the servant of an *ego* or conscious centre of desire or appetite. When the soul departs (Gen. 35. 18), the body becomes untenanted, and the *ego* which has grown with the growth of the body is dislodged from its habitation. It may, however, return again to its old home through the operation of God, as was the case with the widow's child (1 Kings 17. 21; compare Ps. 16. 10).

The fact that the desires to which the soul gives birth are often counter to the will of God fixes *sin* upon the soul; accordingly, we read, 'the soul that sinneth it shall die' (Ezek. 18. 4). Hence the need of atonement for the soul (Lev. 17. 11), and of its conversion or restoration to a life of conformity with God's law (Ps. 19. 7, 34. 22).

In the N. T. ψυχή often signifies life, as in Matt. 2. 20, 'Those who seek the life of the young child;' Matt. 6. 25, 'Be not solicitous for your life' (or animal existence). In Matt. **10**. 28, a distinction is drawn between the destruction of the body, which man can effect, and the perdition or ruin of the soul as well as the body in Gehenna, which only God can bring about. Sometimes there seems to be a play upon the word, as when the Saviour says 'he that loseth his life or soul (in the ordinary sense of the word) shall find it' (in a new and higher sense), Matt. **10**. 39, **16**. 25. When describing His mission, our Lord plainly said that He came to give His soul or life a ransom for many (Matt. **20**. 28). In Acts **2**. 27, St. Peter quotes the Psalm (**16**. 10), 'Thou wilt not leave my soul in Hades.' This passage certainly *might* be taken to signify, 'thou wilt not leave my dead body in the grave;' but it is far more in accordance with the usage of the two important words soul and Hades to understand that the animating principle, the *ego*, of our Saviour was not to remain in the nether world.

§ 2. *The Spirit.*

Very different is the idea which Scripture gives of the Spirit from that which is to be understood by the word soul. With the exception of Job **26**. 4, and Prov. **20**. 27, where **neshamah** (נשמה), 'a breathing being,' is used, the word spirit always represents the Hebrew **Ruach** (רוח).[1] Compare the Assyrian *Rukhu.*

The word **Ruach**, like its Greek equivalents, πνεῦμα and ἄνεμος, the Latin *spiritus*, the English *ghost*, and similar words in other languages, originally signifies wind or breath. It is the only word rendered wind in the O. T. It is rendered whirlwind, in Ezek. **1**. 4; tempest, in Ps. **11**. 6; cool (wind), in Gen. **3**. 8; air, in Job **41**. 16; blast, in Exod. **15**. 8, 2 Kings **19**. 7, Isa. **25**. 4, and **37**. 7. Thus, as *blood* represents the animal life, so does *wind* the spiritual element in life.

Ruach is frequently rendered breath, *e.g.* Gen. **6**. 17, 'the breath of life.' As long as this breath is sustained in a man, he lives (Job **27**. 3); when it goes forth, he returns to his earth (Ps. **146**. 4). The most remarkable passage in which the action of breath and wind is identified with the source of life is the

---

[1] There are two verbs cognate with this word: one signifies the being refreshed (1 Sam. **16**. 23; Job **32**. 20; see also Jer. **22**. 14, where large signifies airy or ventilated); the other signifies to smell, hence to be keen or 'of quick understanding' (Isa. **11**. 3).

vision of the dry bones in Ezek. 37. In this, as in some other
passages, it is not easy to distinguish between the physical and
the super-physical breath, both of which are gifts from God.

In Josh. 2. 11, where we read ' there remained no more courage
in any man,' the word might be rendered *breath*. In Jud. 8. 3,
the deep breathing is a sign of anger, and accordingly the word
is so rendered. In 1 Sam. 1. 15, it is a sign of earnest prayer,
or perhaps of the agitation of the heart. In Gen. 26. 35, it is
a sign of grief; it is here rendered mind instead of spirit,
unfortunately, and this has also been the case in Prov. 29. 11;
Ezek. 11. 5, 20. 32; and Hab. 1. 11.

It is clear that the wind is regarded in Scripture as a fitting
emblem of the mighty penetrating power of the Invisible God;
and that the breath is supposed to symbolise, not only the deep
feelings which are generated within man, such as sorrow and anger,
but also kindred feelings in the Divine nature. God is not set forth
in Scripture as a *soul* [1]—*i.e.* the centre of physical appetite and the
animating principle of a body—but as a *spirit*, that is, an unseen
living being, capable of deep emotions. Moreover, it is revealed
that God, and He alone, has the faculty of communicating His
Spirit or life to His creatures, who are thus enabled to feel, think,
speak, and act in accordance with the Divine will.

§ 3. *The Spirit of God.*

References in the O. T. to the Spirit of God and to the Spirit
of the Lord are more numerous than is sometimes imagined. In
upwards of twenty-five places this Divine Spirit is spoken of as
entering man for the purpose of giving him life, power, wisdom,
or right-feeling. God, moreover, is called 'the God of the spirits
of all flesh' in the O. T., as He is called the 'Father of our spirits'
in the N. T.; and it is everywhere taught or implied that the
personal agency of God is in contact with the centre of life in
every child of man. How He acts, we know not; in what mode
He enlightens, inspires, comforts, and warns, we cannot tell. We
see and feel the results, but we are unable to comprehend the
processes.

---

[1] It is true that the Hebrew word **nephesh** is used in certain idiomatic
expressions with reference to the Divine Being, but not in such a way as to
invalidate what is affirmed above.

§ 4. *Meanings of the Word Spirit in N. T.*

A full examination of the usage of the word πνεῦμα (spirit) in the N. T. would be a work of great interest, but of no little difficulty. The passages in which it occurs may be generally classified as follows :—

First, there are various references to the spirit of man, that part of human nature which is breathed into him by God.

Secondly, mention is often made of evil spirits, which are spoken of as personal beings, capable of allying themselves with men and inflicting various evils upon them.

Thirdly, there are references to the work of the Holy Spirit of God in John the Baptist and others *before* the day of Pentecost.

Fourthly, some passages are found which speak of the Spirit of God dwelling and working in our Saviour during His earthly ministry.

Fifthly, there are a number of passages which imply a special agency of the Holy Spirit, which has come into operation in consequence of the mediatorial work of the ascended Lord.

Lastly, there are texts which speak of the effects produced in man by the Spirit of God, and which combine under the same designation both the Worker and the effect produced.

The first and third of these classes naturally associate themselves with similar passages in the O. T. The second is deeply mysterious and interesting, but does not call here for special discussion. There remain three others upon which a few remarks may be offered.

The Lord Jesus, *as man*, possessed spirit, soul, and body; and His spirit was in a special sense the dwelling-place of the Holy Spirit. He was filled with the Spirit, which was given to Him without measure.[1] He was guided in His movements by the

---

[1] It is almost dangerous, and yet it may be helpful to some minds, to take an illustration of this difficult subject from nature. As it is true that no man hath seen G o d at any time, so it may be said that no one has seen e l e c t r i c i t y. But as a man may be charged with electricity without losing his personal identity, and may thus become, not only an embodiment of that unseen agency, but also capable of communicating it to others by contact, so the Son of Man contained the Fulness of the Spirit. This indwelling Agency had complete possession of the human nature, so that in Him the manhood was taken into the Godhead. By the touch of faith we draw the virtue or Force of the Spirit from Him into ourselves ; we thus become partakers with Him of the Spirit of God. The relationship between the three Persons of the Godhead is utterly beyond human conception. The

Spirit ; His wisdom and discernment, His power over evil demons, and perhaps we may say all His words and deeds, were wrought through the agency of the Spirit. See Matt. 1. 18, 4. 1, 12. 18, 28 ; Luke 4. 1, 14, 18 ; John 3. 34.

A special point in the teaching of John the Baptist was that Jesus, the Lamb of God, should baptize with the Holy Ghost ; and our Lord, in His conversations with Nicodemus, the Samaritan woman, and others, teaches that those who believed in Him would become partakers of a New Life, which would be in a peculiar sense the work of the Holy Ghost. In the course of these conversations He put forth this truth in various forms. There was the heavenly birth, the living water, the bread of life, the resurrection life, the sap of the vine, each in turn taken as the central point in a discourse, leading up to the truth that (after His glorification) those who believe in Him should receive the Holy Ghost. Our Lord's last conversations with His disciples before His crucifixion were full of this subject ; and when He rose from the dead He indicated by the symbolical act of breathing on His disciples the truth that through His mediatorial agency they were to receive the promised blessing of the Spirit. When the day of Pentecost was fully come, this Divine gift was showered down. A life of praise, of sonship, of love, of boldness, and of missionary labour, was inaugurated. The disciples were organised through this new influence into a Church, which breathed the spirit of Christ and did the work of Christ upon earth. For a time the Christian life and preaching were accompanied by special miracles, as our Lord's own life had been. These were intended to give an authoritative seal to the mission of the original disciples, just as similar works had testified a few years earlier to the mission of the Son of God.

If it be asked in what way the work of the Holy Spirit of God differs now from what it was in earlier ages of the world's history, it may be sufficient for the present purpose to answer that, though the Agent is the same, the Truth whereby He operates upon the feelings and affections of man is much more developed now than in old days. Formerly, the way of redemption from sin and corruption was only dimly shadowed forth ; now, the substance has been wrought out : Christ has been lifted up, and all men are being drawn to Him, and those who believe in Him enter thereby

Father is represented in Scripture as the Source of life, will, and affection ; the Son is the obedient Agent of the Father's will working on the creature *ab extra ;* the Spirit works on the creature *ab intra.*

into a special relationship with Him, so that they live in Him and He in them, both being partakers of one Spirit. Formerly, the Spirit operated through the written word, through types and shadows, through laws and ordinances, reproving men of sin, and kindling their hopes of a better time; but now He operates especially through the Living Word, of Whom all the Scripture testifies, and Who is the Way, the Truth, and the Life. He manifests Christ in His completed work to the heart of man, and quickens the believer into newness of life by breathing into him that eternal life which is in the Father, and in His Son, Jesus Christ. Metaphysically, we cannot understand the nature of this agency, but theologically, and as a matter of revelation, we believe and thankfully receive it.

The last class of passages to which reference has to be made consists of those which seem to identify the Spirit of God with the results which He is producing in the heart and life of man. Thus we read of the spirit of sonship or adoption, Rom. 8. 15; the spirit of meekness, 1 Cor. 4. 21; the spirit of faith, 2 Cor. 4. 13; the spirit of wisdom and revelation, Eph. 1. 17; the spirit of truth, 1 John 4. 6; and the spirit of holiness, Rom. 1. 4. It is evident that these passages refer, not to the inherent characteristics of the Holy Spirit, but to those effects which He produces in the believer. They answer to a similar class of passages in the O. T.; see, for example, Isa. 11. 2.

CHAPTER V.

HEART, WILL, CONSCIENCE, UNDERSTANDING.

THE present chapter has for its subject a discussion of those elements in human nature which are the sources or centres of emotion, volition, deliberation, and spiritual apprehension. It is comparatively easy for the physiologist or anatomist to mark out the different organs of the human body, and to learn their structure and manifold uses; but the psychologist has a harder task to perform; he has to analyse and classify his own sensations and emotions, to determine so far as possible which are from the body and which from an immaterial source, to compare his own mental constitution with the effects produced on and by the minds of others, to note how different classes of external entities appeal to and call forth distinct feelings, and move in various spheres of existence, touching finer or ruder chords of human sensibility, according to their nature and the aspect in which they are presented. The mental analyst is in danger of running to one of two extremes, and more especially so when applying his study to Scripture. He is sometimes inclined to take the popular words which represent the inner life, in a very loose and vague sense, using the one for the other as people do in their ordinary conversation, as if there were but one organ of emotion and volition in man, receiving different names according to the different relationship it has to sustain. At other times he is tempted to exercise his powers of mental anatomy in ranging and classifying the different powers of the immaterial existence in several groups, assigning each to a separate organ, and thus making the heart, the will, the conscience, and the understanding to be distinct members of a spiritual organisation. Each of these systems represent an aspect of truth, but each is imperfect if taken by itself. We are not in a position to grasp the subject of immaterial existence, and can only approach it relatively and in those aspects in which it exists in connection with bodily life.[1] We are, as it were,

---

[1] Physiology and psychology are now seen to be closely related, and the brain (which is never referred to in the Bible) is regarded as the medium as well as the seat of mental faculties.

organised grains of dust floating on an ocean of spiritual existence, which permeates our being, connects us with one another, and binds us to that higher sphere of life in which GOD dwells. In this spirit-world we live and breathe and know and feel and think and determine, but we understand little of its nature, and certainly we are not in a position to decide whether there is only one hidden agency at work in our bodies, taking many forms through the medium of the brain and nerves, or whether the nucleus of our conscious life is to be considered as composite in its original nature; in other words, whether human nature is like an Æolian harp, which has many strings, and produces wild and plaintive music through the blind force of the wind; or whether it is like an organ, not only complex in itself, but also played upon by a complex being, who gives expression to his own thought and feeling as he touches its keys.

The Bible does not discuss this subject; it makes use, however, of certain terms which require careful consideration, as they have stamped themselves upon our popular and religious language, and are sometimes used without consideration of the ideas which they were originally intended to convey.

§ 1. *The Heart.*

The general Hebrew word for the heart is **Lev** (לב), answering to the Assyrian *libbu*. It is usually rendered καρδια in the LXX, but sometimes Greek words signifying the soul, the intellect, or the understanding, are taken to represent it.

Two or three other words are occasionally translated '*heart*' in the A. V., *e.g.* **Nephesh**, 'the soul' (Exod. 23. 9, *al.*); **Mai'im** (מעים), the bowels (Ps. 40. 8); **Kir** (קיר), the *wall* of the heart (Jer. 4. 19); and **Kerev** (קרב), the inner or middle part (Jer. 9. 8). Our translators might have adopted a similar rendering in John 7. 38, which would then run thus—'out of his heart shall flow rivers of living water,' the heart representing the innermost part of the body. The R. V. has made no correction.

The heart, according to Scripture, not only includes the motives, feelings, affections, and desires, but also the will, the aims, the principles, the thoughts, and the intellect of man. In fact, it embraces the whole inner man, the head never being regarded as the seat of intelligence. Hence we read of men being 'wise hearted,' Exod. 31. 6, 36. 2; of wisdom being put into the heart,

E

2 Chron. **9**. 23 ; of the heart being awake, Eccles. **2**. 23, Cant. **5**. 2 ; of the thoughts of the heart, Deut. **15**. 9 ; of words being laid up in the heart, 1 Sam. **21**. 12 ; and of mercy being written on the tablets of the heart, Prov. **3**. 3.　In 2 Kings **5**. 26, Elisha says to Gehazi, 'Went not my *heart* with thee' (or after thee); here a combination of knowledge and feeling is implied.　There is also a beautiful expression in the Hebrew 'to speak to the heart,' which we render, 'to speak comfortably or friendly,' Ruth **2**. 13 ; 2 Sam. **19**. 7 ; 2 Chron. **30**. 22 ; Isa. **40**. 2 ('Speak ye comfortably to Jerusalem'); Hos. **2**. 14 ('I will bring her into the wilderness and speak comfortably to her ').

Whilst it is the source of all action, and the centre of all thought and feeling, the heart is also described as receptive of influences both from the outer world and from God Himself.　The wisdom of the wise-hearted was given them by the Lord (2 Chron. **9**. 23); when Saul turned from Samuel, 'God gave him another heart' or 'turned his heart into a new direction' (1 Sam. **10**. 9); the Lord gave to Solomon 'a wise and an understanding heart' (1 Kings **3**. 12); He says concerning His people, 'I will give them one heart and one way, that they may fear me for ever. . . . I will put my fear in their hearts, that they shall not depart from me' (Jer. **32**. 39, 40); 'I will give them one heart, and I will put a new spirit within you ; and I will take away the stony heart out of their flesh, and will give them an heart of flesh' (Ezek. **11**. 19, **36**. 26).　Compare Ps. **51**. 10, 'Create in me a clean heart.'　The word is used in the N. T. in the same way as in the O. T.

§ 2. *The Hardening of the Heart.*

The hardening of the heart is described in Scripture as the work of God.　Pharaoh's case is by no means unique ; it is a sample of the history of all those who neglect the opportunities which God gives them, and thus lead Him to put in exercise that law to which the whole human race is subject—that moral impressions, if not acted upon, become (subjectively) weaker and weaker, until at last the heart of man becomes altogether callous. In the case of Pharaoh three words are used to represent the hardening process : **Chazak** (חזק), to brace up or strengthen,[1] points to the hardihood with which he set himself to act in defiance

---

[1] This word is also used of God's bringing Israel out of Egypt 'with a strong right hand.'　The firmness of the Creator overcame the firmness of the creature.

against God, and closed all the avenues of his heart to those signs and wonders that were wrought by the hand of Moses; **Caved** (כבד), 'to be heavy, dull, or unimpressible,' denotes his insensibility and grossness of perception ; and **Kashah** (קשה), *to be harsh*, marks the restlessness, impatience, petulance, and irritability with which his course was characterised whilst he was resisting the urgent appeals, not of Moses only, but also of his own people. Each of these words is used under similar circumstances in other parts of the O. T. Thus **Chazak** is found in Josh. 11. 20, ' It was of the Lord to harden their hearts.' Compare Jer. 5. 3 ; Ezek. 3. 9. It is usually rendered to be strong, courageous, to hold fast, to be valiant, stout, mighty. **Caved** is used in 1 Sam. 6. 6, ' Wherefore do ye harden your hearts, as the Egyptians and Pharaoh hardened their hearts?' Ezek. 3. 5, 6, 'Of a hard language.' It is usually rendered heavy. **Kashah** is found in Exod. 18. 26 ; Deut. 1. 17, 2. 30, 'The Lord thy God hardened his spirit and made his heart obstinate, that he might deliver him into thy hand;' Deut. 15. 18, 26. 6, 'The Egyptians laid upon us a hard bondage.' Compare 2 Sam. 3. 39 ; 2 Kings 2. 10, 17. 14 ; Neh. 9. 16, 17, 29 ; Job 9. 4 ; Ps. 60. 3, 95. 8 ; Prov. 28. 14, 29. 1 ; Isa. 8. 21, 14. 3 ; Jer. 19. 15 ; Ezek. 3. 7. The usual renderings are hard, grievous, cruel, stiff. It is to be noticed that in God's mission to Ezekiel, in the third chapter, the three words now mentioned occur together. Other words of similar meaning are **Kashach** (קשח), which is found in Job 39. 16, and Isa. 63. 17 ; and **Tekeph** (תקף), which occurs in Dan. 5. 20.

§ 3. *The Will.*

The English word **will** is sometimes merely the sign of the future tense, whilst at other times it expresses the willingness of the agent. In the Hebrew, as in the Greek, those ideas are represented by different words, and in many passages it is important to notice the distinction.

Avah (אבה, Ass. *Abitu*) represents the inclination which leads towards action, rather than the volition which immediately precedes it. In the LXX, **Avah** is rendered both by βούλομαι and θέλω. It is rendered 'will' or 'willing' in the following passages : Gen. 24. 5, 8 ; Exod. 10. 27 (' He would not let them go') ; Lev. 26. 21 ('If ye will not hearken unto me ') ; Deut. 1. 26 ('Ye would not go up') ; Deut. 2. 30 (Sihon 'would not let us pass

by him'), **10**. 10 (the Lord 'would not destroy thee'), **23**. 5, **25**. 7,
29. 20 ; Josh. **24**. 10 ; Jud. **11**. 17, **19**. 10, 25, **20**. 13 ; 1 Sam. **15**. 9,
22. 17, **26**. 23, **31**. 4 ; 2 Sam. **2**. 21, 6. 10. **12**. 17, **13**. 14. 16. 25,
14. 29, 23. 16, 17 ; 1 Kings **22**. 49 ; 2 Kings **8**. 19. **13**. 23, **24**. 4 ;
1 Chron. **10**. 4, **11**. 18, 19, **19**. 19 ; 2 Chron. **21**. 7 ; Job **39**. 9 ;
Ps. **81**. 11 ; Isa. **1**. 19 ('If ye be willing '), **28**. 12, **30**. 9, 15, 42.
24 ; Ezek. **3**. 7 ('The house of Israel will not hearken unto thee,
for they will not hearken unto me') ; see also chap. **20**. 8.

It is remarkable that these passages, with two exceptions (Isa.
1. 19, and Job **39**. 9), are *negative*. Where they refer to the disobedience of Israel, they imply that the refusal to hearken to God's
Word was voluntary, and that they were responsible for it. Where
reference is made to the Divine action, it is implied that God is a
moral governor, and that His dealings with men are deliberate, and
to some extent dependent upon their obedience or disobedience.

In Hos. **13**. 10, 14, we read, 'I will be thy king;' 'O death,
I will be thy plagues ; O grave, I will be thy destruction.' The
word for will (**ehi**, אֵהִי) might probably be better rendered where?
as in the margin and in the R. V. ; and this rendering would
identify the passage all the more closely with St. Paul's words in
1 Cor. **15**. 55.

Chaphets (חָפֵץ), to *delight*, is usually rendered θέλω or βούλομαι
in the LXX. In the A. V., it is rendered 'will' in Ruth **3** 13
('If he will not do the part of a kinsman to thee') ; 1 Sam. **2**. 25 ;
1 Kings **13**. 33 ; 1 Chron. **28**. 9 ; Job **9**. 3 ; Prov. **21**. 1, and **31**. 13.

This word is used in the phrase 'there is a time for every purpose' (Eccles. **3**. 1, 17, **8**. 6) ; also in Eccles. **12**. 10, 'The preacher
sought to find out acceptable words.' The Psalmist uses it when
he says, ' Let them be put to shame that wish me evil ' (Ps. **40**. 14).

Chaphets is rendered please or pleasure in several passages,
including Jud. **13**. 23 ; Job **21**. 21, **22**. 3 ; Ps. **5**. 4, **35**. 27, **115**. 3 ;
Isa. **42**. 21, **53**. 10 ; Ezek. **18**. 23, 32, **33**. 11 ; Mal. **1**. 10.

It is rendered 'favour' in 2 Sam. **20**. 11, Ps. **35**. 27, and **41**. 11.
In these passages there is no reference to what we call 'favouritism,'
i.e. the overlooking of the claims of some so as to gratify the wishes
of special friends ; it is simply recorded that pleasure was found
in certain persons, whatever the ground of it might be.

It is often rendered desire, *e.g.* in 1 Sam. **18**. 25 ; Ps. **34**. 12,
40. 6, **51**. 6, 16 ; Hos. **6**. 6. It is also rendered delight very
frequently ; see especially 1 Sam. **15**. 22, 'Hath the Lord as great
delight in burnt offerings and sacrifices, as in obeying the voice of

the Lord?' 2 Sam. 22. 20, 'He delivered me because he delighted
in me;' Ps. 1. 2, 22. 8, 40. 8; Isa. 1. 11, 62. 4 (**Hephzi-bah**, 'My
delight is in her').

On reviewing all the passages where the word **Chaphets** is used,
the reader will probably come to the conclusion that its true meaning is not so much an intense pleasurable emotion, as a favourable
disposition, or the prompting of the heart to take a certain course
of action from a sense of fitness. It is usually relative rather than
absolute. It teaches us that God is naturally disposed to look for
obedience, trust, and holiness in those who were created after His
own likeness; that He deals tenderly but uprightly with His
creatures; that He confers life rather than death, if morally possible; that He administers judicial punishment where necessary;
and that He has seen fit to inflict suffering upon the Messiah. It
also marks His unwillingness to be put off with ceremonial observances as a substitute for the devotion of the heart.

Ratson (רצון), which properly means good pleasure or acceptance, is occasionally translated 'will,' *e.g.* Gen. 49. 6, 'In their
self-will they digged down a wall;' Lev. 1. 3,[1] 'Of his own voluntary will;' 19. 5, 'At your own will;' 22. 19, 29; Neh. 9. 24,
'As they would;' Esther 9. 5; Ps. 40. 8, 'I delight to do thy
will;' 143. 10, 'Teach me to do thy will;' Dan. 8. 4, 'He did
according to his will;' 11. 3, 16, 36. The word is less abstract
than the previous ones. It sets forth a pleasurable emotion,
whether leading to action or not. Both the substantive and the
verb are used to represent that which is pleasant, delightful, acceptable, or approved of by God.

The LXX usually adopts θέλημα, εὐδοκία, or δεκτός as a rendering for this word.

It is interesting to observe what a number of passages there are
in the N. T. in which reference is made to 'the will of the Lord.'
God's good pleasure is everywhere regarded as the law whereby all
things, human and divine, are ordered. Christ is regarded as its
embodiment and manifestation; and the Christian, being—by profession at least—one with Christ, is supposed to be conformed to
that will in all things.

The θέλημα, answering to **Ratson**, is that which God decides to
have done because it is pleasing to Him; the βουλή, which answers
to **Chaphets**, marks His *disposition* rather than His counsel or pur-

---

[1] Probably these passages in Leviticus ought to be translated otherwise. See
chap. xvi. § 3.

pose. The two words are found together in Eph. 1. 11. The latter
word implies not so much that there has been a consideration of the
circumstances which call for action, as that they are in accordance
with the nature and attributes of God; whilst the former points to
the fact that the course of action determined on gives a real pleasure
to Him.

§ 4. *Freedom of the Will.*

Voluntary action, as opposed to that which is constrained or
compulsory, is indicated by the word **Nadav** (נדב), for which the
LXX uses προθυμέω. This word is applied to the offerings for the
tabernacle which were given 'willingly' (Exod. 25. 2, 35. 5, &c.), to
the 'freewill offerings' for Solomon's temple (1 Chron. 28. 21,
29. 5), and to the 'free offerings' in the days of Josiah (2 Chron.
35. 8).[1] In Lev. 7. 16, and Ezek. 46. 12, it is rendered voluntary.
In Ps. 68. 9, it is used of the 'plentiful rain' which was sent
freely or without stint upon God's inheritance.

This word occurs in Ps. 54. 6, 'I will freely sacrifice unto
thee;' in Hos. 14. 4, 'I will love them freely;' also in Ps. 51. 12,
'Uphold me (with thy) free spirit,' *i.e.* 'sustain in me an uncon-
strained spirit of devotion.' In this last passage the LXX reads
πνεύματι ἡγεμονικῷ, 'with thy guiding or ruling spirit,' the Hebrew
reading followed being perhaps slightly different from our own.

In Ps. 110. 3, we read, 'Thy people shall be willing in the
day of thy power.' These words are sometimes taken as referring
to God's 'preventing grace,' and they have been even cited as
justifying a man in sitting listlessly under God's Word, waiting till
power comes upon him from above. Such an interpretation is held
in forgetfulness of the fact that God works through the will, not
apart from it—that He *turns* the lock, but does not force it. The
form of the word in this passage is the plural substantive, so that
the literal rendering would be, 'thy people shall be *freewill offerings,*'
&c. Luther renders it, 'thy people shall offer willingly' (see
also R. V.); and the words seem to point to the fact that in the
day of the Messiah's exaltation His people shall offer Him uncon-
strained service, yielding their bodies as living sacrifices unto God,
rendering Him a *rational* (as opposed to a *ceremonial*) service. (See
Rom. 12. 1, and compare the Prayer-Book Version of the Psalms.)

The word προθυμία is not often found in the N. T., but there

---

[1] In Assyrian, *nindabu* means a freewill offering (Sayce).

is one passage, viz. 2 Cor. **8.** 11, 12, where it occurs, which calls for some slight elucidation. The A. V. runs thus :—' Now therefore perform the doing of it that, as there was a readiness to will, so there may be a performance also out of that which ye have, for if there be first a willing mind, it is accepted according to that a man hath, and not according to that he hath not.' The words 'a readiness' in the first part of this passage, and 'a willing mind' in the second, stand for the Greek word προθυμία; so that the Apostle would say, 'as there was a willingness to determine (προθυμία τοῦ θέλειν), so let there be a carrying out of that determination by a contribution from what you possess; for where there is a real willingness, such a contribution is acceptable, even though small, because it is given according to what a man does possess, not according to what he does not.' The word προθυμία here answers to **nadav**, whilst the word θέλειν answers rather to **avah**. St. Paul did not accept the will (**avah**) for the deed, but if what is given is given voluntarily (**nadav**), then he gladly accepted the gift in proportion to the means of the giver.

The word which marks volition, or that which immediately precedes action, is **Yaal** (יאל), which the LXX generally represents by ἄρχομαι, to *begin*. We meet with it in Josh. **17.** 12, 'The Canaanites would dwell in that land;' compare Jud. **1.** 27, 34, and Hos. **5.** 11, 'He willingly walked after the commandment.' It is rendered 'assay' in 1 Sam. **17.** 39, 'He assayed[1] to go,' implying that David was on the verge of starting off (Vulg. 'he began to step out') in Saul's armour, but [he put them off, for] he had not proved them. **Yaal** is rendered 'begin' in Deut. **1.** 5. In Gen. **18.** 27, 31, it is found in the expression '*I have taken upon me* to speak unto the Lord.' All these passages exhibit the real meaning of the word as representing the volitional element in an act rather than the feelings, dispositions, or motives which have prompted it.

In a few passages **Yaal** is rendered 'content,' where the word signifies that a certain effort of the will was necessary before the thing required was done. See Exod. **2.** 21; Josh. **7.** 7; Jud. **17.** 11, **19.** 6; 2 Kings **5.** 23, **6.** 3; Job **6.** 28. Where the sentence is in the form of a petition, it seems to answer to our use of the word '*do*' in the sentence 'Oh, *do* come !' In accordance with this sense, it is rendered '*be pleased*' in 1 Sam. **12.** 22; 2 Sam. **7.** 29; 1 Chron. **17.** 27; Job **6.** 9.

---

[1] The R. V. retains this spelling, instead of 'essayed.'

§ 5. *Conscience.*

We look in vain for the word conscience in the O. T., except
in the margin of Eccles. 10. 20, where it represents part of the word
Yada', to know (Assyrian, *idâ*). In the Apocryphal Books we meet
with συνείδησις twice, viz. in Ecclus. 10. 20, where it is rendered
'wittingly;' and in Sap. 17. 11, where it seems to point to the
constraining power of a sense of right. The verb συνείδω is used of
knowledge in Lev. 5. 1; also in Job 27. 6, where the LXX reads
οὐ γὰρ σύνοιδα ἐμαυτῷ ἄτοπα πράξας, 'I am not conscious of having
acted foolishly,' words which have no Hebrew text answering to
them, but which find an echo in St. Paul's phrase, 'I know nothing
against myself' (οὐδὲν ἐμαυτῷ σύνοιδα), 1 Cor. 4. 4.

The verb συνείδω is also used to represent ordinary perception,
without reference to the moral aspect of the thing perceived, in
five passages in the Books of the Maccabees.

Conscience, then, so far as the O. T. throws any light
on it, is to be taken not as a separate faculty which enables a
man to distinguish right and wrong, but as the exercise of *consciousness;* and it will be seen, by noting the passages in the N. T.
in which the word occurs, that this meaning is generally adhered
to. Omitting John 8. 9, the reading of which is doubtful, we
do not meet with the word συνείδησις until we arrive at the end
of the Acts. St. Paul, standing before the council, says, 'In all
good conscience have I lived under the government of God unto
this day' (Acts 23. 1). These words are elucidated by the statement made before Felix, 'In this I exercise myself, having (or to
have) a conscience void of offence towards God and towards man'
(Acts 24. 16). He evidently signified that he was not conscious of
living or aiming to live in any course which was wrong in the sight
of God or really offensive to man. In exact accordance with these
expressions, he writes to the Corinthians, 'I am not conscious
of anything against myself, yet am I not hereby justified, but he
that judgeth me is the Lord' (1 Cor. 4. 4).

The same Apostle refers to his consciousness that what he said
was spoken in sincerity, in Rom. 9. 1, 'My conscience also bearing witness.' Compare Rom. 2. 15; 2 Cor. 4. 2, and 5. 11. In
1 Cor. 8. 7, we read of those who are eating 'with conscience
of the idol'—that is, with a conscious feeling that they are eating
what is offered to idols; and their conscience, *i.e.* their moral sense,
being weak and susceptible, is defiled. See also the tenth verse.

The moral sensibility or conscience is referred to in 1 Cor. **10.**
25, 27, 28, 29, 'Asking no questions because of consciousness;
not your own consciousness, but that of the weak brother who
has not yet attained to that liberty and knowledge which enables
you to disregard heathen superstitions.'

When St. Paul is describing the end or sum and substance
of the charge which Christ lays upon men, he characterises it as
'love out of a pure heart and a good conscience and unfeigned
faith' (1 Tim. **1.** 5); by these words he means that there should
be nothing selfish or sensual in love, that there should be a conscious aim at that which is good in God's sight, and a faithfulness
untainted by a particle of hypocrisy. Compare 1 Tim. **1.** 19, where
faith and a good conscience are again joined together.

The passages in the Epistle to the Hebrews in which the word
occurs are very interesting and important. From Heb. **9.** 9, we
gather that the offerings under the O. T. could not make men 'perfect as pertaining to the conscience,' *i.e.* could not take away the
sense of sin which hinders man from oneness with God. They did
not take away sin, as a matter of fact, and they could not, from the
nature of things; for if the effect of the Levitical dispensation had
been to make men perfect, *i.e.* at one with God (see chap. viii. § 2),
the offerings would not have needed repetition. If the worshippers
had been purged once for all, they would have had no more consciousness of sins (Heb. **10.** 2). But 'the blood of Christ' cleanses
a man's consciousness from dead works, and enables him to serve
the living God (Heb. **9.** 14); and the heart is thus 'sprinkled from
an evil conscience' (**10.** 22). In other words, the faithful acceptance
of the sacrifice of Christ takes away that sense of sin which had been
a bar between man and God, and enables a man to live no longer as
a servant, but as a son.

St. Peter says, 'This is grace (A. V. thankworthy) if from conscience towards God (*i.e.* through consciousness of his duty and of
his relationship to God in Christ) a man endure pains, suffering unjustly' (1 Pet. **2.** 19). He urges that men should keep 'a good
conscience' (**3.** 16), and he reminds them that it is not the external
cleansing, the putting away of the filth of the flesh, that now saves
us, but the answer of a good conscience toward God, or, as we
might render it, the seeking[1] unto God with a good conscience
(1 Pet. **3.** 21).

---

[1] Ἐπερώτημα εἰς Θεόν. This passage has awakened much discussion. I am
inclined to be guided by the fact that ἐπερωτάω sometimes answers to the meaning

The verb συνιδεῖν, to be conscious, is used in only three passages in the N. T., exclusive of that already mentioned in 1 Cor. **4**. 4, viz. in Acts **5**. 2, **12**. 12, and **14**. 6.

Conscience was thus originally identical with consciousness, but while the latter word may be used by us with reference to external facts or to internal feelings, the former is now confined to the knowledge that a man has of the moral aspect of things. A good conscience, according to Scripture, is not only a sense of freedom from past guilt, but also a consciousness of purposing and doing that which is good in God's sight; it implies purity of motive and action; it is inconsistent with a deliberate course of sin, or with departure from the living God, and it is closely connected with faith in Christ.

§ 6. *Words marking Intelligence.*

Coming to the words which designate man's intellectual capacities, we may begin with the word **wisdom**. This word generally answers in the A. V. to the Hebrew **Chacam** (חכם). This is an important word in Scripture, and is used to represent the discernment of good and evil, prudence in secular matters, skill in arts, experience in Divine things, and even dexterity in magic. In the reflexive form it signifies to be wise in one's own eyes, and hence to outwit another. The general rendering of the LXX is σοφία, which is used in the same largeness of sense in the N. T. See especially James 3. 17. It is moral rather than intellectual; it is the adaptation of what we know to what we have to do. In this sense the Lord Jesus grew in wisdom, *i.e.* in its exercise.

The **understanding** is most generally represented by the word **bin** (בין), to perceive, to be intelligent. This word, again, is used with many shades of meaning, such as to **consider**, **discern, feel, know, look, mark, perceive, view**. The LXX usually represents this word by σύνεσις, but occasionally by ἐπιστήμη and φρόνησις.

Sacal (שכל), to **look**, to be **knowing**, and hence to **prosper**, is used to represent a certain kind of wisdom in Gen. **3**. 6, and a good many other passages. The LXX renderings are generally the same as those last mentioned.

of **darash** (דרש), *to seek*, in the O. T. The Vulgate confirms this view by reading *interrogatio conscientiæ bonæ in Deum.* Luther renders 'the contract (Bund) of a good con-cience (Gewissen) with God.' De Sacy takes it as 'the engagement of the conscience to keep pure for God.'

One word remains to be noticed, namely, **tushiah** (תישיה). The LXX renderings for this word are very variable. Some critics understand it as signifying *essentia* or existent being. Hence it is rendered 'that which is' in Job 11. 6, 26. 3, and substance in Job 30. 22. Compare the cognate *yesh* (יש) in Prov. 8. 21. In Isa. 28. 29, it is translated working, 'wonderful in counsel, and excellent in working.' In Job 5. 12, we find the word enterprise adopted. The most general rendering, however, is wisdom, or sound wisdom. Thus we read in Job 6. 13, 'Is wisdom quite driven from me?' Prov. 2. 7, 'He layeth up sound wisdom for the righteous;' 8. 14, 'Counsel is mine, and sound wisdom;' Micah 6. 9, 'The Lord's voice crieth unto the city, and (the man of) wisdom shall see thy name;' the margin has here, 'Thy name shall see that which is.'

CHAPTER VI.

SIN.

The pictorial power of the Hebrew language is seldom exhibited more clearly than in connection with the various aspects of evil. Every word is a piece of philosophy; nay, it is a revelation. The observer of human affairs is painfully struck by the wearisomeness of life, and by the amount of toil and travail which the children of men have to undergo to obtain a bare existence; he sees the hollowness, vanity, and unreality of much that seems bright and charming at first; he notes that human nature, in its personal and social aspects, is distorted and out of course; that the chain of love which ought to bind the great family in one has been snapped asunder; that isolation and desolation have taken the place of unity and happiness; that the relationship between man and his Maker has become obscured, and that even when man knows the will of God, there is something in his nature which prompts him to rebel against it; lastly, he comes to the conviction that this state of things is not original, but is opposed to men's best instincts, and frustrates the original design of their creation.

The Hebrew Bible meets us with a full acknowledgment of these manifold aspects of human suffering, and blends wrongdoing and suffering to a remarkable degree, setting forth sin in its relation to God, to society, and to a man's own self, depicting it in its negative aspect as iniquity or unrighteousness, and in its positive aspect as rebellion and a breach of trust.

§ 1. *Sin.*

The word translated sin throughout the O. T., with very rare exceptions, is derived from the word **Chatha** (חטא), which originally signifies *to miss the mark*, and answers to the Greek ἁμαρτάνω, notifying the fact that all wrong-doing is a *failure* or a *coming*

short of that aim which God intended all His children to reach.[1]
If man was originally made in the image of God, it must have
been implanted in him as a first principle that he should live as
God lives. Every departure, therefore, from the law of Right is
a coming short of the purpose for which man was made, and a
missing of the goal which ought to be reached.

The word usually implies blame-worthiness, and is largely
used in confessions, to express a conviction that wrong has been
done either towards God or towards man. This wrong is not
necessarily wilful, for many sins were committed through negligence
or ignorance (see Lev. 4. 2, 5. 15, Num. 15. 28). Sin is not usually
regarded in the O. T. as a condition (*i.e.* sinfulness), but as a definite
act, whether of thought, word, or deed. The word was applied not
only to moral evil and idolatry, but also to breaches of ceremonial
regulations.

The following are the only passages in which other words
besides **Chatha** have been rendered sin by the translators of the
A. V. In Lev. 4. 13, and Num. 15. 28, 29, we find the word
Shagah (שׁנה), to err; in 1 Kings 17. 18, 'Aven (עון), vanity or
iniquity; in Prov. 10. 12, 19, 28. 13, Pesha' (פשׁע), rebellion or
trangression.

Chatha is occasionally rendered by some other word instead
of sin. Thus it is rendered fault in Gen. 41. 9, and Exod. 5. 16;
trespass in 1 Kings 8. 31; harm in Lev. 5. 16; blame in Gen.
43. 9, and 44. 32; offend in Gen. 20. 9, 40. 1; 1 Kings 1. 21; 2
Kings 18. 14; Eccles. 10. 4; Isa. 29. 21; and Jer. 37. 18.

The verb has a peculiar meaning in the *Piel* or *Intensive* Voice,
as is the case with several other verbs. In this Voice it is rendered
as follows:—to make reconciliation (2 Chron. 29. 24); to bear loss
(Gen. 31. 39); to offer for sin (Leviticus *passim*); to cleanse from
sin (Exod. 29. 36; Lev. 14. 49, 52; Ezek. 43. 20, 22, 23, 45. 18);
to purge or purify (Lev. 8. 15; Num. 8. 7, 21; 19. 9, 12, 13, 17,
19, 20; 31. 19, 20, 23); also in the familiar words of the Psalm
(51. 7), 'Purge me with hyssop and I shall be clean,' and in Job
41. 25, where we read of the Leviathan that 'when he raiseth up
himself, the mighty are afraid; by reason of breakings they purify
themselves.'

The LXX, which is generally very consistent in retaining

---

[1] The word is used in its original sense in Jud. 20. 16, where we read of
'seven hundred chosen men left-handed, every one of whom could sling stones
at an hair's breadth, and not miss.'

the rendering ἁμαρτάνω, has in some ceremonial passages adopted
renderings similar to those now noticed. Thus we find ἐξιλάσκομαι
in 2 Chron. **29**. 24, Ezek. **43**. 22, **45**. 18 ; ἁγνίζω in Num. **8**. 21, **19**.
12, 13, **31**. 19, 23 ; ἀφαγνίζω in Lev. **14**. 49, 52, Num. **19**. 12, 19,
20, **31**. 20 ; καθαρίζω in Exod. **29**. 36, Lev. **8**. 15, **9**. 15 ; ῥαντίζω in
Ps. **51**. 7; ἱλασμός in Ezek. **44**. 27; ἐξιλασμός in Exod. **30**. 10, Ezek.
43. 23, **45**. 19 ; ἄγνισμα in Num. **19**. 19 ; and ἁγνισμός in Num. **8**.
7, **19**. 17.

§ 2. *Wrong.*

The perversion or distortion of nature which is caused by evil-
doing is represented by the word 'avah (עָוָה), to be **bent** or
crooked. The original meaning of the word is found in Isa. **21**.
3, 'I was **bowed down** at the hearing of it;' Lam. **3**. 9, 'He
hath made my ways **crooked**;' and perhaps Ps. **38**. 6, where we
read in the A. V., 'I am **troubled**, I am bowed down greatly.' The
English word **wrong**, *i.e.* that which is **wrung** out of course, gives
the same idea of evil, and is taken as a translation of 'avah in
Esther **1**. 16. We also find the analogous word **perverseness** as
a rendering in 1 Sam. **20**. 30; 2 Sam. **19**. 19; 1 Kings **8**. 47; Job
33. 27; Prov. **12**. 8; Isa. **19**. 14; and Jer. **3**. 21. **Amiss** is found
in 2 Chron. **6**. 37 ; and **iniquity** in 2 Sam. **7**. 14; Ps. **65**. 3, **106**.
6; Jer. **9**. 5; Ezek. **28**. 18; Dan. **4**. 27, **9**. 5; and Mal. **2**. 6.

The chief renderings for 'avah in the LXX are ἁμαρτία, ἀνομία,
and ἀδικία, none of which quite coincide with the original in their
primary meaning.

§ 3. *Travail.*

That sin has made life a **burden** and has turned work into
toil and **travail** is acknowledged by all, and this fact has found
its place among the lessons contained in Hebrew words. The word
'amal (עָמָל) sets forth labour in its toilsome aspect, and is well
represented in the LXX by κόπος, μόχθος, and πόνος. It is
rendered **toil** in Gen. **41**. 51; **trouble** in Job **5**. 6, 7 ; **wearisome** in Job **7**. 3 ; **sorrow** in Job **3**. 10, Ps. **55**. 10; **pain** or
painful (in its old sense, as involving labour) in Ps. **25**. 18, **73**.
16; and **labour** in Ps. **90**. 10, 'Yet is their strength labour and
sorrow.' This last rendering is constantly found in the Book of
Ecclesiastes, which is devoted in great measure to a setting forth
of the burdensomeness of an earthly existence. In Eccles. **4**. 6, 'amal
is rendered **travail**, and this rendering has been adopted in Isa.

53. 11, where we read of the Messiah that 'he shall see (the fruits) of the **travail** of his soul, and shall be satisfied.'

The passages hitherto noted do not trace the weariness of life to its source, but there are others in which this is not obscurely taught. In Isa. **10**. 1, and Hab. **1**. 3, 'amal is rendered **grievousness**; in Num. **23**. 21, **perverseness**, 'he hath not seen perverseness in Israel;' in Hab. **1**. 13, iniquity, 'thou canst not look on iniquity;' in Job **4**. 8, **wickedness**; in Job **15**. 35, **mischief**, 'they conceive mischief and bring forth vanity.' See also Ps. **7**. 14, 16; **10**. 7, 14; **94**. 20; **140**. 9; Prov. **24**. 2; Isa. **59**. 4, in all of which the same rendering is given and the same idea implied.

§ 4. *Iniquity.*

The word 'aval (עָוֶל) is thought to designate the want of integrity and rectitude which is the accompaniment, if not the essential part, of wrong-doing. This word in some of its forms reminds one of the word *evil* (Ger. *Uebel*), and of the contracted word *ill*. The chief renderings for it in the LXX are ἀδικία and ἀνομία, of which the first is probably the best. 'Aval is rendered **unjust** in Ps. **43**. 1, **82**. 2, Prov. **29**. 27, Isa. **26**. 10, Zeph. **3**. 5; **unrighteous** in Lev. **19**. 15, 35, Deut. **25**. 16, Job **27**. 7, Ps. **71**. 4, **92**. 15; **ungodly** in Job **16**. 11; **perverse** in Isa. **59**. 3; **wicked** in twelve passages, including Ps. **89**. 22, 'The enemy shall not exact upon him, nor the son of **wickedness** afflict him.'

'Aval is also rendered **iniquity** in about thirty passages; and this word, taken in its original sense, as a departure from that which is equal and right, is probably the most suitable rendering. The usage of the word is well illustrated by Mal. **2**. 6, where we read of Levi that 'the law of truth was in his mouth, and **iniquity** was not found in his lips; he walked with me in peace and equity, and did turn many away from unrighteousness.'

§ 5. *Transgression.*

The idea of **transgression**, or crossing over the boundary of right and entering the forbidden land of wrong, is marked by the use of the word 'Avar (עָבַר), to cross over (compare the Assyrian *ebiru*, 'to cross'). The word is rendered **transgress** in eighteen passages, *e.g.* Ps. **17**. 3, Hos. **6**. 7, and **8**. 1.

§ 6. *Evil.*

The word generally used for evil and wickedness is **ra'** (רע),
which appears to signify *breaking up* or *ruin.* The LXX rendering
for it is usually κακός or πονηρός. It is one of those words which
binds together in one the wicked deed and its consequences. It is
evil as opposed to good in Gen. 2. 17, *al.* It is rendered calamity
in Ps. 141. 5; distress in Neh. 2. 17; adversity in 1 Sam. 10.
19, Ps. 94. 13, and Eccles. 7. 14; grief in Neh. 2. 10, Prov. 15. 10,
Eccles. 2. 17, Jonah 4. 6; affliction in Num. 11. 11, and ten other
passages; misery in Eccles. 8. 6; sad in Gen. 40. 7, Neh. 2. 1, 2,
Eccles. 7. 3; sorrow in Gen. 44. 29, Neh. 2. 2; trouble in Ps. 41. 1,
and eight other passages; sore in Deut. 6. 22, and eight other passages; noisome in Ezek. 14. 15, 21; hurt in Gen. 26. 29, and
twenty-eight other passages; heavy in Prov. 25. 20; vex in Num.
20. 15, and 2 Sam. 12. 18; wretchedness in Num. 11. 15; also
harm, ill, and mischief in almost every place where these words
are found in the A. V.

These passages sometimes imply injury done to a person, but do
not touch upon its moral aspect. This is to be borne in mind as we
read Isa. 45. 7, 'I create evil,' and similar verses. In other cases,
however, this element is introduced. In Jud. 11. 27, we read, 'I
have not sinned against thee, but thou doest me wrong to war
against me;' here the wrong or injury is regarded as an injustice.
Again, in 1 Sam. 17. 28, 'I know thy pride and the naughtiness
of thy heart,' moral evil seems to be intended. The word is also
rendered 'naught' or 'naughty' in 2 Kings 2. 19, Prov. 20. 14,
and Jer. 24. 2; but in these passages naughty has its original
sense of 'good for nothing,' a sense in which the word is still used
in some parts of England. Perhaps this was all that was implied
in Eliab's rude speech to David.

Ra' is rendered wicked a great many times; it is also frequently
rendered bad, but in the latter class of passages that which is
injurious is referred to rather than that which is morally evil.
Ra', in fact, generally indicates the rough exterior of wrong-doing,
as a breach of harmony, and as a breaking up of what is good and
desirable in man and in society. Whilst the prominent characteristic
of the godly is lovingkindness, one of the most marked features of
the ungodly man is that his course is an injury both to himself and
to every one round him.

§ 7. *Rebellion.*

Pasha' (פִּשַׁע) signifies to revolt or refuse subjection to rightful
authority. It is very generally rendered transgression. The
chief LXX renderings for it are ἀσέβεια, ἀδικία, and ἀνομία. We
meet with the verb in Ps. 51. 13, ' Then will I teach transgressors
thy ways, and sinners shall be converted unto thee;' Prov. 28. 21,
' For a piece of bread a man will transgress' (*i.e.* rebel); Isa. 43. 27,
'Thy teachers have transgressed against me.'

Pasha' is rendered sin in Prov. 10. 12, ' Love covereth all sins,'
where the contrast between the offence and the mercy is brought
out very clearly by the use of the word; again it is found in verse
19, ' In the multitude of words there wanteth not sin ;' 28. 13, ' He
that covereth his sins shall not prosper.' It is rendered trespass
in Gen. 31. 36, 50. 17 ; Exod. 22. 9 ; 1 Sam. 25. 28 ; and Hos. 8. 1,
' They have trespassed against my law.' In 2 Kings 8. 20, 22, it
is used in its primary sense of the revolt of Edom and Libnah ; in
1 Kings 12. 19, of the 'rebellion' of Israel against Judah ; so also
in other passages. We meet with the word in Job 34. 37, where it
is said of him that ' he addeth rebellion unto his sin.' Lastly, it
occurs in the opening of the prophecies of Isaiah, ' I have nourished
and brought up children, and they have rebelled against me'
(Isa. 1. 2).

§ 8. *Wickedness.*

Rasha' (רָשַׁע) is the word most generally rendered wicked [1] in
the A. V. It is supposed originally to refer to the *activity,* the
tossing, and the *confusion* in which the wicked live, and the perpetual
agitation which they cause to others. Thus Isaiah says (57. 20, 21),
'The wicked are like the troubled sea when it cannot rest, whose
waters cast up mire and dirt; there is no peace, saith my God, to
the wicked.' Job also (3. 17) looks forward to the grave as the
place ' where the wicked cease from troubling, and the weary are at
rest.' In the Book of Job the wicked are represented as triumphing
for a time, but as finally put out into darkness ; in the Psalms they
are represented as busily occupied in disturbing the peace of others,

---

[1] The word *wicked* is supposed by some etymologists to be connected with
quick, and to mean *lively ;* if this be its true significance, it answers admirably to
Rasha'. See Dean Hoare's work on *English Roots.*

F

and as trying to destroy them. They are frequently contrasted with the righteous; and their ways are fully described in Ezekiel, chaps. **18.** and **33.** If Kennicott's view of Isa. **53.** 9 could be substantiated, we should read of the Messiah, 'he made his grave with the rich, but with the **wicked** was his death;' and the use of the word to mark the robbers or disturbers of the public peace would have been very appropriate.

Rasha' is usually rendered ἀσεβής, ungodly, in the LXX, but ἄνομος and ἁμαρτωλός are found in several passages.

The *verb* in its Hiphil or causative form is generally taken as signifying to condemn, literally 'to make wicked,' and hence 'to deal with as wicked.' It is found in all but four passages where the word 'condemn' occurs in the A. V.

§ 9. *Breach of Trust.*

The word **Ma'al** (מעל) probably points to the unfaithfulness and treachery of sin, and represents wrong-doing as a breach of trust, whether between man and man or between man and God. It is rendered trespass about thirty times, transgression fifteen times, and falsehood in Job **21.** 34. In the first passage where it occurs (Lev. **5.** 15), it refers to the trespass committed in ignorance; in the second, to any sin committed against one's neighbour (**6.** 2). In Josh. **7.** 1, 22. 20, it is used of Achan's sin; the building of the altar on the east of Jordan was also described by this word (Josh. **22.** 16); it is applied to Uzziah (2 Chron. **26.** 18); to Ahaz (**28.** 22); to Manasseh (**33.** 19); and to the people who married heathen wives (Ezra **9.** 2, 4; Neh. **13.** 27). Lastly, it is found in Prov. **16.** 10, where we read that 'the king's mouth transgresseth not in judgment.' The breach of trust denoted by this word was regarded by God in a very serious light. See Ezek. **14.** 13, **15.** 8, **18.** 24, **39.** 23. The reason of this is manifest. The persons guilty of sin in this particular aspect were chiefly persons in authority. A certain trust had been reposed in them, which they had abused. Much had been given to them, and much was required of them. The nation of Israel as a whole were put in a position of high privilege and consequent responsibility, hence their departure from the way of God was marked specially by this word as an act of unfaithfulness. The word **Bagad** (בגד), to deal treacherously, is sometimes used in the same sense.

§ 10. *Vanity.*

The word most frequently rendered iniquity is **Aven** (אָוֶן) —Assyrian, *'annu.* Some critics connect this word with a root which signifies desire; others, with greater reason, hold that its original meaning is nothingness. Its connection with idolatry is noticeable (see chap. 29. § 2), and originates in the fact that an *idol* is a thing of naught, a vain thing. In Amos 5. 5, we read, 'Bethel shall come to naught' (aven); and, turning to Hos. 4. 15, 5. 8, 10. 5, 8, we find that Bethel, the House of God, is designated as Beth-aven, *i.e.* the house of vanity, because idols were worshipped there.

The word is rendered vanity in several passages: Job 15. 35, 'They conceive mischief and bring forth vanity;' Ps. 10. 7, 'Under his tongue is mischief and vanity;' Prov. 22. 8, 'He that soweth iniquity shall reap vanity.' See also Isa. 41. 29, 58. 9; Jer. 4. 14; Zech. 10. 2.

The word **Aven** is to be found in Prov. 11. 7 (unjust); Isa. 10. 1, 55. 7 (unrighteous); Ps. 90. 10 (sorrow); Deut. 26. 14 (mourning); Job 5. 6 (affliction); Ps. 140. 11 (evil); Prov. 17. 4 (false); Ps. 36. 4 (mischief).

Aven is rendered wickedness in a few passages, and iniquity in thirty-eight places. The most noticeable are: Num. 23. 21; 1 Sam. 15. 23; Job 4. 8, 21. 19, 31. 3, 34. 22; Ps. 5. 5, 6. 8; Isa. 1. 13; Micah 2. 1.

On considering all these passages, we shall be led to the conclusion that the word **Aven** suggests not so much breach of law, or injury done to another, as a course of conduct which will in the end prove unprofitable to the doer. It presents the evil devices of man in their false, hollow, and unreal aspect; and by the use of this word the inspired writers put a stamp of nothingness or unreality upon every departure from the law of God, whether it consists of wrong-doing, evil devising, false speaking, or idolatrous worship.

The leading rendering of **Aven** in the LXX is ἀνομία; ἀδικία is used several times; πόνος and κόπος occasionally.

§ 11. *Guilt.*

We now come to a word about which there has been a good deal of difference of opinion, namely, **Asham** (אָשָׁם), the usual rendering of which in the LXX is πλημμέλεια, a mistake, and in the A. V. trespass or guilt.[1]

---

[1] The English word *guilt* is probably derived from A. S. *geldan*, to pay a fine.

Some critics hold that whilst **Chatha** denotes sins of commission, **Asham** designates sins of omission. Others have come to the conclusion that **Chatha** means sin in general, and **Asham** sin against the Mosaic law. An examination of all the passages in which the word occurs leads to the conclusion that **Asham** is used where a sin, moral or ceremonial, has been committed through error, negligence, or ignorance. A loose code of morality might permit such offences to be passed by, but not so the law of Moses. An offence against the person of another *is* an offence, whether it be known or found out at the time or not. When it comes to our knowledge, we are liable, *i.e.* we are to regard ourselves as having offended, even though it has been unwittingly; and compensation must be made. So also when the offence is a breach of ceremonial law, or if it is an act of idolatry (for which the word **Asham** is frequently used), when the matter is brought to a man's cognisance, he is not to content himself with the excuse that he acted in error, but is to acknowledge himself as **Asham**, and is to offer an **Asham** or guilt-offering [1] for his trespass.

The following passages are the most notable in which the word occurs:—

Lev. 4. 13, 'If the whole congregation of Israel sin through error (A. V. ignorance), and the thing be hid from the eyes of the assembly, and they have done (somewhat against) any of the commandments of the Lord (concerning things) which should not be done, and are **guilty**,' &c.; so also in verses 22 and 27. In these cases a commandment has been broken unwittingly; it afterwards comes to the knowledge of the offender, and he is **Asham**.

Lev. 5. 2, 3, 'If a soul touch any unclean thing, and if it be hidden from him, he also shall be unclean and **guilty** . . . when he knoweth it, he shall be **guilty**;' verse 4, 'Or if a soul swear . . . and it be hid from him, when he knoweth of it, then he shall be **guilty**;' verses 5, 6, 'And it shall be, when he shall be **guilty** in one of these things, that he shall confess that he hath sinned in that thing, and he shall bring his **trespass-offering**;' verse 15, 'If a soul commit a trespass (**ma'al**), and sin through error (or ignorance), in the holy things of the Lord; then he shall bring for his trespass unto the Lord a ram . . . for a **trespass-offering**;' verse 17, 'If a soul sin, and commit any of these things that are forbidden to be done by the commandments of the Lord; though he wist it not, yet he is **guilty**, and shall bear his iniquity; and

---

[1] See chap. xvi.

he shall bring a ram . . . and the priest shall make an atonement for him concerning his ignorance wherein he erred and wist it not, and it shall be forgiven him.[1] It is a trespass-offering: he hath certainly trespassed against the Lord.'

It is unfortunate that unity of rendering has not been preserved in these passages, as there is nothing to show the English reader the connection between the words guilty and trespass. But see R. V. Compare Gen. 42. 21 ; Num. 5. 6, 7 ; Jud. 21. 22 ; 1 Chron. 21. 3 ; 2 Chron. 19. 10, 28. 10, 13 ; Ezra 10. 19 ; Ps. 69. 5 ; Prov. 30. 10 ; Jer. 2. 3, 50. 7 ; Ezek. 22. 4, 25. 12 ; Hos. 4. 15, 5. 15, 10. 2 (compare 2 Sam. 14. 13).

It may be gathered from a consideration of these passages that whilst **Chatha** marks the peculiar nature of sin as a missing of the mark, **Asham** implies a breach of commandment, wrought without due consideration, and which, when brought to the notice of the offender, calls for amends or atonement.

§ 12. *Words for Sin in the N. T.*

Most of the Greek words which have been referred to in the foregoing sections are to be found in the N. T. The original sense of ἁμαρτάνω and **Chatha** seems to be referred to in a most important passage in the Epistle to the Romans (3. 23), 'All have sinned and come short of the glory of God.' The sinner is one who has missed or come short of the mark. An important definition of sin is given by St. James—'to him that knoweth to do good, and doeth it not, to him it is sin' (4. 17). It would seem to be implied that where there is no knowledge of what is right or wrong there is no sin ; and with this agree the words of our Lord to the Pharisees, 'If ye were blind, ye should have no sin : but now ye say, We see ; therefore your sin remaineth' (John 9. 41). The profession of knowledge involved responsibility, and caused the Pharisees to be condemned, out of their own mouth, as sinners. Absolute ignorance is excusable, even though it is a missing of the mark, but negligence is not (see Heb. 2. 3).

The relationship of ἀνομία to ἁμαρτία is clearly shown in 1 John 3. 4, 'Whosoever committeth sin committeth iniquity (ἀνομίαν): and sin is iniquity.' So again with regard to the connection existing between ἀδικία, departure from right, and ἁμαρτία, we read

---

[1] Is it not in some degree implied here that a man is, in a measure at least, responsible for his *ignorance* ?

(1 John 5. 17), ' All unrighteousness is sin.' A similar relationship between ἀσέβεια and ἁμαρτία is implied in the juncture of ἀσεβεῖς and ἁμαρτωλοὶ in 1 Tim. 1. 9, 1 Pet. 4. 18, and Jude 15. With regard to all these words, it is to be noticed that the N. T. leans upon the O. T., and that the vivid teaching of the latter is taken for granted as authoritative by the writers of the Christian Scriptures.

The labour and wearisomeness of sin is not dwelt upon in the N. T., and the words which imply it are usually found in a more noble sense, in connection with toil for Christ. With regard to κόπος, one passage may be referred to as an illustration of this fact, namely, 1 Cor. 3. 8, where we read that every minister shall be rewarded according to his own labour (κόπον). He shall be rewarded not by the results produced—this would have involved the use of the word ἔργον—but by the amount of labour expended; hence κόπος is used. A few verses further down ἔργον is used with great propriety, where we read that the fire shall test a man's work, of what sort it is. Here the point of the passage is that it is not the outward show or bulk, but the real value of the work done, which shall be the test of a man's faithfulness at the Great Day. The words κόπος and μόχθος are found together in 2 Cor. 11. 27, 1 Thess. 2. 9, and 2 Thess. 3. 8. While the former implies pains and labour, the latter signifies toil of such a sort as produces weariness. Where πόνος is used, it is generally to indicate a tax upon one's physical strength, whether arising from toil or from pain. In Rev. 21, 4, we are told that there shall be none of it in the new heaven and earth. The etymological relationship between πόνος and πονηρία is undoubted, though no passages in the N. T. clearly refer to it, and the double use of the word '**Amal** is exactly analogous to it. Πονηρία is often to be understood in the N. T. as signifying rapacity, which is the fruit of covetousness. It is also used of ' evil spirits.'

CHAPTER VII.

REPENTANCE, CONVERSION, AMENDMENT.

THE previous chapters of this book have been occupied with discussion on the names, and consequently on the nature and capacities, of God and of man, and also on the varied aspects of human sin. Attention is now to be called to some of the sacred words used to express the moral or spiritual process whereby man is restored to his true position. Two ideas are set forth in the O. T., and adopted in the N. T., in this connection; the one marks the bringing of a man to *himself*, the other the bringing of a man *to God;* the one is ordinarily designated repentance, the other conversion.

§ 1. *Repentance.*

Very various views have been held with respect to the meaning of the word repentance. Some take it to indicate a change of heart or disposition, others a change of mind or thought (the *Sinnesän-derung* of the Berlenburger Bible), others a change of aim or purpose, and others a change of life or conduct. With the exception of three passages—namely, 1 Kings 8. 47, Ezek. 14. 6, and 18 30 (in which the Hebrew is **Shuv**[1] [שׁוּב], and the Greek ἐπιστρέφω)—the English word repent is used in the A. V. to represent a form of the Hebrew **Nacham** (נחם), from which the name of the prophet Nahum is derived. The original meaning of this word is generally understood to be *to draw a deep breath*, and this is taken as the physical mode of giving expression to a deep feeling, either of relief or sorrow. The one aspect of **Nacham** is represented by the Greek παρακάλεισθαι, the other by μετανοέιν and μεταμέλεσθαι.

Nacham is rendered by μετανοέιν in the following passages: 1 Sam. **15.** 29, 'The Strength of Israel will not lie nor **repent**: for he is not a man, that he should **repent**;' Jer. **4.** 28, 'I have

---

[1] See below, § 3.

purposed it, and will not repent;' Jer. **18**. 8, 'If that nation
against whom I have pronounced turn from their evil, I will
repent of the evil that I thought to do unto them' (compare verse
10, where we read, 'If it do evil in my sight, that it obey not my
voice, then I will repent of the good wherewith I said I would
benefit them'); Joel **2**. 13, 14, 'The Lord . . . repenteth him of
the evil. Who knoweth if he will return and repent;' Amos
7. 3, 6, 'The Lord repented for this. It shall not be, saith the
Lord;' Jonah **3**. 10, 'God repented of the evil that he had said
he would do unto them; and he did it not;' see also **4**. 2; Zech.
8. 14, 'I repented not.'

All these passages refer to God's repentance; the two which
remain refer to man's: Jer. **8**. 6, 'No man repented him of his
wickedness, saying, What have I done?' Jer. **31**. 19, 'Surely after
that I was turned, I repented; and after that I was instructed, I
smote upon my thigh.'

The LXX has μεταμέλομαι for **Nacham** in the following
passages: Gen. **6**. 7, 'It repenteth me that I have made them;'
1 Sam. **15**. 11, 'It repenteth me that I have set up Saul to
be king' (see also verse 35); 1 Chron. **21**. 15, 'The Lord beheld,
and he repented him of the evil, and said to the angel that
destroyed, It is enough, stay now thine hand;' Ps. **106**. 45, 'He
remembered for them his covenant, and repented according to
the multitude of his mercies;' Ps. **110**. 4, 'The Lord hath sworn,
and will not repent;' Jer. **20**. 16, 'Let that man be as the cities
which the Lord overthrew, and repented not;' Hosea **11**. 8,
'Mine heart is turned within me, my repentings are kindled
together.'

In the following passages this Greek word is used in the LXX
of *man's* repentance: Exod. **13**. 17, 'Lest peradventure the people
repent when they see war, and they return to Egypt;' Ezek. **14**. 22,
'Ye shall repent (A. V. be comforted) concerning the evil that I
have brought upon Jerusalem.'

It is evident, from a consideration of these passages, that when
we approach the subject of repentance in the N. T., we must not
tie it down too strictly, either to one formal process, or to one
set time in a man's life, but must understand by it such a state
of deep feeling as leads to a change or amendment of life. The
etymology and the classical usage of the words μετανοεῖν and
μεταμέλεσθαι must give way before the fact that these words were
used by Greek-speaking Jews, as representatives of the passive

and reflexive voices of **Nacham**. It is hard indeed to find one expression in any language which can adequately represent the complex emotions implied by the word. When the word is used with reference to God, there is implied an idea of change, and perhaps of sorrow, but not the consciousness of wrong-doing. When it is used with reference to man, sorrow arises from a sense of sin, a conviction of wrong-doing in its varied aspects fills the heart with bitterness, and change of purpose and of the outward life ensue; also an undercurrent of *relief* accompanies the sorrow, for the penitent draws a deep breath as the sin, which has been leading him astray, shows itself to him in its true colours, and gives way before the announcement of mercy.

There is a remarkable tract on Penitence [1] written by Moses Maimonides, in which the subject is treated, not as a matter of feeling, but of practice. Penitence is described as the condition of a man who, having once fallen into a sin, now abstains from it, although the inducements to return to it are as strong as ever. The Hebrew word which the writer adopts to represent this process is a noun derived from **shuv**, to turn. But the first open step in this change is confession, which is to be expressed in the following form of words: 'O Lord, I have sinned; I have done wrong, and have been a transgressor before Thee, and I have done such and such things; behold, I am sorry (**Nacham**), and am ashamed because of my misdeeds, and I will never commit any such offences again.' It is neither sorrow without change, nor change without sorrow, but it is such a deep feeling of sorrow as gives rise to a determination to change, or, as the English Church Catechism has it, 'repentance whereby we forsake sin.'

The learned Rosenmüller defines r e p e n t a n c e as the admission of wrong-doing followed by grief and leading to a wiser course: '*Post factum sapere, et de errore admisso ita dolere ut sapias.*' [2] He holds to the Latin *resipiscere* as the best rendering of the word; and this view has been very common since the days of Beza, from whom Rosenmüller takes his definition almost word for word. The distinction between μεταμέλεια, r e g r e t, and μετάνοια, r e c o n s i d e r a t i o n, which Beza held, must not be pressed very far, because, as we have seen, these words are used in almost the same sense in the LXX. [3] Besides, as a matter of fact, the noun μεταμέλεια

---

[1] An edition of this tract, with a Latin translation by Mr. Clavering, was published in Oxford in 1705.   [2] Schol. in N. T.

[3] The opinion here advanced has the support of Elsner. See also Archbishop

does not occur in the N. T., and the verb μεταμέλεσθαι falls into the background. It is once used with respect to *God*, viz. in Heb. 7. 21, which is quoted from Ps. 110. 4 ; and four times of *man*, viz. in Matt. 21. 29, 32, 27. 3 ; 2 Cor. 7. 8. See the negative form in Rom. 11. 29 ; 2 Cor. 7. 10.

The objections to the Latin word *Pœnitentia* as a rendering of μετάνοια were more forcibly expressed by Erasmus in his *Annotations*. But he wrote without at all taking into consideration the Hebrew and Judæo-Greek usage, whence we derive the word μετάνοια. Because in his days the Roman sacrament of *penance*, *i.e.* satisfaction for sins committed *after* baptism, was called by the same name as *penitence*, or sorrow for sins committed either *before* or *after* baptism, he thought that some other word should be adopted. He called *pœnitentia* a barbarism and a solecism, and to him must be given the credit of pressing upon his contemporaries the word *resipiscentia*, which had previously been adopted by Lactantius, as the better of the two. Lucas Brugensis, however, well replies that *pœnitentia* had a far wider meaning amongst Latin ecclesiastical writers than was usually supposed ; it implied not only sorrow, but also a change for the better. Whilst, on the other hand, μετάνοια had a wider meaning than *change;* for it included *sorrow*, and compunction of heart.

In the Decrees of the Council of Trent, a careful distinction is drawn between the *pœnitentia* which precedes baptism, and that which follows it. The former is general, and consists of a sorrow for sin with a renunciation of wickedness. Here we have the complex idea of repentance evidently implied in the usage of the word, though not in its etymology. The *pœnitentia* which follows after baptism is not efficacious, according to the theory of the Church of Rome, without confession followed by sacerdotal absolution.[1]

When Martin Luther made his first translation of the N. T.,

Trench's discussions on the word. In his work on the 'Synonyms of the N. T.' he is inclined to draw out the distinction between the two words above named, but in his work on the 'Authorised Version' he rather disclaims Beza's *resipiscentia*.

[1] Satisfaction, according to the Tridentine theology, consists of certain acts of self-denial, whether corporal suffering or otherwise, imposed on the penitent according to the judgment of the priest and the rules of the Church, for the purpose of bringing men into greater conformity with Christ ; because ' If we *suffer* with him, we shall also be glorified together.' These acts are considered to represent the 'fruits meet for repentance,' and to be accepted by God through Christ.

he adopted the phrase *bessert euch*, 'better yourselves' (a phrase answering to 'amend your ways') as a rendering for μετανοεῖτε, repent; but after a few years he returned to the customary phrase of the country, *thut Busse*, a phrase answering to *Do penance* or *Be penitent*. Perhaps he was moved to this change by the feeling that moral amendment in the abstract was no equivalent for repentance, and tended rather to mislead. In seven passages he has *Reue*, regret; thus the 'repentance not to be repented of' (Vulg. *pœnitentiam stabilem*) is rendered '*eine Reue, die Niemand gereuet*,' a regret which no man regrets.

§ 2. *Comfort.*

Where the word **Nacham** signifies to be comforted, the LXX rendering is usually a form of παρακαλέω. But the word comfort in its modern usage hardly conveys the etymological force which it ought to have. It originally signified support and encouragement, quite as much as consolation. The comforter or advocate of the N. T. administers help and strength as well as peace and joy; and the being comforted often involves both a confirmation in the right course, and also a relinquishing of a previous course.

The verb παρακαλεῖν in the N. T. generally signifies to beseech or to encourage. It represents an earnestness and urgency prompted by deep feeling—see, for example, Matt. 8. 5, where the leper falls before Christ, 'beseeching him' to cleanse him; Rom. 12. 1, 'I beseech you by the mercies of God.' Sometimes, however, it signifies to cheer up, as in 2 Cor. 1. 4, 'Who comforteth us in all our tribulations.' Compare Matt. 5. 4, 'Blessed are they that mourn, for they shall be comforted.'

The word παράκλητος occurs five times in the N. T. In four of these passages we have rendered it by the word comforter. In the fifth, although we have our Lord's authority for adopting the same rendering in the one case as in the other,[1] we have rendered it Advocate. The Vulgate has *paraclitus* in John 14. 16, and *advocatus* in 1 John 2. 1; so Luther has *Tröster* and *Fürsprecher*. The word *Beistand* adopted by De Wette and Van Ess gives rather the classical than the Judæo-Greek sense.

---

[1] 'He shall give you *another* Comforter,' implying that they had *one* already, even Himself. St. John in his First Epistle may well be supposed to have this passage in his mind when he uses the word παράκλητος of Christ.

In Rom. **15**. 4, 5, we read of 'patience and comfort' of the Scriptures, and of 'the God of patience and consolation.' The Apostle here beautifully represents the truth that the Scriptures are the *means* of conveying that patience and comfort of which God is the *source*. The R. V. has comfort in both verses.

§ 3. *Conversion.*

Two words answer to the English word conversion in the O. T. **Haphac** (הפך), *to turn*, is used in Isa. **60**. 5, 'The abundance of the sea shall be converted unto thee.' **Shuv** (שוב), *to return*, is the general word. It is found in Ps. **51**. 13, 'Sinners shall be converted unto thee;' Ps. **19**. 7, 'The law of the Lord is perfect, converting (or restoring) the soul;' Isa. **1**. 27, 'Zion shall be redeemed with judgment, and her converts (or they that return of her) with righteousness;' **6**. 10, 'Lest they see with their eyes, and hear with their ears, and understand with their heart, and convert and be healed.' In these passages, with the exception of Ps. **19**. 7, the word is used in the active voice, and in a neuter sense, and might be rendered return. It is frequently used with a second verb to give the sense of 'again' or 'back.'

The LXX usually renders **Shuv** by ἐπιστρέφω, which is the general word used to represent the turning of the heart to God, whether from Judaism, idolatry, or sin, in the N. T. See, for example, Gal. **4**. 9; 1 Thess. **1**. 9; James **5**. 19, 20. The process called conversion or turning to God is in reality a *re-turning*, or a turning back again to Him from whom sin has separated us, but whose we are by virtue of creation, preservation, and redemption. The form στρέφω is used in Matt. **18**. 3.

§ 4. *Amendment.*

The idea of amendment or improvement has been sanctioned by our translators in a few passages. In 2 Chron. **34**. 10, where we read of the amending of the House of the Lord, the Hebrew word is **Chazak**, to be strong. In Jer. **7**. 3, 5, 26. 13, **35**. 15 ('Amend your ways'), we find **Yathav** (יטב), to make good. This word is used in a great variety of senses in the O. T. Thus it is said that 'God saw all that he had made, and behold it was very good,' Gen. **1**. 31; in Exod. **2**. 2, Moses is called 'a goodly child;' the tents of Israel too are called 'goodly,' Num. **24**. 5; it is used of a beautiful woman, 2 Sam. **11**. 2; of the fair daughters of men, Gen. **6**. 2; of fair houses, Isa. **5**. 9; of precious ointment, Ps. **133**. 2, Eccles. **7**. 1; of the idol ready for the sodering, Isa. **41**. 7; of welfare, Neh. **2**. 10; of prosperity, Deut. **23**. 6, Zech. **1**. 17; of wealth, Job **21**. 13; of a good dowry, Gen. **30**. 20; of the tree which was good for food, Gen. **3**. 6; and of a merry heart, 1 Sam. **25**. 36. The thought to be gathered from a consideration of these passages is that goodness is not an absolute moral quality, but signifies that which is agreeable or pleasing, whether to God or man. Hence the verb is rendered to please, or to be pleasant in one's eyes, *e.g.* Neh. **2**. 6, Ps. **69**. 31; to find favour, 1 Sam. **2**. 26, 29. 6; to be accepted, Lev. **10**. 19, 1 Sam. **18**. 5. If this view be correct, we are to understand that when Jeremiah says 'amend your ways,' he does not mean 'improve them' in the abstract, or with relation to what they were before; but rather, 'make your course such as is agreeable to God, and do what is well pleasing in His sight.'

There are several renderings for this word in the LXX, but ἀγαθός, καλός, and χρηστός are the most common. Αγαθός is generally but not always used of moral goodness, as opposed to πονηρία, wickedness, in the N. T., but the idea of what is pleasant in God's sight is implied. In the case of the word καλός, the elements of fairness and nobleness underlie the idea of goodness.

Where χρηστός is used in the N. T., the idea of kindness or kindliness is specially introduced. Thus where the Lord says ὁ ζυγός μου χρηστός (Matt. **11**. 30), we might render His words 'my yoke is *kindly*'—something more than easy; it is grateful to the spiritual sense of the converted man. So of wine, we may read in Luke **5**. 39, 'The old is more kindly;' Luke **6**. 35, 'He is kind to the unthankful;' Rom. **2**. 4, 'The kindness of God leadeth them to repentance;' 1 Cor. **15**. 33, 'Evil communications corrupt kindly manners;' 1 Pet. **2**. 3, 'If so be that ye have tasted that the Lord is kind' (quoted from Ps. **34**. 8).

CHAPTER VIII.

PERFECTION.

§ 1. *Words signifying Perfection.*

THE moral relationship existing between ideas which at first sight appear utterly unconnected with one another, is seldom more beautifully illustrated than in the choice of Hebrew words whereby the ideas of perfection or completeness are portrayed in Scripture.

A few passages may first be noticed in which there is some uncertainty as to the accuracy of our authorised translation. Thus, in 2 Chron. **24. 13**, the word (ארוכה) is generally understood to signify health; but our own language testifies to a relationship here, for health is wholeness. In Jer. **23. 20**, where the A. V. reads, 'Ye shall consider it perfectly,' we might better render the word intelligently (בינה). When the Psalmist says (**138. 8**), 'The Lord will perfect that which concerneth me,' he uses the word **Gamar** (גמר, Assyrian *gamru*), to finish, implying his confidence that God, having begun the good work, will bring it to a successful issue. So Ezra is described as a perfect, *i.e.* a finished, scribe (Ezra **7. 6**).

In Prov. **4. 18**, the A. V. reads, 'The path of the just is as the shining light that shineth more and more unto the perfect day. This verse is sometimes understood as if it meant that the way of the righteous is like the sun, the light of which keeps increasing in brightness until the noonday. But the word here rendered perfect (כון) properly means to fix or establish, and the truth taught is that the way of the righteous is like the dawning light, which increases more and more in steadiness and brightness until the full sun arises and thus establishes the day (LXX, ἕως κατορθώσῃ ἡ ἡμέρα).

Two words, nearly related to each other, and both signifying completion or a consummation, namely, **Calah** (כלה, Assyrian *kalâ*) and **Calal** (כלל, Assyrian *kalâlu*), are found several times in the Scripture. Thus, in Job 11. 7, we read, 'Canst thou find out the Almighty unto perfection,' *i.e.* 'entirely'? Job 28. 3, 'He searcheth out all perfection,' *i.e.* nothing is hid from Him; Ps. 50. 2, 'Out of Zion the perfection (*i.e.* the climax) of beauty God hath shined;' Ps. 119. 96, 'I have seen an end of all perfection (*i.e.* I have thoroughly examined the utmost limits of all things human), but thy commandments are exceeding broad;' Ps. 139. 22, 'I hate them with a perfect (*i.e.* a consummate) hatred;' Lam. 2. 15, 'Is this the city that men call the perfection of beauty?' See also Ezek. 16. 14, 27. 3, 4, 11, and 28. 12.

These two words are usually rendered συντελέω, συντέλεια, ἐξαναλίσκω, παύω, and ἐκλείπω by the LXX.

The word συντέλεια occurs six times in the N. T., and always in one phrase—συντέλεια τοῦ αἰῶνος, or τῶν αἰώνων, 'the end of the world.' Five of these passages are in St. Matthew (13. 39, 40, 49, 24. 3, 28. 20). In Heb. 9. 26, we might render the words 'now once on the completion of the ages or dispensations' (νῦν δὲ ἅπαξ ἐπὶ συντελείᾳ τῶν αἰώνων). The Vulgate, *consummatio sæculi*, the consummation of the age, is an admirable rendering of the Greek, and well sustains the meaning of the Hebrew **Calah**. The German word for *perfection*, Vollkommenheit, answers well to **Calah** and συντέλεισθαι, but it has not been retained in the passages now noticed.

§ 2. *The Word Shalam.*

We now come to one of the most notable words used to represent the idea of perfection, namely, **Shalam** (שלם). It is used of a perfect heart in fourteen passages. Its usual signification is peace, the name **Salem** or **Shalem** being derived from it. Thus we read in Isa. 26. 3, 'Thou wilt keep him in perfect peace' (**Shalom Shalom**). The root may have originally signified *oneness* or *wholeness*, and so *completeness*. Not only does it represent the ideas of peace and perfection, but also of compensation or recompense.[1]

The following renderings have also been given to the verb **Shalam** in the A. V.: to be ended, to be finished, to prosper, to make amends, to pay, to perform, to recompense, to repay, to requite, to make restitution, to restore, to reward.

---

[1] In Assyrian, *salâmu* means to perfect or complete, *salimu* means peace; but the initial letters are slightly different, answering to שׁ and ס.

In all these cases there is implied a bringing of some difficulty to a conclusion, a finishing off of some work, a clearing away, by payment or labour or suffering, of some charge. In Prov. 11. 31, we read, 'the righteous shall be recompensed in the earth; much more the wicked and the sinner.' Here we have for the righteous 'recompense,' or, according to the LXX, 'salvation,' or, we might say, 'peace' on earth; but the messenger of peace to the righteous conveys by implication a presage of wrath to the wicked. The LXX rendering of these words is adopted by St. Peter when he says, 'If the righteous scarcely be saved, where shall the ungodly and the sinner appear?' (1 Pet. 4. 18).

The chief representatives of **Shalam** in the LXX are ἀποδίδωμι, to render; ἀνταποδίδωμι, to recompense;[1] ἀποτίω, to retaliate; ὑγιαίνω, to be whole, or in health; εἰρήνη, peace; σωτήριον, salvation; τέλειος, perfect; and ὁλόκληρος, whole, which last word is found in the phrase 'whole stones' in Deut. 27. 6, and Josh. 8. 31.

§ 3. *The Word Thamam.*

The word **Thamam** (תמם), whence the name of the *Thummim* (perfections) is derived, is best rendered by the words unblemished, entire (*integer*), and sincere. Our translators render it, in one or other of its forms, perfect, plain, undefiled, upright, integrity, simplicity, full, at a venture, without blemish, sincere, sound, without spot, whole, to be consumed, to be accomplished, to end, to fail, to be spent, to be wasted.

The following are the most noteworthy passages in which it occurs:—Gen. 6. 9, 'Noah was a just man, and perfect in his generation.' Gen. 17. 1, 'Walk before me, and be thou perfect' (Luther, *Fromm, i.e.* pious). Lev. 22. 21, 'The sacrifice . . . shall be perfect to be accepted; there shall be no blemish therein.' Deut. 18. 13, 'Thou shalt be perfect with the Lord thy God.' Deut. 32. 4, 'He is the Rock, his work is perfect.' 1 Sam. 14. 41, 'Give a perfect lot' (R. V. Shew the right). 2 Sam. 22. 31. 'As for God, his way is perfect (in verses 24 and 26 the same word is rendered 'upright'). 2 Sam. 22. 33, 'He maketh my way perfect.' Compare Ps. 18. 30, 32. Job 1. 1, 'That man was

---

[1] This word occurs as a rendering for **Shalam** in Deut. 32. 35, 'I will repay, saith the Lord'—words twice quoted in the N. T. See Rom. 12. 19 and Heb. 10. 30.

perfect and upright.' See v. 8; 2. 3. Job 8. 20, 'Behold, God will
not cast away a perfect man.' Job 9. 20, 21, 22, '(If I say) I am
perfect, it shall also prove me perverse. Though if I were perfect,
yet should I not know my soul. . . . He destroyeth the perfect
and the wicked.' See also 22. 3, 36. 4, 37. 16. Ps. 15. 2, 'He
that walketh uprightly.' Compare Prov. 2. 7, 10. 9; Amos 5. 10.
Ps. 19. 7, 'The law of the Lord is perfect.' Ps. 37. 37, 'Mark the
perfect man, and behold the upright.' See also Ps. 64. 4, 101. 2,
6; Prov. 2. 21, 11. 5; Isa. 18. 5, 47. 9; and Ezek. 28. 15.

The LXX represents the **Thummim** three times by ἀλήθεια,[1]
and once by τελείωσις. The verb **thamam** is rendered ἐκλείπω and
συντελέω.

The adjectival form of the word is generally rendered ἄμωμος,
unblemished; but τέλειος occurs in several passages, and ἄμεμπτος
in a few. In 1 Kings 6. 22, we meet with the word συντέλεια; and
in Isa. 1. 6, we find ὁλοκληρία, wholeness.

§ 4. *Teaching of the N. T.*

The ideas included in the word **Shalam** are prominent in the
N. T. There is one remarkable passage in which perfection
and oneness are combined together, namely, John 17. 23, where
the Lord Jesus prays, with respect to His disciples, that they may
be 'perfected in one,' or, more literally, 'completed into one.' The
same idea runs through the N. T.; the perfection of each part of
the body depends upon the completeness of the whole, and *vice versa*
(1 John 4. 2). Christ is 'our peace' because He has made both (*i.e.*
both Jew and Gentile) one, and has done away with the middle wall
of the partition; the twain He has created in Himself into one new
man, so making peace, and has reconciled both in one body to God
by means of the Cross (Eph. 2. 14–16). There is one body, the
Church, and one Spirit, in whom both Jew and Gentile have
access to the Father through Christ. While the Gospel develops
individuality, it represses *isolation*. The whole body of disciples

---

[1] It was remarked by Hody that the rendering ἀλήθεια for Thummim was a
proof of the *Alexandrine* character of the early part of the LXX. Ælian tells
us that Egyptian magistrates used to wear a carved sapphire stone round their
neck, and that it was called ἀλήθεια. The **Urim** and **Thummim** are manifestation and truth in the Greek, doctrine and truth in the Latin, light and
right in the German.

(οἱ πάντες) will become a complete man (Eph. 4. 13); and every man
is to be presented complete, not in himself, but in Christ Jesus
(Col. 1. 28); for from Christ, who is the head, the whole body gets
its sustenance (Eph. 4. 16).

There are some passages in the N. T. in which the word τέλειος
marks an advanced stage of development in spiritual things, and is
applied to those who are 'grown up,' as opposed to those who are
children and only partly informed. Perhaps we may read in this
sense our Lord's words to the young man, 'If thou wilt be perfect
(or mature), go sell all that thou hast' (Matt. 19. 21); compare 1 Cor.
2. 6, 'Though our preaching is foolishness in the eyes of the world,
yet it is wisdom in the judgment of the mature.' 1 Cor. 14. 20,
'In understanding be (not children, but) mature.' Phil. 3. 15,
'As many as are mature, let us be thus minded.' Heb. 5. 14,
'Strong meat is for them that are mature,' *i.e.* that have emerged
out of the state of infancy. In these passages the word answers
to the Hebrew root **calah**, rather than to **shalam.**

The word τελείωσις only occurs twice in the N. T. The first
passage is Luke 1. 45, where it signifies the accomplishment of
God's promises; the other is Heb. 7. 11, where we read that if
there had been τελείωσις, completeness, by means of the Levitical
priesthood, there would have been no necessity for the raising up
of a priest after an order other than that of Aaron. The priest
bore the τελείωσις or **thummim** on his breast-plate, but it was only
a shadow, of which Christ gives us the substance. Completeness is
only attainable through the Saviour. He Himself was perfected[1]
for the work of the priesthood through suffering (Heb. 2. 10), and
being thus perfected, He became the author or cause of eternal
salvation to all that obey Him (5. 9).

The word ἄμωμος, 'free from blemish,' is not only used of Christ,
who offered Himself without spot to God (Heb. 9. 14, and 1 Pet.
1. 19), but also of Christians, who are to be ἅγιοι, or separate from

---

[1] Some render the word τελειόω to consecrate in this and other passages;
and they have the LXX as authority for so doing. See, for example, Exod. 29. 22,
&c.; Lev. 8. 22, &c., where it answers to the Hebrew expression 'to fill the hands,'
i.e. 'to consecrate;' τὰς χείρας being added in some cases, but not in others. But
it must be borne in mind that, in our Lord's case, His being perfected through
suffering was, as a matter of fact, His consecration, and the Levitical formal
solemnity of consecration has given way to the process of 'learning obedience by
the things suffered,' whereby the Lord was constituted a perfect High Priest, one
that could sympathise with all the troubles and temptations of His people, in that
He Himself had suffered being tempted.

the evil of the world, and ἄμωμοι, or free from moral blemishes (Eph. 1. 4, 5. 27 ; Phil. 2. 15 ; Col. 1. 22 ; Jude 24 ; Rev. 14. 5).

The word ἄμεμπτος is used of blameless characters, and is applied in Luke 1. 6 to Zacharias and Elizabeth, and in Phil. 3. 6 to Saul the Pharisee.   In Phil. 2. 15, and 1 Thess. 3. 13, it is set forth as the characteristic of the true Christian, and as applicable to the heart as well as to the outward life.   Compare also the uses of the adverbial form in 1 Thess. 2. 10, and 5. 23.   In Heb. 8. 7, 8, it serves to mark the contrast between the two dispensations : ' If the first had no fault to be found in it (ἄμεμπτος), place would not have been sought for a second ; (but this is not the case) for finding fault (μεμφόμενος), he saith, Behold, the days come,' &c.

The word ὁλοκληρία is used of the wholeness or perfect soundness of the body in Acts 3. 16 ; and the adjective is used in James 1. 4, where it is coupled with τέλειος, and also in 1 Thess. 5. 23, where St. Paul prays for the saints, that their complete spirit, soul, and body may be preserved (so as to be) blameless in the appearing of Christ.

It will thus be seen that the standard of perfection set before all Christians in the N. T. is very high indeed, no room being left for any wrong-doing; but the promise of needful power is equally explicit.   See 2 Cor. 12. 9.

CHAPTER IX.

RIGHTEOUSNESS, FAITH, HOPE.

THE subjects discussed in the present chapter will be found to group themselves round three leading ideas which lie at the foundation of that which is right, as it is set before man in Scripture. First, we are given a conception of rectitude, or the keeping to a straight and even line, as opposed to depravity, which swerves from the appointed course; secondly, we are presented 'with an idea of fixedness, stability, and realisation of the Truth of God, as contrasted with that which is transient, uncertain, and illusory; and, thirdly, there is set forth a spirit of dependence on Him who is the Source of Right and Truth.

§ 1. *Uprightness.*

The idea of rectitude or uprightness is presented by the word **yashar** (ישר), whence the names **Jasher** and **Jeshurun** are derived. (In Assyrian, *esiru* is to go straight, and *isaru* is upright.) This word is found wherever the A. V. uses the word equity, except in Eccles. 2. 21, and Isa. 59. 14 (compare Isa. 26. 10, and 57. 2), where other words of the same significance are used.

Yashar is rendered just in Prov. 29. 10, and righteous in Num. 23. 10, 'Let me die the death of the righteous.' See also Job 4. 7, 23. 7; Ps. 67. 4, 96. 10, 107. 42; Prov. 2. 7, 3. 32, 14. 19, 15. 19, 28. 10.

The LXX renders the verb **yashar** by ἀρέσκω, κατευθύνω, and κατορθόω; also by ὀρθοτομέω, in two passages, namely, Prov. 3. 6, 'He shall *direct* your paths;' and 11. 5, 'The righteousness of the perfect shall *direct* his way.' The noun is usually rendered εὐθύς, but we also find ὀρθός, ἀληθινός, ἀρεστόν, δίκαιος.

The verb κατευθύνω is used only three times in the N. T., namely, in Luke 1. 79, 1 Thess. 3. 11, and 2 Thess. 3. 5; and on each occasion reference is made to the work of God in rightly directing the heart and ways of man. In 2 Tim. 2. 15, where we meet with the word ὀρθοτομεῖν, the A. V. renders the passage 'rightly dividing the word of truth.' Some commentators have illustrated the word in this passage by the work of the carpenter or the stonemason; but it is probable that the LXX is the best guide in the matter. If so, we may render it 'rightly directing the word of truth,' *i.e.* setting it forth in uprightness. Compare Gossner's version, where we find 'verfährt,' and the Vulgate, 'recte tractantem.' The work of the ploughman gives a good illustration of St. Paul's meaning. See R. V., and compare Luke 9. 62.

§ 2. *Righteousness.*

The renderings righteous and just usually stand for some form of the word **tsadak** (צדק), which originally signified to be stiff or straight, and whence the names compounded with **Zedek** are derived. It is rendered lawful in Isa. **49**. 24; moderately in Joel **2**. 23; and right in several passages. It is unfortunate that the English language should have grafted the Latin word *justice*, which is used in somewhat of a forensic sense, into a vocabulary which was already possessed of the good word *righteousness*, as it tends to create a distinction which has no existence in Scripture. This quality indeed may be viewed, according to Scripture, in two lights. In its relative aspect it implies conformity with the line or rule of God's law; in its absolute aspect it is the exhibition of love to God and to one's neighbour, because love is the fulfilling of the law; but in neither of these senses does the word convey what we usually mean by justice. No distinction between the claims of justice and the claims of love is recognised in Scripture; to act in opposition to the principles of love to God and one's neighbour is to commit an injustice, because it is a departure from the course marked out by God in His law.

For a further discussion of the word and of its Greek representative δικαιοσύνη, viewed in relation to the doctrine of justification, see chap. xiv. § 1.

§ 3. *Judgment.*

Mishpath (משפט), which signifies the due administration of judgment (see chap. xxi. § 2), is rendered right in the A. V. in the following passages :—Gen. **18**. 25, 'Shall not the Judge of all the earth do right?' Job 34. 6, 'Should I lie against my right?'

Job **34**. 17, 'Shall even he that hateth right govern?' Job **35**. 2, 'Thinkest thou this to be right?' Ps. **9**. 4, 'Thou hast maintained my right.' Prov. **12**. 5, 'The thoughts of the righteous are right.' Prov. **16**. 8, 'Better is a little with righteousness than great revenues without right.' Isa. **10**. 2, 'To take away the right from the poor of my people.' See also Isa. **32**. 7; Jer. **5**. 28, 17. 11, **32**. 7, 8; Lam. **3**. 35; Ezek. **21**. 27.

Cashar (כשר), that which is fitting, is rendered right in the A. V. in Esther **8**. 5 and Eccles. **4**. 4; and **Con** (כון), stability, is found in Num. **27**. 7; Job **42**. 7, 8; Ps. **78**. 37, and **51**. 10, in which last passage we read, 'renew a right (*i.e.* a stable) spirit within me'—a suitable prayer for one who had fallen through instability. The same word occurs in Ps. **5**. 9, where the A. V. reads, 'There is no faithfulness in their mouth.' Compare the use of the cognate word (כנים) in the expression 'we be all true men,' *i.e.* men to be relied upon, in Gen. **42**. 11, 19, 31, and 34.

§ 4. *Truth.*

The general Hebrew word for truth or truthfulness, and faith or faithfulness, is a derivative of the verb **Aman** (אמן, Ass. *amanu*), whence the word Amen draws its origin. **Aman** in its simple active form signifies to nurse or nourish up; in the passive, to be firm and established, and hence steadfast (Prov. **11**. 13); and in the Hiphil or causative form, to take as established, and hence to regard as true, to realise, or to believe. The last is its most general rendering. The A. V. translates it 'to have assurance' in Deut. **28**. 66; and 'to trust' in Jud. **11**. 20; Job **4**. 18, 12. 20, **15**. 15, 31; and Micah **7**. 5. A form of this word is translated pillars in 2 Kings **18**. 16; compare 1 Tim. **3**. 15, 'the pillar and ground of the truth.'

In Dan. **3**. 14, where the A. V. reads, 'Is it true, O Shadrach?' another word (צדא) is used, which signifies of a purpose or intentionally. In Dan. **3**. 24, 6. 12, **7**. 16 and 19, **itsev** (יצב), to be firm or settled, is rendered true.

The form **emeth** (אמת) is usually rendered truth, but is translated right in Gen. **24**. 48; Neh. **9**. 33; Jer. **2**. 21. The form **Emunah**, generally rendered faithfulness, is found in Hab. **2**. 4,[1]

---

[1] This passage might be rendered 'the righteous (man) shall live in his faithfulness.' The note on the text in Poole's 'Synopsis' is as follows:—'*Qui bonus probusque est manebit constans in expectatione eorum quæ dixi*, 'the good and

where we read, 'The just shall live by his faith'—words which ought to be read in connection with the fifth verse of the first chapter, 'I will work a work in your days which ye will not believe, though it be told you.' **Emunah** is used of the steadiness of the hands of Moses in Exod. **17**. 12; and of the stability of the times in Isa. **33**. 6. In several other passages it is used of God's faithfulness; and it would have been well if this rendering had been adopted (instead of truth) in Deut. **32**. 4; Ps. **33**. 4, **96**. 13, **98**. 3, **100**. 5, and **119**. 30. See also Prov. **12**. 17.

The LXX almost always adopts πιστεύω, to believe, as the rendering for the causative form of **Aman**, as in Gen. **15**. 6, where it first occurs. The adjective is sometimes rendered πιστός, faithful; and sometimes ἀληθινός, real or true. When these two Greek words come together in the N. T. as characterising the glorified Son of God, they express the Hebrew word in all its fulness, and answer to the 'Amen,' by which title He is also described.[1] The substantive is usually πίστις, faith; but sometimes ἀλήθεια, truth.

§ 5. *Trust.*

Passing from the idea of faith to that of trust, a few exceptional renderings in the A. V. may be noted in the first instance. In Ps. **22**. 8, 'He trusted on the Lord,' the word **galal**, 'to roll,' is used. In Job **35**. 14, 'Trust thou in him,' the word is **chul** (חיל), 'stay thou (or 'wait thou') upon him.' **Yachal** (יחל), to hope, occurs in Job **13**. 15, 'Though he slay me, yet will I trust in him;' and Isa. **51**. 5, 'On mine arm shall they trust.'

Chasah (חסה), to flee for refuge, is rendered 'trust' in the A. V. in above thirty passages, out of which number twenty-four occur in the Psalms. It is often used where God is compared to a rock or a shield, or where the saint is described as taking refuge

---

upright man will continue firm in the expectation of those things which I have declared.' Certainly faith, in this passage, is something more than a bare acquiescence in God's word. It is such a belief in the revealed word of God as brings the man into contact with the Divine life, and so breathes righteousness or conformity to God's law into his heart. It worketh, as St. Paul says, by love. Compare Bishop Lightfoot's *excursus* on Faith in his Commentary on the Galatians.

[1] See Rev. **3**. 14, also **19**. 11, **21**. 5, **22**. 6. 'Amen' is usually rendered ἀληθῶς, verily, or γένοιτο, so be it, in the LXX; and only three times do we find the word in its Greek form Ἀμήν. Dr. Sayce points out that at the end of many Babylonian hymns we find *amanu*.

'under the shadow of his wings.' It is used in Ps. 2. 12, 'Blessed are all they that put their trust in him;' where we are taught that the Son affords that same kind of shelter or protection which the Father gives. Compare Ps. 34. 8, where the same words are applied to Jehovah. The word is also used in Ps. 118. 8, 'It is better to trust in the Lord than to put any confidence in man;' in Isa. 14. 32, 57. 13, and Zeph. 3. 12.

The most general word, however, to express trust is bathach (בטח), to confide in, or lean upon.[1] Here it is to be remarked that, though we are in the habit of speaking of faith and trust as the same thing, the Hebrew has two distinct words for them, and so has the LXX. Whilst aman answers to πιστεύω, to believe, or realise, bathach, to trust, is never so rendered, nor is the substantive derived from it ever rendered πίστις. For the verb we generally find ἐλπίζω, to hope, or πείθομαι, to be persuaded; and for the noun we have ἐλπίς, hope. The man who believes God is he who, having received a revelation from Him, realises it, and acts upon it as true. The man who trusts God is he who casts all his hopes for the present and future on God. It is the former quality, not the latter, that God regards as a condition of justification. Faith must precede hope, because a hope for the future which is not grounded upon a present acceptance with God is no hope; and a sense of acceptance which is not accompanied with a living, working faith is an unreality.

§ 6. *Hope.*

The words ordinarily rendered hope in the A. V. are kavah (קוה—Ass. *qû*) and yachal (יחל). The first, which is frequently used in the Psalms, signifies the straining of the mind in a certain direction in an expectant attitude; the second, which occurs several times in the Book of Job, signifies a long patient waiting. The former is generally rendered ὑπομένω; the latter usually ἐλπίζω, but often also ὑπομένω.

§ 7. *Teaching of the N. T.*

We now approach the N. T. with a clear distinction between faith on the one hand, and trust and hope on the other. Faith is the taking God at His word, while trust and patience and also

---

[1] Dr. Sayce says that this root is replaced in Assyrian by *takalu*, e.g. *ina tukulli Assuri*, 'in reliance on Assur.'

hope are the proper fruits of faith, manifesting in various forms the confidence which the believer feels. A message comes to me from the Author of my existence; it may be a threat, a promise, or a command. If I take it as 'yea and amen,' that is Faith; and the act which results is an act of **amunah** or faithfulness towards God. Faith, according to Scripture, seems to imply a word, message, or revelation. So the learned Romaine says in his *Life of Faith :—* ' Faith signifies the believing the truth of the Word of God; it relates to some word spoken or to some promise made by Him, and it expresses the belief which a person who hears it has of its being true; he assents to it, relies upon it, and acts accordingly : this is faith.' Its fruit will vary according to the nature of the message received, and according to the circumstances of the receiver. It led Noah to build an ark, Abraham to offer up his son, Moses to refuse to be called the son of Pharaoh's daughter, the Israelites to march round the walls of Jericho. ' I believe God that it shall be even as it has been told me ' [1]—this is a picture of the process which the Bible calls faith. It is the expectation ($\upsilon\pi\acute{o}\sigma\tau\alpha\sigma\iota\varsigma$) of things *hoped for*, because it accepts God's promises concerning the future as true; and it is the conviction ($\check{\epsilon}\lambda\epsilon\gamma\chi o\varsigma$) of what is (*trusted*, but) not seen, because those who have it do not depend upon the use of their senses, but are able to endure, 'as seeing Him who is invisible.' See Heb. 11.

In the Gospels the Lord Jesus demands to be believed. He asks all men to take Him to be what He claimed to be. If they would only take Him as true, they would be in the way of receiving and entering into a new life. He said, ' I am the Truth.' All that Israel had to believe under the old dispensation was summed up in Him. If they believed Moses, they would believe Him. If they rejected Him, they were doing dishonour to God. Sin sprang from a disbelief of God's word. Christ came to manifest, in a life of love and purity, and in a death of self-sacrifice, what God had really said, and what His feelings towards man actually were. Those that accepted the Truth, as it was revealed in Jesus Christ, entered into life.

The Book of Acts carries this teaching a stage further by exhibiting the special facts which were prominently put forward as things to be believed. These facts were the mission, the death, and the resurrection of Jesus Christ, as the ground of pardon, the way of life, and the pledge of an inheritance beyond the grave.

---

[1] Acts **27**. 25.

The Epistles enter more fully into details, answer different questions, expound doctrines, apply sacred truths to the exigencies of daily life. But all is summed up in Christ; 'Whosoever takes him to be true shall not be ashamed' (Rom. 9. 33, quoted from Isa. 28. 16).

The word hope barely exists in the Gospels, but is frequently to be found in the later books of the N. T. In Rom. 15. 12, the Apostle quotes from the LXX version of Isa. 11. 10 the words, 'In him shall the Gentiles hope,'[1] and then proceeds, 'Now the God of hope fill you with all joy and peace in believing.' In the A. V. the point of the connection is missed by the substitution of the word *trust* for *hope* in the first part of the passage. But there is no objection to this rendering in itself; for though ἐλπίζω represents trust with reference to the future, while πείθομαι represents confidence with regard to the present, yet they are both renderings of one Hebrew word, as we have just seen, and cannot be separated by a very strong line.

In Acts 2. 26, St. Peter quotes from the Sixteenth Psalm the words, 'My flesh also shall rest (or dwell) in hope (κατασκηνώσει ἐπ' ἐλπίδι);' and this expression, 'in hope,' is repeated several times, being applied to Abraham (Rom. 4. 18), to Christians (Acts 26. 6; Rom. 5. 2; Titus 1. 2), to the ministry (1 Cor. 9. 10), and to creation itself (Rom. 8. 20). All hope is concentrated in Christ (1 Tim. 1. 1; Col. 1. 27), and looks for the unseen realities of another world (Rom. 8. 24), even the resurrection (Acts 24. 15), eternal life (Titus 3. 7), and glory (Rom. 5. 2). The word 'hope' as used in ordinary conversation has an element of uncertainty in it, but the Christian's hope is absolute confidence. The two Greek renderings of the Hebrew word **yachal** named above (§ 6), ἐλπίς and ὑπομένη, are found together in 1 Thess. 1. 3.

---

[1] Here the Hebrew word is **darash**, to seek.

CHAPTER X.

GRACE, MERCY, LOVE.

THE Bible is pre-eminently occupied in setting forth the gracious feelings with which God regards the children of men; it depicts them not in the abstract, but as manifested in action. It also teaches that those who have tasted of God's grace and love and mercy are bound to exercise the same dispositions towards their fellow-men. They thus become in reality children of God, and are conformed to the nature of Him from whom their new life is drawn.

§ 1. *Grace.*

Grace is the free bestowal of kindness on one who has neither claim upon our bounty, nor adequate compensation to make for it. Throughout the O. T., with the exception of Hos. **14.** 2, where the word rendered 'graciously' signifies 'goodness' (טוב), it stands for some form of **Chanan** (חנן), to show favour.[1] It is often coupled with **racham** (רחם), a word which signifies a tender feeling of pity. These three words answer to the Assyrian *thabu, 'annu, rêmu*. The adjectival form, **chanun** (חנון), gracious, is used only of God, and denotes the action which springs from His free and unmerited love to His creatures. The verb is rendered 'pity' in Prov. **19.** 17, 'He that hath pity upon the poor lendeth unto the Lord;' where the writer is not speaking of commiseration, but rather of the kindly dealing of one who 'hopes for nothing again.' It is also used in Job **19.** 21, and Prov. **28.** 8, where it might be rendered 'deal graciously.' Other renderings for this word in the A. V. are 'to be favourable,' and 'to be merciful,' and (in the causative form) to beseech, supplicate, and pray. The LXX has ἐλεήμων for the adjective, but χάρις for the noun. The Greek χάρις, and the English 'grace' or favour,' well represent the word, only we have to be on our guard against the supposition that *grace* is an abstract quality; it is an active personal principle, showing itself in our dealings with those by whom we are surrounded.

---

[1] Hence the name Jo-hanan (John), and its inverted form, Hanan-iah.

The adverb 'graciously' is usually rendered δωρεὰν in the LXX; and this word reappears in the N. T., as in Matt. 10. 8, 'Freely ye have received, freely give;' Rom. 3. 24, 'Being justified freely by his grace;' Rev. 22. 17, 'Let him take the water of life freely.' A secondary meaning which the Greek adverb has received is 'without a cause.' In this sense we meet with it in John 15. 25, 'They hated me without a cause,' words quoted from Ps. 69. 4; also Gal. 2. 21, 'Then Christ died in vain, or causelessly.' We occasionally use the English word gratuitous in this sense, as when we speak of 'a gratuitous insult.'

The verbal form is rendered χαρίζομαι in the LXX; and this word occurs several times in the N. T. to indicate an exhibition of free grace, whether in the form of healing (Luke 7. 21), or of remitting a debt (Luke 7. 42), or of the loosing of a prisoner (Acts 3. 14), of making a gift (Rom. 8. 32, 1 Cor. 2. 12), or of pardon (2 Cor. 2. 10, Eph. 4. 32). Χαριτόω, to deal graciously, is not an O. T. word, except in the Apocrypha, but occurs in Luke 1. 28 and Eph. 1. 6.

An act done with any expectation of a return from the object on which it is wrought, or one which is meted out as a matter of justice, recompense, or reward, is not an act of grace. This is specially noted in Rom. 11. 6; compare also the words of our Lord, 'If ye love them that love you, what grace (A. V. reward, R. V. thank) have you?' (Luke 6. 32, 33, 34). So St. Peter says, 'This is grace (A. V. thankworthy, R. V. acceptable), if a man through consciousness of God endure pains, suffering unjustly' (1 Pet. 2. 19).

In the great proportion of passages in which the word grace is found in the N. T., it signifies the unmerited operation of God in the heart of man, effected through the agency of the Holy Spirit. We have gradually come to speak of grace as an inherent quality in man, just as we talk of gifts; whereas it is in reality the communication of Divine goodness by the inworking of the Spirit, and through the medium of Him who is 'full of grace and truth.'

§ 2. *Pity.*

Racham expresses a deep and tender feeling of compassion, such as is aroused by the sight of weakness or suffering in those that are dear to us or need our help. It is rendered pity[1] or pitiful in a few passages. Thus Ps. 103. 13, 'Like as a father pitieth his children, so the Lord pitieth them that fear him;' Ps. 106. 46,

---

[1] The English word pity is really piety.

' He made them also to be pitied of all those that carried them captives ;' Lam. **4.** 10, 'The hands of the pitiful women have sodden their own children.' It is curious that the word 'pitiful' should have had its meaning so altered in modern times as to be hardly understood in the passage last cited.

Racham is rendered 'mercy' several times, and is the origin of the word **Ruhamah**, which occurs in Hos. **2.** 1. Jacob used it to express his strong feeling on sending Benjamin with his brothers into Egypt, 'God Almighty give you mercy before the man, that he may send away your other brother, and Benjamin' (Gen. **43.** 14). It is an element in the character of God, who shows mercy on whom He will show mercy (Exod. **33.** 19), and is merciful as well as gracious (Exod. **34.** 6, Deut. **4.** 31). Accordingly David says, 'Let us fall now into the hands of God, for his mercies are abounding' (2 Sam. **24.** 14). Mercy (*misericordia*) is really the same thing as pity, though the words have gradually assumed rather different senses.

Racham also represents the beautiful expression 'tender mercy' wherever it occurs ; thus the Psalmist prays, 'According to the multitude of thy tender mercies blot out my transgressions' (Ps. **51.** 1). It is the only word rendered 'mercy,' with two exceptions (Jer. **3.** 12, and Dan. **4.** 27), in the prophetical books of the O. T., being specially used in them to mark the tenderness with which God regards His people in their downcast condition. It is rendered 'compassion' and 'bowels of compassion' in all passages where these expressions are found in the A. V., with the exception of Exod. **2.** 6, 1 Sam. **23.** 21, 2 Chron. **36.** 15, 17, and Ezek. **16.** 5, where a less forcible word (חמל) is used. **Racham** has twice been rendered 'love,' viz. in Ps. **18.** 1 and Dan. **1.** 9. With regard to the first of these passages, 'I will love thee, O Lord, my strength,' the word seems at first sight out of place, because there can be no element of pity in man's love to God ; but it expresses here the depth and tenderness of the Psalmist's feeling; and it may be observed that in this passage the word is used not in the Piel or intensive voice (as in all other passages), but in the Kal, or simple active voice.

The most prominent rendering for **racham** in the LXX is οἰκτιρμός. This word occurs five times in the N. T., twice as the attribute of God (Rom. **12.** 1, and 2 Cor. **1.** 3), and three times as a quality to be manifested in our dealings with one another (Phil. **2.** 1 ; Col. **3.** 12 ; see also Heb. **10.** 28).

§ 3. *Love.*

The general word for love in the O. T. is **ahav** (אהב), from which
it has been supposed that its Greek representative ἀγάπη is derived;
but compare **'Agav** below. It indicates desire, inclination, or
affection, whether human or divine. In Amos **4. 5**, it has been
rendered by the weaker English word like. In a few passages the
participial form has been rendered friend, as in 2 Sam. **19. 6**, 'Thou
lovest thine enemies, and hatest thy friends;' 2 Chron. **20. 7**
(compare Isa. **41. 8**), 'Thou gavest thy land to the seed of Abraham
thy friend,' an expression which St. James singled out for comment
in his Epistle (**2. 23**); Zech. **13. 6**, 'I was wounded in the house of
my friends;' see also Esther 5. 10, 14, 6. 13; Prov. **14.** 20, 27. 6;
Jer. 20. 4, 6. In these passages intimacy and affection, the cleaving
of soul to soul, is implied, and 'lovers' rather than 'acquaintances'
are designated. Occasionally the LXX adopts φιλεῖν instead of
ἀγαπᾶν, but never where God's love is concerned.

Other words rendered love in the A. V. are as follows :—**Yedid**
(ידיד), whence the name **Jedidiah**; **re'a** (רע—Ass. *rû*), a companion,
Cant. 1. 9, 15, 2. 10, 13, 5. 2, 6. 4, and Jer. 3. 1; **'Agav** (עגב),
used of impure love, and rendered 'doting' in Ezek. 23. 12,
33. 31, 32; **Chashak** (חשק), *to join together*, Ps. 91. 14; **dodim**
(דודים—Ass. *dadu*), the impulse of the heart, or of sexual affection,
Prov. 7. 18, Ezek. 16. 8; and **chesed**, mercy.

The Greek ἀγάπη is in a measure consecrated by the fact that it
makes its first appearance in the LXX, being apparently unknown
to early classical authors. It is used in the N. T. to designate the
essential nature of God, His regard for mankind, and also the most
marked characteristic of the Divine life as manifested in Christ and
in Christians. It is unfortunate that the English, with some other
languages, should have accepted two renderings for this important
word, the Latin word charity being introduced as an alternative
for the good old Saxon word love, but it has arisen through fear
lest spiritual love should be confused with sensuous affection. The
Greek ἔρως is never used in the Bible except in Prov. 7. 18,
and 30. 16.

The word φιλεῖν is rarely used in the N. T. But see 1 Cor. 16. 22,
and especially John 21. 15–17, where the distinction between love
and friendship is noticeable in the Greek, but is lost in the English
and other versions.

§ 4. *Mercy*.

We have now to consider the word **Chasad** (חסד), which is used in various forms to designate God's dealings with man, and also to indicate the mode in which men ought to deal with one another. The meaning of this word when used as a substantive (**Chesed**) is made clear from the fact that the LXX has rendered it ἔλεος, mercy, in 135 passages. The nature of the quality may be illustrated by the conduct of the Good Samaritan, ' who shewed the mercy' (ὁ ποιήσας τὸ ἔλεος) on him that was attacked by robbers (Luke 10. 37) ; it is a practical exhibition of lovingkindness towards our fellow-man, whose only claim may be misfortune, and whom it is in our power to help, though perhaps at the expense of time, money, convenience, and even religious or national prejudice.

The general English renderings for the word in the A. V. are : kindness, mercy, pity, favour, goodness, and lovingkindness. It is often found united with righteousness, faithfulness, truth, compassion, and other divine qualities.

A few instances may be cited to illustrate its usage : Gen. 24. 12, 'O Lord God, shew kindness unto my master Abraham ;' Gen. 24. 27, 'Blessed be the Lord God of my master Abraham, who hath not left my master destitute of his mercy (LXX δικαιοσύνη) and truth ;' Gen. 24. 49, 'If ye will deal kindly and truly with my master, tell me ;' Gen. 39. 21, 'The Lord was with Joseph, and shewed him mercy ;' Gen. 40. 14, 'Shew kindness unto me, and make mention of me unto Pharaoh ;' Exod. 20. 6, 'Shewing mercy unto thousands of them that love me, and keep my commandments ;' Num. 14. 19, 'Pardon, I beseech thee, the iniquity of this people according unto the greatness of thy mercy ;' Josh. 2. 12, 'Swear unto me by the Lord, since I have shewed you kindness, that ye will also shew kindness unto my father's house ;' Job 6. 14, 'To him that is afflicted pity (should be shewed) from his friend ;' Job 10. 12, 'Thou hast granted me life and favour ;' Ps. 5. 7, 'I will come into thy house in the multitude of thy mercy ;' Ps. 6. 4, 'Oh save me for thy mercies' sake ;' Ps. 13. 5, 'I have trusted in thy mercy ;' Ps. 32. 10, 'He that trusteth in the Lord, mercy shall compass him about ;' Ps. 33. 5, 'The earth is full of the goodness of the Lord ;' Ps. 89. 33, 'My lovingkindness will I not utterly take from him ;' Ps. 89. 49, 'Lord, where are thy former lovingkindnesses ?' Ps. 119. 88, 159, 'Quicken me, O

Lord, according to thy lovingkindness;' Hos. 4. 1, 'There is no truth nor mercy;' Hos. 6. 4, 'Your goodness is as a morning dew;' (the A. V. obscures the connection between this verse and the sixth, where the same word is found—'I desired mercy and not sacrifice;' see R. V. margin); Hos. 10. 12, 'Sow to yourselves in righteousness, reap in mercy;' Hos. 12. 6, 'Keep mercy and judgment;' Micah 6. 8, 'What doth the Lord require of thee, but to do justly, and to love mercy, and to walk humbly with thy God?' Micah 7. 18, 'He delighteth in mercy;' Zech. 7. 9, 'Execute true judgment, and shew mercy and compassions every man to his brother.'

These passages put the general signification of the word **Chesed** beyond the shadow of a doubt. We now have to examine whether this meaning is to be enlarged or modified. The LXX adopts the rendering δικαιοσύνη, 'righteousness,' in Gen. 19. 16, and some other places. We also find ἐλεημοσύνη and ἔλπις in a few passages. In Isa. 40. 6, where the word **Chesed** is applied to the grace or goodliness of man which so soon fades away, the LXX has δόξα, glory; and the passage is quoted by St. Peter in his First Epistle (1. 24) according to this interpretation.

In the passages which remain to be considered, the adjectival form **Chasid** is found. This word must signify not only the reception but also the exercise of **Chesed**, just as **Tsadik**, righteous, signifies the reception and exercise of **Tsedek**, righteousness. If **Chesed**, then, means mercy, **Chasid** must mean merciful; and accordingly it is so translated in the A.V. in 2 Sam. 22. 26, and Ps. 18. 25, 'With the merciful thou wilt shew thyself merciful.' The LXX, however, both in these passages and wherever the word **Chasid** is found, has adopted ὅσιος, holy, as a rendering. This course has had a great influence upon other languages, as it has led translators to confound **Chasid** and **Kadosh**, ὅσιος and ἅγιος, forgetting that to a Jew the meaning of the Greek word ὅσιος would be ruled by the fact that it was to be taken as an interpretation of the Hebrew **Chasid**, merciful. In the two passages just cited, the A.V. retains the right rendering, but the Latin has *cum sancto*, and the German *Bei dem Heiligen.* The Portuguese translator, D'Almeida, both here and in almost all other places adopts the good word *Benigno*, but he is quite an exception to the general rule.

Our translators have followed the multitude in a large number of instances. Thus in Ps. 145. 17, we read, 'The Lord is holy in all his works;' here the margin properly corrects the text by suggesting merciful or bountiful. In Ps. **86**. 2 we read, 'I am holy;' where the margin reads, 'One whom thou favourest,' but it would be better to read, 'I am merciful.' The rendering godly has been adopted in Ps. **4**. 3, *al.*; and saint in 2 Chron. **6**. 41, Ps. **30**. 4, *al.* This last rendering must be regarded as unfortunate, because it serves to obliterate the real meaning of the word, and to confound it with another.

It has been held by distinguished scholars that **Chasid** primarily signifies a *recipient* of mercy, but this meaning is not always applicable, *e.g.* in Jer. **3**. 12, where God says of Himself, 'I am **Chasid**.' *Here* it cannot mean, 'I am a recipient of mercy;' our translators have rightly rendered the words, 'I am merciful.' Nevertheless, the two aspects of mercy, its reception and its exercise, are wonderfully blended in Scripture. The right and wholesome effect of the enjoyment of God's lovingkindness is the exhibition of the same spirit towards our fellows. God is everywhere described as delighting in mercy—'his mercy endureth for ever'—but He requires that those to whom He shows it should, in their turn and according to their opportunities, 'love mercy;' compare Micah **7**. 18 with **6**. 8.

It is a remarkable fact that the word **Chasid**, when applied to man, has usually a possessive pronoun affixed to it, so as to indicate that the persons who are exercising this disposition belong in a special sense to God. They are 'his merciful ones' (A. V. 'his saints'). Merciful men may be very scarce (Ps. **12**. 1; Micah **7**. 2), but wherever they are found they are regarded as God's own. 'He hath set apart him that is merciful for himself' (Ps. **4**. 3); and He gives His special protection to those that are worthy of the name **Chasid** (Ps. **32**. 6, **37**. 28). They show their love to the Lord by hating evil (*i.e.* evil dealings against their neighbour), and the Lord, in His turn, preserves their souls (Ps. **97**. 10). When He comes to judgment He will gather to Himself those who are His merciful ones, and who have made a covenant with Him by sacrifice (Ps. **50**. 5), and they shall not only 'rejoice in glory' (Ps. **149**. 5), but also shall have the honour of executing judgment on the nations (Ps. **149**. 9). In a word, mercy is the main characteristic of God's dealings with man, and hence it is to be looked for as the distinguishing mark of every child of God. 'He that loveth is born of God.' The 'godly' are those who, having received mercy from Him, are exercising it for Him and as His representatives. It is owing to the fact, no doubt, that the word **Chasid** has been rendered ὅσιος in the LXX, that we find it represented by *sanctus* in the Latin, and by

H

saint or godly in the English; yet it is a serious evil that the
primary meaning of the Hebrew word should almost have dis-
appeared from the face of modern translations. The practical
nature of godliness is thereby to some extent obscured, and the
moral demand made upon man by his having become the object of
Divine lovingkindness is thrown into the background.

It only remains to notice the application of the above remarks
to one or two passages of importance in the O. T., and to observe
their bearing on the interpretation of this word ὅσιος in the N. T.

In Deut. 33. 8, Moses says, ' Let thy Thummim and thy Urim be
with thy **Chasid** (ἀνδρὶ ὁσίῳ, A. V. Holy One) whom thou didst
prove at Massah.' The old Portuguese translator, D'Almeida, here
has *amado*, with a note referring the word to Aaron. The same
word is used of Aaron in Ps. 106. 16, where he is called the **Chasid**
of the Lord (A. V. 'the saint of the Lord'). The context in Deut.
33. shows that reference is made to the slaughter of the Israelites
by the House of Levi in the matter of Moab; and the lesson we
learn with regard to the word **Chasid** is that it does not betoken the
weak ' good-nature' which some call ' mercy,' but rather that devotion to God which produces the exercise of true lovingkindness
towards man, and which sometimes involves the taking extreme and
apparently harsh measures so as to prevent the spread of evil. In
this respect man's mercy is to be like God's.

There are several passages relating to David and his seed in
which the words **Chesed** and **Chasid** occur, and which need to be
taken together in order that their whole force may be seen. In 2
Sam. 7. 14, 15, the Lord promises to David with respect to his son,
' I will be his father, and he shall be my son. If he commit iniquity,
I will chasten him with the rod of men, and with the stripes of the
children of men : but my mercy shall not depart away from him ;'
compare the parallel passage, 1 Chron. 17. 13. This promise is
referred to by Solomon at Gibeon in 1 Kings 3. 6 and 2 Chron. 1. 8 ;
and at the dedication of the Temple he closed the service by the
words, 'O Lord God, turn not away the face of thine anointed ;
remember the mercies of David thy servant,' *i.e.* the mercies
which thou hast promised to show unto David (2 Chron. 6. 42). On
turning to the eighty-ninth Psalm, we find several references to these
' mercies.' The Psalmist opens by saying 'The mercies of Jehovah will I sing for ever ;' 'mercy,' he continues in the second verse,
'shall be built up for ever ;' he then proceeds to speak of God's
covenant and oath, which is faithful and sure and true, that David's

seed should be established on the throne for evermore. After ex-
tolling the greatness of God, he continues (verse 14), 'Righteousness
and judgment are the establishment of thy throne: mercy and
truth shall go before thy face.' Returning to the covenant with
David, the Psalmist sketches out its details, saying in verse 24,
'My faithfulness and my mercy shall be with him;' and in verse
28, 'My mercy will I keep for him for evermore;' and in verse 33,
'Nevertheless my mercy (A. V. 'my lovingkindness') will I keep
for him for evermore, and my covenant shall stand fast with him.'
Then the Psalmist breaks out into a lamentation on the troubles
into which Israel was plunged, and cries out (verse 49), 'Lord,
where are thine original mercies (A. V. 'thy old lovingkindnesses') which thou swarest unto David in thy truth?' The
Psalm concludes, as usual, with a note of thanksgiving.

We see here, first, that the word mercy seems to be used with
peculiar significance in relation to God's promise to David and his
seed; and secondly, that it is constantly introduced in connection
with God's faithfulness or truth. In accordance with these passages
we read in Isa. 55. 3, 'Incline your ear, and come unto me: hear, and
your soul shall live; and I will make an everlasting covenant with you,
even the mercies of David, which are sure (or faithful). Behold,
I have given him for a witness to the people, for a leader and law-
giver to the people.'

St. Paul, when addressing the Jews at Antioch, takes up these
words as follows (Acts 13. 32, &c.): 'We declare unto you glad
tidings, how that the promise which was made unto the fathers,
God hath fulfilled the same unto us their children, in that he hath
raised up Jesus (again).[1] For it is written in the second psalm,
Thou art my Son, this day have I begotten thee. And as concerning
that he raised him up from the dead, no more to return to corruption, he said on this wise, I will give you the mercies of David
which are faithful. Wherefore he saith also in another place, Thou
shalt not suffer thy merciful[2] one (A. V. and R. V. 'Thine Holy
One') to see corruption. . . . Be it known unto you therefore that
through this (risen Jesus) there is announced unto you forgiveness
of sins.'

With regard to the rendering of Ps. 16. 10, we are so used to

[1] The R. V. rightly omits the word 'again,' and thus distinguishes the two
'raisings up' of Jesus—first, on His entrance into the world; and secondly, on His
resurrection.

[2] The R. V. has strangely missed the point here.

the expression 'Thy Holy One,' that it is not easy to make such a substitution as the sense requires. It may be noticed, however, that D'Almeida has 'o teu Bem,' thy good or kind one; the old Judæo-Spanish version of the Hebrew Scriptures published at Ferrara has 'tu Bueno,' which has the same meaning; the Spanish translator De Reyna, and also his reviser Valera, had 'tu Misericordioso,' 'thy merciful one,' although this excellent rendering has slipped out of modern editions.

The meaning of the word **Chasid** as representing mercy ought to be borne in mind in other passages where its representative ὅσιος occurs in the N. T. Thus in Heb. 7. 26, the Lord should be described as 'merciful and without malice,' instead of 'holy and harmless;' so in Rev. 15. 4, and 16. 5, the Lord's mercy, not His holiness, is specially referred to. The word ὅσιος is used of the Christian in 1 Tim. 2. 8, where he is told to lift up 'merciful hands, without wrath and contention;' and in Titus 1. 8 it is said that God's steward should be merciful as well as righteous.

CHAPTER XI.

WHATEVER theory one may hold as to the possibility or *a priori* probability of a Divine intervention in human affairs, the Bible is pledged to the fact that such an intervention has taken place. A study of its pages leads to the conclusion that it is as much in accordance with God's nature to help men out of the difficulties in which sin has involved them, as it was to create them after His own likeness in the first instance. Nor will the student of the physical world fail to observe the analogy which here exists between nature and revelation; for if there be a *vis medicatrix* or healing power which is called into play by the wounds, accidents, and diseases to which the body is subject, why should it be thought a thing incredible that the Father of our spirits should provide some means of restoration for those who have become a prey to evil passions, and who through temptation or self-will have become partakers of moral and material corruption?

The patriarchal and Mosaic economies appear to have been intended by the Divine Being to form a groundwork whereupon a restorative work for the benefit of the human race might be built up in the fulness of time; and the pious Jew was trained up in the belief that amidst all his sins and ignorances, his infirmities and misfortunes, he might look up to God and receive from Him those blessings which are summed up in the words redemption and salvation.

§ 1. *Redemption.*

The word which specially indicates redemption is **Gaal** (גאל), best known in the form **Goel**, redeemer.[1] Perhaps the original meaning of the word is to 'demand back,' hence to extricate.

---

[1] Another word, almost the same in sound, sometimes spelt in the same way, and sometimes with a slight change (געל), signifies to defile or pollute.

It first appears in Gen. **48**. 16, 'The angel which redeemed me from all evil bless the lads.' In Exod. **6**. 6, and **15**. 13, it is used of God's redeeming Israel out of Egypt with a stretched-out arm. We meet with it no more till we reach the twenty-fifth and twenty-seventh chapters of Leviticus, where it signifies the liberation of property from a charge, whether that charge was an ordinary debt or whether it had been incurred through a vow. The deliverance was to be effected in this case by payment or by exchange. In cases of poverty, where no payment was possible, the nearest of kin was made responsible for performing the work of redemption. Hence no doubt it came to pass that a **kinsman** came to be called by the name **Goel**, as he is in Num. **5**. 8, 1 Kings **16**. 11, and throughout the Book of Ruth. Compare Jer. **32**. 7, 8.

In the prophets the word is applied not only to the deliverance of God's people from captivity, but to that more important and complete deliverance, of which all other historical interpositions of Divine grace are shadows. See Isa. **35**. 9, **41**. 14, **43**. 1, 14, **44**. 6, 22, 23, 24, **47**. 4, **48**. 17, **49**. 7, 26, **51**. 10, **52**. 3, **62**. 12, **63**. 4, Jer. **31**. 11.

One of the most important passages where the word occurs is in Isa. **59**. 20, 'The **Redeemer** shall come to Zion, and unto them that turn from transgression in Jacob'—words to which St Paul refers as destined to have their fulfilment hereafter at the time of the complete salvation of Israel as a nation (Rom. **11**. 26).[1]

The word occurs once in Job, in the celebrated passage (19. 25), 'I know that my **Redeemer** liveth.' Whatever view may be taken of this passage, whether we regard it as a prediction of the Messiah's coming, or as an intimation of the doctrine of the resurrection, or as referring to a temporal deliverance from disease and trouble, one point is clear, that Job expresses his deep conviction that there was a living God who could and who would take his part, and extricate him from all difficulties; and this is the principle in which the Hebrew reader was to be trained.

In Ps. **19**. 14, the Psalmist calls God his strength and his **Redeemer**; and in Ps. **69**. 18, he appeals to God to draw nigh and **redeem** his soul; and he uses the word again in a personal rather than a national sense, with reference to past or future

---

[1] The text in Romans runs thus: 'The Redeemer shall come from Zion, and shall turn away transgressions from Jacob.' The LXX agrees in the latter part, but in the first part a different Hebrew reading must have been followed by St. Paul.

deliverances, in Ps. **77**. 15, **78**. 35, **103**. 4, **106**. 10, **107**. 2.   In Ps. **119**. 154, **Gaal** is rendered d e l i v e r.

Another application of the word was in the sense of avenging the blood of the slain.   This is treated at length in the thirty-fifth chapter of Numbers, in connection with the subject of the cities of refuge.   It is also referred to in Deut. **19**. 6, 12 ; Josh. **20**. 3, 5, 9 ; and 2 Sam. **14**. 11.

A remarkable combination of the senses of **Goel** is to be found in Prov. **23**. 10, 11, ' Remove not the old landmark ; and enter not into the fields of the fatherless : for their r e d e e m e r is mighty ; he shall plead their cause with thee.'   God takes the place of kinsman and also of avenger to the poor and helpless.

The idea of **Goel** as the avenger of blood comes up again in Isa. **63**. 4, when the Mighty One in blood-stained garments says, ' The day of vengeance is in mine heart, and the year of my r e d e e m e d is come.'   The word occurs again in the ninth and sixteenth verses of the same chapter, where it rather signifies deliverance from captivity.

In most of the passages above enumerated redemption may be considered as synonymous with d e l i v e r a n c e, but always with the idea more or less developed that the Redeemer enters into a certain relationship with the redeemed—allies Himself in some sense with them, and so claims the right of redemption.   The truth thus set forth was doubtless intended to prepare the mind of God's people for the doctrine of the Incarnation.   ' Forasmuch as the children were partakers of flesh and blood, therefore *he* also took part in the same,' and having constituted Himself the kinsman of the human race, He fought their battle against ' him who had the power of death,' and delivered His people from bondage (see Heb. **2**. 14, 15).

The LXX generally renders **Gaal** by λυτρόω, to r e d e e m ; but in fourteen passages we find ῥύομαι, to d e l i v e r ; and in ten, ἀγχιστεύω, to a c t t h e n e i g h b o u r.   The verb ἀπολυτρόω is found in Zeph. **3**. 1 (A. V. ' polluted ') ; λύτρον in Lev. **25**. 24, 51, 54 ; λυτρωτής in Lev. **25**. 31, 32 ; Ps. **18**. 15, 77. 39.

In many of the passages above cited another word is used as a parallel to **gaal**, namely, **padah** (פדה ; Ass. *padû*, ' to spare '), which our translators have rendered by the words d e l i v e r, r e d e e m, r a n s o m,[1] and r e s c u e.   It is used in Exod. **13**. 13, 15, of the redemption of the first-born, who were regarded as representa-

---

[1] The English word r a n s o m is only a contracted form of the word r e d e m p t i o n.

tives of those who had been spared when the first-born of Egypt were destroyed. This redemption extended to all unclean beasts, to all, that is to say, that were precluded from being offered as sacrifice (Num. **18**. 16, 17), and a set price was to be paid for their deliverance or quittance. Redemption-money (A. V. ransom) is described in Exod. **21**. 30 as paid to make amends (**copher**) in certain cases of wrong-doing (see R. V.).

Padah is often adopted to represent the deliverance of a servant from slavery, as in Exod. **21**. 8. It is also used of the people rescuing Jonathan from death, in 1 Sam. **14**. 45.

This word is used in Ps. **31**. 5, 'Into thine hand I commit my spirit: thou hast redeemed me, O Lord God of truth;' Ps. **34**. 22, 'The Lord redeemeth the souls of his servants;' Ps. **49**. 7, 8, 15, 'None can redeem his brother, nor give to God a ransom (**copher**) for him : (for the redemption of their soul is precious). . . . But God will redeem my soul from the power of the grave;' Ps. **130**. 7, 8, 'With the Lord is plenteous redemption; and he shall redeem Israel from all his iniquities;' Isa. **1**. 27, 'Zion shall be redeemed with judgment.' The application of the word to Abraham, in Isa. **29**. 22, is remarkable, 'Thus saith the Lord, who redeemed Abraham.' It seems here to signify his call from the companionship of idolaters and his introduction into the covenant of promise.

From the passages which have now been cited, it will be gathered that the word **padah** is not used in the peculiar technical senses which **gaal** expresses, but that it especially refers to the deliverance from *bondage*. The LXX generally represents it by λυτρόω; five times we find ῥύομαι, twice σώζω, and once ἀπολυτρόω.

The cognate form **pada'** (פָּדַע) is found in connection with **caphar** in Job **33**. 24, 'Deliver him : I have found a ransom' (or mode of atonement); but we find **padah** in verse 28, 'He will deliver his soul from going into the pit.'

§ 2. *N. T. Teaching on Redemption.*

In approaching the Greek words for redemption in the N. T., it is evident that we must not narrow our conceptions to one sole process of deliverance, for the O. T. has led us to look for redemption in many aspects. There may be *physical* deliverance, from disease or death; *social* deliverance, from conventional or legal barriers between man and man, between the sexes, between various

classes of society or various nations of the world; and there may
be *moral* and *spiritual* deliverance, from the power of evil in the
heart, and from the effects of that evil before God. Without
pressing for a strong demarcation between ῥύομαι, to deliver, and
λυτρόω, to redeem, we shall be prepared to find in both cases
that the deliverance of man is costly, involving some gift or act of
self-sacrifice on the part of the Redeemer; nor shall we be surprised
if we find that a certain identification is necessitated between the
Deliverer and those whom He claims a right to deliver.

We find *ῥύομαι* in the sense of deliverance in the following
passages[1]:—Matt. 6. 13, 'Deliver us from evil.' Luke 1. 74, 'That
we being delivered out of the hands of our enemies might serve
him without fear;' connected with the coming of Christ. Rom.
7. 24, 'O wretched man that I am, who shall deliver me from the
body of this death?' but here note the answer, 'through Jesus
Christ.' Rom. 11. 26, referring to Isa. 59. 20, 'The Redeemer
(Goel, ὁ ῥυόμενος) shall come *from* Zion.' See note on this passage
on p. 118. Rom. 15. 31, 'That I may be delivered from them
that are disobedient.' 2 Cor. 1. 10, 'Who delivered us from so
great a death, and doth deliver; and we hope also that he shall
deliver.' Col. 1. 13, 'Who delivered us from the power of darkness, and translated us.' 1 Thess. 1. 10, 'Who delivers us from
the wrath to come.' See also 2 Thess. 3. 2; 2 Tim. 3. 11, 4. 17, 18;
2 Pet. 2. 7, 9.

The verb λυτρόω is used only three times in the N. T. In two
of these passages there is evidently a reference to the cost or sacrifice
which man's delivery has involved. In Titus 2. 14 we are told of
Jesus Christ that He 'gave himself for us, that he might redeem
us from all iniquity.' In 1 Pet. 1. 18, 19, 'Ye were not redeemed
from your vain manner of life with corruptible things, as silver and
gold; but with the precious blood of Christ, as of a lamb without
blemish and without spot.' These passages may be compared with
our Lord's own words which are found in Matt. 20. 28, and Mark
10. 45, 'The Son of man came (*i.e.* identified himself with the
human race), not to be ministered unto, but to minister, and to
give his life a ransom for many,' δοῦναι τὴν ψυχὴν αὐτοῦ λύτρον
ἀντὶ πολλῶν. Thus the Lord became the kinsman of men, so as to
have the right of redeeming them by the sacrifice of His own life.

---

[1] But it is to be remembered that whilst ῥύομαι occasionally stands for **gaal**
and **padah**, it more generally represents the causative form of **natzal** (נצל), to
rescue.

This truth was set forth in most striking words by St. Paul, who
says of the Saviour (1 Tim. 2. 5, 6), 'There is one mediator for God
and men, the man Christ Jesus; who gave himself a ransom for
all (δοὺς ἑαυτὸν ἀντίλυτρον ὑπὲρ πάντων), to be testified in due time.'

Again, the two disciples, on their road to Emmaus, said of
Jesus (Luke 24. 21), 'We trusted that it had been he which should
have redeemed Israel,' ὁ μέλλων λυτροῦσθαι τὸν Ἰσραήλ. By this
expression they implied that a Redeemer was certainly coming, and
that their hopes had been set upon Jesus of Nazareth as the person
they were looking for. By the redemption of Israel perhaps they
meant what the disciples described a few days afterwards as the
restoration of the kingdom to Israel. This redemption had been
looked for with much eagerness among the Jews of that time, possibly owing to the study of Daniel's prophecy of Seventy Weeks.
We have a glimpse of this expectation thirty years earlier in the
prophetic song of Zacharias, which opens with these words (Luke
1. 68): 'Blessed be the Lord God of Israel, for he hath visited and
redeemed (ἐποίησε λύτρωσιν) his people, and hath raised up an horn
of salvation for us in the house of his servant David.' The word
redemption here used by the aged priest appears to gather up in
one all the blessings mentioned in the later portions of the song
—light, pardon, peace, salvation, deliverance from the hand of
enemies, and the power of serving God without fear, 'in holiness
and righteousness before him all the days of our life.' Compare
the words concerning the aged Anna (*i.e.* Hannah [1]) who went
forth to speak of Him to all those that looked for redemption
(λύτρωσιν) in Jerusalem (Luke 2. 38).

The word λύτρωσις occurs once more, namely, in Heb. 9. 12,
where we read of Christ that 'By his own blood he entered in once
for all into the holy place (*i.e.* into the heavens), having obtained
(or found) eternal redemption for us (Job 33. 24).

The noun ἀπολύτρωσις, which does not exist in the LXX, occurs
ten times in the N. T.; once in the Gospels, 'Lift up your heads,
for behold your redemption draweth nigh' (Luke 21. 28). This
passage evidently refers to a great future event, which shall constitute the final deliverance of Israel from desolation. The word is
used with reference to a greater deliverance in Rom. 8. 23, 'Waiting
for the adoption, to wit, the redemption of our body;' also in Eph.
1. 13, 14, and 4. 30.

---

[1] It is a pity that our Revisers did not correct the spelling of this name as
they did in the case of 'alleluia.'

In Rom. 3. 24, Eph. 1. 7, and Col. 1. 14, redemption is apparently identified with present pardon and justification through the blood of Christ. But there is another passage which combines the present and future aspects of redemption in one, viz. Heb. 9. 15. It is here stated that the death of Christ effects a redemption, or perhaps we might render it a quittance or discharge of the account of the transgressions incurred under the first covenant, that they which are called might receive the promise of ·eternal inheritance. In Heb. 11. 35, the word is used with reference to that deliverance from death which the martyrs under the old dispensation might possibly have obtained at the cost of a denial of the faith.

The idea of purchase as connected with salvation is expressed still more strongly in the N. T. than in the O. T., by the use of the words ἀγοράζω and ἐξαγοράζω. The former of these is used several times in the Gospels in its ordinary sense; but in the later books we read, 'Ye are (or *were*) bought with a price' (1 Cor. 6. 20, and 7. 23); 'Denying the Lord that bought them' (2 Pet. 2. 1); 'Thou hast bought us for God by thy blood' (Rev. 5. 9); 'The hundred and forty-four thousand that are bought from the earth' (Rev. 14. 3, 4).

The more complete form ἐξαγοράζω is found in Gal. 3. 13, 'Christ has bought us off from the curse;' and chap. 4. 5, 'Made under the law, that he might buy off them that are under the law.' It primarily refers to the special deliverance which Jews as such needed and obtained through the form and mode of Christ's death, so as to extricate them from the claims which the law of Moses would otherwise have established against them.

Another word is rendered purchase in the N. T., namely, περιποίησις. The verb usually answers to the Hebrew **Chayah** (חיה), to make or keep alive. It is also used in Isa. 43. 21, where we read, 'This people have I formed (or moulded) for myself;' and the noun occurs in Mal. 3. 17, where it signifies a peculiar treasure (A. V. *jewels*). The result of our being saved alive by God is that we become in a special sense His acquired property. Thus we may render Acts 20. 28, 'Feed the church of God which he hath acquired to himself by his own blood;' 1 Pet. 2. 9, 'An acquired people;'[1] Eph. 1. 14, 'Until the redemption of the acquired property;' 1 Thess. 5. 9, 'For the acquisition of salvation;' 2 Thess. 2. 14, 'For the acquisition of glory.'

[1] Thus a *peculiar* people, in the Bible, does not mean an eccentric or a strange people; it gives no excuse to people to affect *peculiarities*.

§ 3. *Salvation.*

The doctrine of **salvation** in the N. T. derives its name from a word which was engrained in the history and language of Israel from the period of the deliverance of the people out of Egypt up to the time of their restoration from captivity. The word **yasha'** (יָשַׁע), to **save**, which generally answers to the Greek σώζω, has given a name not only to Joshua, but to JESUS, who should save His people from their sins. Our translators have rendered **yasha'** by the words **save, help, preserve, rescue, defend,** and **deliver**.

Yasha' is used of the deliverance of Israel from the Egyptians (Exod. **14.** 30; Isa. **43.** 3), and from other enemies (Num. **10.** 9; Deut. **20.** 4). The reference to this fact in 1 Sam. **10.** 19 is very striking : ' Ye have this day rejected your God, who himself **saved** you out of all your adversities and your tribulations.'

This salvation was often effected through the instrumentality of man. Thus the Lord said to Gideon, 'Go in this thy might, and thou shalt **save** Israel from the hand of the Midianites : have not I sent thee?' (Jud. **6.** 14). Again, He says to Samuel concerning Saul, 'Thou shalt anoint him to be captain over my people Israel, that he may **save** my people out of the hand of the Philistines' (1 Sam. **9.** 16). Yet in such cases it was to be clearly understood that the work was God's, not man's; accordingly, Gideon's company was reduced in number, 'lest Israel vaunt themselves against me, saying, My own hand hath **saved** me' (Jud. **7.** 2). Actuated by this conviction, Jonathan reminded his armour-bearer that 'There is no restraint to the Lord to **save** by many or by few' (1 Sam. **14.** 6); and Saul, when appealing to the name of God, describes Him as the Lord who **saveth** Israel (1 Sam. **14.** 39). In 2 Kings **13.** 5 we read that 'the Lord gave Israel a **saviour**, so that they went out from under the hand of the Syrians.' With this passage may be compared the words of Isaiah with regard to Egypt, 'They shall cry unto the Lord because of the oppressors, and he shall send them a **saviour**, and a great one, and he shall deliver them' (Isa. **19.** 20).

Over and above the national salvation depicted in these and many similar passages, there are numerous references in the O. T. to the fact that God exercises a saving care over individuals, especially over those who in their helplessness and trouble need and claim His protection. Eliphaz says of God, 'He **saveth** the poor from the sword, from their mouth, and from the hand of the mighty' (Job **5.** 15); 'He shall **save** the humble person' (**22.** 29). The

Psalmist says, 'He saves the meek' (Ps. 76. 9), the needy (72. 4, 13), the contrite (34. 18), the righteous (Prov. 28. 18), but not the wicked (Ps. 18. 41).

The principle upon which this salvation from trouble is extended to man is simply the merciful disposition of God (Ps. 109. 26) and His own honour (Isa. 37. 35). He saves for His own Name's sake. He says emphatically, 'I, even I, am the Lord; and beside me there is no saviour' (Isa. 43. 11); 'Look unto me, and be ye saved, all the ends of the earth: for I am God, and there is none else' (Isa. 45. 22).

There is nothing in the word **yasha'** which indicates the mode or which limits the extent of salvation. It evidently includes divinely bestowed deliverance from every class of spiritual and temporal evil to which mortal man is subjected. In Ps. 24. 5, and elsewhere, it is set forth in connection with righteousness; in 25. 5, with truth; in 40. 10, with faithfulness; in 51. 12, with joy; in 68. 19, 20, with spiritual gifts; in 69. 13, with the hearing of prayer; and in 79. 9, with the forgiveness of sins.

The Messiah was to be the embodiment of the Divine help and salvation. His coming is thus proclaimed, 'Behold, thy salvation cometh; behold, his reward is with him, and his work before him' (Isa. 62. 11); 'Behold, thy king cometh unto thee: he is just, and having salvation'[1] (Zech. 9. 9); 'Behold, your God will come with vengeance, even God with a recompence; he will come and save you' (Isa. 35. 4).

It is to be noticed that **Chayah** (חיה), to save alive or make alive, is used several times in the O.T., *e.g.* Gen. 12. 12; Ezek. 3. 18; 13. 18, 19; 18. 27. In these and other passages preservation in life is what is generally referred to. Compare 1 Pet. 3. 18, which may be rendered 'being kept alive in the spirit.'

§ 4. *Teaching of the N. T. on Salvation.*

The Greek representative of **yasha'** in the N. T. is σώζω. We find it used of both temporal and spiritual deliverances, though the latter sense strongly predominates. 'To be saved' and 'to be made whole' are sometimes taken as renderings for the same word. Over and over again in this physical sense Christ 'saved others,' though He could not—the Jews supposed—'save Himself.' There are also

---

[1] The word here is passive, and perhaps refers to the resurrection of Christ.

some passages in the Epistles which appear to refer to temporal salvation, whilst others are open to two interpretations.

The references in the N. T. to the ' great salvation' wrought by Christ are very constant and most remarkable. Sometimes this salvation is identified with entrance into the kingdom of God (Mark **10**. 26 ; Luke **13**. 23) ; sometimes it is regarded as a present salvation (Luke **19**. 9 ; 2 Cor. **6**. 2) ; in other passages it is postponed till the Great Day (1 Cor. **3**. 15), which is the day of the Lord Jesus Christ (1 Cor. **5**. 5). It is everywhere set forth as attainable only through Him (John **10**. 9 ; Acts **4**. 12). It follows on repentance (2 Cor. **7**. 10), on belief (Mark **16**. 16), on receiving the love of the truth (2 Thess. **2**. 10), on public confession of Christ's resurrection (Rom. **10**. 9). In some passages salvation is deliverance from sins (Matt. **1**. 21) ; in others it appears to mean a continuous preservation from surrounding evil (2 Tim. **4**. 18 ; Heb. **5**. 9) ; whilst in a third class of passages it is deliverance from the wrath to come (Rom. **5**. 9, **13**. 11 ; 1 Thess. **5**. 8 ; Heb. **9**. 28).

The being saved is brought several times into contrast with the being lost. It is a present loss or perdition from which Christ comes to seek and to save in the first place. He is never represented as saving from final perdition those who deliberately reject His saving work here. His mission was essentially remedial and restorative. So long as He was upon earth He restored health to the sick, sight to the blind, and cleanness to the leper ; now that He has died, risen, and ascended into heaven, He restores the moral being of those who trust Him, not only by healing their backslidings and pardoning their offences, but also by giving them spiritual health, and power to live unto God. Hereafter will come the restoration of the body and of the whole physical fabric of things connected with the body, together with the full development of spiritual life.

CHAPTER XII.

MORAL actions are regarded in Scripture in two lights : first, they tend to influence the character of the agent ; secondly, they affect his relations with his fellow-beings, and also with God. Every breach of law, as a matter of fact, constitutes man an offender, and—if it be known or suspected—causes him to be regarded as such. This principle, with which we are all familiar in human affairs, is true, nay, it may be regarded as a truism, in things pertaining to God ; and since the secrets of every heart are laid bare before Him, it follows that every evil motive, every cherished passion, every wrong word, and every evil deed awaken the Divine displeasure, and call for judicial treatment at God's hands. As in man, however, there exist certain attributes which tend to compensate each other's action, so it is in God. Mercy rejoices against judgment, and the feelings of a Father exist in the bosom of Him whom we instinctively and rightly regard as a Moral Governor. God never forgets whereof we are made ; He knows our frame, and remembers that we are but dust ; and the sins into which we are often hurried through our fallen nature and our inherited constitution, through ignorance, through the force of circumstances, and through the machinations of the Evil One, are weighed by Him in all their aspects, and are seen, if with a magisterial eye, yet through a medium of tender love and pity, which has found its full expression and effect in the atonement.

§ 1. *The Hebrew Word for Atonement.*

The Hebrew word whereby this doctrine is universally set forth in the O. T. is **Caphar** (כפר), the original meaning of which is supposed to be to cover or shelter. A noun formed from it, answering to the modern Arabic **Khephr**, is sometimes used to signify a village as a place of shelter, *e.g.* Caper-naum (the village of Nahum). Another form of this word, namely, **Copher**, usually rendered ransom, is transliterated camphire in Cant. 1. 14, and 4. 13. In Gen. 6. 14 the verb and noun are used, where God is represented as telling Noah to pitch the ark within and without with pitch.

Before referring to the passages in which the word has been rendered to make atonement, we may notice those in which other renderings have been adopted in the A. V. The following are the most important :—

Deut. **21.** 8, 'They shall say, Be merciful unto thy people whom thou hast redeemed, and lay not this innocent blood to their charge ; . . . and the blood shall be forgiven them'—*i.e.* the charge of having shed innocent blood shall be removed from them. 1 Sam. **3.** 14, ' I have sworn that the iniquity of Eli's house shall not be purged with sacrifice nor offering for ever.' No sacrifice for sins of ignorance could cause God to change His determination in this case. It is not the eternal destiny of the individuals, but the official position of the family, that is here spoken of. 2 Chron. **30.** 18, 19, ' Hezekiah prayed for them, saying, The good Lord pardon every one that prepareth his heart to seek God, the Lord God of his fathers, though (he do it) not according to the purification of the sanctuary.' It is added that 'the Lord hearkened to Hezekiah and healed the people.' Here a ceremonial offence was committed, but, through the intercession of Hezekiah, the charge was done away with. Ps. **78.** 38, ' He being full of compassion forgave their iniquity and destroyed them not.' In this case the charge was done away with, not because of man's innocence, but because of God's compassion. Ps. **79.** 9, ' Purge away our sins for thy name's sake.' In this, as in other passages, the purgation is not the moral change, but the removal either of guilt or of the punishment which follows from guilt. The ground of appeal lies not in any latent goodness in the offender, but in the nature of God Himself. This is implied in the familiar but too little heeded phrase, ' for thy name's sake,' which occurs so frequently in the O. T. Prov. **16.** 6, ' By (or *in*) mercy and truth iniquity is purged, and by (or *in*) the fear of the Lord men depart from evil.' This passage teaches that where a man departs from his evil courses and turns into the path of mercy and truth, God is ready to be gracious to him. (Compare Jer. **18.** 23.) Isa. **6.** 7, ' Lo, this hath touched thy lips, and thine iniquity is taken away and thy sin purged.' Isa. **22.** 14, ' Surely this iniquity shall not be purged from you till ye die.' The men of whom this was said, and who had deliberately set themselves in opposition to God's revealed truth, would go into another world with their sins unpardoned. Isa. **27.**

9, 'By this shall the iniquity of Jacob be purged, and this is all the fruit to take away his sin.' (Compare Num. 35. 33; Deut. 32. 43.) Isa. 28. 18, 'Your covenant with death shall be disannulled.' This use of the word **Caphar** is interesting. To be disannulled is to be treated as non-existent; and this is the way in which God covers sin; to use the vivid language of the Bible, He casts it behind His back. Ezek. 16. 62, 63, 'I will establish my covenant with thee, and thou shalt know that I am the Lord; that thou mayest remember and be confounded, and never open thy mouth any more because of thy shame; when I am pacified toward thee for all that thou hast done.' The pacification of God is literally the covering (by atonement) of the sins written against His people. Pacification, *i.e.* atonement, proceeds from Him only. See also Ps. 65. 3; Isa. 47. 11; Ezek. 43. 20.

The word **Caphar**, in one or other of its forms, is rendered atone or atonement in about eighty passages, most of which are in the Levitical law. All men and all things human are represented in the law as needing atonement. Even when a priest, or an altar, or a temple was to be consecrated, there must be atonement made first.

And how was atonement wrought? A spotless victim had to be brought before the Lord to take the part of sinful man. Its death, after the sins of the offerer had been laid upon its head, represented the fact that the innocent must suffer for the guilty. Then came the solemn mystery. The priest, God's agent, must take the blood of the victim and scatter it over God's altar. This process set forth the truth that God and the sinner must be brought into contact through means of Him whom priest and altar typified. The symbol was composite, or many-sided, and its various aspects can only be realised and put together when they are regarded in the light of Christ's death upon the cross. It was not His life that made atonement, but His death, *i.e.* the giving up of His life. One of the ends and objects of His partaking of flesh and blood was that He might taste death. The people of Israel were frequently reminded that their hope lay in the death of a representative. This is brought out very clearly in Lev. 17. 11, 'The life (or soul) of the flesh is in the blood: and I have given it to you upon the altar to make an atonement for your lives; for it is the blood that maketh an atonement for[1] the life.' When therefore the Son of God 'poured out his soul unto death,' shedding His life-blood in behalf

[1] R. V. (?) 'by reason of the life.'

I

of the world, He gave substance and embodiment to the Divine disposition of mercy which was foreshadowed in the Levitical law.

We now have to notice that the word **Caphar** not only sets forth God's merciful disposition to shelter the sinner, and symbolises the process whereby the shelter should be obtained, but also represents the act of the *Priest* in making atonement for the sins of the people. An important conclusion may be drawn from this fact, namely, that this divinely-appointed officer, when making atonement, was really representing, not what man does in approaching God, but what 'God manifest in the flesh' does in sheltering man. The people might bring the sacrifices, but it was the priest alone that could take the blood and sprinkle it on the altar or on the mercy-seat, and when he did so he was setting forth in a dim and shadowy figure the merciful provision of God for the pardon of the sinner. Atonement, then, was not something done by man to pacify or gratify God, nor was it something done by a third party with the intention of representing the sinner before God ; but it is essentially the product of God's pardoning mercy, exhibited in figure through the agency of the priest's sprinkling of the blood, and finally embodied in the work of Christ. 'God was, in Christ, reconciling the world unto himself, not imputing their trespasses unto them' (2 Cor. **5**. 19).

In accordance with the teaching of the O. T. on this subject, we have the doctrine of the Priesthood of Christ, the object of which was 'to make atonement (A. V. 'reconciliation') for the sins of the people,' plainly set forth in the Epistle to the Hebrews (**2**. 17).

The fact that the priest in certain cases (*e.g.* Lev. **10**. 17) consumed the flesh of the atoning sin-offering may have symbolised the identification between priest and victim which was to be accomplished when Christ offered Himself for our sins.

The application of the fire which was continually burning on the altar, together with incense, to make atonement in certain cases (*e.g.* Num. **16**. 46 ; Isa. **6**. 6, 7), seems intended to indicate that the virtue of the atonement once made is continuous, and applicable to all cases.

The word **reconciliation** has been adopted by our translators instead of **atonement**, and must be considered as identical with it in Lev. **6**. 30, **8**. 15, **16**. 20 ; Ezek. **45**. 15, 17, 20 ; Dan. **9**. 24.

The form **Copher** has been rendered **satisfaction** in Num. **35**. 31, 32 ; **bribe** in 1 Sam. **12**. 3, Amos **5**. 12 ; **sum of money** in

Exod. 21. 30 ; ransom in Exod. 30. 12, Job 33. 24, 36. 18, Ps. 49. 7, Prov. 6. 35, 13. 8, 21. 18, and Isa. 43. 3. The usage of the word in these passages, many of which were not ceremonial or symbolical, conveys an idea of *costliness* as an element in atonement, and thus allies it with redemption.[1]

The LXX has translated the verb **Caphar** by ἐξιλάσκομαι, and the noun generally by ἱλασμός, propitiation; occasionally by καθαρισμός, cleansing; and by λύτρον, ransom, in six passages. The prevailing idea set forth both in the LXX and in other translations is that atonement is the doing away with a charge against a person, so that the accused may be received into the Divine favour, and be freed from the consequences of wrong-doing. It should be added that pacification, propitiation, and such words, are by no means adequate for the purpose of conveying the doctrine of atonement; they savour too much of heathenism and superstition, and lead to the supposition that man pacifies God, instead of teaching that God shelters man.

The name of the mercy-seat, **Capporeth** (ἱλαστήριον), is derived from **Caphar**. The description of this remarkable object is to be found in Exod. 25., and its use is indicated in Lev. 16. It was the lid of the ark which contained the law of God. Though made of pure gold, it needed to be sprinkled with blood by the High Priest once a year. This life-blood, shed to represent the punishment due to the Israelites for their sins, was thus brought (by means of sprinkling) into contact with the receptacle of the Law.

The mercy-seat is not only referred to as one of the Levitical 'shadows' in Heb. 9. 5, but is identified with the atoning work of Christ in Rom. 3. 25, where we read, 'God hath set forth (Christ) as a propitiation (Luther, '*zu einem Gnadenstuhl*') through faith in his blood.'

§ 2. *N. T. Teaching on Atonement and Substitution.*

The verb ἐξιλάσκομαι does not appear in the N. T., but both ἱλασμός and καθαρισμός are used of the atoning work of Christ (see 1 John 2. 2, 4. 10, and Heb. 1. 3). The word λύτρον is also applied

---

[1] The free offering of the jewels 'as an *atonement* for the life' by those who had plundered the Midianites was a special case, and must not be regarded as pointing to an independent means of atonement ; moreover, it is to be noticed that the gift was accepted by the priests not as an atonement, but as a memorial (Num. 31. 50, 54).

by Christ to His own death, which was 'a ransom for many' (λύτρον ἀντὶ πολλῶν), Matt. 20. 28, and Mark 10. 45. We have here strongly brought out the truth that the Divine interposition on behalf of sinful man was not a work which cost nothing; it called for no less an offering than the precious life-blood of Christ, who was a 'lamb without blemish and without spot.' As it was an act of self-sacrifice on the Father's part to give His Son freely to bear and suffer what He deemed needful, so it was an act of self-sacrifice on the Son's part to drink the cup which His Father put into His hands. He was at once both a living and a dying sacrifice.

The truth set forth by our Lord in the above-named passages concerning the costliness of atonement is further illustrated by the words of St. Paul in 1 Tim. 2. 5, 6, 'There is one God, and one mediator belonging to God and men, Christ Jesus, (himself) man; who gave himself a ransom for all (ἀντίλυτρον ὑπὲρ πάντων), to be testified in due time.' The word μεσίτης here translated mediator is not to be found in the LXX; it seems to imply not so much what is ordinarily meant by a mediator, as a *medium*, and so a *common ground*. Jesus Christ is a Being in whom Godhead and manhood meet, so that God and man are made one in Him, and are represented by Him. The Son of God, who is One in nature and attributes with the Father, took not only a human *body* but human *nature*, so that every child of Adam may claim Him as kinsman; and then gave Himself a ransom for all. Here St. Paul, not content with the word λύτρον, adopts a composite word to make the passage still more emphatic, ἀντίλυτρον ὑπὲρ πάντων, *a substitutionary ransom on behalf of all*. What men could not do, that Christ Jesus did for them, instead of them, and in their behalf, by the will of God. The obedience of Christ, which culminated in His death, was thus devised, wrought, and accepted by God for the benefit of all men. It may not be needful to assert that He *suffered* what all men deserved to *suffer*, but He certainly *did* what all men were originally intended *to do*, viz. His Father's will in all its fulness; and that will, in His case, involved that He should suffer death for the sin of the world, destroying thereby the body of sin, whilst by His resurrection He opened the kingdom of heaven to all believers.

The Hebrew preposition rendered by the word *for* in connection with the doctrine of acceptance and atonement does not mean *instead of*, but *over, on, because of*, or *on account of*. The preposition which properly marks *substitution* is never used in connection with the word caphar. To make atonement for a sin is literally to

cover *over* the sin, the preposition ('al, עַל) being constantly used
with verbs signifying to cover, *e.g.* in Hab. 2. 14. 'As the waters
cover the sea.'   Ba'ad (בְּעַד), *because of*, is used in some passages,
as in Exod. 32. 30.   In one passage only does the strict idea of
substitution, as distinguished from representation, appear in
the O. T. in connection with sacrifice, namely, in Gen. 22. 13, where
we are told that Abraham offered up a ram *instead* of his son.   The
absence of this peculiar mode of expression from the Levitical law
is significant ; and it teaches us to be cautious in the use of language
relative to the *transfer* of sins and of righteousness effected in the
atonement.   In connection with this point, the following weighty
words from Archbishop Magee's work on the Atonement deserve
consideration :—'The expression *to bear the sins of others* is fami-
liarised to denote *the suffering evils inflicted on account of those sins.*
I will not contend that this should be called suffering *the punishment* of those sins, because the idea of punishment cannot be
abstracted from that of guilt ; and in this respect I differ from
many respectable authorities, and even from Dr. Blayney, who uses
the word punishment in his translation.   But it is evident that it
is, notwithstanding, a judicial infliction ; and it may perhaps be
figuratively denominated *punishment*, if thereby be implied a reference to the actual transgressor, and be understood that suffering
which was due to the offender himself ; and which, if inflicted on
him, would then take the name of punishment.   In no other sense
can the suffering inflicted on one on account of the transgressions of
another be called a punishment ; and in this light the bearing the
punishment of another's sins is to be understood as bearing that
which in relation to the sins and to the sinner admits the name
of punishment, but with respect to the individual on whom it is
actually inflicted, abstractedly considered, can be viewed but in the
light of suffering.'

The same writer observes that 'those that hold the doctrine of
a vicarious punishment feel it not necessary to contend that the evil
inflicted on the victim should be exactly the same in quality and
degree with that denounced against the offender; it depending,
they say, upon the will of the legislator what satisfaction he will
accept in place of the punishment of the offender.'   Once more, he
remarks that 'a strict vicarious substitution or literal equivalent is
not contended for, no such notion belonging to the doctrine of the
atonement.'

To sum up the Scriptural view on this doctrine, we may say that

atonement signifies *shelter by means of representation.* Applying
this general definition to the case of *sin,* Scripture teaches that
shelter for the sinner is secured through his being represented by
Christ before the Father; and in order that he should be so represented, Christ became our kinsman, and wrought out that perfect
righteousness which man has failed to attain; further, He endured
death on the cross, and more than death—the hiding of His Father's
countenance, which was the curse due to sin. Thus He who knew
not sin was made (or dealt with as) sin for us, that we might be
made the righteousness of God in Him. It is a real substitution,
for what He did and suffered took the place of what we ought to
have done and suffered.

The only time that the word atonement is used in the
A. V. of the N. T. is in Rom. 5. 11. Here it stands for the Greek
καταλλαγή, which ought to have been rendered *reconciliation* in
accordance with the previous verse (see R. V.). It is to be remarked
that καταλλαγή is never used of the atonement in the O. T. The
verb καταλλάσσω is found in the following passages in the second
book of Maccabees: (1. 5), 'May God *be at one* with you;' (5. 20),
'The great Lord being *reconciled;*' (7. 33), 'He shall *be at one*
with his servants;' (8. 29), 'They besought the merciful Lord *to
be reconciled* with his servants.' While these four Apocryphal
passages speak of God's reconciliation to man, in the N. T. we read
only of man's being reconciled to God. The minister of reconciliation has to beseech men to be reconciled to God (2 Cor. 5. 20), and
in so doing he is expressing in words that which Christ expressed
in deeds. For 'God reconciled us to himself through Christ'
(2 Cor. 5. 18), and the process by which He did it, namely, the
death on the cross (Rom. 5. 10), is available for the whole world
(2 Cor. 5. 19; Rom. 11. 15).

When we speak of Christ reconciling His Father to us,[1] we are
not to picture up an angry Judge being propitiated by a benevolent
Son; this would be an entire misrepresentation of the Christian
Faith. Rather we should regard the Son as sent by His Father to
die for the sins of the world, in order that He might remove the
bar which hindered the free action of Divine love on the heart of
man. As the Father has committed the work of Judgment to the
Son, so has He committed the work of Atonement; and the Son of
Man is as much the agent of His Father's will in the latter case as
in the former.

[1] See the second article of the Church of England.

§ 3. *Forgiveness.*

Passing from the subject of atonement to that of forgiveness, we meet with the word **Salach** (סלח, Ass. *sulû*), a term of great importance, because it is reserved especially to mark the pardon extended to the sinner by God, and is never used to denote that inferior kind and measure of forgiveness which is exercised by one man towards another. This word is used about forty-five times. The LXX sometimes renders it by ἀφίημι, to remit, but the usual rendering is ἵλεως εἰμὶ or ἱλάσκομαι, to be propitious, the word used by the publican when he said, 'God be merciful to me a sinner' (Luke **18**. 13).

Salach is to be found in the following amongst other passages:— Exod. **34**. 9, 'If now I have found grace in thy sight, O Lord, let my Lord go among us; for it is a stiff-necked people; and pardon our iniquity and our sin, and take us for thine inheritance.' Lev. **4**. 20, 'The priest shall make an atonement for them (*i.e.* for the congregation when they had sinned through ignorance), and it shall be forgiven them;' see also verses 26, 31, 35, and chap. **5**. 10, 16, 18. Num. **14**. 19, 20, 'Pardon, I beseech thee, the iniquity of this people according to the greatness of thy mercy, and as thou hast forgiven this people, from Egypt until now. And the Lord said, I have pardoned according to thy word.' Deut. **29**. 20, With respect to the apostate and licentious man, it is said, 'The Lord will not spare him, but the anger of the Lord and his jealousy shall smoke against that man, and all the curses that are written in this book shall lie upon him, and the Lord shall blot out his name from under heaven.' 1 Kings **8**. 30, 39, 'When thou hearest, forgive.' 2 Kings **5**. 18, 'The Lord pardon thy servant, (that) when my master goeth into the house of Rimmon to worship there, and he leaneth on my hand, and I bow myself in the house of Rimmon . . . the Lord pardon thy servant in this thing.' 2 Kings **24**. 3, 4, 'Surely at the commandment of the Lord came (this punishment) upon Judah, to remove them out of his sight, for the sins of Manasseh, according to all that he did; and also for the innocent blood that he shed: which the Lord would not pardon.' Neh. **9**. 17, 'Thou art a God ready to pardon' (lit. a God of pardons). Ps. **25**. 11, 'For thy name sake, O Lord, pardon mine iniquity, for it is great.' Ps. **86**. 5, 'Thou, Lord, art good, and ready to forgive.' Ps. **103**. 3, 'Who forgiveth all thine iniquities, and healeth all thy diseases.' Ps. **130**. 4, 'There is forgiveness

(ὁ ἱλασμός, the propitiation) with thee, that thou mayest be feared.'
Isa. 55. 7, 'Let the wicked forsake his way, and the unrighteous
man his thoughts: and let him return unto the Lord, and he will
have mercy upon him; and to our God, for he will abundantly
pardon.' Jer. 5. 1, 'Seek in the broad places (of Jerusalem) if
ye can find a man, if there be any that executeth judgment,
that seeketh the truth; and I will pardon it.' Jer. 5. 7, 'How
shall I pardon thee for this?' Jer. 31. 34, 'I will forgive
their iniquity, and will remember their sin no more.' Jer. 33. 8,
'I will cleanse them from all their iniquity, whereby they have
sinned against me; and I will pardon all their iniquities, whereby
they have sinned, and whereby they have transgressed against me.'
Jer. 36. 3, 'It may be that the house of Judah will hear all the
evil that I purpose to do unto them; that they may return every
man from his evil way, that I may forgive their iniquity and their
sin.' Jer. 50. 20, 'The iniquity of Israel shall be sought for, and
there shall be none; and the sins of Judah, and they shall not
be found: for I will pardon them whom I reserve.' Lam. 3. 42,
'We have transgressed and rebelled: thou hast not pardoned.'
Dan. 9. 9, 'To the Lord our God belong mercies and forgivenesses,
though we have rebelled against him.' Amos 7. 2, 3, 'When the
grasshoppers had made an end of eating the grass of the land, then
I said, O Lord God, forgive, I beseech thee: by whom shall Jacob
arise? for he is small. The Lord repented for this: It shall not
be, saith the Lord.'

It appears, on the whole, that the process represented by this
word **Salach** is the Divine restoration of an offender into favour,
whether through his own repentance or the intercession of another.
Though not identical with atonement, the two are nearly related.
In fact, the covering of the sin and the forgiveness of the sinner
can only be understood as two aspects of one truth; for both found
their fulness in God's provision of mercy through Christ. The
Apostle brings atonement and pardon closely together when he
says, in summing up the symbolic value of the Levitical system,
'Without shedding of blood (the preliminary to atonement) there
is no forgiveness (ἄφεσις),' Heb. 9. 22.

The words ἀφίημι and ἄφεσις are constantly used in the N. T.
to denote the forgiveness of sins, whether by God or by man. One
of the chief objects of the mission of Christ was that forgiveness of
sins might be proclaimed through His name; and His death upon
the cross has been the means of obtaining it. See Matt. 26. 28;

Mark 1. 4; Luke 1. 77, 24. 47; Acts 2. 38, 5. 31, 13. 38, 26. 18; Eph. 1. 7; Col. 1. 14.

§ 4. *Sin Bearing.*

Nasa (נשׂא, Ass. *nasâ*), to bear, though found in connection with the putting away of sin, is by no means confined to this purpose. It is used very frequently of the bearing of the ark, also of an armour-bearer; it implies first the *lifting-up*; secondly, the *carrying*; and thirdly, the *taking away* of a burden. Nasa is often used of the endurance of punishment, or of the incurring of responsibility. Thus, in Gen. 4. 13, Cain says, 'My punishment (or *fault*) is greater than I can bear;' here the LXX less correctly renders, 'My fault is too great to be forgiven.' (See also the Vulgate and Luther.) We also frequently meet with the expression, 'He shall bear his iniquity,' *i.e.* he shall incur the responsibility of his sin, *e.g.* Lev. 5. 17, 'He is guilty, and shall bear his iniquity.' In some passages the stern consequence of a man having to bear his iniquity is plainly set forth; thus, in Lev. 19. 8, we read, 'He shall bear his iniquity, because he hath profaned the hallowed things of the Lord; and that soul shall be cut off from among his people.'

The word **nasa**, however, is also used of the undertaking the responsibilities or sins of others by substitution or representation. The high priest was to bear the name of Israel before God (Exod. 28. 12). The scapegoat was to bear the iniquity of the people (Lev. 16. 22). In Lev. 10. 17, the expression, 'To bear the iniquity of the congregation,' is identified with the making atonement for them before the Lord. A different Hebrew word, **Saval** (סבל), 'to bear a burden' (rather than 'to lift'), is used in Isa. 53. 11, 'He shall bear their iniquities;' but in the following verse the word **nasa** occurs, 'He bare the sins of many,' and the two Hebrew words are found together in the fourth verse. The expression is very instructive. Christ did not *drive* sins away; He *bare* them. Moreover, the emphatic personal pronoun is added. Compare 1 Pet. 2. 24, 'Who his own self bare our sins.'

The transition from the vicarious bearing of sin to the idea of pardon is very natural, but it is remarkable that this transition should have been effected as early as the days of the patriarchs. Joseph's brethren used the word **nasa** when they say, 'Forgive the trespass of the servants of the God of thy fathers' (Gen. 50. 17). Pharaoh says, 'Forgive, I pray thee, my sin only this once' (Exod. 10. 17). Moses says to God (Exod. 32. 32), 'If thou wilt

forgive their sin.' Among God's attributes it is recorded that
He forgives iniquity and transgression and sin (Exod. 34. 7 ;
Num. 14. 18; Micah 7. 18). Again, Moses intercedes, 'Pardon
the iniquity of this people' (Num. 14. 19). Joshua uses the
word of God, 'He will not forgive your transgressions nor your
sins' (Josh. 24. 19). In some of these passages the English word
bear or *put up with* might possibly express the meaning as well as
the word forgive. Nasa is also used in Ps. 25. 18, 32. 1, 5, 85. 2,
99. 8 ; Isa. 2. 9, 33. 24.

In other passages our translators have rendered nasa by spare
or pardon. See Gen. 18. 24; Exod. 23. 21 ; 1 Sam. 15. 25; Job 7.
21 ; Isa. 44. 21 ; Jer. 23. 39 ; Lam. 3. 17.

The usual Greek renderings for nasa are αἴρω and λαμβάνω, and
these are reproduced in the N. T. Thus, in St. Matt. 8. 17, we read
that the Lord, in healing various people that came to Him, fulfilled
the words of the prophet, 'Himself bare our infirmities and carried
our sorrows.' Here the Greek ἀσθενείας ἡμῶν ἔλαβε is not quoted
from the LXX, but is a translation of the original words in
Isa. 53. 4.

In John 1. 29 we have the words of the Baptist, 'Behold the
Lamb of God, that taketh away the sins of the world.' Here the
word αἴρω answers to nasa, and implies the lifting up or taking a
burden upon oneself, and consequently the delivering others from
it. This sentence seems to be referred to by St. John when he
says concerning the Lord, 'He was manifested that he might
take away our sins' (1 John 3. 5).

The word ἀναφέρω, which occurs in the LXX in Isa. 53. 11, is
used of the offering of sacrifices in Heb. 7. 27, 13. 15 ; James 2.
21 ; 1 Pet. 2. 5. It is also twice used of the bearing of sin,
i.e. the taking of the responsibility of the sin of others upon
oneself ; in Heb. 9. 28, 'Christ was once offered (προσφέρω) to
bear (ἀναφέρω) the sins of many ;' and again, in 1 Pet. 2. 24,
'Who himself bare our sins in his own body on the tree, that we,
being dead (ἀπογενόμενοι [1]) to sins, might live to righteousness.'

§ 5. *Acceptance.*

Several words are taken to represent the doctrine of the Divine
acceptance of man. In Prov. 21. 3, we read, 'To do justice and
judgment is more acceptable to the Lord than sacrifice.' Here

---

[1] This word is unique, and marks severance rather than death.

the word **Bachar** (בחר) signifies to choose or select, whether for work or for honour. This is the word used of the 'chosen people,' and answers to the word ἐκλεκτός, 'elect,' in the LXX and the N. T. In some passages the LXX has rendered it αἱρετίζω. It has been rendered 'elect' in Isa. 42. 1, 45. 4, and 65. 9, 22, in all which passages there is reference either to Israel or to the Messiah.

In Lev. 10. 19, 'Should it have been accepted in the sight of the Lord?' we might render, 'Should it have been good or pleasing (טוב) in his sight?' In Ps. 20. 3, 'The Lord . . . remember all thy offerings, and accept thy burnt sacrifice;' here, as we read in the margin, the word for accept (דשן) may signify either make fat or turn to ashes, the latter being the most probable. In Eccles. 12. 10, 'The preacher sought to find out acceptable words,' the word (Chaphets) signifies pleasant or desirable.

In 1 Sam. 26. 19, David says to Saul, 'If the Lord have stirred thee up against me, let him accept an offering.' Here the word to *smell* (רוח, Ass. *ruḥḥu*) is used, so that the passage may be compared with others, such as Gen. 8. 21, where God is described as smelling a sweet savour, that is to say, being pleased with the offering, and hence with the offerer.

Nasa (נשא), which has been discussed above, is frequently used to represent acceptance, with the addition of the word 'face' or 'person' (פנים). It occurs in Gen. 19. 21, where the angel says to Lot, 'I have accepted thee concerning this thing;' in Gen. 32. 20, where Jacob says of Esau, 'Perhaps he will accept of me;' and in Job 42. 8, 9, when God says of Job, 'Him will I accept.' See also 1 Sam. 25. 35; Job 13. 8, 10, 32. 21, 34. 19; Ps. 82. 2; Prov. 18. 5; Mal. 1. 8.

A noun formed from the verb **Nasa** is used without the additional word 'face' or 'person' in Gen. 4. 7, 'If thou doest well, shalt thou not be accepted?' Perhaps the word might be rendered excellency (as in the margin), or superiority, rather than acceptance. Our translators have rendered it dignity in Gen. 49. 3, excellency in Job 13. 11, and highness in 31. 23.

The most important word for acceptance is **ratsah** (רצה), to be well pleased. It is used of God's acceptance of Aaron's ministrations in behalf of Israel (Exod. 28. 38; Deut. 33. 11), and is applied to the Divine regard for the offerer who comes before God in the appointed way. Thus, we read in Lev. 1. 4, 'He shall put his hand upon the head of the burnt offering, and it shall be accepted for him (לו), to make atonement for him.' In the third verse of the same chapter, instead of reading with the A. V. 'of his own voluntary will,' there is little doubt that we should read 'for his acceptance;' and so in other passages. See R. V.

The following passages illustrate the usage of **ratsah**:—Lev. 7. 18, **19**. 7, 'If it (the peace offering) be eaten at all on the third day, it shall not be accepted, neither shall it be imputed unto him that offereth it: it shall be an abomination, and the soul that eateth it shall bear his iniquity' (compare 22. 21, 23. 11). 2 Sam. 24. 23, 'And Araunah said unto the king, The Lord thy God accept thee.' Ps. 19. 14, 'Let the words of my mouth and the meditation of my heart be acceptable in thy sight.' Ps. 69. 13, 'As for me, my prayer is unto thee, O Lord, in an acceptable time,' *i.e.* at a season agreeable to Thee (compare Isa. 49. 8). Ps. 119. 108. 'Accept, I beseech thee, the freewill offerings of my mouth.' See also Prov. 10. 32; Eccles. 9. 7; Isa. 56. 7, 58. 5, 60. 7, 61. 2; Jer. 6. 20, 14. 10, 12; Ezek. 20. 40, 41, 43. 27; Hos. 8. 13; Amos 5. 22; Mal. 1. 10, 13.

It is evident that by the Divine acceptance is to be understood the pleasure with which God welcomes into personal contact with Himself those who approach Him in His own appointed way, and in a spirit cognate to His own. An evil-doer, as such, is not acceptable to God, even though he offer sacrifices. He must be sheltered by atonement, and must thus have the germ at least of a Divine life working in him if he would be regarded by God with pleasure.

The LXX frequently adopts εὐδοκέω, to be well pleased, for **ratsah**, especially in the Psalms. We also find προσδέχομαι and δέχομαι, to accept, in several passages. The adjectival form is usually δεκτός, and the substantive is εὐδοκία and θέλημα.

In the utterance, 'Thou art my beloved Son, in whom I am well pleased,' which is repeated in six passages in the N. T. in slightly different forms, there may be an implied reference to Isa. **42**. 1 ('Mine elect, in whom my soul delighteth'), where the word **ratsah** is found. If so, we might gather that the purport of the announcement was that Christ Jesus was accepted by God as the minister of the true sanctuary and as the offering for the sins of the world. It is more probable, however, that the Greek word here used answers rather to the Hebrew **chaphets**, and signifies that Christ is one in whom God takes pleasure.

The verb προσδέχομαι in the N. T. generally means either to expect or to receive. It is used in the passage, 'This man

receiveth sinners and eateth with them' (Luke 15. 2). In Phil.
4. 18, Christian service is spoken of as 'an acceptable sacrifice'
(θυσία δεκτή). That which is acceptable in God's sight is spoken
of as εὐδοκία in Matt. 11. 26, and Luke 10. 21, 'So it seemed good
in thy sight;' compare also Eph. 1. 9, and Phil. 2. 13. In Eph.
1. 5, the two Greek renderings of ratson are combined in one
phrase—'according to the *good pleasure* of his *will.*' In the angels'
song (Luke 2. 14), if we accept the reading 'good will towards men,'
we must understand God's willingness to accept men ; if we read
'towards men of good will,' we ought to understand His good will ;
so that the meaning is practically the same; and, after all, we are
only dealing with a Greek rendering of what must have been a
Hebrew song.

With regard to the word θέλημα, we have, in Heb. 10. 7, a
quotation from the Psalms which rules the meaning of the word in
other passages, 'Lo, I come to do thy will, O God.' Here θέλημα
answers to ratson, that which is acceptable in thy sight. 'By the
which will,' continues the writer, 'we are sanctified.' Forasmuch
as sacrifices of bulls and goats did not prove acceptable to God, the
Divine Son came to do what would be acceptable. He substituted
the offering of Himself for the types, and this offering being accepted by God, believers in Him were sanctified thereby (see Matt.
26. 39). In Heb. 10. 36, the responsibility of doing the will of
God is laid on the believer ; and so in chap. 13. 21, where we learn
that what we do is wrought in us by God, and is acceptable to Him
through Jesus Christ. Compare Rom. 12. 1.

On reviewing the passages of the N. T. in which the idea of
acceptance is presented, they will be seen to confirm the view
taken of the Hebrew word, as signifying the favourable and pleasurable reception given to man by God. God's acceptance of the man
who believes in His Son is not to be regarded as a mere fictitious
theory; it is a solid fact, a spiritual reality. Just as men here
below have pleasure in one another under certain circumstances, so
the unseen Author of Existence takes pleasure in those who fear
Him, draws near to them when they draw near to Him, and in the
Person of Christ 'receiveth sinners and eateth with them.' It is
indeed a mystery ; but it is gloriously true, and will be more fully
realised hereafter, when the Tabernacle of God shall be with men.

CHAPTER XIII.

PURIFICATION, BAPTISM.

ONE of the essential attributes of God is His *purity*. This truth is constantly set forth in Scripture, both in plain declarations and also in symbolical representations. 'God is light, and in him is no darkness at all' (1 John 1. 5). In the remarkable vision recorded in Exod. 24. 10, we read, 'They saw the God of Israel: and there was under his feet as it were a (paved) work of a sapphire-stone, and as it were the body[1] of heaven in his clearness.' With this description we may compare the vision of the Divine glory which St. John had, 'Before the throne there was a sea of glass like unto crystal' (Rev. 4. 6). What is compared in the one place to the brilliancy of the firmament,[2] is described in the other as an ocean of blazing crystal. That spotless purity which is the basis of the Divine character, and the atmosphere in which God exists, cannot indeed be adequately pictured forth by either of these figures. Even the heavens, though they declare His glory, are not pure in His sight. The ethereal splendour of the noonday is turned to darkness in the presence of Him who is 'the Father of lights.' Saul of Tarsus knew well the dazzling brightness of an Eastern sun at mid-day, but when the Divine glory of the Sun of Righteousness shone round about him, he found it to be 'above the brightness of the sun' (Acts 26. 13).

The ideal condition of man is to be godlike, that is, to be pure and unpolluted in heart, word, and deed. But he fails to live up to this ideal. There is a fearful gulf between the purity of the Divine Being and that defilement which is, in greater or less degree, the sad inheritance of every child of Adam. How is this gulf to be spanned? Who is there that can bring a clean thing out of an

---

[1] Literally the *bone* of heaven, *i.e.* the very heaven itself. The Hebrews often used the word 'bone,' as we use 'marrow,' for the *essence* of a thing. Our word *bone* is literally *beon* or essence.

[2] LXX, ὥσπερ εἶδος στερεώματος τοῦ οὐρανοῦ τῇ καθαρότητι.

unclean ?   'If I wash myself with snow water, and make my hands
never so clean, yet shalt thou plunge me in the ditch' (Job 9. 30, 31).
'Though thou wash thee with nitre, and take thee much soap, yet
thine iniquity is marked before me, saith the Lord God' (Jer. 2. 22).
But what man cannot do, God Himself has done, according to the
Scriptures.   He has opened a fountain for sin and for uncleanness.

§ 1. *Purification.*

The process whereby moral impurity was to be done away was
typified or shadowed forth by the purifications of the Levitical
ritual ; and the word which is in general use in the O. T. to express
the process is **thahér** (טהר), which signifies, in the intensive form, to
make clear, bright, or shining, and hence to make or pronounce
clean.   It is used of clearness in the passage quoted at the
beginning of this chapter.

External purification was taken at a very early time as a symbol
of internal cleansing.   Thus Jacob says to his household, 'Put away
the strange gods that are among you, and be clean, and change
your garments : and let us arise, and go up to Bethel' (Gen. 35. 2).
The cleansing and the change of dress were evidently intended to
set forth the resolution to put away those false gods by which their
lives had been contaminated.   Nor were the people of God peculiar
in the use of this symbolical rite.   It has been found in all ages and
in almost all countries, especially where there is a hot climate.   The
word which is adopted for the purifications appointed by God is also
used to express idolatrous purgations in Isa. 66. 17.   The purification
in the gardens there spoken of was simply misdirected symbolism.

Among the elements used for ceremonial cleansing in the Levitical system, three are especially to be noticed, namely, *fire, water,*
and *blood.*   Precious metals taken from idolatrous nations were to
be passed through the fire ; this process, together with an application of water, was considered to have purged them of their defilement.   Clothing and all things that could not abide the fire were
to be made to go through the water ; and the persons of those who
had come in contact with the heathen were to be reckoned unclean
until this process was accomplished (Num. 31. 23, 24).   Cleansing by
blood was needed in various cases of ceremonial defilement; in fact,
'almost all things are by the law purged with blood' (Heb. 9. 22).

No instance of ceremonial cleansing is more fully detailed or
more interesting than that of the leper.   Here we have to distin-

guish between three processes, each of which was called by the same name. There was, first, the actual cure of the disease; secondly, the authoritative pronunciation by the priest; and, thirdly, the external washings, offerings, and other rites which signed and sealed the same, and gave the healed man admittance into the congregation. With regard to the cleansing away of the disease, we have no exact account in Scripture. Leprosy appears to have come and gone, no one knew how. It was regarded as incurable by human means, and was considered to be a special visitation from God. Hence it was often designated as *the plague* or *stroke*.[1] The cure of Naaman is thus described, 'His flesh came again like unto the flesh of a little child, and he was *clean*' (2 Kings 5. 14). It was with reference to this actual cure that the leper said to the Lord Jesus, 'Lord, if thou wilt, thou canst make me *clean*.' What the waters of Jordan were appointed to do in the one case, to indicate that salvation was of the Jews, the word and touch of Jesus of Nazareth did in the other, to shew that saving power was vested in Him. Secondly came the inspection by the priest. 'Go, shew thyself to the priest.' If he was satisfied, by the presence of certain symptoms clearly described in the Law, that the man before him was cured, or 'clean' (in the first sense of the term), then he 'pronounced him clean'—literally, 'cleansed him.' The official and authoritative declaration of the fact is thus identified in language with the fact itself.[2] In order, however, that the man thus doubly 'cleansed' might be received into the congregation and restored to those privileges from which he had been debarred, it was needful that he should be 'cleansed' in a third sense through the offering of certain gifts and the performance of sundry remarkable rites, including the being sprinkled with blood and washed with water (see Lev. chaps. 13. and 14).

A few other leading instances of the use of the ceremonial word

---

[1] In the opinion of some scholars leprosy is referred to in Isa. 53. 4, where we read, 'yet we did esteem him stricken, smitten of God, and afflicted.' Jerome's translation is 'et nos putavimus eum *quasi leprosum* et percussum a Deo et humiliatum,' 'we regarded him as if he were leprous, smitten of God, and humbled.'

[2] This identification in language is well worth observing in connection with the form of Absolution in the Service for the Visitation of the Sick in the Church of England. In the General Absolution we read that God 'hath given power and commandment to his ministers to declare and pronounce to his people, being penitent, the Absolution and Remission of their sins.' In the Visitation Service, after the Priest or Presbyter has 'moved the sick person to make a special confession of his sins, if he feel his conscience troubled with any weighty matter,' he 'shall absolve him,' *i.e.* declare him absolved (see Hooker, *E.P.* Book VI.).

thahér for purification may be noticed. It is used to distinguish the clean from the unclean beasts (Gen. 7. 2, 8, 8. 20, Lev. 20. 25); to express the cleansing of the priests and Levites (Ezra 6. 20); the cleansing of the people, the gates, and the walls of Jerusalem (Neh. 12. 30, 13. 9, 22, 30); of the land (Ezek. 39. 12, 14, 16). It also represents the pure gold used in the construction of the tabernacle vessels, &c. (Exod. 25.); the pure perfume (Exod. 30. 35); the clean place where the ashes of the offerings were cast (Lev. 4. 12, 6. 11); and clean persons, who were to perform certain rites (Lev. 7. 19, 10. 10, 11. 32, &c.).

When we turn to the Psalms and the Prophets, we find **thahér** used several times in a moral and spiritual sense. The following are the most important passages :—Ps. 12. 6, 'The words of the Lord are pure words, as silver tried in an earthen furnace, purified seven times.' Ps. 19. 9, 'The fear of the Lord is clean, enduring for ever.' Ps. 51. 2, ' Wash me throughly from mine iniquity, and cleanse me from my sin.' Ps. 51. 7, 'Purge me with hyssop, and I shall be clean : wash me, and I shall be whiter than snow.' Ps. 51. 10, 'Create in me a clean heart, O God, and renew a right spirit within me.' Prov. 15. 26, 'The words of the pure are pleasant words.' Prov. 22. 11, 'He that loveth pureness (or cleanness) of heart.' Jer. 13. 27, 'O Jerusalem, wilt thou not be made clean?' Jer. 33. 8, 'I will cleanse them from all their iniquity, and I will pardon all their iniquities.' Ezek. 36. 25, 33, 'Then will I sprinkle clean water upon you, and ye shall be clean : from all your filthiness, and from all your idols, will I cleanse you;' 'In the day that I shall have cleansed you from all your iniquities I will also cause you to dwell in the cities.' Ezek. 37. 23, 'I will save them out of all their dwelling-places, wherein they have sinned, and will cleanse them.' Mal. 1. 11, 'In every place incense shall be offered unto my name, and a pure offering,' in contrast with the polluted offering of verse 7. Mal. 3. 3, 'He shall sit as a refiner and purifier of silver : and he shall purify the sons of Levi, and purge them as gold and silver, that they may offer unto the Lord an offering in righteousness.'

§ 2. *Purification according to the N. T.*

With the exception of a few passages, **thahér** has been rendered by καθαρίζω in the LXX. The exceptions are as follows :—
In 2 Chron. 29. 16, 18, and 30. 17, 18, we find ἀγνίζω ; in these

K

passages reference is made to the cleansing or purification of the temple and the worshippers at the Feast of the Passover; ἀφαγνίζω occurs in Num. 8. 6, 21, where the cleansing of the Levites is spoken of; βρέχω, in Ezek. 22. 24, where the prophet speaks of the land not being cleansed with rain; ἁγνεία, in 2 Chron. 30. 19; ἁγνισμός, in Num. 8. 7; δίκαιος, in Prov. 30. 12; and δοκιμός, in 2 Chron. 9. 17.

Tracing the Greek word καθαρίζω through the N. T., we find that the Levitical purifications marked by this word were fulfilled in Christ. He made a καθαρισμός, or purgation, whereby our sins are done away (Heb. 1. 3). His blood cleanseth from all sin (1 John 1. 7). Consequently, ' If we confess our sins, God is faithful and righteous to forgive us our sins, and to cleanse us from all iniquity ' (1 John 1. 9). The blood of Christ, who through the Eternal Spirit offered Himself without spot to God, purges the conscience from dead works, so that the purged person is in a position to serve (λατρεύειν) the living God (Heb. 9. 14). Christ loved the Church, and gave Himself for it, that He might sanctify and cleanse it with the washing of water by the word (Eph. 5. 26). He gave Himself for us, that He might redeem us from all iniquity, and purify unto Himself a peculiar people, zealous of good works (Titus 2. 14).

In connection with these announcements we have the corresponding exhortations, ' Let us cleanse ourselves from all filthiness of the flesh and spirit, perfecting holiness in the fear of God ' (2 Cor. 7. 1); ' Let us draw near with a true heart, in full assurance of faith, having our hearts sprinkled from an evil conscience, and our bodies washed with pure water ' (Heb. 10. 22).

These passages teach that the offering of Christ is not only the pledge of pardon, but also the appointed means of cleansing for all who feel their moral pollution. The defilement of sin was to find its cure in that one great work. Nor were its benefits confined to Jews. What God had cleansed was not to be regarded any longer as common or unclean. The middle wall of partition between Jew and Gentile was broken down. God made no difference; He purified the hearts of both through faith (Acts 15. 9).

The cleansing thus effected through Christ answers to all the aspects of the ceremonial cleansing of the O. T.: there is the actual moral change in the individual, the clean heart, the renewed spirit, the godly life; there is the changed social position, membership in the body of Christ becoming a reality; and there is the being pronounced and regarded as clean in the sight of God through the mediatorial agency of the High Priest.

§ 3. *Washing.*

The Hebrew words for washing deserve attention from the fact that they too are used ceremonially and morally as well as literally.

Duach (רוח), to cast off, and hence to purge from impurity, is used only four times in the O. T. Twice it is rendered wash, viz. in 2 Chron. 4. 6, and Ezek. 40. 38 ; in each of these places reference is made to the putting off the pollution contracted by the priests and Levites while preparing the animals for offering. The first of these passages may be thus understood : ' He made also ten lavers, and put five on the right hand, and five on the left, to wash in them ; the defilement contracted by the operations connected with the burnt offering they cleansed in them ; and the sea was for the priests to wash in.' The Levites washed in the lavers, and the priests in the larger vessel called the sea. The R. V. has failed to draw out the distinction.

Duach is used in a spiritual sense in Isa. 4. 4, ' When the Lord shall have washed away the filth of the daughters of Zion, and shall have purged the blood of Jerusalem from the midst thereof by the spirit of judgment and by the spirit of burning.' The other passage where the word occurs is Jer. 51. 34. Here the Lord, identifying Himself with His people, says, ' Nebuchadnezzar hath devoured me, . . . he hath cast me out,' *i.e.* hath treated me as if I were the ' off-scouring ' of the earth.

Shathaph (שטף), to flood, overflow, or pour copiously, is used, in 1 Kings 22. 38, of the cleansing of Ahab's chariot ;[1] in Job 14. 19, of the destruction of the surface of the land by floods of water ; and in Ezek. 16. 9, of the ' thorough washing ' which represented the care with which God dealt with His people Israel at their first beginning.

We now come to the two words which were in most ordinary use among the Jews, namely, **cavas** (כבס), for which the LXX has πλύνω or ἀποπλύνω, which was applied to the washing of garments ; and **rachats** (רחץ, Ass. *rahatsu*), generally rendered νίπτω or λούω,

---

[1] Different Hebrew words are used for the washing of Ahab's chariot and for the cleansing of his armour. Were the two washed at the same place ? The chariot was washed in the pool of Samaria ; but probably his armour was taken to be cleaned at his palace at Jezreel, and doubtless the dogs licked the blood that was rinsed from it at or near the pool of Jezreel, according to the prophecy of Elijah, which otherwise would not have been literally fulfilled. But see R. V.

but in seven passages πλύνω, which represented the bathing or washing of the body.

Cavas is the term applied to the 'fuller,' and is supposed to refer in the first place to the treading whereby clothes were cleaned. This cleansing of garments was an important ceremonial action. We have already seen its meaning under a slightly different form in Gen. **35**. 2, where Jacob told his household to put away their false gods, and *to change their garments ;* evidently the latter action was taken as the external symbol of the former. Of the 'divers washings' of the Levitical dispensation, some had to do with the *garments*, and are described under the word **cavas**; while others had to do with the *flesh*, and are represented by **rachats**. The following come under the first head : the ceremonial cleansing of the garments before the people were allowed to approach Mount Sinai (Exod. **19**. 10, 14); the cleansing of the garment sprinkled with the blood of the offering (Lev. **6**. 27); the cleansing of men's clothing after leprosy or after contact with that which was pronounced unclean (Lev. **17**. 15); the cleansing of the Levites' clothing for their service (Num. **8**. 7), where it was connected with the sprinkling of 'holy water' over their flesh.

Under the second head (**rachats**, the washing of the flesh) come the washing or bathing of the body, the hands, and the feet generally ; the washing of the sacrifices (Exod. **29**. 17); of the priests before their consecration, and also before their daily ministration (Exod. **29**. 4, and **30**. 19, 21) ; and the washing of the elders' hands over the beheaded heifer (Deut. **21**. 6). This word is also used figuratively in Job **29**. 6, and Ps. **58**. 10. In the triumphant expression, 'Moab is my washpot' (Ps. **60**. 8, and **108**. 9), the image is taken from the laver for the cleansing of the body, not from the trough for the washing of garments.

Each of these expressions is applied to spiritual washing. The word **cavas**, which implies the cleansing of garments, is found in the four following passages :—Ps. **51**. 2, 'Wash me throughly from my sin ;' Ps. **51**. 7, 'Wash me, and I shall be whiter than snow ;' Jer. **2**. 22, 'Though thou wash thee with nitre, and take thee much soap, yet thine iniquity is marked before me, saith the Lord God ;' Jer. **4**. 14, 'O Jerusalem, wash thine heart from wickedness, that thou mayest be saved.'

The word **rachats**, which signifies the washing of the body, is used in a spiritual sense in Ps. **26**. 6, 'I will wash my hands in innocency ;' Ps. **73**. 13, 'I have washed my hands in innocency ;'

Prov. **30**. 12, 'There is a generation that are pure in their own eyes, and yet is not washed from their filthiness;' Isa. **1**. 16, 'Wash you, make you clean;' Isa. **4**. 4, ' When the Lord shall have washed away the filth of the daughter of Zion.'

The word wash, whether applied to the body or to its clothing, is never used except with reference to *water*, and it appears to symbolise the purgation of the inclinations, the character and the external life, from moral pollution. Compare Heb. **10**. 22, 'having our hearts sprinkled from an evil conscience, and our bodies washed with pure water.'

In the N. T., νίπτω is used of washing the face (Matt. **6**. 17) ; the hands (Matt. **15**. 2); the eyes (John **9**. 7, 11, 15); and the feet (John **13**. 5, 6, 8, 10, 12, 14; 1 Tim. **5**. 10). The word λούω is used of the bathing of the body in Acts **9**. 37, **16**. 33, and 2 Pet. **2**. 22. In John **13**. 10 we read, 'He that is bathed (λελουμένος) needeth not save to wash (νίψασθαι) his feet, but is clean every whit' (καθαρὸς ὅλος). It is evident that our Lord here referred, in the first instance, to the well-known fact that after a complete bath a man needed only to cleanse away the impurity which he contracted in walking from it if he wished to be accounted entirely clean ; the significance of the act to the disciples seems to have been that whereas they were in a measure clean *through the word* which He had spoken unto them, there was yet need that He should humble Himself still lower in their behalf, in order to cleanse them in the sight of God. The act of washing their feet symbolised the humiliation of Him who took the form of a servant, and it set forth the necessity of yielding to His cleansing work as the only means of having part with Him in His future kingdom. Washing with water is also connected with the Word in Eph. **5**. 26. Here we read that Christ gave Himself (*i.e.* died) for His Church, that He might sanctify and cleanse it with the washing [1] of the water in the word (τῷ λουτρῷ τοῦ ὕδατος ἐν ῥήματι). Washing (λουτρόν) is also used as a symbol of regeneration in Titus **3**. 5. With these passages we may connect Acts **22**. 16, 'Arise, and be baptized, and wash away (ἀπόλουσαι) thy sins;' and 1 Cor. **6**. 11, ' Such were some of you, but ye are washed' (ἀπελούσασθε). In the Received Text of Rev. **1**. 5 we read, 'Who washed us from our sins in his own blood.' Others here read λύσαντι (liberated) for λούσαντι (washed).

The word πλύνω, which is applied to the washing of garments,

---

[1] The laver (כִּיּוֹר) is rendered λουτήρ in the LXX. The word λουτρον only occurs in Cant. **4**. 2 and **6**. 5 for רַחְצָה, of the washing of sheep.

is used symbolically in Rev. 7. 14; also in the oldest MSS., together
with the Vulgate and the versions made from it, in Rev. 22. 14,
'Blessed are they that wash their robes, that they may have a right
to the tree of life.'

§ 4. *Purity.*

Barar (ברר, Ass. *baru*), literally to separate, and hence to
manifest or make clean, is sometimes used in the sense of cleansing.
In David's hymn (2 Sam. 22. 21, 25, 27; Ps. 18. 20, 24, 26) it is
used in respect of the cleanness of his hands, *i.e.* his freedom from
evil deeds. Job says, 'If I make my hands never so clean, yet shalt
thou plunge me in the ditch' (9. 30); here the word is made the
more emphatic by being used with Zacac (on which see below). In
Ps. 73. 1 we read, 'Truly God is good to Israel, even to such as are
of a clean heart;' the word is used in the expression, 'Fair as the
moon and clear as the sun,' in Cant. 6. 10; also in Isa. 52. 11, 'Be
ye clean, that bear the vessels of the Lord.' These passages chiefly
refer to moral purity, not to ceremonial cleanness, in which sense
the word is never used. It evidently applies to the thoughts of the
heart as well as to the outward actions, and it is sometimes used of
that moral cleansing or purgation which consists of separating the
evil from the good, the dross from the ore; see Ps. 24. 4; Isa. 1.
25; Ezek. 20. 38; Dan. 11. 35, 12. 10. The word is used of 'a
pure language' in Zeph. 3. 9, where perhaps clearness or plainness
is what is referred to.

There are three roots closely connected together which all represent purity, cleanness, or freedom from pollution, namely (1)
Zakak (זקק), which is used in Ps. 12. 6, and Mal. 3. 3; (2) **Zacac**
(זכך), which is found in Job 8. 6, 11. 4, 16. 17 ('My prayer is pure'),
15. 15 ('The heavens are not clean in his sight'), 33. 9; Prov. 16.
2, 20. 11, 21. 8; Lam. 4. 7 ('Purer than snow'); also Exod. 27.
20, 30. 34; Lev. 24. 4, 7; (3) **Zacah** (זכה), which we find in Job
15. 14 ('What is man, that he should be clean?'); 25. 4 ('How can
he be clean that is born of a woman?'); Prov. 20. 9 ('Who can say,
I have made my heart clean, I am pure from my sin?'); Ps. 51. 4
('That thou mightest be clear when thou judgest'); 73. 13 ('I have
cleansed my heart in vain'); 119. 9 ('Wherewithal shall a young
man cleanse his way?'); Isa. 1. 16 ('Wash you, make you clean').

These passages refer to moral purity and transparency of heart.
They point to a character free from taint or sully, as the object

which man aims at, but which he fails to obtain by his own devices;
and even at the best, that which seems perfectly pure in his sight is
proved vile when seen in the light of God.

§ 5. *Sprinkling.*

Two Hebrew words are rendered to sprinkle in the O. T.
Zarak (זרק) occurs thirty-five times, and is always so rendered,
except in Isa. **28.** 25, where it is translated scatter, and 2 Chron.
34. 4, where we find strew. It is curious that the LXX almost
always renders it προσχέω, to pour,[1] giving the idea of shedding or
scattering rather than of sprinkling. The act set forth by this
word was usually performed by means of a vessel, the name of which
was derived from it, and which the LXX renders φιάλη, a phial
(A. V. vial). It is first applied to the scattering of the ashes of
the furnace, in Exod. **9.** 8 ; then to the pouring of the blood of the
offering on the altar and on the people, in Exod. **24.** 6, 8 ; see also
Exod. **29.** 16, 20 ; Lev. **1.** 5, 11, **3.** 2, 8, 13, **7.** 2, 14, **8.** 19, 24,
9. 12, 18, **17.** 6 ; Num. **18.** 17 ; 2 Kings **16.** 13, 15; 2 Chron. **29.** 22,
30. 16, **35.** 11. In Num. **19.** 13, 20, it is applied to the sprinkling
of the water of separation ; and in Job **2.** 12, to the sprinkling of
dust on the head ; in Isa. **28.** 25, to the scattering cummin ; and in
Hos. **7.** 9, to the grey hairs which are *here and there* (margin,
sprinkled) on the head.

The word is once used in a spiritual sense, namely, in Ezek. **36.**
25, 'Then will I sprinkle clean water upon you, and ye shall be
clean.'

Nazah (נזה) occurs twenty-four times, and is always rendered to
sprinkle. It is not necessarily used in a ceremonial sense. The
LXX renders it by ῥαίνω, ῥαντίζω, and their compounds. It is
applied to the priest's sprinkling of blood with the finger before the
vail, or on the side of the altar, or on the mercy-seat, on the occasion of the sin offering, in Lev. **4.** 6, 17, **5.** 9, **16.** 14, 15, 19. It is
also applied to the sprinkling of the blood of the bird on the leper
with hyssop, Lev. **14.** 7, 51; to the sprinkling the water of purifying and separation, Num. **8.** 7, **19.** 21 ; and to the sprinkling of oil
with the finger, Lev. **8.** 11, 30, **14.** 16, 27. The word is used with
a spiritual significance in Isa. **52.** 15, 'So shall he sprinkle many

---

[1] This verb is not to be found in the N. T., but the noun derived from it
(πρόσχυσις) is used in Heb. **11.** 28, of the *shedding* or *sprinkling* of the blood of
the paschal lamb on the door-posts.

nations.' It signifies dropping, whilst **Zarak** marks pouring forth.

The sprinklings (ῥαντισμοί) specially referred to in the Epistle to the Hebrews are of two kinds—that which was performed with the ashes of a red heifer on persons who had contracted certain defilement (Heb. 9. 13), and that which was performed with blood on the people and the Book in making the old covenant; also on the tabernacle and various vessels connected with the sacred service (Heb. 9. 19, 21). The substance of which these are the shadows is the sprinkling of the blood of Jesus, which speaketh better things than that of Abel (Heb. 12. 24).

St. Peter connects this 'sprinkling of the blood of Jesus Christ' with obedience, and both of these with 'sanctification of the spirit' (1 Pet. 1. 2). This sprinkling has its effect both in the sight of God, where it signifies reconciliation, and on the conscience of man, which it purges from dead works to serve the living God (Heb. 9. 14). Accordingly, the Christian is invited to approach God with a true heart sprinkled from an evil conscience (Heb. 10. 22).

§ 6. *Baptism.*

Many are the controversies that have gathered around the rite of Baptism. Questions have been raised as to the mode of administration, as to the right age and condition of those to whom it is to be administered, as to the persons who may perform the ordinance, as to the privileges and responsibilities involved in it, as to the exact bearing of the symbol, and as to the nature of the *nexus* which exists between the sign and the thing signified. Only one of these questions need be discussed here. When our Lord gave orders to His followers to baptize, how would the word which He used be understood? Did it prescribe the exact mode in which the ordinance was to be administered? or had it already arrived at that secondary or technical sense in which undoubtedly it has been largely used in after-times?

Classical authors have been diligently searched by contending parties with the hope of finding some solution of the question. But the more they have been scrutinised, the more clearly has it appeared that the word βαπτίζω has been used with very great latitude, and that it can neither be confined to its primary use of staining or dyeing, nor be restricted to the case of religious or ceremonial acts of cleansing.

The conclusion arrived at by a writer [1] who was himself a 'Baptist,' that is, one who holds to the practice of immersion, is as follows :—

'The English translators did not translate the word "baptize," and they acted wisely ; for there is no one word in the English language which is an exact counterpart of the Greek word, *as the New Testament uses it*, containing the precise ideas of the Evangelist, neither less nor more. The difficulty, or rather the excellency, of the word is that it contains two ideas, inclusive of the whole doctrine of baptism. "Baptize" is a dyer's word, and signifies *to dip so as to colour*. Such as render the word dip give one true idea; but the word stood for two, and one is wanting in this rendering. This defect is in the German Testament, Matt. 3. 1 : "In those days came John *der Täufer*"—John the Dipper ; and the Dutch, "In those days came John *der Dooper*"—John the Dipper. This is the truth, but it is not the whole truth. The Anglo-Saxon Testament adds another idea by naming John *le fulluhterc*—the fuller ; and the Icelandic language translates Baptism, *skirn*, washing. These convey two ideas, *cleansing* by *washing*, but neither do these accurately express the two ideas of the Greek baptize.' [2]

As the question under discussion concerns a rite the performance of which has been held essential in all ages of Christianity, it certainly might have been supposed that this is one of the cases in which an examination of the early versions would decide the matter, but the search has led to no definite result. The old Latin version, indeed, rendered βαπτίζω by *tingo*, to moisten, bathe, dye, or stain ; but Jerome adopted *baptizo*, a Latinised form of the Greek original, feeling, no doubt, that no Latin word could rightly convey its meaning ; and from the Latin of Jerome the same word spread, through the influence of the church to which he belonged, into the Italian, Spanish, Portuguese, French, and English languages. The Syriac version has a very good word for dipping, but never uses it for baptism, preferring a word which originally signifies to stand, and which was adopted possibly from the position which the catechumen took when the water was poured

---

[1] Mr. R. Robinson, of Cambridge, quoted by Elihu (a Baptist) in his Vindication of the Bible Society.

[2] An anonymous writer, quoted in the pamphlet from which this passage is extracted, says, 'To *scrape* is the action employed when Paganini plays ; but surely he would be offended if we were to use that homely word respecting his performance. In like manner, I think it would be bad grammar, and bad taste, to say *dip* instead of *baptize*.'

over him. In the Sclavonic, modern Russ, and kindred languages, a term is used which is connected with '*crossing*,' or possibly with *christening*. In Arabic and Persian, as also in Icelandic, we find words which signify washing or cleansing; and in Anglo-Saxon, as we have seen above, the word is almost the same. Wycliffe used *wash* and *baptize* indifferently; thus in Matt. 3. we read, 'I *waishe* yhou in watir into pennance, but he that schal come after me is strenger than i, whos schoon y am not worthi to bere, he schal *baptise* you in the hooly Goost and fire.' The German and kindred languages have been cited in favour of the rendering *dip*, but it has been shown by Dr. Henderson that there is a slight distinction between the words for dip and baptize in these languages; thus the German word for dip is generally *tauchen*, but the word for baptize *taufen*. Moreover, in these languages the preposition following the verb is usually not *in*, which would be expected if the verb answered to our English dip, but *with*, showing that the verb is used in a ceremonial rather than an etymological sense, for the administration of a cleansing rite.

It is evident that the versions of the Scriptures will not lead us to any definite conclusion, and we are thrown back once more upon the Bible itself. Although the English word *baptize* does not occur in the O. T., yet on examining the LXX we find the Greek βαπτίζω used twice in the canonical scriptures, and twice in the Apocrypha. In Judith 12. 7 we read, 'She washed herself (ἐβαπτίζετο) at the fountain of water.' Apparently this was for ceremonial cleansing. In Sirach 34. 25 we are told of one who was βαπτιζόμενος ἀπὸ νεκροῦ, *i.e.* washed or bathed, in order to be cleansed from the ceremonial pollution which arises from contact with a dead body. This was done by sprinkling (Num. 8. 7). In Isa. 21. 4 the prophet says, 'Fearfulness hath affrighted me,' which the LXX renders ἡ ἀνομία μὲ βαπτίζει. Here the word stands for the Hebrew Ba'ath (בעת), and seems to be used figuratively of one who was flooded, overwhelmed with evil.

The most important passage, however, where the word occurs is in the history of Naaman the Syrian, in 2 Kings 5. 14. Elisha had told the Syrian that if he would 'wash' seven times in the Jordan he should be cleansed from the leprosy. Accordingly, he went and 'dipped' (ἐβαπτίσατο) seven times in the river. The Hebrew verb in this passage is **thaval** (טבל), to dip. It is the word used of Joseph's coat which was dipped in goat's blood (Gen. 37. 31; LXX, μολύνω); of the priest's finger being dipped in blood (Lev. 4.

6, 17, **9**. 9); of the living bird which was dipped in the blood of the slain bird (Lev. **14**. 6); of the finger being dipped in oil (Lev. **14**. 16); of hyssop being dipped in water (Num. **19**. 18); of the feet of the priests dipped in the brim of the water (Josh. **3**. 15); of Ruth dipping her morsel in the vinegar (Ruth **2**. 14); of Jonathan dipping the end of his rod in the honeycomb (1 Sam. **14**. 27); of Hazael dipping a cloth in water (2 Kings **8**. 15). We also meet with it in Job **9**. 30, 31, where we read, 'If I wash myself with snow water, and make my hands never so clean, yet shalt thou plunge me in the ditch.'

The meaning of the word **thaval** in these passages is clear and indubitable; it does not, however, follow that βαπτίζομαι signifies to *dip* when adopted by the LXX in 2 Kings **5**. 14. In none of the passages above cited was the dipping effected for the purpose of *washing* the object dipped; in some quite the contrary; but in the case of Naaman the order was ' Go, wash,' where the word **rachats** is used to signify the cleansing of the body (see § 3); hence in this passage the verb **thaval** was used to express a process identical with the act of washing. Moreover, in none of the other passages is the word βαπτίζω adopted as a rendering of **thaval**; we always find either βάπτω[1] or παραβάπτω. It may be concluded from this fact that the special word βαπτίζω was used in the passage under consideration in order to show that Naaman's washing in the river Jordan was to be regarded as partaking of the nature of a symbolical or ceremonial cleansing.

On the whole, the usage of the word βαπτίζω in the LXX cannot be said to decide whether the washing indicated by it must needs take place by a process of dipping (though this process would certainly be most in accordance with the passages referred to), or whether its requirements would be satisfied by having water poured over the person. Nor does the N. T. finally decide the matter. The word was used by the Jews in our Lord's time of ceremonial washing, rather than of mere dipping, as will be clearly seen by reference to Mark **7**. 4 and Luke **11**. 38, where the baptizing of the person is regarded as a sort of ritual observance; whilst in Mark **7**. 4 and 8, the baptism of cups and other vessels is spoken of in the same way.

---

[1] The word βάπτω, to dip or tinge, is used only four times in the N. T. In Luke **16**. 24, it refers to the dipping the tip of the finger in water; in John **13**. 26, it is twice used of the dipping the sop; in Rev. **19**. 13, we read of 'a vesture *dipped in blood*,' but here it would be better to render the words, *stained with blood* (βεβαμμένον αἵματι). The Vulgate rendering in this passage is 'vestis *aspersa* sanguine.'

The 'divers baptisms' (A. V. 'washings') spoken of in Heb. 9. 10, may comprehend such observances as those just referred to, but they rather seem to indicate the various rites of purification which formed part of the Levitical system. These rites were of two kinds; there were those which a man had to perform for himself, and those which others were to administer to him. It would be the last class which would be probably referred to; they were performed by priests or other 'clean' persons, who poured or sprinkled oil, blood, water, or water impregnated with the ashes of a red heifer, upon the persons who were to be purified. The application of the word βαπτισμοί to these rites tends to confirm the view already indicated, that whatever the etymology and primary usage of the term baptize may have been, it had practically come to be used of *ceremonial washing* in our Lord's time, and that it was not exclusively or necessarily applied to *dipping*. If the true rendering of the expression βαπτισμῶν διδαχῆς, in Heb. 6. 2, be not 'the doctrine of baptisms,' as the A. V. has it, but 'cleansings of teaching,' *i.e.* the purging from old prejudices and superstitions through the teaching of the truth, then we have further confirmatory evidence in the same direction.

The exact mode in which John the Baptist administered the rite is not described in the N. T. The writers seem to take it for granted that such a description was not called for. Those who submitted to it acknowledged thereby their sorrow for their past sins, and their determination to live a changed life, and to prepare for the coming of Him who should fulfil the promise made by God to the fathers. A cleansing ordinance would suitably indicate the change of heart and life thus entered upon.

When our Lord was baptized, it was not because He needed cleansing, but in order that He might give a personal sanction to the ordinance, submitting to it with the same humility as He evinced when falling in with other Jewish rites. The descent of the Spirit upon Him immediately afterwards was intended not only to mark that He was 'anointed to preach the gospel,' but also to indicate that it was He who should 'baptize' with the Holy Ghost, which He did when He 'shed forth' the Spirit from on high like floods upon a dry ground. The usage of the word in this connection suggests the symbolical action of sprinkling or effusion rather than of dipping.

The second baptism which our Lord underwent (Matt. 20. 22, 23; Luke 12. 50) was no ceremony, but a solemn reality;

He was to be perfected through sufferings, and the waves of trouble which poured upon His soul were signified outwardly by the sweat which was 'as it were great drops of blood falling down to the ground' (Luke 22. 44).

The usage of the word baptize thus leads to the conclusion that the act of dipping cannot be held as *essential* to Christian baptism unless it is proved to be so by the additional use of βάπτω, or some such word, as an adjunct or an alternative. This, however, is confessedly not the case. Nor does the symbolical teaching connected with the rite suggest any other conclusion than that which we have now arrived at. Baptism is pre-eminently symbolical of cleansing, whether by the blood of Christ or by the inspiration of the Holy Ghost; and so the ceremonial act is regarded by St. Peter as analogous with 'the putting away of the filth of the flesh' (1 Pet. 3. 21). When a believer, or the child of a believer, is baptized, we are to understand that, by profession at least, he has become a disciple of Christ, and is one with Him by faith; he dies to sin, in union with the Captain of Salvation; he is buried with Him; he puts on the Lord Jesus Christ, as one puts on armour or clothing; he walks in newness of life; and he is admitted into the society or body of those who are similarly cleansed.

If this, the death unto sin and the new birth unto righteousness by the quickening power of the Spirit through faith in Christ Jesus, be indeed what is set forth in the rite of baptism, and if the word has gradually passed into this technical or ceremonial sense, then the exact mode in which the rite is administered, whether by immersion or effusion, is not a point of primary importance, and may be left open to that discretion which has usually been permitted in non-essentials. Immersion ought not to be rigorously enforced; still less ought it to be rigorously denied. The ceremonial application of clean water to the person, as a symbol of the purifying efficacy of Christ's blood and of the quickening power of the Holy Spirit, and the submission to the ordinance, as a mark of discipleship to the Father, the Son, and the Holy Ghost—these are the grand points to be observed; whilst the exact mode of administration is a matter of church order and discipline, concerning which there ought to be much forbearance and also considerable latitude for the carrying out of personal conviction; and this is the case, theoretically at least, in the Church of England, as well as in other Churches.

CHAPTER XIV.

JUSTIFICATION.

§ 1. *Ideas connected with the Word.*

THE idea of justification appears to be in some measure legal or forensic rather than moral or psychological. It is frequently taken in Scripture to be the opposite of condemnation; and in some of its aspects it answers fairly to our word acquittal. But it has often been observed that human legal analogies are very inadequate for the purpose of representing the relation of the restored man to his God. Acquittal is the judicial declaration that an accused man is *not guilty* of a certain crime, so far as the law under which he has been tried is concerned. He may have committed the offence, but either it cannot be brought home to him by adequate testimony, or else the law under which he is tried has not provided for the charge laid against him. This, however, is a most imperfect representation of God's work in justifying, as it leaves out of sight the fact that His law is perfect and applicable to all cases, also that no outside testimony of man's guilt is necessary, because God is acquainted with the very secrets of the heart; and, what is still more important, it leaves out of sight the truth which is to be gathered from Scripture as a whole, that the process of Divine acquittal is so blended with the entrance of spiritual life into the person acquitted, that, though they are theoretically distinct, one cannot be fully stated or even comprehended without reference to the other. The controversy between the Church of Rome and various Protestant bodies has arisen, in part at least, from the complexity of the relationship which thus exists between God and man.

Another difficulty has arisen in England from the poverty of our language. We have no one word which can convey the idea of *righteousness* and that of *justification*, as they are set forth in Scripture. In this case, as in many others, we see the wisdom of God in selecting Hebrew as the means of communication with His creatures, because here the ideas of *righteousness, justification,* and *acquittal* all cluster round one verbal root, and are seen to be parts of one whole.

The Hebrew word which expresses the being just or righteous is **Tsadak** (צדק), which is supposed to convey originally an idea of straightness or stiffness (see chap. ix. § 2.)

The verb is once used in the Hithpael or reflexive voice, namely, in Gen. **44.** 16, 'What shall we speak? or how shall we clear ourselves?' As a matter of fact, Judah and his brethren were innocent, but he asked this question under the impression that they were guilty. It is once used in the Niphal or passive, viz. in Dan. **8.** 14, 'Thus shall the sanctuary be cleansed.' It appears here to be used in a secondary or derived sense. Five times it occurs in the Piel or intensive, viz.: in Job **32.** 2, 'He justified his own soul rather than God;' 33. 32, 'If thou hast anything to say, answer me: speak, for I desire to justify thee;' Jer. **3.** 11, 'The backsliding Israel hath justified her soul more than treacherous Judah;' Ezek. **16.** 51, 52, 'Thou hast multiplied thine abominations more than they, and hast justified thy sisters in all thine abominations which thou hast done. They are righteous in comparison with thee. Yea, be thou also confounded, and bear thy shame in that thou hast justified thy sisters.' The conduct of the inhabitants of Judah had been so much worse than that of Samaria or Sodom that they caused these nations to appear or to be accounted righteous in comparison.

Tsadak is used twelve times in the Hiphil or causative voice: Exod. **23.** 7, 'I will not justify the wicked.' This principle of the Divine action is laid down as an example to be imitated by the earthly judge in Deut. **25.** 1, 'Then shall they justify the righteous and condemn the wicked.' 2 Sam. **15.** 4, 'Oh that I were made judge in the land, that every man which hath any suit or cause might come to me, and I would do him justice!' 1 Kings **8.** 32, and 2 Chron. **6.** 23, 'Condemning the wicked, to bring his way upon his head; and justifying the righteous, to give him according to his righteousness.' This passage is important as giving a fulness of meaning to the word justification which otherwise might be missed. It is here not only acquittal, but the consequences of acquittal. Job **27.** 5, 'God forbid that I should justify you.' Ps. **82.** 3, 'Do justice to the afflicted and needy.' Prov. **17.** 15, 'He that justifieth the wicked, and he that con-

demneth the just, even they both are abomination to the Lord.'
Isa. 5. 23, 'Woe unto them . . . which justify the wicked for
reward, and take away the righteousness of the righteous from
him.' Isa. 50. 8, 'He is near that justifieth me; who will
contend with me?' Isa. 53. 11, 'By his knowledge shall my
righteous servant justify many; and it is he that shall bear
their iniquities.' This passage is usually explained as if 'his
knowledge' meant 'the knowledge which others should have concerning him;' but there is no necessity to fall back upon this
explanation. The Messiah was to be 'acquainted with grief;'
nay more, he was to bear man's iniquities, and they became in
some mysterious sense identified with Him. It was this which
became the means of justifying many.[1] Dan. 12. 3, 'They that
turn many to righteousness shall shine as the stars for ever
and ever.' Compare the teaching of the last verses of St. James's
Epistle.

It remains to notice the passages where the verb is used in
the active voice. They are as follows:—Gen. 38. 26, 'She hath
been more righteous than I.' Job 4. 17, 'Shall a mortal man
be more just than God?' Job 9. 2, 'How should man be just
before God?' Job 9. 15, 'Though I were righteous I would
not answer.' Job 9. 20, 'If I justify myself (lit. if I be
righteous), my own mouth shall condemn me.' Job 10. 15,
'If I be righteous, yet will I not lift up my head.' Job 11. 2,
'Should a man full of talk be justified' (lit. be righteous)?
Job 13. 18, 'Behold now, I have ordered my cause; I know that I
shall be justified' (lit. that I am righteous). Job 15. 14,
'What is he that is born of a woman, that he should be

---

[1] 'No man, except Christ, has ever yet been able rightly to discern the nature
and extent of sin; because only one whose penetrating gaze can apprehend the
whole of the glory and worth of which God created humanity capable, the whole
tenor of its downward way, and the high end it may yet attain; none but Jesus
has ever sounded the whole extent of the aberrations, degradations, and disorder
of our race. He, however, *has* sounded all these depths, His heart has been
pierced with adequate sorrow for all that dishonouring of God's holy name, of
which the beings, whose brother He became, were guilty; and consequently He
has fully apprehended the righteous severity of Divine justice in connecting sin
with death in its various forms. And because He has manifested the righteousness and justice of the Divine sentence, not in words only, but practically by
His silent and holy endurance of its penalty, He has accomplished the purpose
of Divine punishment, and has terminated it—on behalf of whom? on behalf
of all those who by faith appropriate this His holy endurance of the Divine
judgment as their own.'—*Essay on the Atonement*, by Wolfgang Friedrich Gess.

righteous?' Job 22. 3, 'Is it any pleasure to the Almighty
that thou art righteous?' Job 25. 4, 'How can man be
justified (lit. righteous) with God?' Job 33. 12, 'Behold
in this thou art not just.' Job 34. 5, 'Job hath said, I am
righteous.' Job 35. 7, 'If thou be righteous, what givest
thou him?' Job 40. 8, 'Wilt thou condemn me, that thou mayest
be righteous?' Ps. 19. 9, 'The judgments of the Lord are true,
and righteous altogether.' Ps. 51. 4, 'That thou mightest be
justified (lit. be righteous) when thou speakest, and clear
when thou judgest.' Ps. 143. 2, 'Enter not into judgment with
thy servant, O Lord: for in thy sight shall no man living be
justified' (or righteous). Isa. 43. 9, 'Let them bring forth
their witnesses, that they may be justified (or righteous): or
let them hear, and say, It is truth.' Isa. 43. 26, 'Declare thou,
that thou mayest be justified' (or righteous). Isa. 45. 25,
'In the Lord shall all the seed of Israel be justified' (or
righteous), and shall glory.' Ezek. 16. 52, 'They are righteous
in comparison with thee.'

The passages which have been cited above show that justification is a term applicable to something more than the discharge
of an accused person uncondemned. As in our courts of law
there are civil as well as criminal cases, so it was in old time;
and a large number of the passages adduced seem to refer to
trials of the former description, in which some question of property,
right, or inheritance was under discussion between two parties.
The judge, by justifying one of the parties, decided that the
property in question was to be regarded as his. Applying this
aspect of the matter to the justification of man in the sight of
God, we gather from Scripture that whilst through sin man has
forfeited legal claim to any right or inheritance which God might
have to bestow upon His creatures, so through justification he is
restored to his high position and regarded as an heir of God.

The adjective **tsadik** is almost always rendered δίκαιος,
righteous, in the LXX, and the substantives **tsedek** and **tse-
dakah** generally δικαιοσύνη, righteousness. The word ἔλεος,
mercy, has been adopted in Isa. 56. 1, 'My salvation is near to
come, and my righteousness to be revealed; also in Ezek. 18. 19,
21, where we read of man doing 'what is lawful and right.'
The righteousness of the law was specially manifested in mercy,
so that the Greek translators were right in point of fact, though
incorrect in their rendering in these passages.

In several passages the LXX has adopted ἐλεημοσύνη, a word which has passed from its original meaning as the feeling of mercy or pity to the active development of that feeling in eleemosynary acts, or alms-giving. This is the case in Deut. 6. 25, where our translation is, 'It shall be our righteousness if we observe to do all these commandments.' Here the LXX, followed by the Vulgate and the translations made from it, say, 'There shall be mercy for us if we observe,' &c. The passage literally translated would be, 'There shall be righteousness for us,' &c. Perhaps the LXX has preserved the true meaning of the passage, and certainly it is in accordance with the general tenor of God's Word. The same rendering is found in Deut. 24. 13; Ps. 24. 5, 33. 5, 103. 6; Isa. 1. 27, 28. 17, 59. 16; Dan. 4. 27, 9. 16.

The verb **tsadak** is rendered δικαιόω, to make righteous or to acquit, almost everywhere by the LXX; but the various voices in which the word is used were not capable of being accurately distinguished in the Greek. This difficulty has reappeared in at least one passage in the N. T. In Rev. 22. 11, the words 'He that is righteous let him *be righteous* still' are, if literally rendered, 'He that is righteous let him *be justified* still'— a rendering which was adopted by the Latin Vulgate, and is to be found in most, if not all, versions made from that venerable work. This literal rendering is certainly very beautiful and instructive, though the usage of the LXX affords our translators some plea for departing from it. The R. V. has changed, but hardly improved, the rendering.

§ 2. *Righteousness in Relation to Justification.*

The nature of righteousness, or conformity to the Divine law of love, has been pointed out in chap. ix., but we must here notice its relationship with justification.

We read in Gen. 15. 6, 'Abraham believed God, and it was reckoned to him (for) righteousness.' In this passage three words enter upon the sacred pages for the first time—belief, righteousness, and reckoning or imputation—words which were destined to play a conspicuous part in Christian terminology. That element of Abraham's feeling and conduct towards God which we usually call belief, faith, or faithfulness,[1] was regarded by God as a reason why he should be accepted as righteous or justified. Not

---

[1] See chap. ix.

only does all right action spring from belief in the Word of God, but also our Heavenly Father justifies or acquits those persons who exercise it. Abraham's faith, according to the Hebrew text, 'was reckoned unto him righteousness;' but the LXX, followed by St. Paul, interprets this phrase as meaning '*for*' (εἰς), not '*as*' (ὡς) righteousness.'[1] It would follow that the passage does not teach us that Abraham's faith was regarded or estimated by God *as if it were* righteousness—the one quality being taken for the other—but that owing to the fact that he had faith in the promises, God accepted him, acquitted him from the charge of sin, pronounced him righteous, and conferred on him an inheritance. Thus, as St. Paul says, Abraham was justified *by faith* (ἐκ πιστέως), *i.e. owing to the fact that he had faith.* The ground on God's part, and the method of justification, are not touched by the word. It simply points to the aspect in which the Judge of all the earth regards the believer, and the way in which He deals with him.

It is not a little remarkable that the privilege thus granted to Abraham was accorded to another person in exactly the same terms, but apparently on a different ground. In Ps. **106**. 30, 31, we read, 'Then stood up Phinehas and executed judgment: and the plague was stayed. And that was counted unto him for[2] righteousness unto all generations for evermore.' When we turn to the history (Num. **25**.) on which these verses are a comment, we find that Phinehas was zealous for God's sake against those who were committing whoredom and idolatry, going so far as to slay 'a prince of a chief house among the Simeonites,' together with the daughter of the 'head over a people and of a chief house in Midian.' What was it that prompted him to this bold and decided action, which atoned for the sins of the people? The prophet Malachi answers, speaking in God's name, 'He feared me, and was afraid before my name. The law of truth was in his mouth, and iniquity was not found in his lips' (Mal. **2**. 5, 6). He 'said unto his father and to his mother, I have not seen him; neither did he acknowledge his brethren, nor knew his own children' (Deut. **33**. 9). He had respect to the unseen God,

---

[1] This important distinction, which has sometimes been neglected in controversy, has been observed in the Vulgate (*ad* justitiam); so Luther has '*zur* Gerechtigkeit;' De Sacy, '*à* justice;' D'Almeida, '*por* justiça.' Beza made a mistake in putting *pro* justitia in Rom. **4**. 3, &c.

[2] The Hebrew preposition *for* (לְ) is inserted here, justifying the interpretation of the LXX in the passage previously discussed.

and despised the fear of man and the ties of kindred; in other words, he had *faith*, and his deed is of a class with many of those which are recorded in the eleventh chapter of Hebrews. It was his conviction of the truth of God's Word that caused him to be loyal when a whole nation seemed to be drifting into carnality and idolatry; and so 'it was reckoned to him for righteousness.'

The second passage in which the substantive occurs is Gen. 18. 19, where God says of Abraham, 'I know him, that he will command his children and his household after him, and they shall keep the way of the Lord, to do justice and judgment.' Here justice (*i.e.* righteousness) seems to mark a course of action in conformity with the grand principle of right, the loving God with all one's heart, and one's neighbour as oneself. This righteousness was not *absolute*, *i.e.* such as would commend Abraham to God as a rightful claimant of the inheritance of sonship, because, in that case, he would not have been said to have been justified by faith; it was therefore *relative*, and was the result of his faith in God (see Rom. 4. 2-4, and compare 2 Sam. 22. 21).

Jacob appeals to this relative and practical principle in Gen. 30. 33, with reference to his dealings with Laban (whether fairly or not), where he says, 'So shall my righteousness answer for me in time to come, when it shall come for my hire before thy face.' He implies that he had been honest, and more than honest; that he had borne losses which might fairly have gone to the account of Laban. This righteousness is something more than what we ordinarily mean by the word justice; it is not the doing to others *as they have done to us*, but the doing to them what we would like them to do to us if our respective positions were changed. It exceeds 'the righteousness of the Scribes and Pharisees,' which consisted in doing good either where a return was to be expected, or where the object was to make a fair show before men.

Another noteworthy passage is Deut. 9. 4, 5, 6, where the people of Israel were guarded in the plainest terms from the supposition that they were being brought into Canaan for their own righteousness. They were thus trained in the idea that the inheritance was not to be regarded as a reward for human merit, but was to be received as a gift from the covenant-keeping God.

The expression, 'O God of my righteousness,' which is occasionally found in the Psalms, *e.g.* Ps. 4. 1, has been diversely explained. Some critics suppose that it means, ' O God, who art my righteous

judge;' others, 'O God, who justifies me.'[1] But perhaps its explanation is more simple. As 'the temple of God's holiness,' in Ps.
138. 2, signifies 'God's holy temple,' so the phrase 'God of my
righteousness' may mean 'my righteous God,' whilst it is in
harmony with the doctrine that God possesses in fulness Himself
that righteousness which He bestows on man.

In Deut. 33. 19, and Ps. 4. 5, we read, 'offer the sacrifices
of righteousness.' This cannot signify 'substitute righteousness
for sacrifices,' but rather 'offer righteous sacrifices,' *i.e.* do not
let your sacrifices be formal or impure, but bring them in a right
spirit, in loving conformity with God's law. The form of the
expression is exactly parallel to that which the A. V. translates
'just balances' (lit. balances of righteousness) in Lev. 19. 36, Job
31. 6, and Ezek. 45. 10. That this is the right interpretation of
the passage may be confirmed from a reference to Ps. 51. 19,
where, after saying, 'Thou desirest not sacrifice; else would I
give it: thou delightest not in burnt offering,' and again, 'The
sacrifices of God are a broken spirit: a broken and a contrite
heart, O God, thou wilt not despise,' the Psalmist looks forward
to a state of things when sacrifices should be once more acceptable,
' Build thou the walls of Jerusalem ; then shalt thou be pleased
with the sacrifices of righteousness, with burnt offerings and
whole burnt offerings : then shall they offer young bullocks upon
thine altar.' Compare Mal. 3. 3, where we are told that the
angel of the covenant 'shall purify the sons of Levi, and purge
them as gold and silver, that they may offer unto the Lord an
offering in righteousness.' In all these passages the spirit of the
offerers rather than the nature of the offering is described by the
qualifying word 'righteousness.'

In some passages in which God's righteousness is appealed to,
it appears that its merciful aspect, as referred to so often by
the LXX, is in the Psalmist's mind. Thus he says, 'Lead me,
O Lord, in thy righteousness' (Ps. 5. 8) ; 'Deliver me, in thy
righteousness' (31. 1). In these passages the writer throws himself upon the revealed character of God as containing something
more than abstract justice ; there is in Him an element of pity
for the suffering, and of mercy for the fallen ; there *must be*, for
these principles have found expression in the law which He has
prescribed for men's dealings with one another.

In Prov. 10. 2 ('Righteousness delivereth from death') we

---

[1] De Sacy renders, 'Dieu, *qui est le principe de ma justice.*'

have one of a class of passages very common in the O. T., pointing out the blessings which as a matter of fact follow from conformity to the will of God. When the prophet Ezekiel says (18. 20), 'The righteousness of the righteous shall be *upon* him, and the wickedness of the wicked shall be *upon* him,' he teaches that a man is dealt with by God according to his own personal character and course of action, and that he must not delude himself with the idea that he can possess any hereditary immunity from evil.

Lastly, we read, in Mal. 4. 2, of a Being who is described as the Sun of Righteousness, who should rise with healing in His wings for them that fear the name of God. Just as the material sun in the heavens gives forth light and heat, and becomes a centre of attraction for all other bodies that come within its sphere, so from the Messiah there was to issue healing power which should become an efficient remedy for all spiritual diseases and for physical corruption.

§ 3. *N. T. Teaching on Justification and Righteousness.*

Turning now from the O. T. to the N. T., it is noticeable that the word 'righteousness' is rare in the Gospels. St. Mark never employs it; St. Luke only once (four times in the Acts); St. John, twice; and St. Matthew, eight times at most. In the Epistles of St Paul the word is used sixty-six times, and in various senses.

(i.) There is one absolute and eternal standard of right, which is of the essence of the nature of God, so that we say whatever He does must be right, because Right is summed up in Him.[1] With respect to this element in the character of God, St. Paul speaks of our own righteousness commending God's righteousness (Rom. 3. 5). This is the only passage in St. Paul's Epistles in which the words are put in the order, Θεοῦ δικαιοσύνη; in all the others he — no doubt with a purpose — wrote, δικαιοσύνη Θεοῦ.

(ii.) If we could obtain a thorough conformity with this Divine

---

[1] The question is sometimes asked, Is a thing right because God does it? or does He do it because it is right? This is a metaphysical query far beyond the limits of the present work. Suffice it to say that if God has done a thing, it is certain to be right; and if a thing is certainly wrong, we may be sure that God does not approve of it. God and right, the Law-giver and the law, are, so far as we can understand, not *two*, but *one*.

standard by the spiritual observance of the various principles and precepts contained in the law, we should be righteous even as He is righteous ; but in this sense 'There is none righteous, no, not one' (Rom. 3. 10).

(iii.) Nevertheless, some have sought to establish their own righteousness by attempting to fulfil the letter of the law of Moses. This was the case with many of the Jews (Rom. 10. 3), and it had been the aim of St. Paul himself in his early days ; so far, in fact, had he succeeded that he could say, 'as touching the righteousness which is of the law,' I was 'blameless,' *i.e.* no fault could be found in me by those who measured me by the letter of the law (Phil. 3. 6). Yet when the commandments contained in the law were opened out to him in their application to the thoughts of his heart,[1] he found that sin, though repressed, was not conquered : 'Sin revived, and I died' (Rom. 7. 9).

(iv.) One Being, however, has partaken of human nature, of whom God could say, in the full meaning of the words, 'Thou hast loved righteousness and hated iniquity' (Heb. 1. 9). Jesus Christ is emphatically called 'the righteous one' (Acts 22. 14 ; 1 John 2. 1). He, in human nature, lived up to the perfect standard of the Divine law, so that His righteousness was of the same complexion and character as the righteousness of God.

(v.) But Jesus Christ has become righteousness unto us (1 Cor. 1. 30). Hence we read of those 'who receive the gift of righteousness' (Rom. 5. 17).

(vi.) This gift is made available to us—so far as *God's* part is concerned—by Christ's atoning death upon the cross. God made Him, who knew not sin, to be sin (*i.e.* dealt with Him as sin should be dealt with), that we might become the righteousness of God in Him (2 Cor. 5. 21).

(vii.) The gift of God's righteousness is available to us—so far as *our* part is concerned—through faith. We must *yield* to it (Rom. 10. 3). It is conferred 'upon all them that believe.' They are then 'freely justified by his grace, through the redemption that is in Christ Jesus, whom God has set forth as a mercy-seat or propitiation, through faith in his blood' (Rom. 3. 22, 24, 25). Hence it is called the righteousness *of faith.*

---

[1] A student of Luther's works will probably be led to the conclusion that there was no point in which he was more strong, more clear, and more excellent than in the application of the law of God to the whole man instead of confining it to external actions and so-called religious observances.

(viii.) Thus, by the term 'the righteousness of God,' St. Paul generally implies that righteousness which comes up to God's standard, and which flows from God to man when he rests on Christ crucified as his ground of pardon, and is united with Christ risen as the spring of his spiritual life.

(ix.) Lastly, the possession of it necessarily leads a man into practical conformity with the will of God, because it sets his heart in the right direction, and makes him a partaker of the Divine life which flows into him through the agency of the Holy Spirit of God. The Christian becomes in a practical sense 'the righteousness of God in Christ' (2 Cor. 5. 21); being made free from sin, he is made servant to righteousness (Rom. 6. 18); and he who has been hungering and thirsting after righteousness is filled out of the fulness which is in Christ Jesus our Lord.

The word righteous or just (δίκαιος) is almost always taken in the N. T. to represent that upright and merciful character in conformity with law which we have already met with in the O. T.; and this is the case whether the word is applied to God, the righteous Judge, to Jesus Christ 'the holy one and the just,' or to those who shall rise at 'the resurrection of the just.'

In the opening of the Epistle to the Romans, St. Paul takes as his text the words of Habakkuk (2. 4), 'a righteous man shall live by faith.' From this passage he teaches that Divine life is not granted to a righteous man as a reward for his justice and obedience to the law of Moses, but it accrues to him by virtue of that faithfulness whereby he takes hold of Christ, and thus avails himself of the grace and righteousness of God. In this sense also are we to understand the words 'by the obedience of one many shall be constituted righteous' (Rom. 5. 19); it is not their own obedience which causeth them to be righteous in God's sight, but through the work of Christ, who was 'obedient unto (or, *up to*) death,' they are accounted righteous before God.

Little needs to be added concerning the N. T. usage of the word justify. We have seen that it signifies a decision in a person's favour, and that it involves a consequent freedom from penalty, and a claim to an inheritance. St. Paul sums up the whole matter very tersely in his speech at Antioch, where alone the word occurs in the Acts (13. 39): 'Be it known unto you that through this (Jesus) is remission of sins proclaimed to you; and every one who believes in him is justified from all things, from which ye could not be justified under the law of Moses.' Neither charge

nor penalty exists for the believer.   He is now justified in [1] Christ's
blood (Rom. 5. 9).   His faith in the sacrifice of Christ is of such a
nature as to identify him with Christ in his death to sin,[2] and thus
' he that is dead (*i.e.* dead in this sense with Christ) is justified
from sin ' (Rom. 6. 7, margin).

We see that to be justified, to be accounted righteous, and to
have the gift of the righteousness of God, are three aspects of one
and the same thing, and set forth most forcibly some of the benefits
which we obtain through faith in Christ's offering of Himself.

§ 4. *Innocence.*

The word **Nakah** (נקה, Ass. *naqû*) signifies (in the passive) to
be cleansed or made free from pollution, and so to be guiltless, innocent, and unpunished.   It implies that a man's innocence
with respect to a particular charge is established in the sight of
others, so that the charge falls to the ground.   The first passage in
which it occurs is Gen. 24. 8, 41, 'Thou shalt be clear from this
my oath.'

We read in Exod. 34. 7, Num. 14. 18, and Nahum 1. 3, that
'the Lord will by no means clear (the guilty).'   These words,
coming as they do after the representation of God as 'forgiving
iniquity and transgression and sin,' are remarkable.   They are
illustrated by the following clause, 'visiting the iniquity of the
fathers upon the children, and upon the children's children, unto
the third and to the fourth (generation).'   They imply that, though
God is ready to pardon sin, He by no means ignores or disregards it.
The sinner is regarded as guilty in God's sight until the revealed
way of removing that guilt is found and appealed to.   This truth is
also taught in the following passages where the word is used:—
Exod. 20. 7, Deut. 5. 11, 'The Lord will not hold him guiltless
that taketh his name in vain.'   Num. 5. 31, 'Then shall the man

---

[1] It is often hard to give an exact rendering to the preposition ἐν (in), especially in St. Paul's Epistles.   It marks position, relationship, or union.   The
expression 'in Christ' usually signifies 'by virtue of union with Christ by faith.'

[2] Christ died to sin once.   He was crucified by sinners, and slain by wicked
hands.   The sin which slew Him was the sin of the world, summed up in one act
of intense hatred of God and of goodness.   He was constituted 'accursed' under
the law of Moses, not by wrong-doing, but by being fastened to a cross, and was
further identified with sinners by being crucified between two thieves.   All this
was foreordained.   He endured the cross and despised the shame because He
knew that He, the innocent, was dying for a guilty world by the will of God.

be guiltless from iniquity,' *i.e.* shall be acquitted from the charge
of wrong-doing. Num. **32**. 22, 'Then afterwards ye shall return
and be guiltless before the Lord and before Israel.' Josh. **2**. 19,
' His blood shall be upon his head, and we will be guiltless,' *i.e.*
with respect to the oath made to spare Rahab's kindred (compare
verse 17, where the same word is rendered 'blameless'). 1 Sam.
26. 9, 'Who can stretch forth his hand against the Lord's anointed
and be guiltless?' 2 Sam. **3**. 28, 'I and my kingdom are guiltless before the Lord for ever from the blood of Abner, the son of
Ner.' 2 Sam. **14**. 9, 'The woman of Tekoah said unto the king,
The iniquity be on me and on my father's house; and the king and
his throne be guiltless.' 1 Kings **2**. 9, 'Now therefore hold him
not guiltless.' Job **10**. 14, 'If I sin, then thou markest me, and
thou wilt not acquit me from mine iniquity.' Every sin constitutes
a distinct charge against a man in the sight of God, and it must
be dealt with as such. Ps. **24**. 4, 'He that hath clean hands
and a pure heart.' Clean hands are those which are innocent of
blood-guiltiness. Joel **3**. 21, 'I will cleanse their blood which I
have not cleansed.'

Some other renderings of the words may be noticed :—Gen. **20**.
5, 'In the integrity of my heart and in the innocency of my
hands have I done this.' Gen. **44**. 10, 'Ye shall be blameless.'
Exod. **23**. 7, 'The innocent and righteous slay thou not.' Deut.
19. 9, 10, 'Thou shalt add three cities more for thee besides these
three, that innocent blood be not shed in thy land, and so blood
be upon thee.' Deut. **19**. 13, 'Thine eye shall not pity him, but
thou shalt put away (the guilt of) innocent blood from Israel.'
Deut. **21**. 8, 9, 'Lay not innocent blood to the charge of thy
people Israel. . . . So shalt thou put away (the guilt of) innocent
blood from among you.' Deut. **27**. 25, 'Cursed be he that taketh
reward to slay an innocent person' (compare 1 Sam. **19**. 5; 2
Kings **21**. 16, **24**. 4). Jud. **15**. 3, 'Now shall I be more blameless
than the Philistines.' Job **4**. 7, 'Remember, I pray thee, who ever
perished, being innocent?' (see also Job **9**. 23, 28, **17**. 8, **22**. 19,
30, **27**. 17). Ps. **10**. 8, 'He doth murder the innocent' (see Ps. **15**.
5, **94**. 21, **106**. 38; Prov. **1**. 11, **6**. 17; Isa. **59**. 7; Jer. **2**. 34, **7**. 6,
19. 4, **22**. 3, 17, **26**. 15; Joel **3**. 19; Jonah **1**. 14). Ps. **19**. 13, 'Keep
back thy servant also from presumptuous (sins); let them not
have dominion over me : then shall I be upright, and I shall be
innocent from the great transgression.' Ps. **26**. 6, 'I will wash
my hands in innocency: so will I compass thine altar' (see **73**.

13). Prov. **6**. 29, 'Whosoever toucheth (his neighbour's wife) shall not be innocent' (see **11**. 21, **16** 5, **17**. 5, **19**. 5, 9, **28**. 20 ; Jer. **2**. 35). Jer. **25**. 29, **49**. 12, 'Should ye be utterly unpunished? Ye shall not be unpunished.' Jer. **30**. 11, **46**. 28, 'I will correct thee in measure, and will not leave thee altogether unpunished.'

The above are almost all the passages in which the word **Nakah** occurs. It generally appears to signify proved innocence from specified charges, whether those charges are brought by God or man. The offences, if committed, were punishable ; but when they have not been committed, if that innocence can be made clear, the person against whom the charge is made goes off free from blame and punishment. It is evident that the innocence implied by this word is from one point of view not such a perfect state as what is called justification ; for whilst the former leaves one in the negative position of not having done certain things, the latter advances a step further, and constitutes one upright in the sight of God. Where **Nakah** is used, man is regarded as actually clear from a charge ; where **Tsadak** is used, man is regarded as having obtained deliverance from condemnation, and as being thus entitled to a certain inheritance.

In the Piel or intensive voice, the word is only used in *negative* sentences, with the exception of Ps. **19**. 12, 'Cleanse thou me from my hidden (faults),' *i.e.* hold me guiltless.

The LXX renders **Nakah** by ἀθόω, καθαρίζω, καθαρός εἰμι, and, in a few passages, by ἀναίτιος and δίκαιος.

§ 5. *Imputation.*

With the exception of 1 Sam. **22**. 15, where the word **Sum** (שׂוּם, Ass. *samu*), signifying to set, place, or appoint, is used, the idea of imputation is always represented by **Chashav** (חָשַׁב). This word is largely used, and in slightly different senses. Our translators have rendered it by the word 'think' thirty-seven times ; 'imagine,' twelve times ; 'devise,' thirty times ; and purpose,' ten times. Hence it may be gathered that it signifies a mental process whereby some course is planned or conceived. Thus, it is applied to the 'cunning' workmen who contrived the various parts of the tabernacle, and refers not so much to their skill in manipulating their materials as to their inspired genius in devising the arrangements. It is rendered 'find out' in 2 Chron. **2**. 14, where we read of a certain person employed on the temple who was skilful to grave any manner of graving, and to 'find out'—*i.e.* picture up in the imagination—'every device which shall be put to him.' It is used in Gen. 50. 20, where Joseph says to his brethren, 'God meant it (*i.e.* planned it) for good, to bring to pass, as it is this day, to save much people alive.' In Dan. 11. 24, 25, the word is repeated in order to give it emphasis, where we read, 'He shall forecast his devices against the strongholds; . . . they shall forecast devices against him.' A similar use of the word in its doubled form is in Jer. 49. 30, 'The king of Babylon hath taken counsel against you, and hath conceived a purpose against you.'

It is easy to see that a word which represents this process of the thought or imagination may be applied in various senses. Thus it is rendered regard, *i.e.* 'pay attention to,' in Isa. 13. 17, 33. 8. It is also used to express the estimation in which one person is held by another. Thus Job says (18. 3), 'Wherefore are we counted as beasts and reputed as vile in thy sight?' Compare Job 13. 24, 19. 15, 33. 10, 41. 27, 29; Isa. 29. 16, 17, 53. 3, 4; Lam. 4. 2. The Anakims 'were accounted giants' (Deut. 2. 11, 20); silver 'was nothing accounted of in the days of Solomon' (1 Kings 10. 21; 2 Chron. 9. 20); 'Cease ye from man, whose breath is in his nostrils : for wherein is he to be accounted of?' (Isa. 2. 22).

The following passages may be adduced in further illustration of the meaning of the word :—Gen. 31. 15, 'Are we not counted of him strangers? for he hath sold us, and hath quite devoured also our money.' Lev. 25. 31, 'The houses of the villages which have no walls shall be counted as the fields of the country,' *i.e.* shall be dealt with on the same principle as the fields. Num. 18. 27, 'Your heave offering shall be reckoned unto you as the corn of the threshing-floor, and the fulness of the winepress.' Num. 18. 30, 'When ye have heaved the best thereof, then it shall be counted unto the Levites as the increase of the threshing-floor, and as the increase of the winepress.' Josh. 13. 3, 'From Sihor unto the borders of Ekron, which is counted to the Canaanite.' 2 Sam. 4. 2, 'Beeroth also was reckoned to Benjamin.' 2 Sam. 19. 19, 'Let not my lord impute iniquity unto me, neither do thou remember that which thy servant did perversely.' Neh. 13. 13, 'They were counted faithful.' Ps. 44. 22, 'We are counted as sheep for the slaughter.' Ps. 88. 4, 'I am counted with them that go down into the pit.' Prov. 17. 28, 'Even a fool when he holdeth his peace is counted wise.' Prov. 27. 14, 'He that blesseth his friend with a loud voice, it shall be counted a curse to him.' Isa. **40**. 15, 17, 'The nations are counted by him as the small dust in the balance . . . they are counted less than nothing, and vanity.' Hos. **8**. 12, 'I have written to him the great things of my law, but they were counted as a strange thing.'

In all these passages a mental process is involved whereby a certain thing or a course of action is subjected to a sort of estimation as to value or position. It is not an artificial proceeding, a mere fancy, but a distinct judgment, founded either upon the nature of things, or upon the mind of him who is passing certain things under review.

Sometimes the word is used in our ordinary sense of reckoning —that is to say, to represent the arithmetical process of counting up—*e.g.* Lev. **25**. 27, **27**. 18 ; 2 Kings **12**. 15.

A few passages remain to be noticed, and they are important from their theological meaning :—

Gen. **15**. 6, Abraham 'believed in the Lord, and he counted it to him (for) righteousness.' God reckoned him as righteous, on the ground of his faith.

Lev. **7**. 18, 'It shall not be accepted, neither shall it be imputed.' The offering shall not be reckoned as having been made.

Lev. **17**. 4, 'Blood shall be imputed to that man ; he hath shed blood ; and that man shall be cut off from among his people.'

Ps. **106**. 31, 'Then stood up Phinehas and executed judgment (P. B. prayed), and that was counted unto him for righteousness.' The faith of Phinehas caused God to regard him as righteous.

Ps. **32**. 2, 'Blessed is the man unto whom the Lord imputeth not iniquity, and in whose spirit there is no guile.' This non-imputation of iniquity is regarded by St. Paul as identical with imputation of righteousness (Rom. **4**. 6).

The word **Chashav** is generally rendered λογίζομαι in the LXX, and the use of this word in the N. T. exactly accords with what we have gathered from the O. T.[1] There are several samples of the ordinary use of the word. Thus, in Rom. **6**. 11, we read, 'Reckon yourselves dead indeed to sin,' that is, regard yourselves in this aspect. In 1 Cor. **13**. 5, the words, 'charity thinketh no evil,' might perhaps be rendered 'doth not impute evil,' that is to say, 'doth not take account of injuries done to it.' A few verses

---

[1] In Mark **15**. 28, the words, 'he was reckoned among transgressors,' are quoted from Isa. **53**. 12, where, however, the Hebrew word is not **chasav**, but **manah**, to number.

below we read, 'I thought as a child,' by which we are to understand, 'I took account of things as a child does.' In Phil. 3. 13 the Apostle says, 'I reckon not myself to have attained,' that is, 'I do not regard myself as having attained.' In the more distinctly doctrinal sense, we have in Rom. 2. 26, 'If the uncircumcision keep the righteousness of the law, shall not his uncircumcision be reckoned as circumcision' (εἰς περιτομὴν)? 2 Cor. 5. 19, 'God was in Christ, reconciling the world unto himself, not imputing their trespasses unto them.' In Rom. 4. 3, the words concerning Abraham in Gen. 15. 6 are introduced and discussed at some length, the passage from Ps. 32. being also quoted in confirmation of the Apostle's argument. In the fourth verse stress is especially laid on the fact that the reckoning of Abraham's faith for righteousness was not a matter of justice due to Abraham, but was a work of grace springing out of God's free love.

We see therefore that to reckon, to impute, and to account are one and the same thing, and that the word is used in Scripture to indicate what may be called a mental process whereby the love and mercy which exists in the Divine nature, and which was embodied in Christ, is brought to bear upon the case of every individual who believes in (and acts upon) the Word of God. There is nothing unnatural or artificial about the imputation of righteousness by faith. On the contrary, it commends itself to man's deepest convictions.

CHAPTER XV.

SANCTIFICATION, ANOINTING.

§ 1. Sanctify, Sacred, Holy.

FEW religious words are more prominent in the Hebrew Scriptures than those which spring from the root **Kadash** (קדש, Ass. *qadasu*), which is used in some form or other to represent the being set apart for the work of God. It generally answers to the Greek ἁγιάζω and ἅγιος. Perhaps the English word s a c r e d represents the idea more nearly than h o l y, which is the general rendering in the A. V. The terms sanctification and holiness are now used so frequently to represent moral and spiritual qualities, that they hardly convey to the reader the idea of *position* or *relationship* as existing between God and some person or thing consecrated to Him; yet this appears to be the real meaning of the word.[1]

(*a.*) The word **Kadash** is applied to places, *e.g.* to the camp of Israel (Deut. 23. 14); to the hill of Zion (Ps. 2. 6, &c.); to the ground where God manifested Himself to Moses (Exod. 3. 5); to the city of Jerusalem[2] (Neh. 11. 1; compare Matt. 4. 5); to heaven (Ps. 20. 6); to the 'Holy Land' (Zech. 2. 12); to the tabernacle (Exod. 29. 43); to the temple (1 Kings 9. 3); to the inner part of the temple or tabernacle, commonly called the s a n c t u a r y or the H o l y of H o l i e s (Exod. 25. 8); to the king's 'chapel' (Amos 7. 13); to the altar (Exod. 29. 36); and consequently, as our Lord reminded the Jews,[3] to the gifts (Exod. 28. 38) and offerings (Exod. 29. 27)

---

[1] In accordance with the above view, Dr. Henderson renders Jer. 1. 5 thus: 'Before thou camest forth from the womb I *separated* thee;' and in his note he says, 'When Jehovah declares that He had sanctified the prophet before his birth, the meaning is not that He had cleansed him from the pollution of original sin, or that He had regenerated him by His Spirit, but that He had separated him in His eternal counsel to the work in which He was to be engaged.' The Apostle Paul, he adds, uses language very nearly parallel when he says of God that He *separated him* (ἀφορίσας) from his mother's womb. See Gal. 1. 15; Rom. 1. 1; Acts 13. 2.

[2] Jerusalem is still called *El-Khuds*, *i.e.* The Holy.

[3] Matt. 23. 17.

which were placed thereon; also to a house or field set apart for God (Lev. 27. 14, 16).

(*b*) The word is applied to times, *e.g.* to the Sabbath (Gen. 2. 3, Exod. 20. 8, 11); to a day set apart as a fast (Joel 1. 14); to the fiftieth year (Lev. 25. 10).

(*c.*) It is applied to persons, *e.g.* to the firstborn (Exod. 13. 2); to the priests (Exod. 28. 41); to the people (Deut. 7. 6); to the assembly of the people (Ps. 89. 7, Joel 2. 16); to a man of God (2 Kings 4. 9); to Jeremiah 'sanctified' in the womb (Jer. 1. 5); to the guests at a sacrificial feast (Zeph. 1. 7, margin); and to the saints or people dedicated to God, whether angels or men (Job 5. 1, 15. 15; Ps. 16. 3, 34. 9; Isa. 4. 3; Dan. 4. 13, 7. 18, 21, 22, 25, 27, 8. 13, 24; Zech. 14. 5).

The point involved in every case is relation or contact with God. Thus the Sabbath day was holy because God rested thereon, and it was to be set apart by Israel as a pledge that He had sanctified or set apart the people to Himself (Exod. 31. 13); the mountain of the Lord was to be called holy because He would dwell there (Zech. 8. 3); the 'sanctuary' was to be made that the Lord might dwell among the people (Exod. 25. 8); the firstborn, by being hallowed or set apart, were regarded by God as His own (Num. 3. 13); and even the censers in which sinful men offered incense to God became hallowed by that very act (Num. 16. 38).

God Himself was regarded as holy, *i.e.* as a Being who from His nature, position, and attributes is to be set apart and revered as distinct from all others; and Israel was to separate itself from the world and the things of the world because God was thus separated; they were to be holy, for He was holy (Lev. 11. 44, 19. 2, 20. 7, 26, 21. 8). Joshua says, 'Ye cannot serve the Lord, for he is an holy God (*i.e.* a God set apart and distinct from all other beings); he is a jealous God, he will not forgive (or put up with) your transgressions nor your sins' (Josh. 24. 19). In accordance with this teaching, the Lord was to be 'sanctified,' *i.e.* regarded as occupying a unique position both morally and as regards His essential nature. Thus we read in Lev. 10. 3, 'I will be sanctified in them that come nigh me;' 1 Sam. 6. 20, 'Who is able to stand before this holy Lord God?' Ps. 111. 9, 'Holy and reverend is his name;' Isa. 6. 3, 'Holy, holy, holy is the Lord of Hosts;' Isa. 8. 13, 14, 'Sanctify the Lord of Hosts himself,[1] and let him be your fear,

---

[1] This passage is quoted in 1 Pet. 3. 15. Compare also the words of the Lord's Prayer (Matt. 6. 9), 'Hallowed (or sanctified) be thy Name.'

and let him be your dread, and he shall be for a sanctuary;' Isa.
29. 23, 'They shall sanctify my name, and sanctify the Holy One
of Jacob,' *i.e.* the Being whom Jacob sanctified or set apart as his
God.   In harmony with these passages, we find the Lord several
times described as 'the Holy One of Israel,' *i.e.* the Being to
whom alone Israel gave special and peculiar honour (2 Kings 19. 22 ;
Ps. 71. 22 ; Isa. 10. 17, 49. 7).   In Ezek. 11. 16 the Lord says,
'Although I have cast them far off among the heathen, and although I have scattered them among the countries, yet will I be
unto them as a sanctuary for a little time (A. V. *as a little sanctuary*) in the countries whither they shall come;' that is to say,
'Although they will have no temple for a little while, yet I will be
with them, and they shall learn to reverence me;' thus God Himself took the place of the 'sanctuary' built by Solomon (1 Chron.
22. 18. 19).   The holy temple of the Lord represented His Presence,
but that Presence could go with the people into captivity even
though the temple were to be destroyed.

The Spirit of God is called Holy in Ps. 51. 11, 'Take not thy
holy Spirit from me;' Isa. 63. 10, 11, 'They rebelled and vexed
his holy Spirit . . . Where is he that put his holy Spirit within
him ?'   Compare the expression 'The spirit of the holy gods' (Dan.
4. 8, 9).

In all these passages it is implied that He whom Israel was to
worship was to be regarded as entirely separate from all other
beings, and also as pure from every thought and deed of evil.   What
a contrast with the theology of heathendom !

The process of setting apart for sacred uses which is described by
the words dedication and consecration is also represented by
Kadash.   See, for example, Jud. 17. 3 ; 2 Sam. 8. 11 ; 2 Kings 10.
20 ; 1 Chron. 18. 11 ; 2 Chron. 31. 6.   It was also used to denote
the setting apart of certain people for warfare, as in Jer. 51. 27,
'Prepare the nations against her;' Joel 3. 9, 'Prepare war;'
Micah 3. 5, 'They even prepare war against him.'

In 2 Sam. 11. 4 **Kadash** is rendered purify, to signify the
doing away with ceremonial defilement.   But the same word is also
used in Deut. 22. 9, where we read, 'Thou shalt not sow thy vineyard with divers seeds : lest the fruit of thy seed which thou hast
sown, and the fruit of thy vineyard, be defiled;' and in Job 36. 14,
'Their life is among the unclean.'   In these passages we have
samples of the use of the word **Kadash** in an opposite sense to the
true one.

M

The familiar expression 'beauty of holiness' is found in
1 Chron. 16. 29; 2 Chron. 20. 21; Ps. 29. 2, 96. 9, 110. 3.   Other
suggested renderings are 'the glorious sanctuary' and 'holy array.'
The word rendered 'beauty' frequently means majesty or excellency,
and probably points to the glory of God rather than to the garments
of man.

In Exod. 28. 36, Jer. 31. 40, and other passages, we meet with
the expression 'Holiness to the Lord,' or as it is sometimes
rendered, 'Holiness of the Lord,' or 'Holy to the Lord.'   This expression indicates that the object thus inscribed is dedicated to
God.

The word holy is sometimes opposed to the unholy or profane
(חל, βέβηλος), as in Lev. 10. 10, and Ezek. 44. 23, where the latter
word signifies that which is devoted to ordinary uses.   It also
occurs in connection with the separation of the Nazarite in Num.
6. 5, 8; and of the 'holy seed' of Israel as compared with the
Canaanites (Ezra 9. 2).   It was set forth as of the greatest importance that Israel should regard themselves as a *separate people*.   In
this respect the Nazarite from the days of Joseph onwards (Gen. 49.
26) was a type of the whole nation.   They were 'a peculiar treasure'
(Exod. 19. 5; Deut. 14. 2, 26. 18; Ps. 135. 4), redeemed by God for
His own purposes (Exod. 33. 15, 16); ordained to keep His law (Lev.
20. 7, 8), and to live to His praise and glory (Lev. 20. 24–26).

With regard to the mode in which ceremonial sanctification [1]
was accomplished, we find it varying according to the circumstances
of the case.   When Aaron and his sons were hallowed or sanctified for the priesthood, 'Moses took of the anointing oil, and of the
blood which was upon the altar, and sprinkled upon Aaron and
upon his garments, and upon his son's garments with him.'   The
A. V. has unfortunately rendered **Kadash** 'consecrate' instead of
'hallow' in Exod. 28. 3, 30. 30; Josh. 6. 19; 2 Chron. 26. 18, 29.
33, 31. 6; Ezra 3. 5.

The word used for consecration in Num. 6. 9, 12, is **Nazar**
(נזר), to separate, and is rightly used of the **Nazarite** or separated
person.   Another form of this word is rendered crown in several
passages, perhaps because the wearing a crown was a special mark
of distinction or separation.   It is used of the golden crown on the
High Priest's mitre, on which the words 'Holiness to the Lord'

---

[1] The technical act of consecration was a different process.   It was literally
the *filling of the hand*, part of the sacrifice being put into the hand and waved,
and then borne to the altar.

were written (Exod. **39**. 30) ; and of the 'crown of the anointing oil' which separated him for the work of God (Lev. **21**. 12) ; it was the mark of the anointed king (Ps. **89**. 38, 39, **132**. 17, 18) ; and in Zech. **9**. 16 we are told that the Lord's people shall be 'as the stones of a crown, lifted up as an ensign on his land.' In most of the passages in which this word occurs, the LXX renders it ἁγίασμα.

Chanac (חנך), to initiate or inaugurate, is used in Num. **7**. 10, 11, 84, 88, of the dedication of the altar; in 1 Kings **8**. 63, 2 Chron. **7**. 5, 9, of the dedicating of the house of the Lord; in Ezra **6**. 16, 17, with reference to the rebuilt temple; in Neh. **12**. 27, of the wall of Jerusalem ; and in Dan. **3**. 2, 3, of the dedication of the image which Nebuchadnezzar set up. This word is applied to the training or dedication of children in Prov. **22**. 6 ; see also Gen. **14**. 14.

The word **ordain** occurs seventeen times in the O. T., and represents eleven different Hebrew words. In some of these passages there is a reference to the **appointment** of rites, and of religious or secular officers, but nothing in the words used indicates any peculiarities in the *mode* of appointment.

§ 2. *Teaching of the N. T. on Sanctification.*

We now turn to the N. T. in order to trace the usage of the word ἁγιάζω, the Greek representative of **Kadash**. First, it is applied to the sanctification and consecration of the Son by the Father in John **10**. 36 ; compare chap. **17**. 19, 'In their behalf I sanctify myself,' *i.e.* set myself apart for the special work of God. The Lord was 'set apart' from the foundation of the world for the work of redemption, and His incarnation, temptations, and sufferings were the processes whereby His atoning death was prepared for and rendered valid.

Secondly, the sanctification of Christians is referred to as the work of the Father in John **17**. 17, 'Sanctify them *in* (or *by*) the truth ;' see also 1 Thess. **5**. 23 and Jude 1. But whilst the Father is the source, the Son is the agent, for His object in sanctifying Himself was that they also might be sanctified by the truth. Compare 1 Cor. **1**. 2 ; Eph. **5**. 26. In Heb. **2**. 11 we read of Christ and Christians, that 'Both he that sanctifieth and they that are sanctified are all of one' (*i.e.* from one source) : 'for which cause he is not ashamed to call them brethren.'

The means whereby the Christian is sanctified is the blood, *i.e.* the offering of the life-blood of Christ (Heb. **9**. 14, **10**. 10, 14).

In Rom. **15**. 16, the agency of the Holy Spirit is mentioned in connection with sanctification. Here reference is made to the power whereby St. Paul's ministrations were effective in preaching to the Gentiles, and presenting them as an offering to God.

In 2 Tim. **2**. 21, the man who is purged from iniquity is compared to a sanctified vessel. The sanctification of food, *i.e.* its being regarded as free from ceremonial pollution, is referred to in 1 Tim. **4**. 5, as accomplished by means of the word of God and prayer. In 1 Cor. **7**. 14, we are told that 'The unbelieving husband is sanctified by the wife, and the unbelieving wife is sanctified by the husband; else were your children unclean, but now are they holy.' According to this passage, we are to understand that the marriage tie extends sanctity or sacredness from the husband to the wife, or from the wife to the husband, and so to the children. In these passages we have the idea of sacredness, affecting the *position* and *use* rather than the *nature* of that to which it refers. The preposition which is generally the connecting link between the object sanctified and that which sanctifies it, is not *by* or *with*, but *in*. This seems to imply that sanctification takes place through the *contact* of one object with another. The gift by being placed on the altar becomes in a ceremonial sense *one* with it. The Christian is sanctified by becoming one with Christ, faith in His blood being that which makes both one; and Christ is sanctified in that He is one with the Father. We find the preposition ἐν with ἁγιάζω in the following passages of the LXX : Exod. 29. 43 ; Lev. 10. 3 ; Num. **20**. 13 ; Deut. 32. 51 ; Ezek. 20. 41, 28. 22, 25, **36**. 23, 38. 16, 39. 27, and **44**. 19.

The noun ἁγιασμός occurs ten times in the N. T., and would best be rendered sanctification. The passages are as follows :— Rom. **6**. 19, 'Yield your members servants to righteousness unto holiness,' *i.e.* with a view to sanctification; so verse 22. 1 Cor. **1**. 30, 'Christ Jesus is made unto us . . . sanctification,' *i.e.* a means or ground of it. 1 Thess. **4**. 3, 4, 7, 'This is the will of God, even your sanctification, . . . that every one of you should know how to possess his vessel in sanctification and honour . . . for God hath not called us unto uncleanness, but in sanctification.' The A. V., by rendering this last expression '*unto holiness*,' obscures the connection of the verses. 2 Thess. **2**. 13, 'God hath

chosen you to salvation in sanctification of (the) spirit.'[1] 1 Tim.
2. 15, 'If they continue in faith and charity and sanctification
with sobriety.' Heb. **12**. 14, 'Follow after sanctification, without which no man shall see God.' 1 Pet. **1**. 2, 'In sanctification
of (the) spirit.'[1] Thus, true sanctification involves the separation
of the spirit from all that is impure and polluting, and a renunciation of the sins towards which the desires of the flesh and of the
mind lead us.

Whilst ἁγιασμός may be regarded as the process of sanctification,
ἁγιότης and ἁγιωσύνη are rather the result of the process. The
former occurs in 1 Cor. **1**. 30, and Heb. **12**. 10; the latter in Rom.
1. 4, 2 Cor. **7**. 1, and 1 Thess. **3**. 13. These passages, if examined,
will show that the quality of holiness, or perfect freedom from
pollution and impurity, is essential to the nature of God, was exhibited by His Son Jesus Christ, and is imparted to the Christian
in proportion to his faith.

The adjective ἅγιος, holy, is used nearly a hundred times with
reference to the Holy Spirit of God—that Spirit which was in
Christ without measure, and which is now imparted to all that
trust Him. Again, both in consequence of the indwelling of the
Holy Spirit, or because of their professed separation from evil and
dedication to God, all Christians are regarded as ἅγιοι, holy or
saints. The word is also applied to Christ, who was the holy one
of God, and our Lord applies it to His 'holy Father,' and to the
'holy angels.' We find it used in a more ceremonial sense of the
holy city Jerusalem (Matt. **27**. 53), and the holy place (Matt.
24. 15); of the Covenant with Abraham (Luke **1**. 72); of the
Scriptures (Rom. **1**. 2); of the law and commandment (Rom. **7**. 12);
of a kiss (Rom. **16**. 16); and of food which was separated from
ordinary uses, and was therefore not to be cast to the dogs
(Matt. **7**. 6).

The word ἁγνεία, which is found in Gal. **5**. 22 (in some MSS.),
also in 1 Tim. **4**. 12, and 1 Tim. **5**. 2, answers very well to our word
purity, in its double sense of chastity and freedom from wrong
motives.

The verb ἁγνίζειν is used with reference to ceremonial purifications in John **11**. 55, Acts **21**. 24, 26, and **24**. 18. It is also used

---

[1] There is no article here in the Greek, so that the expression possibly signifies
the sanctification of a man's own spirit, or, in a general sense, *spiritual sanctification*, as opposed to that which is *external* or *ceremonial*. R. V. retains the
article.

in a spiritual sense in three passages, namely: James **4**. 8, 'Purify your hearts, ye double-minded;' 1 Pet. **1**. 22, 'Seeing ye have purified your souls in obeying the truth through the Spirit unto unfeigned love of the brethren, love one another with a pure heart fervently;' 1 John **3**. 3, 'He that hath this hope in Him (*i.e.* not in himself, but in Christ) purifieth himself, even as He is pure.'

The adjective ἁγνός occurs eight times in the N. T. in the sense of moral chastity and purity; and ἁγνότης, which is derived from it, and which is peculiar to the N. T., is found in 2 Cor. **6**. 6, and, according to some MSS., in 2 Cor. **11**. 2; whilst the adverb ἁγνῶς occurs in Phil. **1**. 16.

§ 3. *Anointing.*

In considering the ceremonial anointing of the O. T., we have only to do with one word, viz. **Mashach** (משח), from which the name Messiah is derived, and which is almost always rendered χρίω in the LXX. Other words, indeed, are used, but not in a ceremonial sense. Among passages where such occur, two may be noted: the first is Isa. **10**. 27, 'The yoke shall be destroyed because of the anointing,' or literally, 'from the face of the oil;' the other is Zech. **4**. 14, 'These are the two anointed ones (literally, sons of oil or brightness) that stand by the Lord of the whole earth.'

Mashach is first used of the anointing of the pillar at Bethel (Gen. **28**. 18, 31. 13), and it does not occur again till Exod. **25**. 6, where 'the anointing oil' is spoken of. We next meet with it in connection with the consecration and sanctification of Aaron (Exod. **28**. 41). The anointing came *after* the offering of atoning victims in Aaron's case, as in the case of the altar (Exod. **29**. 36). The tabernacle, the ark, the table, and various vessels were to be anointed (Exod. **30**. 26–28). They were then regarded as sanctified or set apart, and whatever touched them had this sanctification communicated to it. The unleavened wafers and some other meat offerings were to be anointed (Lev. **2**. 4). In all these cases the unction was the mode of setting apart or sanctifying.

The anointing of a king is first mentioned in the parable of Jotham (Jud. **9**. 8, 15). It next occurs in the inspired hymn of Hannah (1 Sam. **2**. 10), 'He shall give strength unto his king, and exalt the horn of his anointed.' Saul was anointed captain over God's people, that he might save them out of the hand of the Philistines (1 Sam. **9**. 16). Various references are found to the Lord's anointed, that is to say, the king, both in the historical and poetical books. The following are the most important : Ps. **2**. 2, 'The rulers take counsel together against the Lord and against his anointed ;' Ps. **18**. 50, 'He sheweth mercy to his anointed, to David, and to his seed for evermore ;' **20**. 6, 'Now know I that the Lord saveth his anointed ;' **45**. 7, 'God hath anointed thee with the oil of gladness above thy fellows ;' **92**. 10, 'I shall be anointed with fresh oil.'

The reference in Ps. **105**. 15, 'Touch not mine anointed (ones), and do my prophets no harm,' is thought to be to the priests (compare Hab. **3**. 13). The meaning of the phrase 'Anoint the shield' (Isa. **21**. 5) is doubtful. In Isa. **45**. 1, Cyrus is called the Lord's anointed, because he was appointed king for a special purpose. In Isa. **61**. 1, the word receives a larger meaning, and teaches that the holy oil wherewith the priest and king and the vessels of the tabernacle were anointed was a symbol of the Holy Spirit. For we read, 'The Spirit of the Lord God is upon me, because he hath anointed me to preach good tidings unto the meek.'

In Ezek. **28**. 14, the king of Tyrus is described as 'the anointed cherub.' Some here translate the word 'extended' instead of anointed; but compare Isa. **45**. 1. In Dan. **9**. 24, we are told that seventy weeks were determined . . . to anoint the Most Holy,' *i.e.* either the Most Holy Being or the Most Holy Place. In Amos **6**. 6, the word appears to be used of personal decoration with oil, and not of the ceremonial anointing. If this be the case, it is the only place in the whole O. T. in which the word is so used. Possibly there is a reference here to the abuse of holy things, a view which would be most in accordance with the accusations implied in the two previous verses.

The verb χρίειν is used five times in the N. T. In four of these passages it refers to the anointing of Christ by His Father, namely : Luke **4**. 18, which is quoted from Isa. **61**. 1 ; Heb. **1**. 9, quoted from Ps. **45**. 7 ; Acts **4**. 27, where it is used with special reference to the quotation from the second Psalm, which immediately precedes it ; and Acts **10**. 38, where we are told that God anointed Jesus with the Spirit. What, then, is the idea which we ought to connect with the name Christ or Messiah ? It points to One who is King by Divine authority, and signifies that God would set His mark upon Him by giving Him the Holy Ghost without measure.

Perhaps also it teaches that the ministrations of the prophet, priest, altar, and tabernacle with all its vessels, were foreshadowings of the work which He was to accomplish.

The anointing of Christians is spoken of in 2 Cor. 1. 21, where we are told that ' He who hath anointed us is God ; ' and in accordance with this fact, St. John three times in his First Epistle reminds those to whom he writes that they have a *chrism* or *unction* from the Holy One (chap. 2. 20, 27). This chrism includes not only the special temporary gifts of the Spirit, but also the indwelling and working presence of the Holy Ghost which the Christian receives from the Father through the Son.

The anointing of the sick is described by a different Greek word, namely, $\dot{\alpha}\lambda\epsilon\dot{\iota}\phi\omega$. It was a medical rather than a ceremonial act, and was performed by friction or rubbing, not by pouring. So far from St. James's words (5. 14) discouraging the use of medical help, they order it. The same word is used of the anointing of the head and of the body for purposes of decoration or preservation.

CHAPTER XVI.

OFFERINGS, ALTAR.

FEW elements in the Mosaic dispensation are more interesting to the Christian student than the system of offerings therein prescribed. The practice of slaying animals for a religious purpose appears to have been called into existence at a very early stage of human history, but the Levitical system claims to have been elaborated under Divine direction during the sojourning in the wilderness, and that with a fulness of detail which must arrest the attention of every reader. If it be true that even in earthly matters 'coming events cast their shadows before,' much more is it to be expected that when the Author of all existence was about to make a special intervention in the affairs of men, He would not only intimate His purpose to some of those whom He was about to benefit, but would also prefigure the course which He was about to adopt. The system of offerings appointed to Israel may thus be regarded as a book of pictures, sketched in shadowy outline, indicating to God's people the work which was to be accomplished by Divine grace when the fulness of the time should have come.

There is a further reason for a patient and accurate examination of this system. Among the controversies of the present day, few have given rise to such vehemence and acrimony as the questions, how far any part of the Levitical system of offerings is, or ought to be, reproduced in connection with the sacrament of the Lord's Supper, and whether the rite in question is a sacrifice, the holy table an altar, and the minister a priest.

§ 1. *The Korban.*

The word **Korban** (קרבן, Ass. *Kurbannu*), with which we are familiar from its occurrence in the N. T. (Mark 7. 11), is used for the offering in about seventy passages in the O. T. It is not restricted to any sacrifice in particular, but represents the various ways in which the offerer found a way of approach and acceptance. We might almost render it *a way of access*. The verb **Karav** (קרב), whence it is derived, signifies to approach or draw near, and is often used of man's entrance into the presence of the living God (so also in Assyrian). It is no ordinary nearness that is represented by it, but rather that of the closest and most intimate kind (see, *e.g.*, Num. **16**. 9 ; Ps. **65**. 4 ; Jer. **30**. 21). The very word just used ('intimate') reminds us of the meaning of the word in one of its forms (קֶרֶב), as applied to the innermost part of the body; whilst in another form (קרוב) it signifies a near neighbour or a kinsman. The word is also used of close hand-to-hand conflict, and hence is rendered **battle** or **war** in nine passages in the O. T. So also in Assyrian.

Korban is also rendered **sacrifice** in Lev. **27**. 11, and **oblation** ten times in Leviticus, and twice in Numbers. It would be better to have a uniform rendering in these passages. The verb in its causative form is rendered **offer** more than fifty times in Leviticus, and twenty-five times in Numbers. It occurs in a non-sacrificial sense in Jud. **3**. 18, where we read of Ehud's **offering** a present to Eglon ; also in 1 Chron. **16**. 1, and 2 Chron. **35**. 12, *al.*

The LXX renders the verb ἐγγίζω, προσφέρω, προσέρχομαι, προσάγω ; and the noun always δῶρον.

The verb **Nagash** (נגש) has much the same meaning as **Karav**, and is applied to the presentation of offerings in Amos **5**. 25, Mal. **1**. 7, 8, 11, 13, and **3**. 3. This word is coupled with **Karav** in Jer. **30**. 21, which runs thus : 'Their noble (A. V. nobles) shall be from themselves, and their ruler shall issue from amidst them, and I *will cause him to draw near* (**Karav**), and he shall *approach* (**Nagash**) unto me.'

§ 2. *N. T. Teaching.*

We find ἐγγίζω used once in the N. T. in a special sense, namely, in Heb. **7**. 19, 'The bringing in of a better hope, by which *we draw near* unto God.'

The word προσφέρω is used of the **offering** of gifts of many kinds. Thus we meet with it in Matt. **2**. 11, with respect to the offerings made by the Wise Men ; in Matt. **5**. 23, of the offering or gift upon the altar, where reference is evidently made to the ordinary offerings prescribed under the name in Leviticus. In Matt. **8**. 4, Mark **1**. 44, and Luke **5**. 14, it is applied to the offering to be made by the cleansed leper. In John **16**. 2 we read, 'Whosoever killeth you will think that he offereth religious service to God' (λατρείαν προσφέρειν τῷ θεῷ). The only Epistle in which the word occurs is that which was addressed to the Hebrews, in which it is found twenty times, and, with one exception,[1] always in a sacrificial or religious sense. Thus it is said of the Lord Jesus that He offered Himself without blemish to God through the Eternal Spirit (Heb. 9. 14), and that He was once for all offered to bear the sins of many (9. 28).

The word προσέρχομαι is used of the sinner's approach to God on the basis of an offering in Heb. 4. 16, 7. 25, 10. 1, 22, and 11. 6.

There is one remarkable passage in which προσάγειν is used, namely, 1 Pet. 3. 18, 'Christ died, the just for the unjust, that he might bring us to God.' Here the Vulgate rendering is striking, 'that he might offer us to God,' the offering being the means of the sinner's approach. The noun προσαγωγή, derived from this verb, is used of the access or way of approach which the Christian obtains through Christ, in Rom. 5. 2, Eph. 2. 18, and 3. 12.

In St. Matthew's Gospel we find δῶρον for a sacrificial gift several times; and St. Mark, in chap. 7. 11, specially interprets **Korban** by this word. In the Epistle to the Hebrews this word is put side by side with θυσίαι, sacrifices.

The general lesson which we gain from the frequent and remarkable use of the word **Korban** (in the Levitical law), and of its Greek representatives in the N. T., is that a way of access to God is made open, not through the efforts of man, but through the good will and ordinance of our heavenly Father, who has caused us to come near to Himself in and through His Son Jesus Christ.

§ 3. *Burnt-Offering.*

The word generally rendered burnt-offering[2] in the A. V. is **'Olah** (עלה). The verb **'Alah**, whence it is derived, is rendered to burn in Exod. 27. 20, Lev. 2. 12, 24. 2, and to offer in a few other passages ; but the original meaning of the word in the Active Voice

---

[1] Namely, Heb. 12. 7, 'God *deals with* you (ὑμῖν προσφέρεται) as with sons.' The word is here in the Middle Voice, and signifies the entrance into a certain relationship.

[2] This is one of a large class of expressions in which a hyphen ought to be introduced. The R. V. is no better than the A. V. in this respect.

is to ascend, hence in the Causative Voice it signifies to *make to ascend*, or *cause to go up*. Some scholars have held that the best rendering for 'olah would be *altar-offering*, because the offering was *lifted up* and placed upon the altar. This interpretation, however, has not been generally accepted. The Vulgate rendering (derived from the Greek) *holocausta*, that which is wholly burnt, and the German *Brandopfer*, signifying burnt-offering, fall in with our own rendering, but they are descriptions rather than translations. The fact that flame *ascends*, and that 'the sparks fly *upwards*,' furnishes us with the true solution of the name. The 'Olah, when turned into a cloud of vapour by the action of the fire, ascended into the heavens, and was gradually dispersed amidst the upper air; and whilst beholding this striking sight, the offerer, who had identified himself with the victim by the pressure of his hands, realised his acceptance by God, who dwelleth in the heavens. The best rendering of the word would be *an ascending-offering*. Arias Montanus rendered it *ascensio*.

The word is used frequently, both in the Levitical ritual and in the historical books. Its first occurrence is in Gen. 8. 20, where Noah is said to have offered burnt-offerings on the altar. We next meet with it in Gen. 22. 2–13, where Abraham is told to offer up Isaac as a burnt-offering. It is also used in Job 1. 5, and 42. 8, where the patriarch is described as offering for his sons, and where his friends are ordered to make an offering. The Levitical law, however, drew a clearer distinction between the two. The word is first used in connection with the people of Israel in Exod. 24. 5. In this important passage we are told that Moses 'sent young men of the children of Israel, which offered burnt-offerings and sacrificed peace-offerings unto the Lord,' the first kind being wholly burnt, and the last eaten; and it was with the blood of these offerings that the people and the Book of the Covenant were sprinkled. This transaction was previous to the appointment of the Aaronic priesthood. The making of the Covenant was a national, not a sacerdotal work; moreover, it had not to do directly *with sin*, for neither the burnt-offering nor the peace-offering were sin-offerings; they represented acceptance rather than pardon.[1]

Passing by the historical books, we find 'olah used in a few other passages, namely, Ps. 51. 19, 66. 15; Isa. 57. 6, 66. 3; Ezek. 43. 18, 24; and Amos 5. 22.

The most general renderings for the verb 'alah in the LXX are ἀναβαίνω, ἀναφέρω, ἀναβιβάζω, and ἀνάγω; the noun 'olah is almost

---

[1] Though these were closely related.

always rendered either ὁλοκαύτωμα, or ὁλοκαύτωσις, *i.e.* that which
is wholly burnt.

Calil (כָּלִיל), that˙ which is complete, is used of the whole
burnt-offering in Lev. 6. 22, 23; Deut. 33. 10; 1 Sam. 7. 9; and
Ps. 51. 19.

On examining the N. T., we do not find the substantive applied
directly to Christ through its Greek representatives, but the idea of
ascending or going up, from which the burnt-offering received its
Hebrew name, and which is so fully sustained in the Greek verbs
above-mentioned, reappears in relation to the Lord's work in various
ways, which may be briefly noticed.

With regard to the word ἀναβαίνω, it may be deemed fanciful
to refer to our Lord's expression, ' Behold, we *go up* to Jerusalem '
(see Matt. 20. 18; Mark 10. 32, 33; Luke 18. 31, and 19. 28),
because it was the ordinary and natural phrase to use when describing a journey to that city which was the Crown of the Holy Land.
Yet it may be noticed that no site could be more aptly marked out
as the altar of earth on which the Great Offering should be consum-
mated. It had probably been the scene of sacrifice as early as the
time of Abraham ; it lies ' beautiful for situation, the joy of the
whole earth,' 2400 feet above the Mediterranean, which washes the
western shore of the land, and 3700 feet above the Dead Sea, which
lies in leaden solitude in a cleft between the torrid mountains of
Judah and the long purple wall of Moab.

Our Lord's ascension or ' going up' to His Father in heaven is
described by the word ἀναβαίνω in John 20. 17, and Eph. 4. 9, 10.

The sacrificial word ἀναφέρω is also used of our Lord's being
'carried up' into heaven in Luke 24. 51 ; whilst it is applied to His
offering of Himself in Heb. 7. 27. It is also adopted with reference
to the offering up of a sacrifice of praise (Heb. 13. 15), and of
spiritual sacrifices which are acceptable to God through Christ
(1 Pet. 2. 5).

The word ἀνάγω is used only twice in the Epistles, namely, in
Rom. 10. 7, and Heb. 13. 20, in both of which passages it is adopted
to express the bringing of Christ up from the dead—an essential
element in the Lord's appointed work.

It may be gathered from these passages that whilst the slaying
of the victim, which was to be a male without blemish, represented
Christ's devotion of Himself to death, and while the pouring forth
of the blood upon the altar foreshadowed the atonement wrought by
virtue of His death, the ascent of the slain animal in the form of a

cloud of smoke into the heavens typified the bringing of Christ up
from the grave, and His ascension to the right hand of God. But
since the offerer, by pressing his hand upon the victim before slaying
it in the presence of God, identified himself with it, he must be considered as symbolically going through the same process as it had to
undergo. So also the Christian, identifying himself with his Saviour
by faith, is 'crucified with Christ,' dies with Him, is buried with
Him, rises with Him under the influence of the Spirit of life, and
is seated with Him in heavenly places, His life of devotion being
compared to an offering made by fire, an odour of a sweet savour
unto God.

§ 4. *The Meat or Meal Offering.*

The general Hebrew word for a gift, whether to God (Gen. 4. 3)
or to man (Gen. 32. 13) is **Minchah,** (מנחה); it is also the word which
our translators have rendered meat-offering—'meat' being here
used in its old sense of 'food,' and not signifying 'flesh.' The
LXX has θυσία (sacrifice) for it in 140 places, and δῶρον (a gift)
in 32 places.[1] **Minchah** is the word used of the offerings of Cain
and Abel in Gen. 4. 3, 4, 5, in which passage it is not restricted to
its Levitical use as an unbloody sacrifice; it is first rendered 'meat-
offering' in Lev. 2. 1, where it is described as a mixture of flour,
oil, and frankincense—the flour being the essential part, the oil and
frankincense being added that it might burn with a sweet savour.
The word is used of the '*jealousy-offering*' in Num. 5. 15, 18, 25, 26.
It is also to be found in the following passages :—Num. 16. 15,
'Respect thou not their offering.' 1 Sam. 2. 17, 'Men abhorred
the offering of the Lord;' verse 29, 'Wherefore kick ye at my
sacrifice, and at mine offering?' 1 Sam. 3. 14, 'The iniquity of
Eli's house shall not be purged with sacrifice nor offering for
ever.' 1 Sam. 26. 19, 'If the Lord have stirred thee up against me,
let him accept (or smell) an offering.' 1 Chron. 16. 29, Ps. 96. 8,
'Bring an offering, and come before him.' Ps. 20. 3, 'Remember
all thy offerings.' Isa. 43. 23, 'I have not caused thee to serve
with an offering.' Isa. 66. 20, 'They shall bring all your brethren
for an offering unto the Lord out of all nations . . . as the children
of Israel bring an offering in a clean vessel into the house of the
Lord.' Jer. 41. 5, 'There came certain from Shechem, from Shiloh,

---

[1] The Assyrian word is *manitu*. The LXX also occasionally reproduces the
original word in the form μαναά. The Vulgate adopts *munus* and *oblatio* as
renderings ; and Luther has *Opfer* and *Speisopfer*. Meat is literally that which
we chew or grind.

and from Samaria, even fourscore men, having their beards shaven, and their clothes rent, and having cut themselves, with offerings and incense (or rather frankincense) in their hand, to bring them to the house of the Lord.' Amos 5. 25, 'Have ye offered unto me sacrifices and offerings in the wilderness forty years?' Zeph. 3. 10, 'From beyond the rivers of Ethiopia my suppliants, even the daughters of my dispersed, shall bring mine offering.' Mal. 1. 10, 'Neither will I accept an offering at your hand;' see also verse 11, 'In every place incense shall be offered unto my name, and a pure offering.' Mal. 3. 3, 4, 'He shall purify the sons of Levi, that they may offer an offering in righteousness. Then shall the offering of Judah and Jerusalem be pleasant unto the Lord, as in the days of old.'

Minchah is rendered gift in Ps. 45. 12; sacrifice in 1 Kings 18. 29, 36, the time of the offering of the (evening) sacrifice;[1] Ps. 141. 2, 'Let my prayer be set forth before thee as incense; and the lifting up of my hands as the evening sacrifice;' oblation in Isa. 1. 13, 19. 21, 66. 3, Jer. 14. 12.

The minchah, which was closely connected with the 'olah, must be regarded as a token of love, gratitude, and thanksgiving to God, who is Himself the giver of all good gifts. It was an acknowledgment on the part of man that 'the earth is the Lord's and the fulness thereof.' Part of it was called the 'memorial,'[2] and was burnt with fire, and the rest was eaten by the priest and his family, not by the offerer.

§ 5. *The Sacrificial Feast.*

We now come to the word **Zevach**[3] (זֶבַח), which is generally rendered sacrifice in the English, and θυσία, θύω, and θυσιάζω in the LXX. We certainly need greater uniformity of rendering for the Levitical terms than we possess at present. If the word sacrifice had been confined to the **zevach**, instead of being also occasionally applied to the **minchah**, the **korban**, the **isheh**, the **chag** or feast (Ps. 118. 27, and Isa. 29. 1), the **todah** or praise

---

[1] The word *evening* is inserted in italics both here and in some other places. (Compare 2 Kings 16. 15; Ps. 141. 2; Ezek. 9. 4, 5; Dan. 9. 21.) Reference is supposed to be made to the offering of a lamb every evening, prescribed in Num. 28. 8. The lamb itself was an 'olah, but no doubt it was accompanied by a minchah.

[2] The meaning is plain from Ps. 20. 3, '(God) remember all thy minchahs.'

[3] Assyrian, *zibû*; but *naqu* usually represents the word.

(Jer. **17**. 26, and **33**. 11), and the verbs 'aseh and **kathar,** present controversies might have assumed a very much milder form. The R. V. unfortunately does not help us much here.

The idea of a sacrifice is instinctively connected in our minds with that of a priest;[1] but this is a mistake. The verb **zavach** properly means to slay an animal for the purpose of food, and accordingly it is rendered kill or slay in Deut. **12**. 15, 21; 1 Sam. **28**. 24; 2 Chron. **18**. 2; and Ezek. **34**. 3. Although the verb has been also rendered to offer in thirty-seven passages, usually where the kindred substantive is found with it, yet in these passages it does not represent the act of the priest as such, but the act of the lay offerer, *e.g.* the head of the family, who presented and slew the animal before God's sanctuary. The word is generally used in connection with a sacred feast, in which the family or nation which offered the sacrifice (through their heads or representatives) proceeded to partake of the flesh of the victims, entering thereby into communion with God. Thus the **zevach** or sacrifice was utterly distinct from the 'olah or ascending-offering, which was wholly burnt or turned into vapour, and from the sin-offering, which was partly burnt and partly eaten by the priest.

The various ceremonies connected with the sacrifice are described in Lev. **17**. 5–7 and other passages. A man brought an unblemished animal to the door of the sacred tent, pressed his hands on its head, and slew it. The priest, who in this and all other things acted on God's behalf, took the blood, which represented the life of the animal (and therefore the life of the offerer), and shed it forth upon the altar as an atonement. He also burnt or vaporised the fat—to represent the fact that the richness or goodness of animal life proceeded from God, and was due to Him. A certain fixed portion of the flesh was then given to the priest, to be eaten by himself and his family, and the rest was eaten by the offerer and his household. Whether the feast was public or private, and whether the animal was offered by the elders of the nation or by the head of a family, these ceremonies were appointed in order to symbolise the union between God and man, who were thus made partakers of the same food. If it was impossible to perform the full rites connected with the sacrifice through distance from the ' tabernacle of the congregation,' or from the place which God should subsequently choose to put His

---

[1] In some French translations of the Bible a priest is called *sacrificateur.*

name there, *i.e.* the Temple,[1] one point at any rate was to be observed—the blood of the slain animal was to be poured upon the earth and covered with dust (verse 13).

There can be little doubt that the rites connected with the **zevach** were designed to produce a moral effect upon the children of Israel. Every time that they slew an unblemished animal for food they were reminded of God's merciful disposition towards them; they were thus stimulated to live in conformity with His law, and to deal mercifully with their poorer brethren. Nor can it be doubted that the death of the animal, followed by the sprinkling of the blood and the burning of the fat, would impress the pious Israelite with a recollection of the fact that sin brought death into the world, and that he himself had sinned. He would thus have what the Scripture calls '*a broken spirit*' (Ps. **51.** 17); and his sacrifice would be a strong call to *righteousness* (Ps. **4.** 5), to *obedience* (1 Sam. **15.** 22), to *joy* (27. 6), and to *mercy* (Hos. 6. 6). Where the sacrifice had not this spirit, it lost all its value and significance.

The connection between the **zevach** and the making a Covenant is brought out in various parts of Scripture, the sharing in food being a symbol of the oneness of the eaters. See, for example, Gen. **31.** 54, and Ps. **50.** 5. The Passover and the Peace-offering, which were special kinds of **zevach**, are referred to below.

§ 6. *The Altar*

The Hebrew name for an *altar*, מזבח (**Mizbeach**), is derived from **zavach**, and is literally a place of slaughter. It is rendered θυσιαστήριον in the LXX, except where a heathen altar is referred to, and then the Greek word βωμός is adopted.[2] The primary idea which a Hebrew would attach to an altar would depend upon his view of the word **zavach**; according to Levitical usage, it would be the appointed place on which the blood of slain beasts was to be sprinkled and their fat burnt. In a short but interesting essay on the Jewish altar by David Mill,[3] it is noticed that the

---

[1] See 2 Sam. **7.** 1, 1 Kings **8.** 16, 29, where we have direct and unimpeachable references to Deut. **12.** 10, 11, *al.*

[2] The word **ariel** (Isa. **29.** 1, 2; Ezek. **43.** 15, 26) is supposed by some to mean 'altar of God,' an Arabic root akin to the Latin *ara* being produced in support of the translation; but this is doubtful.

[3] David Mill was Reland's successor as Oriental Professor at Utrecht, where his *Dissertationes Selectæ* were published.

N

Rabbinical writers used to regard it not only as God's table[1] (see
Mal. **1**. 7), but also as a symbol of mediation; accordingly, they
called it a *Paraclete* (פרקלט, Παράκλητος), *i.e.* an intercessor; it
was regarded as a centre for mediation, peace-making, expiation,
and sanctification. Whatever was burnt upon the altar was considered to be consumed by God, a guarantee that the offerer was
accepted by Him.

It seems probable from the general use of **Mizbeach** for an
altar, that in the Patriarchal age the animals which were offered
to the Lord as burnt-offerings were laid on the altar and sacrificed
(*i.e.* slain) there. The account of the burnt-offering in Gen. **22**.
exactly falls in with this supposition. In this matter, however,
as in many others, the law of Moses departed from the earlier
practice, while retaining the principal features of the system.

§ 7. *Altar and Sacrifice in the N. T.*

The word θύω is used in the N. T. both with respect to the
slaying of the Passover Lamb and to the killing of animals for
the purpose of food, *e.g.* Luke **15**. 23; Acts **10**. 13. The noun
θυσία occurs several times in the N. T. with reference to Levitical
rites, *e.g.* 1 Cor. **10**. 18; to the Christian life of self-sacrifice
(Rom. **12**. 1; Phil. **2**. 17, **4**. 18; Heb. **13**. 16; and 1 Pet. **2**. 5);
and to the sacrifice of Christ on the cross (Eph. **5**. 2; Heb. **9**. 26,
10. 12).

The altar, θυσιαστήριον, is mentioned in about twenty passages,
in most of which the Jewish altar is referred to. In 1 Cor. **10**. 18,
St. Paul reminds the Corinthians that in the case of Israel those
who eat the sacrifices become in so doing partakers of (or with)
the altar. By this he means that while the altar (which represented God) had part of the victim, the sacrificer had another
part; thus the sacrificial victim being consumed partly by God
and partly by man, forms a bond of union between the one and
the other.

In Heb. **13**. 10, the writer points out that there were certain
offerings of which neither priest nor offerer might eat. They were
not burnt, *i.e.* turned to vapour on the altar, but were entirely

---

[1] The table was not provided in the Levitical law, but is referred to in
Ezek. **40**. 39. It served a different purpose from the altar. The animal was
slain and cut up on the table, but its blood was sprinkled, its fat burnt, and, in
the case of the 'olah, all the pieces were burnt on the altar.

consumed,[1] so that there was no communion with the altar or with God in these cases. 'We Jews,' the writer seems to say, 'have an altar with which neither the offerer nor the priests who minister in the tabernacle have a right to share. Where part of the blood of the victim was brought into the Holy Place as a sin-offering by the High Priest on the Great Day of Atonement, it was sprinkled on and before the mercy-seat or place of propitiation. In this case none of the body was eaten, the whole being utterly consumed in a clean place outside the camp.' He then applies this feature in the Levitical law to the Christian dispensation, and shows that we are in an analogous position. Christ's blood is presented in the Holy Place now as an atonement for us. His body, therefore, is to be devoted to consumption outside the camp. But what is His body ? '*We* Christians,' he implies, 'are the body of Christ; and as His crucifixion literally happened outside the city walls, so we are to go forth to Him bearing His reproach, sharing the ill-treatment He received, being mocked and jeered at by the world as it passes by, having no continuing city here, but seeking that city which is to come.'

§ 8. *Technical Sense of the word 'Do.'*

The word **'Asah** (עשׂה), *to do*, which usually allies itself in meaning with the words with which it stands connected, has amongst its extended significations an application to offerings. It is rendered o f f e r in forty passages, most of which are in Leviticus and Numbers, *e.g.* Lev. 5. 10, 'He shall offer the second for a burnt-offering, according to the ordinance, and the priest shall make an atonement for him.' Sometimes it refers to the service of the priest, and sometimes to the action of him

---

[1] It is important to notice that throughout the Levitical ritual two distinct words are used to represent *burning*. **Kathar** (קטר), which properly means *to turn into smoke or vapour*, is used of the burning of the 'olah, of the memorial portion of the **minchah**, and of the fat of the **zevach**, all of which were intended as offerings for God's good pleasure, and not for sin. This burning took place on the altar at the door of the tabernacle. **Saraph** (שׂרף, Assyrian *sarapu*), to *consume* or *burn up*, is used of the burning of the bodies of certain sin-offerings. Nothing is said of their smoke ascending as a sweet savour to God, because they represent 'the body of sin,' an object which is by no means pleasing in His sight. This is the aspect of the matter presented by the sin-offering which the priest offered for himself, and still more emphatically by the offering of the goat for the sins of the people on the Great Day of Atonement. Ordinary sin-offerings were eaten by the priest.

who brings the offering and appoints what particular animal he will offer. Naaman, the Syrian, is represented as using the word in 2 Kings 5. 17 ; and it is used of Jehu's offering in the house of Baal, 2 Kings 10. 24, 25. We also find it in Ps. 66. 15, 'I will offer bullocks with goats.'

The word first occurs in this sense in Exod. 10. 25, where Moses says, 'Thou must give us also sacrifices and burnt-offerings, that we may sacrifice unto the Lord our God.' In Exod. 29. 36 it is regularly introduced into the Levitical system : 'Thou shalt offer every day a bullock for a sin-offering for atonement ;' verses 38, 39, 'Thou shalt offer . . . two lambs of the first year day by day continually. The one lamb thou shalt offer in the morning ; and the other lamb thou shalt offer at even.' See also Lev. 14. 19, 30, 15. 15, 30, 23. 12, 19 ; Num. 6. 11, 16, 17, 15. 3, 14, 24, 28. 4, 8, 20, 21, 23, 24, 31. The word is used of 'preparing' or arranging the animal or meat offering or drink-offering in Num. 15. 5, 6, 8, 12 ; Jud. 13. 15, 16 ; Ezek. 43. 25, 27, 45. 17, 23, 24, 46. 7, 12, 13, 14, 15. It may be added that 'Asah is used of the making or ordaining of feasts in Jud. 14. 10 ; 1 Kings 3. 15, 12. 32 ; Ezra 3. 4, 6. 19 ; Neh. 8. 18 ; Esther 2. 18, 5. 8.

The Greek rendering in these passages is invariably ποιεῖν, *to do*, or *make*[1]; the Vulgate usually has *facere*, but sometimes *offerre ;* and Luther usually has *machen*, but occasionally *opfern*.

It has been supposed by some commentators that our Lord used the word ποιέω in a sacrificial sense when He said '*Do this* in remembrance of me' (Luke 22. 19). It seems most reasonable to suppose that the word is to be taken here in that ceremonial sense in which it is frequently found in the O. T. The question, however, remains to be asked, to what special religious rite was the Lord referring? When He said 'Do this,' He must at least have meant 'Keep this rite'; but did He mean 'Offer this bread and wine as an offering'? or was there some special Mosaic rite to which the words would bear reference? In answering this question it must be remembered that our Lord was approaching His death, and was instituting an ordinance which bore a direct relationship to it, so that whenever it is duly observed we 'shew forth the Lord's death.' Also it must be granted that the giving up of the Saviour's life upon the cross was pre-eminently vicarious and redemptive, and that in it all the offerings of the old dispen-

---

[1] This use of the word ποιέω must not be forgotten in the interpretation of uch a passage as 2 Cor. 5. 21, ' He made him (to be) sin on our behalf.'

sation had their fulfilment.   What objection, therefore, can lie against the conclusion that the Lord meant, 'Perform this sacrificial rite;' and that while the blood of bulls and goats, together with various meat and drink offerings, *prefigured* the Lord's death, the simple elements of bread and wine were to take their place for all time to come as *memorials* of the same?   But even if we adopted the expression 'offer this' as a rendering, would this imply that the offerer was in any sense a *priest*?   Certainly not; because the Hebrew and Greek words for '*do*' are used of the *people* as well as of the *priests*; see, for examples of this usage, Lev. 23. 12, 19; Deut. 12. 27; 1 Kings 8. 64; 2 Kings 5. 17; 2 Chron. 7. 7; Ps. 66. 15.   Again, would the expression 'offer this' give additional force to the arguments by which the theory of transubstantiation is upheld?   Certainly not.   On the contrary, though the offerings under the old dispensation foreshadowed the Lord's atoning offering in its various aspects, yet they were not identical with it, so that the Christian offering (if such an expression may be permitted for the sake of argument) would by analogy be at most a representation of the same—the breaking of the bread setting forth the laceration of the body, and the pouring out of the wine setting forth the shedding of the blood.[1]

It has been observed, however, that wherever the word *do* is used in a sacrificial sense in the O. T., there lies in the context some noun substantive which indicates the nature of the rite. This, then, we must look for in the N. T. when investigating the ceremonial significance of the expression before us.

Our Lord was at a Passover Supper; and at the table were the lamb, also the bread and wine, which were the regular adjuncts of the feast.   It was not the lamb, however, which He took as the basis of His new rite; if it had been so, then there might have been a clearer connection between the Lord's Supper and the O. T. animal sacrifices.   It was the unleavened bread and the wine which He took in His hands, calling the one His body and the other His blood.[2]   We may hence gather that it was the *nutritious* efficacy of His sacrifice to which the Lord was specially referring when He instituted His Supper: 'The strengthening and

---

[1] Wine is called 'the *blood* of grapes' in Gen. 49. 11, *al.*

[2] Our Lord did not say τοῦτο γίγνεται, 'this has become or is turned into,' but τοῦτο ἐστι, which in ritual connection can only mean 'this represents or stands for.'   The Roman Church, in advocating the doctrine of transubstantiation, departs from the literal sense of Scripture.

refreshing of our souls by the body and blood of Christ, as our bodies are (strengthened and refreshed) by the bread and wine.' It may therefore be inferred that when the Saviour said 'Do this,' He did not mean 'Offer this atoning victim,' but 'Keep this memorial Communion Feast.'

That this is a just view of our Lord's words will be seen more clearly when it is considered that the *keeping* of the Passover Feast was constantly spoken of in the O. T. as a *doing*, the words 'Asah and ποιέω being almost invariably used with respect to it. Instances are as follows :—Exod. 12. 48, 'Will keep the passover to the Lord.' Num. 9. 2, 'Let the children of Israel also keep the passover.' Num. 9. 3, 'Ye shall keep it in his appointed season.' Num. 9. 4, 'That they should keep the passover.' Num. 9. 5, 'And they kept the passover.' Num. 9. 6, 'That they could not keep the passover.' Num. 9. 10, 'Yet shall he keep the passover.' Num. 9. 11, 'At even they shall keep it.' Num. 9. 12, 'According to all the ordinances of the passover they shall keep it.' Num. 9. 13, 'Forbeareth to keep the passover.' Num. 9. 14, 'If a stranger shall sojourn . . . and will keep the passover.' Num. 9. 14, 'According to the ordinance of the passover . . . so shall we do.' 2 Chron. 30. 1, 2, 5, 'To keep the passover.' 2 Chron. 30. 3, 'They could not keep it.' 2 Chron. 30. 13, 'To keep the feast of unleavened bread.' 2 Chron. 35. 18, 'Neither did all the kings of Israel keep such a passover as Josiah kept.' Ezra 6. 19, 'And kept the passover.'

In all these passages the word do or keep answers to that which our Lord used when He said 'Do this.' Compare Matt. 26. 18, where our Lord definitely uses it of the Passover. It can hardly be doubted, then, that His words had direct reference to the Passover Feast. The institution was necessarily proleptic, and anticipated His death. The Passover Lamb was to be slain ; the sacrifice upon the cross fulfilled *this* part of the paschal celebration. Thenceforward the death of Christ upon the cross was to be not only the means of atonement and pardon, but also the source of spiritual sustenance.

The faithful realisation and the personal appropriation of what is meant by 'Christ crucified' is the appointed means for sustaining and stimulating in the heart that Divine life which flows from God to the believer and enables him to walk even as Christ walked. Thus the *memorial* is a real *feast*, and the ordinance furnishes a special opportunity for feeding upon Christ in the heart by faith, as a means of renewing spiritual life in all its aspects.

§ 9. *To Slay a Victim.*

Shachath (שׁחט, Assyrian *sakhatu*), to kill or slay, is first found in Gen. 22. 10, 'And Abraham stretched forth his hand and took the knife to slay his son.' The only other place in Genesis where it occurs is in chap. 37. 31, 'And they took Joseph's coat, and killed a kid of the goats, and dipped the coat in the blood.' It is used of the killing of the Passover Lamb in Exod. 12. 6, &c., and in the directions for sacrifices it constantly occurs. It is rendered offer in Exod. 34. 25, 'Thou shalt not offer the blood of any sacrifice with leaven.'

In Jud. 12. 6, it is applied to the slaughter of *men;* also in 1 Kings 18. 40, where the slaughter of the priests of Baal is referred to; see also 2 Kings 10. 7, 14, 25. 7; Jer. 39. 6, 41. 7, 52. 10. In Isa. 57. 5, the slaughter of children in the valleys was probably sacrificial, to propitiate false gods, as in Ezek. 23. 39, and perhaps Hos. 5. 2.

The general rendering for the word in the LXX is σφάζω, but in a few passages we find θύω.

According to the Received Text, in Rev. 5. 6 we read of a lamb as it were slain (ἐσφαγμένον); the fruits, if not the outward marks, of sacrifice abiding in the exalted Saviour (compare Rev. 5. 9, 12, 13. 8).

§ 10. *The Passover.*

Pasach (פסח) gives its name to the **Pascha** or Passover Feast.[1] It is used of the angel passing over the houses of Israel in Exod. 12. 13, 23, and 27, and it occurs perhaps with significant reference to the great deliverance from Egypt in Isa. 31. 5, 'As birds flying, so will the Lord of hosts defend Jerusalem; defending also he will deliver it; and passing over he will preserve it.' It is not a little remarkable that the word means not only to leap, and hence to pass over, but also to limp. It is the only word rendered 'lame' in the O. T., and is also found in 1 Kings 18. 21, when Elijah says, 'How long halt ye between two opinions?' and in verse 26 it occurs in the Piel or intensive voice, with reference to the priests of Baal 'leaping' on the altar.

The Paschal Feast is πάσχα in the LXX, except in the Books of Chronicles, where the more exact form φασέκ is adopted.

---

[1] Dr. Geddes gravely proposed that this word should be translated skip-offering. But leap-offering would be more exact; compare the word leap-year.

While the whole Gospel narrative points to the relationship between Christ and the Paschal Lamb, there is only one passage in the N. T. which definitely asserts it, but that single sentence is clear enough, 'Christ our passover is sacrificed (*i.e.* slain) for us' (1 Cor. 5. 7).

§ 11. *The Peace-Offering.*

The *peace-offering* is always **Shelem**, from **Shalam** (שלם, Assyrian *sulmannu*). It has been noticed in a previous chapter that this word has various meanings (see chap. viii.). It conveys the idea of *completeness* or *perfection*, and also of *compensation*, as well as that of *peace*. The verb is used of the *payment of vows* and praises to the Lord, *e.g.* in Ps. 50. 14, 56. 12, 76. 11, 116. 14; Isa. 19. 21; Jonah 2. 9; Nahum 1. 15; and this fact may give a clue to the real nature of the **Shelem**. It was a special kind of **Zevach**, or sacrificial feast, occasioned by some particular event in family life which called for a thankful acknowledgment of God's goodness, and a rendering to Him what return was due and possible. It might be rendered recompense-offering. The ceremonial offering of the **Zevach** of the **Shelem** (A. V. sacrifice of the peace-offering) was ordained by God so as to unite religious worship with the enjoyment of domestic happiness. It is remarkable that **Shelem** is only used in the plural. The LXX renders it by εἰρηνικὰ and θυσία σωτηρίου.

§ 12. *The Sin-Offering.*

The *sin-offering* is always **Chattath** (חטאת), for which the LXX has περὶ ἁμαρτίας. The verb **Chatha**, whence it derives its name, signifies *to sin*, but in the Piel voice to *cleanse* or *purge*, or to *offer for sin*, as in Lev. 6. 26 and 9. 15; also in Ps. 51. 7, '*Purge* me with hyssop, and I shall be clean.' It is used of *purification* in Num. 19. 9, 17; see also Job 41. 25. The main peculiarities of the sin-offering have been referred to above in chap. vi.; but it may be added that whilst the 'Olah, which was an offering of devotion, went *upwards*, both the blood and the flesh being lifted on the altar and turned to vapour, the sin-offering, which was mystically identified with sin, went *downwards*—the blood was poured down at the side of the altar, the animal, if not eaten by the priest, was burnt up on the ground, and as there was nothing pleasing to God in the sin which it represented, the smoke is not described as rising up to God as a sweet odour.

The identification of Christ with the sin-offering (περὶ ἁμαρτίας) seems clear from Rom. **8.** 3, where we are told that 'God sending his Son in the likeness of sinful flesh (or of flesh which is the seat of sin), and for sin (*i.e.* as a sin-offering), condemned sin in the flesh.' The flesh, which had been the seat of sin in all other persons, was the seat of righteousness in Christ. In all the points in which St. Paul (in the previous chapters) had shown the flesh to be wanting, Christ proved more than conqueror. His members were instruments of righteousness, His feet were swift to go on errands of mercy, His words were sweeter than honey and the honeycomb, His heart was pure from all taint of sin. Hence the force of His own question, 'Which of you convinceth me of sin (περὶ ἁμαρτίας);' and hence the efficacy of His being a sin-offering (περὶ ἁμαρτίας). His life in the flesh was a practical condemnation of sin and a victory over it; and His death as a sin-offering was, by the will of God, the means of imparting that victory to all who are one with Him by faith.

In 2 Cor. 5. 21, we read, in confirmation of the passage just commented on, God 'made him who knew not sin to be sin for us.' God identified Him with sin, dealt with Him as sin deserves to be dealt with, and thus fulfilled in Him that of which the sin-offering of the O. T. was a type.

The phrase περὶ ἁμαρτίας or περὶ ἁμαρτιῶν is also used with reference to the type or antitype in Gal. **1.** 4; Heb. **10.** 6, 12, 18, 26, **13.** 11; 1 Pet. **3.** 18; 1 John **2.** 2, **4.** 10.

§ 13. *The Trespass-Offering.*

The trespass-offering[1] is **Asham** (אשׁם). Here, as in the case of the sin-offering, the offence and the sacrifice are identical in name. The exact nature of the trespass or guilt indicated by this word has already been discussed (see chap. vi.). The trespass-offering of the Philistines, mentioned several times in 1 Sam. **6.**, is called βάσανος, torment, in the LXX; but the general rendering is πλημμελεία, a discord or mistake. In Isa. **53.** 10, where the A. V. and R. V. read 'Thou shalt make his soul *an offering for sin*,' **Asham** is used, thus extending the efficacy of Christ's sacrifice to

---

[1] If trespass is the right word for **Asham**, the word *guilt* should be changed; but if on the whole guilt gives the best idea, it would be best to render the word here the guilt-offering; otherwise the English reader loses the connection between the offence and the offering.

the class of sin designated by this Hebrew word. The LXX, however, renders the wording περὶ ἁμαρτίας. It also occurs in Prov. 14. 9, ' Fools make a mock at sin.' These words have received various renderings. We might translate ' Fools scorn the trespass-offering,' or perhaps, 'As for fools, (God) scorneth their trespass-offering; but among the upright there is acceptance.' See R. V.

§ 14. *Fire-Offering.*

The offering made by fire is **Isheh** (אשׁה, Ass. *isatu*), from **esh**, fire. It is used freely from Exodus to Samuel, but never later. It is generally rendered κάρπωμα, fruit or offering, in the LXX, but sometimes ὁλοκαύτωμα, or that which is wholly burnt. In one passage **Isheh** is used with reference to a sacrifice which was not burnt at all ; see Lev. 24. 7, 9.

§ 15. *Drink-Offering.*

The drink-offering is **nesec** (נסך, Ass. *nasaku*), from **nasac**, to *pour out*. The LXX always renders it σπόνδη. The use of the verb **nasac** in Ps. 2. 6 is remarkable—'I have poured out (as a drink-offering?) my king upon my holy hill of Zion.' Compare Prov. 8. 23, where wisdom is described as ' poured out from everlasting.' The word *set* adopted by the A. V. is intelligible, but hardly adequate. The verb σπένδομαι is twice used by St. Paul of himself as ready to be *poured forth* as an offering (Phil. 2. 17 ; 2 Tim. 4. 6).

§ 16. *Incense.*

The burning of perfume or incense is always expressed by the word **Kathar** (קטר), *to burn* or *turn into vapour*, the incense being called **Kethoreth.** In the Hiphil, the verb is used of the burning of animal sacrifices (see p. 194, note). In the Piel voice it is rendered *offer*, in connection with incense, in Num. 16. 40 ; 1 Chron. 6. 49 ; Jer. 11. 12, 17, 32. 29 ; and Amos 4. 5. The word θυμιάω is generally adopted for it in the LXX. See Rev. 5. 8, 8. 3, 4, 18. 13, for the use of this word in the N. T. We must distinguish incense from frankincense (**levonah**), which was one of its components. The R. V. has corrected the six places where they are confused by the A. V., namely, Isa. 43. 23, 60. 6, 66. 3 ; Jer. 6. 20, 17. 26, 41. 5.

§ 17. *The Freewill-Offering.*

The freewill-offering is always that which is given willingly, bountifully, liberally, or as a prince would give. The word **Nedavah** (נדבה, Ass. *nindabu*) refers not to the nature of the offering or to the external mode in which it is offered, but to the motive and spirit of the offerer. The most usual rendering in the LXX is ἑκούσιος. The verb occurs in Exod. **35**. 29, 'The children of Israel brought a willing offering unto the Lord ;' **36**. 3, 'They brought yet unto him free offerings every morning.'[1] In Lev. **7**. 16 it is called 'a voluntary offering.' In Jud. **5**. 2, 9, in Deborah's song the people are praised for offering themselves willingly. Again the word occurs in 1 Chron. **29**. 6, 9, 14, 17, with reference to the offerings made for the construction of the temple ; also in 2 Chron. **17**. 11 ; Ezra 1. 6, 2. 68, 3. 5, 7. 15, 16 ; Neh. **11**. 2. 'Free offerings' are also referred to in Ps. **54**. 6, **110**. 3, **119**. 108 ; Amos **4**. 5. It is used of the rain as a free gift of God in Ps. **68**. 9 ; and of His free love in Hos. **14**. 4.

§ 18. *The Wave-Offering and Heave-Offering.*

The wave-offering, **Tenuphah** (תנופה), was supposed to be shaken to and fro, whilst the heave-offering, **Terumah** (תרמה), was elevated. The LXX usually has ἀφαίρεμα, ἀφόρισμα, or ἐπίθεμα for the wave-offering, and ἀπαρχή, first-fruits, for the heave-offering. The verb which gives the name to the first is rendered to wave wherever this word is used in the A. V. ; in 2 Kings **5**. 11, Naaman expresses his supposition that Elisha would 'strike his hand over the place,' or as our margin has it, 'move his hand up and down.' Compare Isa. **30**. 28, where we read of God's 'sifting the nations with the sieve of vanity.' It is rendered shake in Isa. **10**. 15, *al.* The word is found in Ps. **68**. 9, 'Thou didst send (*i.e.* sift out from the clouds) a gracious rain upon thine inheritance.' In Exod. **20**. 25, Deut. **27**. 5, and Josh. **8**. 31, the lifting up (*i.e.* the movement to and fro) of the graving tool is spoken of.

The noun is rendered oblation in 2 Chron. **31**. 14, Isa. **40**. 20, and Ezek. **44**. 30 ; it is rendered 'offering' in Exod. **25**. 2, *al.*

---

[1] It is important to notice that when in Lev. **1**. 3 and elsewhere the A. V. reads, 'He shall offer it of his own *voluntary will*,' an entirely different word is used. These passages ought to be rendered, 'He shall offer it *for his acceptance*.'

CHAPTER XVII.

WORD, LAW, COVENANT.

IT was observed by the late Dr. McCaul[1] that 'whether we take the Hebrew Scriptures as true or not, it is an incontrovertible fact that the fundamental idea of the Hebrew religion is that Jehovah is a God who reveals Himself to His creatures; that He has not left the human race to grope their way to the regions of religion or morality as they best can, but that from the beginning He has taken His children by the hand, cared for their welfare, made known to them His will, and marked out for them the way to happiness.' In accordance with this undeniable fact, the Divine Being is represented as speaking by word of mouth with His creatures.

Under the general title 'the Word of the Lord' in the O. T. we find not only the law of the ten commandments (literally, *the ten words*) uttered by the Divine Voice on Mount Sinai, but also all the promises, warnings, precepts, prophecies, revelations of the Divine character, and messages of mercy, which proceeded from God through the medium of 'holy men of old.' In the Psalms and prophetical books the whole body of revealed truth, including all historical manifestations of God's righteous and merciful rule, appears to be referred to as the Word of the Lord. Occasionally the utterance of speech on God's part is taken as identical with the exertion of His power, as when we read that 'By the word of the Lord were the heavens made' (Ps. **33.** 6); and again, 'Man doth not live by bread alone, but by every word that proceedeth out of the mouth of God' (Deut. **8.** 3); and again, 'He sent his word and healed them' (Ps. **107.** 20). Throughout Scripture a distinction is drawn between *the Will of God* and the expression of that will or *the Word of God.* He was not content with willing that there should be light, but He *said,* 'Let there be light,' and there was light; thus without the Word was not anything made that was made (see John **1.** 3).

The mode of transmitting the message from God to man was

---

[1] See his Essay on 'Prophecy' in *Aids to Faith.*

by no means uniform. God said to Moses, 'Who hath made man's mouth? or who maketh the dumb or deaf or the seeing or the blind? have not I, the Lord? now therefore go, and I will be with thy mouth, and teach thee what thou shalt say' (Exod. 4. 11, 12). A little further we learn that Moses was to transmit the Divine message to his brother Aaron, and that he was to pass it on to the people; thus Moses was to be to Aaron in the place of God. This would imply the suggestion of the substance of what was to be said, though not necessarily the dictation of the words. In the remarkable instance of Jeremiah's prophecy (Jer. 36.) God spoke the words to Jeremiah, and he dictated them to Baruch, who wrote them down. In the vision in which Ezekiel received his special appointment as a messenger from God to Israel, he is directed to eat the roll on which the woes to be inflicted upon the people were recorded. Having thus made the message his own, he was to go forth with the words 'Thus saith the Lord.'

§ 1. *The Word.*

The most ordinary Hebrew terms setting forth the Divine utterances are **amar** (אמר), to say, and **davar** [1] (דבר), to speak. The former refers rather to the mode of revelation, and the latter to the substance. Hence **davar** is frequently rendered thing, as in Gen. 15. 1, 19. 8; compare Luke 1. 37. **Milah** (מלה) has also been rendered word in thirty passages, nineteen of which are in Job and seven in Daniel. It is used in 2 Sam. 23. 2, 'The spirit of the Lord spake by me, and his word was in my tongue;' Ps. 19. 4, 'Their words unto the end of the world.' In the LXX the verb **amar** is generally rendered ἔπω and λέγω, and the noun ῥῆμα and λόγιον; **davar** is generally rendered λαλέω, and the noun generally λόγος, sometimes ῥῆμα, and in thirty-five passages πρᾶγμα. **Milah** is rendered λόγος and ῥῆμα; and **Nam** (נאם), to utter or assert, which is rare in the earlier books and frequent in the later, is rendered λέγω. **Peh** (פה), mouth, is rendered word in Gen. 41. 40 and fourteen other passages.

In the N. T. 'the word of God' frequently stands for the truths contained in the O. T.; but it often stands for 'the Gospel,' *i.e.* the story of the life, teaching, death, resurrection, ascension, and second

---

[1] Whence **devir** (דביר) oracle, is derived. See 1 Kings 6. 5, and later passages.

coming of Christ, together with their bearing on human life and destiny.

Christ Himself is called 'THE WORD,' both at the beginning of St. John's Gospel and elsewhere; and though it is usually supposed that this title was given to Him by the Evangelist with especial reference to the philosophical theology current in his time, the usage of the O. T. is quite enough to justify and to suggest it.

The LXX usage of ῥῆμα and λόγος does not justify a profound distinction between these words in the N. T. The first, perhaps, stands for the utterance, and the second for the drift and reason of what is uttered. See 1 Pet. 1. 23, 25, where they are combined.

§ 2. *The Law.*

The general word for Law is **Torah** (תורה, Ass. *toretu*, the law of the gods). By this word the Pentateuch is universally described among the Jews to the present day. The verb (ירה) whence it is derived signifies to project, and hence to point out or teach. The law of God is that which points out or indicates His will to man. It is not an arbitrary rule, still less is it a subjective impulse; it is rather to be regarded as a course of guidance from above. The verb and noun are found together in Exod. 24. 12, 'I will give thee a law, and commandments which I have written, that thou mayest teach them.' It is generally, though imperfectly, represented in the LXX by the word νόμος.

Torah has been rendered law in all places but one, namely, 2 Sam. 7. 19, 'The manner of man,' literally, 'The law of the man.' In the parallel passage (1 Chron. 17. 17), **tor** (תור), which is evidently the same word, is rendered 'estate.'

Torah is first found in Gen. 26. 5, in connection with Abraham's loyalty to God. It frequently signifies ritual, custom, or prescriptive right. It is applied to specific ordinances, to groups of regulations and instructions, and to the books which contain them.

The word **Dath** (דת), an edict, usually a late word, is used as part of a compound word in Deut. 33. 2, 'From his right hand went a fiery-law for them.' This term is frequently adopted in Ezra, Esther, and Daniel. **Chok** (חק), a statute or decree, is frequently used, either in its masculine or feminine form, for the Divine statutes. It is rendered law in the following passages:— Gen. 47. 26, 'Joseph made it a law over the land of Egypt unto this day.' Gen. 49. 10, 'The sceptre shall not depart from Judah,

nor a law-giver from between his feet, until Shiloh come.' Num.
21. 18, 'The princes digged the well, the nobles of the people digged
it, by (the direction of) the law-giver.' Deut. 33. 21, 'He provided
the first part for himself, because there, in a portion of the law-giver,
was he seated.' 1 Chron. 16. 17, Ps. 105. 10, 'He confirmed the
same to Jacob for a law, and to Israel for an everlasting covenant.'
Ps. 60. 7, 108. 8, 'Judah is my law-giver' (a passage interesting
in connection with Gen. 49. 10, cited above). Ps. 94. 20, 'Shall
the throne of iniquity have fellowship with thee, which frameth
mischief by a law?' Prov. 31. 5, 'It is not for kings to drink
wine . . . lest they forget the law, and pervert the judgment of
any of the afflicted.' Isa. 33. 22, 'The Lord is our judge, the Lord
is our law-giver, the Lord is our king; he will save us.'

The most usual renderings of **Chok** in the LXX are δικαίωμα,
πρόσταγμα, and νόμιμον.

In Isa. 49. 24, 'the lawful captive' is literally 'the captivity
of the righteous;' in Jer. 32. 11 a word is used which signifies
'commandment;' in Ezra 7. 24, 'lawful' means 'permissible;'
whilst 'judgment' is the literal rendering in Lev. 24. 22; Ps. 81.
4; Ezra 18. 5, 19, 21, 27, 33. 14, 16, 19 ('lawful and right').

§ 3. *Commandment.*

The most general word for command or commandment is
some form of **tsavah** (צוה), which appears to signify literally *to set
up* or *appoint*. It is largely used from Gen. 2. 16 onward, and
applies to any order, human or divine. The general Greek renderings are ἐντέλλομαι, προστάττω, and ἐντολή.

Amar (אמר), to speak, is rendered 'command' in Exod. 8.
27 and forty-four other passages; and **Davar** (דבר), to speak, is
so rendered twenty times. What is spoken either by the Lord or
by any one of high authority is naturally looked upon as a commandment. With God, to speak is to command; and with man, to hear
ought to be to obey.[1] **Amar** is used in Job 9. 7, where we read
that God 'commandeth the sun and it riseth not'—the laws of
nature, their continuance, and their cessation, being equally regarded as the utterance of the Divine word. So God 'commandeth
and raiseth the stormy wind' (Ps. 107. 25); 'He sendeth forth his
commandment upon earth, his word runneth very swiftly' (Ps.
147. 15).

---

[1] The ordinary word for obedience in the O. T. literally signifies hearing.

Peh (פֶּה), mouth, is rendered 'commandment' in Gen. **45.**
21, Exod. **17.** 1, and thirty-two other passages. It is possibly an
Egyptian idiom, and may be compared with the use of the 'mouth'
as signifying *self* in Coptic. It occurs in Job **39.** 27, 'Doth the
eagle mount up at thy command?' in Prov. **8.** 29, 'He gave to the
sea his decree that the waters should not pass his commandment;'
Eccles. **8.** 2, 'Keep the king's commandment;' Lam. **1.** 18, 'I
have rebelled against his commandment.'

§ 4. *Charge or Precept.*

The word **Pekud** (פָּקוּד, Ass. *paqadu*) is properly a charge. It
is only found in the plural, and is always rendered precept except
in Ps. **103.** 18, **111.** 7. The general renderings of the verb are
ἐπισκέπτω, to visit, ἐκδικέω, to avenge, and καθίστημι, to appoint.
It is used of visitation, whether for purposes of mercy or for
purposes of chastisement. The substantive in the feminine form,
Pekudah (answering to ἐπίσκεψις or ἐπισκοπή), is found in the former
sense in Jer. **27.** 22 ; but in the latter sense in Isa. **10.** 3, 29. 6 ;
Jer. **6.** 15, 8. 12, 10. 15, 11. 23, 23. 12, 48. 44. In these cases the
context plainly decides the matter ; and though it is noticeable that
the instances of the *noun* being used of judgment preponderate, if
the passages where the *verb* is used were also cited this would not
be the case.

But the word has a further sense. It is often rendered ἐντολή
and δικαίωμα, and signifies a charge. Sometimes it denotes the
oversight or care which a responsible person is enjoined to take.
Thus we read in Num. **4.** 16 that Eleazar had the 'oversight'
(ἐπισκοπή) of all the tabernacle. It was put in his charge, and he
was responsible for its safe keeping. In Ps. **109.** 8 we read, 'Let
another take his office' (ἐπισκοπή), *i.e.* let another perform the
duties which are laid upon him. It is a pity that this passage has
not been translated more literally where it is quoted in the N. T.,
in Acts **1.** 20, where we read, 'His bishoprick let another take.'
The margin here very properly has 'office' or 'charge.' Whilst it
is true that a 'bishoprick' is an ἐπισκοπή, not only etymologically
but really, yet it does not follow that an ἐπισκοπή is a (modern)
'bishoprick.' This rendering, like many others, has come to us
from the Latin Vulgate. It was accepted by Wycliffe and Tyndale
without hesitation. See R. V.

The word ἐπίσκοπος answers to another form of **pakad**, and indicates the persons who have a charge or responsibility laid upon them, whether for military, civil, or religious purposes. The following are among the passages in which it occurs :—Num. **31**. 14, 'Moses was wroth with the o f f i c e r s of the host;' Jud. **9**. 28, 'Is not Abimelech the son of Jerubbaal? and Zebul his o f f i c e r?' 2 Chron. **34**. 12, 'The men did the work faithfully; and the over-seers of them were Jahath and Obadiah;' verse 17, 'They have delivered the money into the hand of the o v e r s e e r s, and to the hand of the workmen.' See also Neh. **11**. 9, 14.

§ 5. *Combination of Words in the* 119*th Psalm.*

In reading the 119th Psalm we are struck with the constant recurrence of various titles by which God's revelation of Right is described. In the first nine verses we find eight different titles given to the truth of God.[1] They are as follows :—

(1.) The law or **Torah**.

(2.) The word.

(3.) The commandments.

(4.) The statutes.

(5.) The precepts, **pekudim** (פקודים).

(6.) The ways. The word used throughout this Psalm for 'way' is **orech** (ארח), a course, journey, or pilgrimage; whilst in other parts of the Scripture **derec** (דרך), a path, is the expression used. Either word implies that man's course of life, thought, and desire ought to be brought into harmony and made coincident with God's.

(7.) The judgments. The word **mishpath** (משפט) is used twenty-one times in the Psalm, and seems to point to rules of righteous administration.

(8.) The testimonies. The word for 'testimony' is derived from 'od (עוד), to bear witness. It is used fourteen times in this Psalm, and in various other parts of the O. T. The law of God is His testimony, because it is His own affirmation concerning His nature, attributes, and consequent demands.

With exquisite beauty and with inspired depth of thought the writer of the 119th Psalm draws out these varied aspects of the Divine Truth, and presents the law of God in every light in which

[1] Compare Ps. **19**. 7, 8, 9, in which five words are used to designate God's law, namely, decree, testimony, statutes, commandments, and judgments.

the experience of a godly man can regard it. Certainly no student
of the Psalms can doubt that the pious Israelite found the revealed
will of God anything but a heavy burden or an intolerable yoke.
Whosoever trusted in the Most High soon learned to take pleasure
in God's commandments, and to realise their breadth and spirituality,
and he was thus enabled to love God's law as well as to long for
His salvation.

§ 6. *Teaching of the N. T.*

The word νόμος is very frequently used of the law of Moses,
which is regarded, both in the O. and N. T., as *one*, though containing many ἐντολαί or specified commandments (see Matt. 22. 36).
This law is also called the law of the Lord, because, though it was
given by Moses (John 1. 17), and by the disposition of angels (Acts
7. 53), it really represented the will of the Lord God (Luke 2. 23).

In the four Gospels and Acts the law is referred to fifty times,
and generally in the sense now mentioned; in some passages, however, it specially designates the books of Moses, according to the
ordinary Jewish mode of dividing the O. T.

In Rom. 2. 14 we have another sense of the word introduced.
The heathen nations have not [the [1]] law; but if it should be found
that they do the things of the law (*i.e.* act on those great principles
which lie at the root of the whole Mosaic legislation), then, though
they have not [the] law, they become a law to themselves, inasmuch
as they show forth in their outer life the results which the law
aimed at producing, and which were written not indeed on external
tables, but on their hearts; moreover, their consciousness and their
inmost convictions, which lead them to disapprove of one course of
action and approve of another, will bear witness with these outward
results in the Day when God shall form a judicial estimate of the
secrets of the heart.

With regard to the persons thus described, St. Paul says again,
in verses 26, 27, that the uncircumcision, *i.e.* the Gentiles, who
accomplish the law, will be reckoned as true Jews, and will judge
those Jews who have the letter of the law and circumcision, but
who nevertheless are transgressors.

---

[1] There is no definite article here, and hence some critics have doubted whether
the reference is made to the law of Moses, or whether the principle of *law* in the
abstract is to be understood. But this is probably one of the cases in which the
absence of the article ought not to be pressed.

In Rom. **5**. 14, St. Paul says that 'Up to the time that the law was given, *i.e.* from Adam to Moses, sin was in the world (and among the heathen nations which have not heard of Christ's salvation sin is still in the world; nor did the command that all men everywhere should repent go forth till the Day of Pentecost); but sin is not reckoned where there is no law; and yet death, the fruit and penalty of sin, reigned all this time, even on those whose sins were committed under far less aggravated circumstances than the transgression of Adam.' Hence we are left to imply that there is some law which all the heathen have transgressed, and that in all the children of men there has been such a departure from God as has justified Him in inflicting death. Sin was in them, though not in the form of rebellion against the law of Moses.

In other passages the word νόμος rather signifies order or principle. This is sometimes the case with **davar**, *word*, in the O. T., as in the familiar sentence, 'Thou art a priest for ever after the order of Melchizedek.'[1] In Rom. **3**. 27, St. Paul asks, 'On what principle (A. V. by what law) is a man accounted righteous? on the principle of works? no; on the principle of faith.' So again in Rom. **8**. 2, 'The binding principle of the spirit of life in Christ Jesus hath made me free from the binding principle of sin and death.'

In Rom. **7**. 2 the word is used in two senses, 'The married woman is bound by law (*i.e.* by the law of Moses) to her living husband; but if the husband dies she is liberated[2] from the bond or tie which had existed between the two parties.' So, carrying out the parallel, we may understand verse 6, 'Now we are liberated from the bond which connected us with the flesh, sin, and the letter of the law, for we have been identified through faith with the death of Christ—a death whereby sin was overcome, the flesh was made an instrument of good instead of evil, and the letter of the law had its complete fulfilment and consequent abolition.'

When St. Paul said, 'I was living without the law once' (Rom. **7**. 9), he seems to be referring to a part of his previous history during which sin lay dormant in him. But when the commandment came—*i.e.* some special commandment of the law which went against Paul's manner of life and natural dispositions—sin burst

---

[1] Some render these words, 'after *my word*, O Melchizedek.'

[2] The word κατηργήται is not an easy word to translate. It signifies a complete abolition of that relationship which had previously existed.

forth into a new life,[1] whilst I died, *i.e.* trespassed and so brought death on myself ; and the commandment in question which if I had kept it would have kept me in the way of life, proved practically a means of leading me to death. For sin, receiving an impetus (ἀφορμήν) from the commandment, deceived me (as it is the way of all sin to do, see Gen. 3. 13, 1 Tim. 2. 14, James 1. 14), and made use of the law of God to slay me. Perhaps Paul's reference to a point of his past history in Gal. 2. 19, may be explained in the same way, 'I through the law died to the law, that I might live to Christ,' *i.e.* the law taught me my sinfulness and led me to believe in Christ, and accordingly I did what all converted Jews must do— I died to the law, identifying myself with Christ in His death, that I might live no longer to myself, but to Him who died for me. The words διὰ νόμου might, however, be explained by a similar phrase in Rom. 2. 27 (διὰ γράμματος), as 'although I had the law,' or 'in spite of the law.'

We find δικαίωμα ten times in the N. T. In seven of these passages it conveys the O. T. word precept, namely, Luke 1. 6 ; Rom. 1. 32, 2. 26, 8. 4 (A. V. the righteousness of the law) ; Heb. 9. 1, 10 ; Rev. 15. 4. In Rev. 19. 8, we are obliged to render the word 'the righteousnesses of the saints ;' so in Rom. 5. 16, 'The gift is of many offences unto righteousness (A. V. justification) ; verse 18, 'by one righteousness' (A. V. by the righteousness of one).

The words ἐντέλλεσθαι and ἐντολή are used of the charges contained in the law. They are also applied to the orders given by Christ Himself, the new Lawgiver ; see Matt. 28. 20 ; John 15. 14, 17 ; Acts 1. 2, 13. 47. The latter class of passages shows that the Lord laid great stress on the keeping of His commandments. The ἐντολή spoken of in various verses of Rom. 7. was doubtless some portion of the Mosaic commandments ; but the 'holy commandment' of 2 Pet. 2. 21 must be referred to the charge laid down by our Lord ; see also 2 Pet. 3. 2.

The verb ἐπισκέπτομαι is used ten times in the N. T., and generally, if not always, signifies visitation for purposes of mercy. The kindred term ἐπισκοπεῖν is used in Heb. 12. 15 and 1 Pet. 5. 2, and denotes responsibility and watchfulness rather than rule.

---

[1] The word ἀνέζησε seems to imply that he had felt its power before, but that he had, as he thought, quite overcome it, so that he supposed it was dead. He had brought himself into complete harmony with the law as he imagined, but suddenly a special commandment in the law was pressed upon his attention, and brought out the old Adam in renewed vigour.

The Lord is called the Shepherd and Watcher over our souls or lives, 1 Pet. 2. 25. The apostles had a charge of the same kind, though more limited, Acts 1. 20; and the Ephesian elders are told to take heed to the flock over which the Holy Ghost had appointed them as watchers, Acts 20. 28. The word ἐπίσκοπος, which is found in these two places, gradually assumed a more technical sense, and stood for the *whole* office, of which this careful watching was only a part (1 Tim. 3. 1, 2, and Titus 1. 7).[1]

The word ἐπισκοπή occurs in Luke 19. 44, where the Lord spoke of the doom which was coming on Jerusalem, because she knew not the time of her v i s i t a t i o n. This was the visitation of God's mercy and grace in the Person of Christ, of whom it is said that 'He came unto his own (property), and his own (people) received him not.' Compare Luke 1. 68, 78, with John 1. 11. There is another day of visitation yet to come, in which the mercy of God in Christ will be more gloriously manifested. See 1 Pet. 2. 12.

§ 7. *Covenant.*

The Hebrew word for *covenant* is always **Berith** (ברית). This word is rendered διαθήκη in the LXX in every passage where it occurs, except Deut. 9. 15, where it is rendered μαρτύριον, testimony, and 1 Kings 11. 11, where it is rendered ἐντολή, commandment.

The word διαθήκη is confined to this one use in the LXX, with the exception of four passages, namely, Exod. 31. 7 and Lev. 26. 11, where it may represent a different Hebrew reading from that which we now possess; also Deut. 9. 5, where it stands for a 'word;' and Zech. 11. 14, where it is used of the 'brotherhood' (אחוה, Ass. *akhutu*) between Judah and Israel.

Translators have found much difficulty in giving a uniform rendering to the word **berith** even in the O. T. Expressions answering to the words a l l i a n c e, b o n d, c o m p a c t, c o v e n a n t, d i s p o s i-t i o n, t r e a t y, have been resorted to, but none of them are perfectly satisfactory, and for this reason, that while they represent the

---

[1] It has been said that 'in the incumbent of a large London parish, with curates, Scripture readers, district visitors, lay agents, and Sunday school teachers, dependent on his piety, zeal, vigour, ability, and force of character, for direction, stimulus, encouragement, superintendence and tone, we seem to have the best representative now in existence of the Primitive Bishop.' See *Church Missionary Intelligencer* for April 1871 ; and on the whole subject of the Primitive Christian ministry consult Dr. Lightfoot's Essay in his 'Commentary on the Epistle to the Philippians.'

nature of a covenant between man and man, none of them are adequate for the purpose of setting forth the nature of God's gracious dealings with man.   The translators of the LXX evidently felt the difficulty, and instead of using συνθήκη, which would be the natural word for a covenant, used διαθήκη, which means a legal Disposition, and hence a Testament.[1]   The Syriac version transliterates the Greek word.   The Arabic substitutes *'ahad*, a compact. The Spanish translator De Reyna, after discussing in the Preface to his Bible the words *Concierto*, *Pacto*, and *Allianza*, comes to the conclusion that none of them are good, because what is needed is a word which signifies an agreement ' made in conjunction with the ceremonial death [2] of an animal ' (*hecho con solemne rito de muerte de algun animal*).   On the whole, however, he thought it better to use a word which was an imperfect representation of **berith** than to reproduce the word and thus convey no sense at all.

The Lord Jesus is called the mediator of the new Covenant, because He is the medium wherein the Disposition of God is carried into effect, whether as regards the individual or the race as a whole (Heb. 8. 6, 9. 15, and 12. 24).   The inheritance which was given by *promise* to Christ (Gal. 3. 16) was conveyed by *covenant* (through His blood-shedding) to all believers (Gal. 3. 17, 29), who are made *one* with Him by faith; and it is this union of God with man, and of man with God, in Christ, which is summed up in the N. T. sense of the word **berith**.

The crucial passage in the N. T. is Heb. 9. 17, which the R. V. renders, ' A testament is of force where there has been death : for doth it ever avail while he that made it liveth ?'   This rendering does not go far to reduce the difficulty.   The real point which the passage brings out is that the victim represents the makers of the covenant, *i.e.* the contracting parties, and they could only be united representatively in the victim by means of its death.   So in the death of Christ man and God are made one.   It is a covenant, not a last will and testament, which is in the writer's mind.

---

[1] *Testamentum*, literally something attested or borne witness to, but always used of a will whereby we dispose of our goods.

[2] The idea of blood-shedding in connection with the Abrahamic covenant was sustained in the memory of Israel by the rite of circumcision.   See Acts 7. 8.

CHAPTER XVIII.

WORSHIP, PRAISE, PREACH.

Two classes of words are put together in this chapter. *First,* there are those adopted in Scripture to set forth man's public and private expression of his dependence on God, and of his thankfulness to the Being who 'giveth to all men liberally and upbraideth not.' Prayer and praise are uniformly regarded in Scripture as actions well-pleasing to God; they are based on an acknowledgment of His Personality, of His greatness, and of His power and willingness to interfere in the temporal and spiritual affairs of men. *Secondly,* there are the words by which the Hebrews set forth the mode of conveying truth from man to man. In each case there is something of that pictorial power to which attention has been called in previous chapters.

§ 1. *Worship.*

The word **worship** is the general representative of the Hebrew **Shachah** (שחה), and of the Greek προσκυνεῖν. The following are the only exceptions:—The Chaldean word **Segid** (סגד) is used in Dan. 2. 46, where we read that the king prostrated himself before Daniel, and commanded that they should offer sweet odours and an oblation unto him; it is also used throughout the third chapter for the prostration or worship which was to be offered to the image of gold. **'Atsav** (עצב) is found in Jer. 44. 19, where it appears to signify the fashioning of cakes as images of 'the queen of heaven.' The words 'did we make her cakes to worship her?' might be rendered 'did we make her cakes to represent her?' In 2 Kings 10. the word used for the worshippers of Baal is **'Eved,** which signifies a servant or slave.

Shachah originally signified prostration as a mark of respect, and is applied in Scripture not only to God and to false gods, but also to men, just as the English word 'worship' is used of the husband's reverence for his wife in the marriage service of the English

Church, and is retained as a title of respect for a civil magistrate. **Shachah** is also rendered in the A. V. by the words bow, stoop, crouch, fall down, beseech humbly, make obeisance, and do reverence. It is used of Abraham's reverent prostration before his three angelic visitors (Gen. **18.** 2), and of his obeisance before the Hittites (Gen. **23.** 7, 12); it occurs in the blessing which Isaac gave to Jacob, 'Let nations bow down to thee : let thy mother's sons bow down to thee' (Gen. **27.** 29); Jacob himself bows down or prostrates seven times on meeting Esau (Gen. **33.** 3, 6, 7); Joseph dreams that he receives this worship from his parents and brethren (Gen. **37.** 10), and he *does* receive it (Gen. **42.** 6). See also Gen. **48.** 12, **49.** 8; Exod. **11.** 8; Ruth **2.** 10; 1 Sam. **20.** 41, **24.** 8.

In Gen. **47.** 31 we read that Israel bowed himself (worshipped or prostrated) on the bed's head, or, according to the LXX, as quoted in Heb. **11.** 21, on the top of his staff. Various explanations are given of this statement. The difference between the LXX and the Hebrew depends not upon the letters, but upon the vowel points. On comparing the passage with others in which the same verb is used with the same preposition in Hebrew and in the LXX, it will be seen that the top of the rod was not that which he *leaned* upon, as might seem to be implied by the italics in the A. V., but that which he *touched with his forehead* in the act of prostration ; and the only question remains, whether the worship thus offered was directed to Joseph, in fulfilment of the dream and in reverence for his high office, or whether it was directed to God, in accordance with whose promise Jacob exacted an oath from Joseph concerning the transmission of his bones to Canaan ; or finally, whether by faith he saw in Joseph a type or foreshadowing of the true deliverer of the people. De Sacy, in his French version, gives an interpretation to which Calvin is very much inclined also. Bearing in mind the Egyptian custom of carrying a staff of authority, such as may still be seen graven on the walls of the ancient temples, he holds that Jacob bowed to the staff which Joseph bore in his hand, and thereby recognised his son's secular authority and fulfilled the dream of Joseph.

Turning to the more directly religious use of the word **Shachah**, it may be observed that the worship of God was to be carried out by the people themselves, and was not done for them by the priest. It was not only to consist of outward prostration, such as they offered as a mark of reverence to one another, or such as the heathen offered to their false gods, but was to be accompanied by the devotion of the heart. The annual keeping of the three feasts was considered a mark of worship (1 Sam. **1**. 3). See also 1 Sam. **15**. 25 ; 2 Sam. **12**. 20 ; 2 Kings **18**. 22 ; Ps. **5**. 7, **29**. 2, **132**. 7, **138**. 2 ; Isa. **27**. 13.

Reverent worship was to be offered in later days to the Messiah, as seems evident from Ps. **22**. 27, ' All the kindreds of the nations shall worship before thee ; ' verse 29, 'All they that be fat upon earth shall eat and worship ; all they that go down to the dust shall bow before him ; ' Ps. **45**. 11, ' He is thy Lord ; and worship thou him ; ' Isa. **49**. 7, ' Thus saith the Lord, . . . to him whom man despiseth, to him whom the nation abhorreth, to a servant of rulers, Kings shall see and arise, princes also shall worship, because of the Lord.'

With regard to the heathen, the prophet's assurance is not only that their old worship is evil, but that ' Men shall worship God, every one from his own place, even all the isles of the heathen ' (Zeph. **2**. 11). Each man, whether in this mountain or in that, was to render true allegiance to God. And this prediction is fully consistent with others which speak of all going up to Jerusalem and to the temple of the Lord to worship, as in Isa. **66**. 20–23 ; Ezek. **46**. 2–9 ; Zech. **14**. 16, 17.

§ 2. *N. T. Teaching.*

The witness of the N. T. is very interesting in connection with the prophetic passages cited above. We find, for instance, that our Lord received w o r s h i p from the Magi (Matt. **2**. 8, 11), from the leper (Matt. **8**. 2), from the ruler (Matt. **9**. 18), from His disciples after He had calmed the storm (Matt. **14**. 33), from the Canaanitish woman (Matt. **15**. 25), from Salome (Matt. **20**. 20), from the blind man (John **9**. 38), and from His disciples after His resurrection (Matt. **28**. 9, 17). It has been thought that this was only civil worship, and that it was paid to Jesus as a mark of respect or gratitude. But was it so in all cases ? Did not the man whose eyes had been opened by Jesus Christ mean something more than civil worship when he prostrated himself before Him on hearing that He was the Son of God ? Did not the disciples mean something more than civil worship when they bowed before their risen Lord ? And it may be fairly asked whether the Lord would have permitted it to be paid to Him unless He were worthy to receive it ? Surely not. He would have said, as Peter did to Cornelius when he fell at his feet and worshipped, ' Stand up, for I also am a man '

(Acts **10**. 26). He would have said, as the angel did to St. John, when acting in the same way, 'See thou do it not, for I am thy fellow servant: worship God' (Rev. **19**. 10, **22**. 9). The truth is that in receiving worship from men, the Lord Jesus Christ was assuming to Himself the right of the First Begotten, of whom the Lord had said, 'Let all the angels of God worship him' (Heb. **1**. 6). Compare Rev. **5**. 11–14, where there is an ascription of 'Blessing and honour and glory and power for ever and ever to him that sitteth on the throne *and to the Lamb.*'

Various instances of worship or adoration are found in the N. T. in addition to the passages now referred to. When Satan tempted the Lord to fall down and worship him, the answer given from Deut. **6**. 13 was, 'Thou shalt w o r s h i p the Lord thy God, and him only shalt thou serve.' Evidently stress is here laid on the word *worship*, and yet when we turn to the Hebrew and to the LXX in the passage in question, we find 'Thou shalt f e a r,' &c. Worship, then, is regarded by our Lord as the expression of reverential fear; and what Satan called for was recognised as an act of that kind which should only be offered to God.

In our Lord's conversation with the woman of Samaria, the word προσκυνεῖν occurs nine times in the course of five verses, and the true principle of worship is clearly enunciated. The spirituality of worship, however, was not intended to supersede all external forms in religion, as may be shown by the fact that the worship of God, as manifested in outward prostration, is referred to in later times (see 1 Cor. **14**. 25 ; Rev. **4**. 10, **5**. 14, **19**. 10). The movements of the body may therefore still be allowed to represent outwardly the feelings of the spirit. External ceremonial is not done away with in the present dispensation, though its relative importance is considerably reduced, and every place is hallowed ground.

The word σέβομαι, answering to **yara** (ירא), to fear, is occasionally found in the LXX, and is used several times in the Acts (never in the Epistles), generally with reference to outsiders who had been led to look with reverence on the God of Israel. See Acts **13**. 43, 50, **16**. 14, **17**. 4, 17, **18**. 7, 13, **19**. 27.

The word δόξα is used in Luke **14**. 10, where the A. V. has 'Thou shalt have w o r s h i p in the presence of them that sit at meat with thee.' This rendering is as old as Coverdale, but Tyndale's rendering 'praise' is better, and 'glory' would be still more literal. See R. V.

§ 3. *Prayer.*

Twelve Hebrew words have been rendered by the English word 'pray' in the O. T. Two are interjections, namely, **ana** (אנא) and **na** (נא), the former of which is found in Gen. **50.** 17, and the latter in Gen. **12.** 13, **18.** 4, and Jud. **9.** 38. **Chanan** (חן), to be gracious, when used in the reflexive or causative sense, signifies to seek the favour of another; see, for example, 2 Chron. **6.** 37.

Palal (פלל), in the reflexive, 'to cause another to intervene or arbitrate in one's case,' is found very frequently, and is generally represented by the Greek προσεύχομαι. This word conveys a very *objective* idea about prayer. It shows that men were not in the habit of praying merely as a relief to their feelings, but in order to ask another Being, wiser and mightier than they, to take up their cause.

In Job **22.** 27 and **33.** 26, the word **'atar** (עתר), to entreat, is used. In Job **21.** 15 a different word is used, namely, **paga** (פגע), which signifies to meet, 'What profit shall we have if we meet [1] him' (to supplicate his mercy)? In Isa. **26.** 16 we read, 'Lord, in trouble have they visited thee, they poured out a prayer when thy chastening was upon them.' Here **lachash** (לחש), to whisper, is used, in order to convey the idea of the secret and sorrowful sighing of the oppressed. This word is usually rendered enchantment.

Shaal (שאל, Ass. *sâlu*), to ask, whether in the sense of inquiry or petition, whence the name of *Saul* is derived, occurs in Ps. **122.** 6, where it is adopted for the sake of alliteration, 'Pray for the peace of Jerusalem;' **Sichah** (שיחה), meditation or complaint, is used in Job **15.** 4; Ps. **55.** 17, **64.** 1.

In Ezra **6.** 10 we find **Tsala** (צלא), to request; in Dan. **6.** 11, **Ve'ah** (בעה) to seek; and in Dan. **9.** 13 a composite phrase is adopted, which probably means to conciliate the face of a person, and hence to pray with some prospect of success.

With regard to the act of prayer as represented by the word προσεύχομαι in the N. T., it may be noticed in passing that it is never mentioned in St. John's Gospel or Epistles. Prayer was to

---

[1] This word is used in Isa. **47.** 3, 'I will not meet (thee as) a man;' Isa. **64.** 5, 'Thou meetest him that rejoiceth.' Also in Isa. **53.** 6 (Hiphil), 'The Lord hath laid (margin, 'made to meet') on him the iniquity of us all;' and in verse 12, 'He made intercession for the transgressors;' He was as it were a common meeting-ground between God and the sinner.

be offered⁻'in spirit' (Eph. **6.** 18).[1] It appears to have been
generally directed to God the Father.   The only exception is Acts
1. 24, where the disciples are apparently described as praying
to their Ascended Master.   Compare Acts **7.** 59, where Stephen
appealed to the Lord Jesus.

§ 4. *Praise and Blessing.*

The praises of God are set forth very largely in the O. T., and
are represented by two or three words.   The most general is **Hallal**
(הלל, Ass. *ellu*, 'bright'), whence comes the word *Hallelu-jah,*[2]
'Praise the Lord.'   Its original meaning is to s h i n e, then to m a k e
clear, and afterwards to e x c l a i m in a loud tone.   It is perhaps
something more than a coincidence that the Greek δοξάζω, to
glorify, which is often used of the praise of God, should also refer
in the first instance to the making clear, bright, or shining.
The LXX rendering for **Hallal**, however, is not δοξάζω, but αἰνέω,
ἐπαινέω, or καυχάομαι.

Another word largely used in the Psalms, and from which the
Hebrew name for a psalm is derived, is **Zamar** (זמר), to sing praise
to God.   With the exception of the Book of Psalms, it is only found
in Jud. **5.** 3 and 2 Sam. **22.** 50.   This word is rendered ψάλλω in
the LXX, whence the English 'psalm.'   See Rom. **15.** 9; 1 Cor.
14. 15; Eph. **5.** 19; and James **5.** 13.

Barac (ברך, Ass. *baraku*), to bless (whence the name **Beracah**
in 2 Chron. **20.** 26), literally, to k n e e l, is translated 'praise' in
Jud. **5.** 2 and Ps. **72.** 15; and it is to be noticed that blessing
signifies not only the act of a superior to an inferior, but also
the expression of grateful praise proceeding from the inferior and
ascending to the superior.   The usual Greek translation of this word
is εὐλογέω.

Barac is the word used in the important promise, 'In thy seed
shall all the families of the earth be blessed.'   This promise was
uttered on five different occasions; in three passages (Gen. **12.** 3,
18. 18, and **28.** 14) the verb is used in the Niphal or passive voice;

---

[1] A. V. 'in *the* Spirit.'   There is no article in the Greek; the words therefore seem an exact parallel to our Lord's description of worship, that it is to be
' in spirit and in truth.'   But see Jude 20.

[2] This word is sometimes spelt *alleluia* in modern hymn-books, in imitation of
the mode of spelling which found favour in mediæval times.   The letter H ought
certainly to be restored at both ends.

in the other two, however (namely, Gen. 22. 18 and 26. 4), the Hithpael or reflexive voice is adopted, so that we might render 'In thy seed shall all the nations of the earth bless themselves.' The same is the case in Deut. 29. 19 ; Jer. 4. 2 ; Ps. 72. 17 ; and Isa. 65. 16. But, after all, the difference is not so great, for whilst the passive signifies that the blessing is a gift of God, the Hithpael appears to signify that the blessing received from God produces fruit in the life; and those who bless themselves in God indicate by this expression that they acknowledge their blessings to be summed up in Him.

Yadah (ידה), to set forth, or confess publicly, whether in the way of praise or otherwise, whence the name **Judah**, is found in a great many passages, the first instances being in Gen. 29. 35 and 49. 8. It occurs chiefly in the Psalms. The verb is generally rendered ἐξομολογέω in the LXX, the noun αἴνεσις.

The only other word to be noticed is **Shavach** (שבח), to praise and commend, which is used four times in the Psalms, once in Ecclesiastes (4. 2), and five times in Daniel.

The verb αἰνέω is only used in the N. T. with reference to the praise of God ; but the compound ἐπαινέω is not so restricted. The verb καυχάομαι occurs very frequently in St. Paul's Epistles, but is not found in any other book of the N. T., except in James 1. 9 and 4. 16. When used in a good sense, it signifies that sort of boasting or rejoicing which manifests itself in giving praise to God. Whilst εὐχαριστία is the rendering of thanks to God, εὐλογία generally signifies in the N. T. the bestowing of blessing on man. There is, however, a close relationship between these acts. When our Lord broke the bread and distributed it through the disciples among the five thousand, He *gave thanks* (εὐχαριστήσας), John 6. 11 ; but St. Matthew (14. 19) tells us that on the same occasion He *blessed* (εὐλόγησε). Again, at the Last Supper, we read that when He had *given thanks*, He broke the bread (Luke 22. 19, 1 Cor. 11. 24), and also taking the cup when He had *given thanks* He gave it to them (Mark 14. 23) ; but we are also told that He *blessed* and brake the bread (Mark 14. 22), and the cup is described as the cup of *blessing* which we bless (1 Cor. 10. 16). Thus the giving of thanks to God is the means of conferring a blessing on men. It is true that the word bless, when used with God as its object, signifies the praising Him or speaking good of His name, but still the relationship just pointed out really exists, and may fairly be gathered from the word.

The word εὐλογητός, blessed, is only used of God and of Christ; but εὐλογημένος is used more generally. The verb is often used to express the blessing promised to Abraham and conveyed to the faithful in Christ.

The word ἐξομολογεῖν is used in the N. T. of an open or public confession, whether of sins [1] (Matt. 3. 6, Mark 1. 5, Acts 19. 18, James 5. 16), or of the praise of God (Matt. 11. 25, Luke 10. 21, Rom. 14. 11, 15. 9, Phil. 2. 11, Rev. 3. 5). The use of the word in Luke 22. 6 implies that Judas made an open avowal before the priests that he would betray the Lord.

§ 5. *Preaching.*

The word preach means either to *tell good tidings* or to *proclaim.* The first idea is represented by **Basar** (בשׂר), εὐαγγελίζομαι. to evangelise; the second by **Kara** (קרא, Ass. *qaru*), κηρύσσω. Basar is used in Isa. 61. 1, 'To preach good tidings to the meek;' and in the same verse **Kara** is rendered 'proclaim' —'to proclaim liberty to the captives.' Basar is rendered preach in one other passage, namely, Ps. 40. 9, 'I have preached righteousness in the great congregation.' Here the use of the word is important. It was not a mere proclamation of righteousness, but the announcing of good tidings concerning righteousness that the Psalmist refers to; and this point is confirmed and expounded by the following verse, where we read, 'I have not hid thy righteousness within my heart: I have declared thy faithfulness and thy salvation: I have not concealed thy lovingkindness and thy truth from the great congregation.'

This word is translated 'publish' in 1 Sam. 31. 9, and in 2 Sam. 1. 20; also in Ps. 68. 11, where we read, 'The Lord gave the word: great was the company of those that published it' (Prayer Book version, 'Great was the company of the preachers'). The word is here in the feminine gender, and reference is made to the bands of women who proclaimed the good tidings of a victory. An

---

[1] Only three kinds of confession are recognised in Scripture,—secret confession to God, which is followed by pardon from Him; confession to our neighbour when we have injured him; and public confession before the congregation where a public offence has been committed. In the lapse of time it was found that these public confessions sometimes created scandals, and private confessions were allowed to take their place; but these have gradually grown into a system, called, indeed, the confessional, but which is not, properly speaking, so much open confession as secret examination.

instance of this custom may be found in 1 Sam. **18**. 6, 7. The same word is used in 1 Chron. **16**. 23, Ps. **96**. 2, and Isa. **60**. 5, 6.

Basar is only once used where evil tidings were to be given, namely, in 1 Sam. **4**. 17, where we read that 'The messenger answered and said, Israel is fled before the Philistines.'

Kara, to call or proclaim, is rendered 'preach' in Neh. **6**. 7, 'Thou hast appointed prophets to preach (*i.e.* proclaim) of thee at Jerusalem, saying, There is a king in Judah;' Jonah **3**. 2, 'Arise, go unto Nineveh, that great city, and preach unto it the preaching that I bid thee.' It is usually rendered to call, cry, name, bid, invite, proclaim, publish. It also signifies to read aloud, the only kind of reading ever referred to in the O. T. In this sense it is used more than thirty times. Hence the name **Karaite**, as applied to that sect of Jews which confines its teaching to that which may be gained from the reading of the O. T.; and **Keri**, the word which signifies what is to be read as opposed to what is written (**Chetib**) in those passages of the Hebrew Scriptures in which MSS. differ. Another sense in which the word **Kara** is frequently used is to mark naming; also invocation, or calling upon the name of the Lord, *e.g.* Gen. **4**. 26, which our translators have rendered, 'Then began men to call upon the name of the Lord' (margin, 'to call themselves by the name of the Lord'). Luther renders, 'Then began men to preach concerning the name of the Lord.'[1]

In 1 Kings **8**. 43 we find **Kara** used in both its senses. 'Hear thou in heaven thy dwelling-place, and do according to all that the stranger calleth to thee for, that all the peoples of the earth may know thy name to fear thee, as do thy people Israel; and that they may know that this house which I have builded is called by thy name.'

The LXX usually retained the distinction between these two aspects of the verb **Kara**, which is represented by προσκαλέω. In the active and passive voices this Greek word is always used for to name and to be named; but in the middle voice it signifies to invoke or call upon a person. Instances of the former sense will be found in Num. **21**. 3, 'He called the name of the place Hormah;' Deut. **15**. 2, 'It is called the Lord's release;' Isa. **43**. 7, 'Every one that is called by my name;' Dan. **9**. 18, 'Behold the city which is called by thy name;' Amos **9**. 12, 'All the heathen that are called by my name.' The middle

---

[1] '*Zu predigen von des Herrn Namen.*' The LXX has ἐπικαλεῖσθαι.

voice is adopted in the following passages :—Gen. **12.** 8, 'He builded an altar unto Jehovah, and called upon the name of Jehovah ;' Deut. **4.** 7, 'What nation is there so great, who hath God so nigh unto them, as Jehovah our God is in all things that we call upon him for?' See also Prov. **21.** 13; Isa. **55.** 6, **64.** 7; Jonah **1.** 6; Zech. **13.** 9.

The word rendered **Preacher** in the Book of Ecclesiastes is **Koheleth** (קהלת), which is rendered ἐκκλησιάστης in the LXX, whence we have derived the name of the book. It is generally supposed to signify one who convokes an assembly, from **Kahal** (see chap. xix.). The noun is in the feminine form, perhaps to mark dignity or office. Some critics, however, connect the word with a cognate Arabic root, and translate it *the Penitent*.

The verb κηρύσσω, to proclaim, is found about sixty times in the N. T., and κήρυγμα eight times. It is used of the public reading of the law of Moses (Acts **15.** 21), and of the declaration of the Gospel of Christ. Where this word is used, more stress is laid on the publicity of the proclamation than on the nature of the news itself. It has been observed that it is this word, not εὐαγγελίζομαι, which is found in 1 Pet. **3.** 19, a passage which is usually considered to refer to the notification of the fulfilment of the Divine purposes in Christ, made to a special portion of the spirits of the departed.[1]

§ 6. *Teaching.*

Twelve Hebrew words are used to convey the idea of teaching in the O. T. In Deut. **6.** 7, 'Thou shalt teach them diligently unto thy children,' the word **Shanan** (שנן), to whet or sharpen, is used. Here the idea seems to be not so much the sharpening of the children's understanding as the plying of the Divine statutes to and fro in their hearts, and the setting forth God's truth in all its aspects. In 2 Chron. **30.** 22, where we are told that the Levites 'taught the good knowledge of the Lord,' the word **Sacal** (שכל, Ass. *sukhallu*, 'intelligence'), to make wise,'[2] is used, to mark

---

[1] In 1 Pet. **4.** 6 the word εὐαγγελίζομαι is used. See Alford's note.

[2] This word, which is almost always used in the Hiphil voice, seems to signify sometimes the receiving and sometimes the giving of instruction. In Dan. **12.** 3, the words 'they that *be wise*' might be rendered 'they *that teach.*' **Sacal** has sometimes been rendered **prosper**, as in Jer. **23.** 5, 'A king shall reign and prosper;' but it may here signify do wisely, or give instruction. The title of several of the Psalms, **maschil**, is derived from it. The LXX usually renders it συνίημι and σύνεσις.

the fact that the Levites were not content with superficial teaching. The same word is found in Prov. **16**. 23, ' The heart of the wise teacheth his mouth.' In Isa. **43**. 27, ' Thy teachers have transgressed against me,' the marginal rendering 'interpreters' is probably the best, reference being made to the expositors (מלּיץ) of the law. In Prov. **31**. 1, and Ezek. **23**. 48, **Yasar** (יסר), ' to chasten,' is used, a word which answers to the Greek παιδεύω, by which it is usually rendered, the instruction often involving chastisement. In Ps. **105**. 22 we find **Chacam** (חכם), a word often heard in a modern Jewish school, and cognate with the Arabic **hakim**, a wise man. In Exod. **18**. 20 the word used is **Zahar** (זהר), to illuminate, and hence to warn. Thus the analogy of spiritual and intellectual light was set before Israel at the beginning of their history. This is the word rendered shine in Dan. **12**. 3.

Alaph (אלף), a verb connected with the first letter of the Hebrew alphabet, is found in Job 33. 33, ' I shall teach thee wisdom,' and 35. 11, (God) ' teacheth us more than the beasts of the earth, and maketh us wiser than the fowls of heaven.' It is also found in chap. **15**. 5, ' Thy mouth uttereth (margin, teacheth) thine iniquity.' Compare Prov. **22**. 25, ' Lest thou learn his ways.' Evil, like good, has its alphabet. **Davar** (דבר), to speak or to broach a subject, is used in Jer. **28**. 16, and **29**. 32, ' Thou hast taught rebellion against the Lord.' The so-called prophetic utterances of Hananiah had really been rebellious words. **Bin** (בין), ' to make to understand,' is found in 1 Chron. **25**. 8, where the teacher is put in contrast, or rather in company, with the scholar ; it also occurs in 2 Chron. **35**. 3, and Neh. **8**. 9, with reference to the teaching of the Levites. **Yada'** (ידע, Ass. *idu*), ' to make to know,' is used in Deut. **4**. 9, and Jud. **8**. 16, ' He taught the men of Succoth,' *i.e.* gave them a lesson which they would not readily forget. Compare 2 Chron. **23**. 13 ; Ezra **7**. 25 ; Job 32. 7, 37. 19 ; Ps. **90**. 12 ; Prov. **9**. 9 ; and Isa. **40**. 13.

Lamad (למד, Ass. *lamadu*), whence the name **Talmud** is derived, is frequently used ; it signifies to *chastise*, and hence to *teach*, and is rendered διδάσκω and μανθάνω. Also **Yarah** (ירה), to *cast forth*, hence to *guide or direct*, is applied to teaching several times. The master and the scholar in Mal. **2**. 12 are literally the awakener and the answerer. It is the teacher's business to awaken thought in the heart of the pupil, and it is the scholar's business to answer to the test to which his understanding is put.

CHAPTER XIX.

TEMPLE, TABERNACLE, CONGREGATION, CHURCH.

THE identification in name between a building set apart for sacred purposes and the worshippers who meet therein may be traced back to the days of Moses, perhaps to an earlier period. The people of Israel were to be a spiritual house, and God was to dwell among them, as in a tabernacle. In the N. T., Christians are described in almost the same terms.

§ 1. *Temple.*

The ordinary Hebrew name for the temple was **Haical** (היכל, Ass. *ekallu,* 'palace'); this word, however, does not necessarily denote a sacred edifice. It is translated palace[1] in 1 Kings 21. 1; 2 Kings 20. 18; Ps. 45. 15; Isa. 13. 22, 39. 7, 44. 28, *al.* It ought also to have been so translated in Hos. 8. 14, where we read in the A. V., 'Israel hath forgotten his Maker, and buildeth temples;' the context shows that palaces are here referred to. (See R. V.) In these passages the LXX usually adopts the rendering οἶκος, house. The **Haical** was evidently regarded as the King's house, the dwelling-place of One who is highly exalted. The more general word for a palace (ארמון) is never used of the temple, as it rather signifies a fortress than a dwelling-place. This word first occurs in 1 Kings 16. 18 and 2 Kings 15. 25, where the palace, *i.e.* the fortified part of the King's house, is referred to. Before the temple was built the tabernacle was regarded as God's **Haical** (1 Sam. 1. 9, 3. 3; 2 Sam. 22. 7), though a curtained tent might seem unworthy of such a title. The general Greek rendering for the word **Haical**, when applied to the temple, is ναός.

Another word rendered temple is **Beth** (בית, Ass. *bitu*), a house. This is the only word used for a house in the O. T., except in Ps. 83. 12, where we find the word **Naoth** (נאות), which signifies

---

[1] The word palace is derived from the name of one of the seven hills on which Rome was built.

pastures or pleasant places; and in Job 1. 3, where not a house, but a household of servants (עבדה), is really spoken of. **Beth** is rendered temple in 2 Kings 11. 10, 11, 13; 1 Chron. 6. 10, 10. 10; 2 Chron. 23. 10, 35. 20.

The sanctuary is literally that which is holy (קדש), or, in other words, that which is set apart for sacred uses; see chap. xv.

§ 2. *Tabernacle.*

The usual word for a tabernacle is **Ohel** (אהל), which properly means a tent. Another word frequently rendered tent is **Mishcan** (משכן, Ass. *maskanu*), the ordinary word for a dwelling-place,[1] which is found in Cant. 1. 8, 'Besides the shepherds' tents.' **Kubbah** (קבה, Ass. *qubbu*), a dome or vault (compare the modern Arabic **kubbet**), is found in Num. 25. 8, where we read, 'He went after the man of Israel into the tent;' **Sucah** (סכה, Ass. *sukku*), a booth (whence the name **Succoth**), is used by David in 2 Sam. 11. 11, where he says, 'The ark, and Israel, and Judah, abide in tents.' **Machaneh** (מחנה) is a camp, or company, hence the name **Mahanaim** (two hosts). See Gen. 32. 2, 7, 8, 10, 21, and compare 1 Chron. 12. 22, 2 Chron. 14. 13, 31. 2, Cant. 6. 13. It is translated 'tent' in Num. 13. 19; 1 Sam. 17. 53; 2 Kings 7. 16; Zech. 14. 15; and also in 2 Chron. 31. 2, where it is applied in the plural form to the temple of God.

The LXX has various renderings for **Ohel**, but the most general are σκηνή, σκήνωμα, and οἶκος. **Mishcan**, a dwelling-place, which stands for the same Greek word, is rendered tabernacle in about a hundred and twenty passages in the A. V.

Where the Feast of Tabernacles is referred to, **Sucah** is used. It probably means a place of shade or shelter, hence a booth, tent, or pavilion. The rendering cottage in Isa. 1. 8 is hardly accurate. In Job 36. 29 we read, 'Can any one understand the spreadings of the clouds, or the noise of his tabernacle?' Here reference is made to the heavens, either as God's place of shelter—His hiding-

---

[1] These words are found together in Exod. 26. 7, the covering (**Ohel**) upon the tabernacle (**Mishcan**), and in other passages. The **Mishcan** is evidently the structure as a whole, regarded as the **Shekinah** or dwelling-place of God; whilst the **Ohel** was the awning of goat's hair. The word which the A. V. and R. V. perversely render the door of the tabernacle is not a door at all, but an opening or entrance.

place—or to the clouds as a shade for the earth.[1]　The word is used again in Ps. 76. 2, 'In Salem is his tabernacle, and his dwelling-place in Zion.'　See also Isa. 4. 6.

In Amos 5. 26, 'Ye have borne the tabernacle of Moloch,' there may be reference to a movable tent in which the images of false gods were placed.　The marginal rendering, '**Siccuth** your king,' is endorsed by the Masoretic punctuation, is accepted by Luther and by the R.V., and may be illustrated by the name of the Assyrian god *Sakkut*.　But the quotation in St. Stephen's speech (Acts 7. 43) follows the LXX, and is confirmed by the implied contrast with another tabernacle of which we read in Amos 9. 11, where the same word is used, 'I will raise up the tabernacle of David that is fallen down, and will close up the breaches thereof.'　With this passage may be compared the complaint of Jeremiah concerning the temple at Jerusalem: God 'hath violently taken away his tabernacle (σκήνωμα), as if it were a garden: he hath destroyed his places of assembly; the Lord hath caused the solemn feasts and sabbaths to be forgotten in Zion.'　The word for 'tabernacle' here, **Sak** (שׂך), though spelt differently, is from a cognate root.　Some render it **hedge** or **fence**, but perhaps it signifies **shelter** or **covering**, and so is applicable to the 'tabernacle of David.'

§ 3. *Congregation.*

The general word for congregation is **Kahal** (קהל).　It properly signifies an assembly or assemblage, and is applied to all sorts of gatherings, whether for war, for complaint, for listening to instruction, or for any similar purpose.

The verb is first used of the gathering of the people against Moses (Exod. 32. 1); compare Num. 16. 3, 19 (the LXX has συνίστημι in each case).　In Num. 20. 2, the LXX has συνα-θροίζω, to mark the tumultuous nature of the gathering; in the fourth verse the congregation is συναγωγή; and in the eighth the verb ἐκκλησιάζω is used, whilst the Hebrew word is the same throughout.　Gatherings for wicked purposes are referred to in Gen. 49. 6, Prov. 5. 14, and Ps. 26. 5.

The first passage of special interest in which the noun occurs is Gen. 28. 3, where Isaac says to Jacob, 'God Almighty bless thee,

---

[1] Compare its use in 2 Sam. 22. 12, 'He made darkness pavilions round about him;' also Ps. 18. 11, 'His pavilion round about him were dark waters and thick clouds of the skies.'

and make thee fruitful, and multiply thee, that thou mayest be an assemblage of peoples'[1] (εἰς συναγωγάς ἐθνῶν). In Gen. **35.** 11 this blessing is repeated by God Himself, 'I am God Almighty : bo fruitful and multiply; a nation and a company of nations shall be of thee;' and Jacob, when an old man, cited the words of the blessing in his conversation with Joseph, 'I will make of thee a multitude of peoples (**48.** 4). The word **multitude** is unfortunate. The R. V. has **company.**

The congregation or assembly of Israel, which is so often spoken of in the O. T., is sometimes referred to as συναγωγή (synagogue), sometimes as ἐκκλησία (ecclesia), in the LXX. Once, where the judicial function of the congregation is referred to, the LXX renders the word συνέδριον (whence the word Sanhedrim), namely, in Prov. **26.** 26, 'His wickedness shall be shewed before the congregation.'

The assembly or congregation of Israel is well defined in Josh. **8.** 35, 'There was not a word of all that Moses commanded, which Joshua did not read before all the congregation of Israel, with the women, and the little ones, and the strangers which were conversant with them.' The **congregation**, then, properly meant all the male adults of the nation. In Ezra **2.** 64, 65, 'the whole congregation' was numbered at 42,360, exclusive of men-servants and maid-servants. In chap. **10.** 1 we read of 'a congregation of men, women, and children.' In Neh. **8.** 2 we are told of 'a congregation both of men and women.' In Joel **2.** 16 the prophet says, 'Gather the people, sanctify (*i.e.* call with sacred solemnity) the congregation, assemble the elders, gather the children, and those that suck the breasts.'

Israel was regarded as a vast family, the women and children forming an integral portion of it, except for public or judicial purposes, and none excluded except through wilful disobedience of the law of Moses, or (for a time) through ceremonial uncleanness. This great family was addressed, both by Moses and the prophets, in the *singular* number, as if they might be regarded as one, in spite of their diversities of age, circumstances, and dwelling-places. This fact illustrates the teaching of the N. T., where we find that there was One Person who concentrated in Himself the fulfilment of much that had been spoken to Israel in its corporate capacity, and became in His turn a centre of unity to a spiritual Israel, gathering

---

[1] The words 'Am and Goi had not yet received their differentiated and technical meaning. See chap. xxii.

together into one all the children of God that were scattered abroad (John 11. 52).

The first great assembly of Israel was at the giving of the Law at Mount Sinai. The reference to it in Deut. **18.** 16 is interesting from its connection with the prophecy concerning Him who was to build up a new *ecclesia*, 'The Lord thy God will raise up unto thee a Prophet, from the midst of thee, of thy brethren, like unto me; unto him ye shall hearken. According to all that thou desiredst of the Lord thy God in Horeb in the day of the assembly (ἐκκλησία), saying, Let me not hear again the voice of the Lord my God, neither let me see this great fire any more, lest I die. And the Lord said unto me, They have well spoken that which they have spoken. I will raise them up a Prophet from among their brethren like unto thee, and will put my words into his mouth, and he shall speak unto them all that I shall command him.' The assembly on the occasion here referred to was a representative assembly, but the whole of Israel, even all their generations, were regarded as pledged by what was then transacted. This is brought out clearly, both in Exodus and Deuteronomy. Thus in Deut. **4.** 10 we read, 'The Lord said unto me, Gather me the people together, and I will make them hear my words, . . . and ye came near, and stood under the mountain;' and in Deut. **5.** 22, after recapitulating the commandments, Moses says, 'Those words the Lord spake unto all your assembly in the mount. . . . And it came to pass, when ye heard the voice . . . that ye came near, even all the heads of your tribes and your elders.' What the representatives did was evidently regarded as done by the whole people, and not by one generation only, for in the same chapter and the third verse we are told that 'the Lord made not the covenant with our fathers (only), but with us, even us (also), who are all of us here this day;' and yet the actual generation of men with whom the covenant was originally made had passed away.

Although theoretically 'the congregation of Israel' signified the whole people of Israel, yet for practical purposes they were represented by elders. Other examples will be found in 1 Kings **8.** 1, 2, 3, and 2 Chron. **5.** 2, 3. The same was probably the case in the gathering (**Kahal**) of all the congregation at the entrances of the tabernacle for the observance of special national ceremonies. See Lev. **8.** 3, 4.

In Lev. **4.** 13, 14, 21, the whole congregation is described as sinning; a national offence has been committed, and a national sin-offering is to be offered. Accordingly, the elders of the congregation in their representative capacity laid their hands on the head of the bullock which was to be offered, to signify the transmission of the nation's evil deed to the atoning victim.

The gatherings at religious feasts are probably referred to in Ps. **22**. 22, 25, **26**. 12, **35**. 18, **40**. 9, 10, **68**. 26, **107**. 32, **149**. 1.

The being 'cut off from the congregation of Israel,' and the being forbidden to enter it (Num. **19**. 20; Deut. **23**. 1), seem to have implied severance from the privileges, religious and social, which the nation as such enjoyed. In some places, however, it was synonymous with death. In Prov. **21**. 16 we read of 'the congregation (συναγωγή) of the dead,' a striking picture of that vast gathering which is being daily enlarged as men are 'gathered to their fathers,' and which remains an integral portion of the family of man.

In Ps. **58**. 1, where we read, 'Do ye indeed speak righteousness, O congregation,' the word used is **Alam** (אלם), which signifies either to bind into a sheaf, or to be dumb. The former meaning would present a very suitable symbol of a congregation, but the latter meaning, 'ye dumb folk,' would also give good sense. See R. V.

In Ps. **68**. 10 the Psalmist says, 'Thy congregation shall dwell therein;' and in **74**. 19, 'Forget not the congregation of the poor for ever.' Here the word (חיה) means a living being. Translators have not been agreed as to its meaning here, but our version gives a fair sense. In some versions we here find the strange rendering, 'Thy beasts shall dwell therein.'

Besides **Kahal**, an assemblage, there is another word which occurs about a hundred and fifty times in the O. T., with almost the same width of meaning, namely, **'Adah** (עדה). This word first appears in Exod. **12**. 3, and is almost always rendered congregation. It is frequently used in the early books, but rarely in the later. Whilst **Kahal** generally refers to the *representative* gathering, **'Adah** often signifies an informal massing of the people. **'Adah** is used of the company of Korah (Num. **16**. 5; Ps. **106**. 17); in Jud. **14**. 8 it is used of a swarm of bees; in Ps. **68**. 30, of a multitude of bulls. It only occurs three times in the prophets, namely, in Jer. **6**. 18, **30**. 20, and Hos. **7**. 12; whilst **Kahal** occurs twenty-two times, chiefly in Ezekiel. The LXX usually has συναγωγή as a rendering for **'Adah**.

The word **'Adah** not only signifies congregation, but also

witness or testimony, and in another form ('**Aduth**) it is used
of 'the ark of the testimony.' This chest was so called because
it contained the tables of the Law which testified to God's character and attributes (Exod. **25.** 21, 22). The same form is used in
connection with the tent which contained the ark, and which was
consequently called the tent or tabernacle of the testimony or of
witness in Exod. **38.** 21; Num. **1.** 50, 53, **10.** 11, **17.** 7, 8, **18.** 2;
and 2 Chron. **24.** 6.

Wherever we read of 'the tabernacle of the congregation,' the
word **mo'ed** (מוֹעֵד) is used. It is generally supposed that this word
is derived from **ya'ad** (יָעַד), to appoint, and, in the passive, to meet
or make an appointment. This verb is used of God's meeting
Moses and communing with him from above the mercy-seat in
Exod. **25.** 22; and in Exod. **29.** 42, 43, it is apparently adopted
to explain the true meaning of the word **mo'ed**, for we here read,
'This shall be a continual burnt-offering throughout your generations, at the door (*i.e.* opening) of the tabernacle of the congregation before the Lord, where I will meet you to speak there unto
thee, and there I will meet with the children of Israel, and it
shall be sanctified by my glory.' See also Exod. **30.** 6, 36, where
the same Hebrew words are used in the same relationship. The
'tabernacle of the congregation' was therefore the appointed place
of meeting between God and Israel; they were brought near together in that Holy Place, just as God and man are said to be
brought near together in the Body of Christ, which is the true
Tabernacle not made with hands.

The LXX has almost always rendered this expression by the
words σκηνή τοῦ μαρτυρίου, 'the tent of witness,' thus connecting
the word **mo'ed** with '**adah**, which has been discussed above. There
is a good deal to be said in favour of this view of the matter, for
the roots of the words are cognate, if not the same. See Acts **7.** 44,
Rev. **15.** 5.

The word **mo'ed** is also used to represent seasons (Gen. **1.** 14),
appointed times (Gen. **18.** 14), feasts (Lev. **23.** 2), and solem-
nities (Deut. **31.** 10). In all these renderings, which frequently
recur in the O. T., there is an idea of some *time* or *place* appointed
by God.

What, then, was the Tabernacle of the Congregation? Not
the tent or collection of tents in which the congregation of Israel
dwelt, but the tent or tabernacle in the most sacred part of which
the ark of the testimony was placed, and which was set apart as

the dwelling-place of God, the centre whence issued the promises, warnings, and commands of the Most High. The R. V. rightly renders it 'the Tent of Meeting.'

§ 4. *Convocation.*

The word used in the expression 'a holy convocation' is **Mikra** (מקרא), from **kara**, to call or convoke. See Exod. 12. 16, Lev. 23. 2, *al.*; and compare Num. 10. 2. The sabbaths and feast days were occasions for this convocation. The word has been rendered assembly in Isa. 1. 13 and 4. 5. It seems to imply that assemblies were convened on these days for purposes of public worship, or for the reading and exposition of the Law. It may be, however, that the word answers to our word institution or solemnity, and signified that the days so designated were intended to be kept free from secular work, and to be regarded as sacred by Divine command. The LXX usually has κλητὴ ἁγία, which, according to N. T. usage, might be rendered 'called to be holy;' compare the κλητοὶ ἁγίοι of St. Paul's Epistles (A. V. 'called to be saints').

§ 5. *N. T. Teaching on the Temple and Tabernacle.*

The most notable words that we have been considering reappear in the N. T., sometimes with a more spiritual significance. Whilst the literal ναός or temple was built by Solomon, it was reserved for Christ, the true Son of David, to build the spiritual ναός, which is composed of living stones based upon Him as their foundation. The first hint in the N. T. that there should be such a spiritual temple is in John 2. 19, where the Lord says, 'Destroy this temple,[1] and in three days I will raise it up.' He spoke, however, as the Evangelist tells us, of the temple of His body; but His body was itself a figure of that organisation of which all Christians form a part, so that His resurrection was regarded as the rising of the Head, the First-fruits, whilst the Body is to be raised hereafter. This idea of the living Temple is touched upon by St. Paul several times (see 1 Cor. 3. 16, 17, 6. 19; 2 Cor. 6. 16; Eph. 2. 21); each Christian is regarded as a dwelling-place of the Holy Ghost, and, when viewed in connection with others, he is

---

[1] We have to distinguish between the ναός, which is the Temple proper, and the ἱερόν, or sacred precincts and courts. The latter is never referred to in a spiritual sense in the Epistles.

described as a living [1] stone in the great Temple, of which Christ
is the foundation and the chief corner stone (1 Pet. 2. 5). Every
Christian, whether Jew or Gentile, whether bond or free, is built
up and 'fitly framed' in harmony with the rest; and each community of Christians may be regarded as a chamber (κατοικητήριον,
Eph. 2. 22) in the great edifice.

In the Epistle to the Hebrews the σκηνή or tabernacle of the
Mosaic dispensation is contrasted with that which the Lord pitched,
of which Christ was the minister (Heb. 8. 2); and in Rev. 21. 3 we
read, with respect to the same heavenly tabernacle, that hereafter
it shall be set up among men.

The σκήνωμα is twice mentioned by St. Peter as a symbol of the
earthly body, or dwelling-place for the soul (2 Pet. 1. 13, 14). In
this sense St. Paul uses the form σκῆνος in 2 Cor. 5. 1, 4, where he
speaks of 'our earthly house of this tabernacle' being dissolved.

Besides the references to the temple as the house (οἶκος) of God
in the N. T., we have the identification of the Church, *i.e.* the Body
of believers, with the House of God in 1 Tim. 3. 15 and 1 Pet. 4.
17; whilst in Heb. 3. a comparison is instituted between the faithfulness of Moses as a servant over his house, *i.e.* the house of Israel
which was committed to his charge by God, and the faithfulness
of Christ the Son of God in taking charge of those who believe
in Him, and who thus constitute His house. In Heb. 10. 21 He
is called a High Priest over the house of God, which is not a
material but a spiritual house. See 1 Pet. 2. 5.

The word συναγωγή in the N. T. is generally used of the building
rather than of those that assemble in it; there are, however, a few
passages in which the synagogue meant the judicial and religious
assembly. See, for instance, Mark 13. 9, Luke 21. 12, and Acts 13.
43.[2] In James 2. 2 the word is apparently applied to the Christian
place of meeting, where they were not to forsake the assembling of
themselves together (Heb. 10. 25).

§ 6. *The Ecclesia.*

To the Christian the word *ecclesia* is far more important than
the word synagogue. On examining the Gospels we find the word
only in Matt. 16. 18 and 18. 17. The former passage revealed

---

[1] 'It seems unfortunate that the word translated living in the one verse
should be rendered lively in the other, the very object of the Apostle being
to show the oneness of nature between Christ and believers.

[2] Compare also the technical word ἀποσυνάγωγος (John 9. 22, *al.*).

Christ's intention to supersede the *ecclesia*[1] of the O. T. dispe
by one which should be peculiarly His own, and which shou
for ever. The latter points to the functions which this new ~~~~,
or some local section of it, was to exercise through its representatives in cases of dispute between man and man (compare 1 Cor.
6. 1).

When we pass to the Acts and Epistles, we find that Christians
are formed into *ecclesiæ*, or congregating bodies, in every town to
which the Apostles went, whilst all these smaller organisations
were regarded as local representatives of a great spiritual and spotless *ecclesia* or Body, the Head of which was invisible, being at the
right hand of God (Eph. 1. 22). Membership in the *ecclesia* of
Christ was obtained by faith in Him, and was sealed and signified
by baptism.

Believers in Christ are regarded as one Body. They have one
Master, one faith, one baptism, one God and Father. Originally
they continued steadfast in the Apostles' teaching, and in fellowship (*i.e.* sharing their goods with one another), and in breaking
of bread, and in prayers (Acts 2. 42). As time went on there
would be different local arrangements, different places of meeting,
'diversities of administrations,' but the word of the Apostolic body,
as representing the teaching of Christ, was to be supreme. Christ
was over all, and the Spirit was in all. This unity was to embrace
not only *belief*, but also *life*. If any one preached a false gospel, he
was to be regarded as *anathema*, *i.e.* as an outcast; and if any one
did not love the Lord Jesus Christ, he too was to be regarded as
anathema. Those that loved God and their brethren, and walked
worthy of their profession, showed thereby that they were truly
born of God, and were really members of the one Body in which
the Spirit of Christ dwelt; but those whose religion consisted only
of profession and talk, and who did not deny themselves for their
brother's good, were regarded as having a name to live, whilst
really dead.

The fact that this body was called the *ecclesia* of Christ shows that
it answers in some respects to the *ecclesia* of the O. T., the Israel of God.
Believers in Christ are delivered out of a bondage worse than that of

[1] There have been various controversies as to the right rendering of this
word. In many versions it has been reproduced without any attempt at translation. Others, like ourselves, have taken the word Κυριάκη, the Lord's household, to represent it. Tyndale rightly translated the word *congregation* or
assembly, thus retaining the relationship between the O. T. and the N. T.
Luther's word *Gemeine*, 'community,' is a very good one.

Egypt; they have a Leader greater than Moses, a Priest higher than Aaron, an atoning-offering more precious than the blood of bulls or of goats, a tabernacle more lasting than the tabernacle of witness; they have the true Manna or Bread of Life to eat, and the true Rock supplies them with the Water of Life; from the hands of One higher than Joshua they hope to receive their promised inheritance, and One greater than David is their King. They are divided into many generations, and distributed through all parts of the world, yet they are *one;* and wherever Christ is loved and honoured as Saviour and Leader, wherever He is trusted as Priest and Sacrifice, wherever He is obeyed as King, and hoped in as the Giver of an everlasting habitation—*there* are members of the one great *ecclesia,* the Holy Catholic Church.

The various local communities referred to as Churches in the N. T. may be regarded as nurseries for the true Church of which Christ is the Head. An *ecclesia* was first formed in Jerusalem, and afterwards in every large town to which the Gospel came. Each *ecclesia* had its elders, who may be regarded, according to the analogy of the O. T., as its representatives, and who, like the elders of the Jewish *ecclesia,* had to exercise spiritual and prophetical, though not sacerdotal, functions.[1] The various *ecclesiæ* formed through the Roman world were confederate Churches, bound together by the common ties of Apostolic teaching and unity of Spirit; Jerusalem being still regarded as the Mother Church. There might be many places of meeting or *ecclesiæ* in one city, but they were not independent of one another; such an event as the arrival of an Apostle would bring them all together as one brotherhood. As the Word of God grew and multiplied, it extended into the more outlying country districts, and the Churches thus formed were affiliated with the city communities, and thus what we may call dioceses were formed, all, however, acting in harmony with the directions which emanated from the Apostolic body at Jerusalem. When this venerable city was destroyed, the local centre of unity vanished; at the same time the Apostles and their coadjutors passed away; but they left their writings behind, and these letters and authorised narratives of our Lord's history were received as the utterances of the Spirit of Christ, and took the same place in the Christian system which the Scriptures of the O. T. had occupied in the Jewish Church.

How, in the lapse of ages, Rome gradually assumed to itself both the authority of the Apostles and the local dignity which

---

[1] See chap. xx.

originally belonged to Jerusalem, is a matter of history which need not here be touched upon. It may be observed, however, that all schisms *in* the various Churches, or *from* them, arose partly from the fact that, as generations passed away, the Churches lost something of that vital hold of simple Apostolic truth which they originally possessed, and partly because it does not seem, humanly speaking, possible that there should be upon earth anything approaching to a perfect Church. There have always been offences, heresies, false teachers, and false professors, and there will be to the end of this dispensation. Every attempt to form a new community on the Apostolic model has ended in the same way. A root of bitterness has sprung up in spite of all precautions; and men have learnt over and over again by sad experience that they must be content to put up with an imperfect organisation and with indifferent teachers, whilst they have been also led to see that, amidst all human imperfections, the true Head of the Church remains 'the same yesterday, to-day, and for ever,' ministering grace to all that love Him in sincerity and truth.

The word *ecclesia* is used in other senses besides that now discussed, in a few passages of the N. T. Thus, in Acts 19. 32, 39, 41, a civil assembly is called by this name. In 1 Cor. 14. the *ecclesia* appears to be the assembly of Christians for Divine worship, answering to one of the senses of συναγωγή noted above. In Heb. 12. 23 we read of the ἐκκλησία of the first-born, whose names are written in heaven. Reference is here made perhaps to the true Israel of the old dispensation, that is, to the congregation [1] or *ecclesia* in the wilderness with whom God was pleased, [2] to those who did not bow the knee to Baal, and to those 'who feared the Lord,' and 'spake often one to another.' Others suppose that the *ecclesia* of Christ is here referred to; they hold that the Church is a representative body, and that the world at large will reap the fruit of the faith and love of the spiritual first-born.

---

[1] Acts 7. 38. The A. V. here most unfortunately renders ἐκκλησία *church* instead of *congregation*. See R. V., margin.

[2] Heb. 3. 16, '*Some* did provoke . . . but not *all*.' There was a Church within a Church, Jews who were Jews inwardly, Israelites indeed, a remnant according to the election of grace. Rom. 2. 29, 11. 4, 5, Mal. 3 16 Israel is called God's first-born in Exod. 4. 22.

CHAPTER XX.

PROPHET, PRIEST, ELDER, MINISTER.

IT has always been part of the system of the Divine government to employ *men* as instruments for the conveyance of heavenly truth and blessing to the world at large. Whether it be as the announcers of the Revealed Message, as the writers of the inspired Scripture, as the official representatives of God in matters relating to the atonement, or as teachers and guides of the people, human instruments have been employed, human voices have been heard, 'the pen of a man' has been used, the agent has been 'taken from among men,' the treasure has been conveyed in 'earthen vessels.' There has, indeed, been a constant tendency in those that have been selected for these important services to constitute themselves into a caste, and to assume to themselves powers and rights which God never gave them; and by a natural reaction, many persons, resenting such claims, have thrown discredit on sacred offices, and have sought to break through the distinctions which God Himself has marked out.

The practical advantages of a settled order of ministry are denied by comparatively few; but how many there are who differ, and that hotly, concerning the names, relative positions, and spiritual powers of the ministry! Metaphysical questions have intruded themselves, to add to the entanglement. Not only has the nature of the special prophetic gifts of the O. and N. T. been earnestly investigated, but such points as the following are raised:—Does the grace of God's Spirit come direct to each member of the Church, or only through certain privileged persons? Does the spiritual efficacy of baptism and the Lord's Supper depend upon the presence and superintendence of a person who has received special gifts by the laying on of hands? Are the spiritual gifts referred to in the N. T. transmitted through Episcopal consecration? or are they vested in the Holy Catholic Church as a body, to be exercised through such representatives as may be appointed from time to time by the Christians of each locality? Is a threefold order of ministry—bishops, presbyters, and deacons—essential to the exercise of such gifts? Is Episcopal succession from the Apostles' days, by a continuous laying on of hands, necessary in order to convey these gifts?

The animosity raised by such questions is endless, and we need over and over again to be reminded that the great object of the ministry is not that men should set themselves up as a privileged caste, but that they should lead others to Christ; whilst the object of Christ in dispensing His gifts to men is to make them conformable to the will of God. Whatever helps forward that conformity, whether it be the faithful use of the Lord's Supper, the reading and meditating on Scripture, public prayer and preaching, or private spiritual intercourse between man and man, that is to be regarded as a *gift*, and as a means whereby the life of God penetrates the soul.

§ 1. *The Prophet.*

The general name for a prophet in the O. T. is **Nabi** [1] (נביא). The original meaning of this word is uncertain; but it is generally supposed to signify the bubbling-up of the Divine message, as water issues from a hidden fountain. It is used both of prediction, properly so called, and of the announcement of a Divine message with regard to the past or present; also of the utterance of songs of praise. It is applied to messengers of false gods (*e.g.* 'the prophets of Baal'), and to a man who acts as the mouthpiece of another, as when the Lord says to Moses (Exod. 7. 1), 'Aaron thy brother shall be thy prophet.' The first passage in which the word occurs is Gen. 20. 7, where it is used of Abraham. In Deut. 18. 15, 18, the title is applied to the Messiah, who was to have God's words in His mouth, and who thus became the Mediator of the New Covenant, taking a position analogous in some respects to that of Moses. The LXX almost always adopts the rendering προφητεύω and προφήτης for **Nabi**.

In Micah 2. 6, 11, the word **nathaph** (נטף), to drop, is used. Some commentators suppose that it is adopted as a word of contempt. It is used, however, of a discourse distilling in drops in the following passages:—Job 29. 22, 'My speech dropped upon them;' Prov. 5. 3, 'The lips of a strange woman drop as an honeycomb;' Cant. 4. 11, 'Thy lips, O my spouse, drop as the

---

[1] In Assyrian the *Nabû* proclaimed the will of the gods; hence *Nabû* or *Nebo* (? *annap*) 'the prophet-god.' The predicter of the future was the *asipu* (אשף).

honeycomb;' 5. 13, 'His lips, like lilies, dropping sweet-smelling myrrh;' Ezek. 20. 46, 'Drop thy word towards the south;' 21. 2, 'Drop thy word towards the holy places;' Amos 7. 16, 'Drop not thy word against the house of Isaac.'

The word **Masa** (משׂא), a burden, is used in Prov. 30. 1 and 31. 1, where the A. V. renders it 'prophecy.' By a burden we are to understand the message laid upon the mind of the prophet, and by him pressed on the attention of the people. The message of the Lord ought not to have been regarded as a burden by the people (see Jer. 23. 33–38); but it could not fail to be realised as such by the prophets, who at times felt heavily laden with the weight of their message. See Jer. 20. 9, and compare Nah. 1. 1, Hab. 1. 1, and Mal. 1. 1.

In Hos. 9. 7 the prophet is described as the 'man of the spirit,' or the 'spiritual man,' an expression which reminds us of St. Peter's declaration that 'holy men of old spake as they were moved by the Holy Ghost.'

§ 2. *The Seer.*

The seer is **Chozeh** (חזה, Ass. *khazu*), one who sees a vision, not with the eye of sense, but with the spiritual and intellectual faculties. This term is usually (but not always) found in passages which refer to visions vouchsafed by God.

Chozeh is rendered 'prophet' only once, namely, in Isa. 30. 10, 'Which say to the prophets, Prophesy not unto us right things, speak unto us smooth things, prophesy deceits.' A cognate noun is used of visions in almost all passages in which they are mentioned. The verb is frequently found in the same sense, as in Exod. 24. 11, 'They saw God,' where it explains and somewhat modifies the fact recorded in the previous verse, in which the ordinary word for sight is used. Again, it is used in Num. 24. 4, 16, where Balaam speaks of himself as 'seeing-the-vision of the Almighty, falling (into a trance), but having his eyes open.' In 2 Sam. 24. 11 it is used of Gad, David's 'seer;' see also 2 Kings 17. 13, 1 Chron. 21. 9, 25. 5, 29. 29; 2 Chron. 9. 29, 33. 18, 19, 35. 15.

The verb is used of spiritual apprehension in Job 24. 1, 27. 12, 34. 32, 36. 25.

In Ps. 63. 2 two words are used, the first being the more general one, the second that which we are now considering. The Psalmist expresses his longing to see (raah) God's power and glory as he has seen **(Chazah)** God in the sanctuary. He wished to see face to face that Being whom now he only saw through a glass darkly.

Chazah is used in Isa. **13.** 1, and similar passages, of the burden or vision which the prophet saw. It occurs in Isa. **33.** 17, ' Thine eyes shall see the king in his beauty,' and implies that there would be something more in that beatific vision than what would be presented to the outer eye. It is used of false visions in Ezek. **13.** 6, 7, 8, 9, 16 ; compare 1 Kings 22. 22. It is also used by Amos, Micah, and Habakkuk of their visions, and by Daniel in reference to dreams.

In some passages the word is found in a more general sense, as in Ps. **58.** 8, 10; Prov. **22.** 29, 24. 32, 29. 20; Cant. **6.** 13; Isa. **48.** 6, and **57.** 8.

The more general word **Roeh** (ראה), to see, is used of prophetic or spiritual sight in a few passages, two of which have been already referred to. It represents the 'visions' mentioned in Gen. **46.** 2 ; Num. **12.** 6; 1 Sam. **3.** 15; 2 Chron. **26.** 5; Isa. **28.** 7; Ezek. **1.** 1, 8. 3, 4, **11.** 24, **40.** 2, **43.** 3 ; and Dan. **8.** 16, 27.

§ 3. *N. T. Use of the Word Prophet.*

The words προφήτης and προφητεύω are used in the N. T. not only with respect to the prophets of the O. T., but also with reference to those persons who ' prophesy in Christ's name' (Matt. **7.** 22) under the new dispensation. The prophecy of Zacharias (Luke **1.** 67) is an inspired hymn gathering together the O. T. predictions, and announcing that they were about to be fulfilled in Christ. The prophecy of Caiaphas (John **11.** 51) was an utterance capable of a meaning further than that which was in the mind of the speaker, and it was intended by Him who overrules all things to have this double significance. When the Jews blindfolded the Lord and smote Him with their hands, they said, ' Prophesy to us who smote thee' (Matt. **26.** 68, Mark **14.** 65, Luke **22.** 64), implying that prophecy is the utterance of that which cannot be discovered by such means of knowledge as are ordinarily available. Among the special gifts of Pentecost, we find that both men and women should prophesy (Acts **2.** 17), and the utterance of the wonderful works of God is said to have been a fulfilment of the prediction. Prayer, preaching, and singing seem to be all expressions of prophecy. It was also related to the gift of tongues. See Acts **19**. 6, **21**. 9 ; Rom. **12**. 6 ; 1 Cor. **11**. 4, 5, **12**. 10, **14**. *passim* ; 1 Thess. **5**. 20 ; 1 Tim. **1**. 18, **4**. 14 ; Rev. **10**. 11, **11**. 3.

Both John the Baptist and the Lord Jesus were regarded by many among the Jews as prophets (Matt. **21**. 11, 26, 46), and rightly so, for John was 'more than a prophet,' whilst the Lord was 'the prophet who should come into the world' (John **6**. 14 ; Acts **3**. 22, 23). The Apostles are coupled with prophets sent by Christ in Luke **11**. 49 (compare Matt. **23**. 34, where *wise men* are substituted for Apostles). See also Acts **11**. 27, **13**. 1, **15**. 32, **21**. 10 ; 1 Cor. **12**. 28 ; Eph. **2**. 20, **3**. 5, **4**. 11 ; Rev. **18**. 20, **22**. 9.

There is no office in the Church at the present time quite analogous to the prophetic. This gift, in some of its aspects, must be classed along with others which were called into existence by the will of God for a special time and purpose, its object being the directing and strengthening of the faith of the infant Church, which was thus provided for temporarily, as every new-born child is, until God saw fit to leave His people to those less obtrusive but more permanent operations of the Spirit which are referred to in such passages as Gal. **5**. 22, 23.

§ 4. *The Priest.*

The Hebrew name for a priest is **Cohen** (כהן) throughout the O. T., with the exception of three passages, where a word derived from **Camar** (כמר), which means to *make hot* or *black*, is used, namely, 2 Kings **23**. 5, Hos. **10**. 5, and Zeph. **1**. 4. In these passages idolatrous priests are referred to.

The original meaning of the word **Cohen** is lost in obscurity. In 1 Kings **4**. 5 the A. V. renders it 'principal officer' (compare the marginal rendering of verse 2) ; in 2 Sam. **8**. 18 and **20**. 26 it has been rendered 'chief ruler' (margin, 'princes'). David's own sons were thus designated, but it seems impossible now to decide what duties were involved under this name. In Job **12**. 19 it is rendered 'princes.' Possibly the usage of the word in the passages now quoted is a remnant of its original signification, at a time when one man combined in Himself the priestly and the kingly office.

The Greek ἱερεύς and the Latin *sacerdos* are far better (because more indefinite) renderings of **Cohen** than either the French 'sacrificateur' or the English 'priest,' which last confuses two things kept carefully distinct, both in the O. T. and N. T.

The verb **Cahan**, 'to minister in the priest's office,' is used several times in Scripture. In one passage it is rendered to 'deck;' the bridegroom decks himself with ornaments, as the priest clothes himself with his special robes of office (Isa. **61.** 10). The LXX is very uniform in the use of ἱερεὺς for the noun and ἱερατεύειν for the verb. Only once is λειτουργεῖν, to minister, used for it, namely, in 2 Chron. **11.** 14.

The word **Cohen** is not confined as a title to the priests of the Levitical order. It is applied to Melchizedek, to Potipherah (Gen. **41.** 45), to the priests of Midian (Exod. **3.** 1), and to the priests who conducted idolatrous worship. Moses is included among God's priests in Ps. **99.** 6.

The verb ἱερατεύω is only used once in the N. T., namely, where Zacharias is described as 'executing the priest's office' (Luke **1.** 8). In the following verse ἱερατεία is found, and it occurs again in Heb. **7.** 5. In 1 Pet. **2.** 5, 9, we meet with ἱεράτευμα, which is used of Christians, regarded as a *holy priesthood*, and also as a *royal priesthood*, the last expression being an adaptation of the title given (conditionally) to Israel in Exod. **19.** 6, where the words 'kingdom of priests' are rendered 'royal priesthood' in the LXX. Compare Rev. **1.** 6, **5.** 10, **20.** 6. The word ἱερουργεῖν, not ἱερατεύειν, is used in Rom. **15.** 16, and means the performance of sacred duties, not necessarily the exercise of sacerdotal functions.

It is remarkable that the word ἱερεὺς occurs nowhere through the whole range of the Epistles, except in the Epistle to the Hebrews, where the contrast between Christ's priestly work and that of Aaron is drawn out. If the ministry of the Christian Church were intended to occupy a position at all analogous to that of the Levitical priesthood, can it be doubted that the Epistle to the Hebrews would have contained some notification of the fact? But the minister is comparatively kept out of sight (except where matters of order were concerned), and attention is concentrated on One who cannot be seen with the outward eye, but who is our one and only High Priest, acting in our interests 'within the veil.' Sacerdotal terms were freely used of the ministry in the next ages of the Church. This is not to be wondered at when we remember that to Greeks and Romans sacerdotalism was almost identified with religion. Their usage does not imply that they saw any real analogy between the *Jewish* and the Christian ministry, though it does imply that the latter took the place of the *heathen* priesthood.

§ 5. *The Elder.*

The elder is always **Zakén** (זָקֵן), literally an old man, and is represented in the LXX by πρεσβύτερος, *Presbyter*. The word is frequently used in each language to express old age, for which in the LXX πρεσβύτης is also used; but gradually it was restricted to an official sense. The first intimation of such a sense is in Gen. 50. 7, where we read that 'Joseph went up to bury his father, and with him went up all the servants of Pharaoh, the elders of his house, and all the elders of the land of Egypt.' The office was in those days a natural, social, and civil one. In Exod. 17. 5 the elders are again referred to as lay-representatives of the people. So again in Exod. 18. 12, 19. 7, 24. 1, 9.

In Num. 11. 16 the Lord says to Moses, 'Gather unto me seventy men of the elders of Israel, whom thou knowest to be the elders of the people, and officers over them, and bring them unto the tabernacle of the congregation, that they may stand there with me.' These men represented the various tribes of Israel, and were quite distinct from the Levites and priests (Josh. 24. 1 ; 1 Kings 8. 1–3). They acted on behalf of Israel on great occasions, whether civil or religious, and in the first instance their appointment was sanctioned by an outpouring of the Spirit upon them, as we read in Num. 11. 25, 'And the Lord came down in a cloud, and spake unto Moses, and took of the spirit that was upon him, and gave it unto the seventy elders : and it came to pass, that, when the spirit rested upon them, they prophesied, and did not cease.' It was on the occasion now referred to that there remained two of the men in the camp, Eldad and Medad ; 'and the spirit rested upon them ; and they were of them that were written, but went not out unto the tabernacle : and they prophesied in the camp.' When Joshua, in his eagerness, wished Moses to forbid them, the lawgiver gave that noble and remarkable answer, 'Enviest thou (*i.e.* art thou jealous) for my sake ? Would God that all the Lord's people were prophets, and that the Lord would put his spirit upon them.' This passage implies that the outpouring of the Spirit on the presbyters caused them to become prophets, constituting them a *spiritual*, though not a *sacerdotal*, order.

The word is rendered 'ancients' in Isa. 3. 14, 24. 23. The latter passage is one of peculiar interest. We here read that 'the Lord shall reign in Mount Zion, and in Jerusalem, and before his

ancients gloriously,' or (as it is in the margin) 'there shall be glory
before his ancients.'   Are not these 'ancients' or 'elders' the
same as those whom St. John saw in vision (Rev. 4. 4) before the
throne of God, giving glory to God and to the Lamb?   May they
not be taken as the representatives of all God's people?

§ 6.   *The Office of Elder in the N. T.*

The importance of a right judgment of the position and functions of these elders cannot well be overrated when we come to
discuss the nature of the analogous office of presbyter in the N. T.
On the one hand, the elder was neither a priest nor a Levite, but
a representative of the people; on the other hand, he had special
duties and responsibilities in consequence of this position, and he
also had special grace conferred on him (in the first instance, at
least) to enable him to perform those duties aright.

The word presbytery, πρεσβυτέριον, is used three times in the
N. T.: twice of the Sanhedrim (Luke 22. 66; Acts 22. 5), and once
of the gathering of Christian elders who laid their hands on Timothy
(1 Tim. 4. 14).[1]

Christian presbyters or elders are first named in Acts 11. 30,
where reference is made to the elders in Judæa or Jerusalem.   St.
Paul appointed elders, apparently by the laying on of hands, and
after nomination by the people, in every Church which he founded
(Acts 14. 23).   We find these elders in conclave with the apostles in
Acts 15.; and we have a most instructive address, illustrating their
office and work, in Acts 20. 17, &c.

Elders are not mentioned in the Epistles until we reach the
First Epistle to Timothy, though they are probably the persons
referred to in 1 Thess. 5. 12.[2]   It seems strange that they are not
in the list of gifted persons mentioned in Eph. 4. 11; but this may
be accounted for by the fact that the work of an elder, *as such*, did
not call for extraordinary gifts, and was to be carried on long after
those gifts had ceased.   They may, however, have been included

---

[1] Paul himself laid hands also on Timothy (2 Tim. 1. 6), but perhaps at a different time and with a different object.   It may be observed that the great Apostle
of the Gentiles was formally appointed to his missionary work, not by apostolic
ordination, but by the laying on of the hands of the ministers at Antioch (Acts
13. 3), although he had previously received a mission, accompanied by the special
gifts of the Holy Spirit, by the laying on of hands on Ananias.

[2] Compare the προϊστάμενοι here with the προεστῶτες πρεσβ. in 1 Tim. 5. 17.

under the name *Prophets*. From the First Epistle to Timothy we learn the character and position of the elder; whilst from Titus 1. 5 it would appear that the system of appointing elders in every city where there was a Church, was still sustained. Both Peter and John describe themselves by this title (2 John 1; 3 John 1; 1 Pet. 5. 1).

The advice to the elders given by St. Peter falls in exactly with the exhortations given by St. Paul to those of Ephesus. St. James also doubtless refers to those who held the rank of elder in the Church, in the remarkable passage (5. 14) in which he speaks of healing the sick by the medical use of oil, in connection with the pardon of sin.

According to the analogy of the O. T., the elders would be spiritual but non-sacerdotal representatives and leaders of the various local communities which are feeders to the one Church (see chap. xix.). They would exercise their spiritual and ministerial functions in the name of the congregation, being counsellors and helpers, guides and feeders of the flock over which the Holy Ghost had appointed them. Many of them at first were no doubt possessed of the gifts of prophecy and tongues, and were selected for the responsible position which they held, either because of their age, wisdom, and piety, or because of the special gifts they possessed. But they no more held the peculiar position of the **Cohen** or *priest* than did the elders under the O. T. dispensation. Although they would naturally take the chief part in the administration of the Lord's Supper, this was not a sacerdotal act. Just as the Passover Supper was administered in every family by the head of the household, so the Lord's Supper is administered by the presbyter as leader of a community, but not as a *sacerdos*, and at *a table*, not at *an altar*. See chap. xvi. § 7.

§ 7. *The Ministry.*

The minister in the O. T. is **Shereth** (שרת), a word which the LXX has almost always rendered λειτουργός.[1] The office of minister was not necessarily sacred, but it was always honourable. The minister differed from the servant or slave, in that the latter performed what we call menial duties, or at any rate was expected to toil for his master, whereas the former was a person in attendance

---

[1] The verb is rendered διακονεῖν only in Esther 1. 10, 2. 2, 6. 3.

on a king, prince, or great personage, to render such honourable
service as would be acceptable. In this sense, Joseph was minister
to Potiphar (Gen. **39.** 4), and afterwards was in attendance on
the prisoners in behalf of the governor of the prison (Gen. **40.** 4);
so, too, Joshua ministered to Moses, Samuel to Eli, and Abishag
to David.

The word is constantly used of the ministrations of the
priests and Levites, especially of the latter, and signifies that they
were fulfilling high functions in respect of that unseen Being in
whose honour they were employed. The term is equally applicable
to angels, who are described in the Epistle to the Hebrews as
ministering spirits (πνεύματα λειτουργικά) sent forth by their
Heavenly Master to minister to them who should be heirs of
salvation.

In Ezek. **20.** 32 the heathen are said to serve or minister to
wood and stone. Here the use of the word **Shereth** is ironical;
they are engaged in ministrations—but to whom? to the King of
kings? —no, to blocks of wood and stone.

The words λειτουργός, λειτουργία, and λειτουργεῖν are used of
Christian ministrations several times in the N. T. In some of
these passages they denote the ministering in worldly things. See
Rom. **15.** 27; 2 Cor. **9.** 12, Phil. **2.** 25, 30. In Rom. **13.** 6 those
in civil authority are honoured by this title when described as God's
ministers.

In Phil. **2.** 17 and Rom. **15.** 16 the work of the Christian
ministry, properly so called, is spoken of in terms derived from
the sacerdotal and ministerial system of the old dispensation; but
when these passages are carefully examined, they will not be found
to justify the claims which have been sometimes made by the
ministerial order in later times. In Phil. **2.** 17 Paul describes
himself as ready to be offered like a libation on the sacrifice and
ministry of his convert's faith (compare 2 Tim. **4.** 6); that is to
say, that he might be sacrificed on their behalf. In Rom. **15.** 16
he speaks of himself as ministering the Gospel of God, that the
offering up of the Gentiles might be regarded by God as an
acceptable sacrifice, being sanctified by the Holy Ghost. In each
of these cases the sacrifices are *persons;* and the passages are closely
related to Rom. **12.** 1, where Christians are directed to offer their
bodies as living sacrifices; but there is no reference whatsoever to
what is now sometimes called 'the Christian sacrifice.'

§ 8. *Service.*

With regard to the word **serve** or **service**, the LXX often keeps up a distinction which is not to be found in the Hebrew. It has both δουλεία, which is bond service, and which may be used in a religious sense or not; and λάτρεια, sacred service, a word only used in a religious sense, but not confined to the priesthood. For these two renderings the Hebrew has only one word, 'avad (עבד[1]), which is used of every kind of service, good and bad, whether exercised towards man, idols, or God. The distinction which is sometimes drawn between the words *douleia* and *latreia*, in connection with the worship of God and of created beings, cannot be substantiated by reference to the O. T.

The verb δουλεύω, as well as the noun δοῦλος, is frequently used in the N. T. of the service due from every Christian to God and to Christ (see, for example, Col. 3. 24; 1 Thess. 1. 9), whether that service take the form of ministry or not.

Λατρεία is used of that religious service of the Christians which consists in self-dedication to God, in Rom. 12. 1; Phil. 3. 3; Heb. 9. 14, 12. 28. St. Paul uses it of his own life of service in Acts 24. 14, 26. 7, 27. 23; Rom. 1. 9; 2 Tim. 1. 3. It is also used to indicate the ceaseless employment of God's servants in heaven (Rev. 7. 15, 22. 3).

Διάκονος (whence the word deacon) and kindred forms are used in the N. T. in a general and non-technical sense of all kinds of ministry or service for the good of others. See Matt. 20. 18; John 12. 2, 25. It is not applied to the seven so-called deacons, and only gradually grew up into a technical sense. See Phil. 1. 1, and 1 Tim. 3. 8, 12.

---

[1] The Assyrian replaces *ebed* (slave) by *ardu*.

CHAPTER XXI.

KING, JUDGE, PUNISH.

§ 1. *Kings and Rulers.*

THE Hebrew words translated king and kingdom in the A. V. are connected with the root **Malac** (מלך, Ass. *malaku*), which appears in various proper names, such as Ebed-Melech and Milcom. The verb is generally rendered reign (in Ezek. 20. 33, rule).

Another word largely used in the same sense is **Mashal** (משל, Ass. *masalu*), which refers not so much to the office as to the government which that office implies. It is generally rendered rule, sometimes reign or dominion, and occasionally govern, as in Gen. 1. 18, where the heavenly bodies are described as governing the day and the night.

Shalath (שלט, Ass. *saladhu*), to get the mastery, is used with much force in Ps. 119. 133, 'Let not any iniquity have dominion over me.' It is also rendered 'dominion' nine times in Daniel, and 'rule' fourteen times in the same book. This word is used of Joseph when he is described as 'the governor of Egypt' (Gen. 42. 6). **Sheleth**, which is derived from it, signifies a shield, and is rendered ruler in Hos. 4. 18 ; and **Sholtan** (Ass. *sildhannu*), which reminds us of the modern word **Sultan**, is rendered dominion in Dan. 4. 3, &c.

Nagid (נגיד), a leader or guide, is generally translated prince or captain, and is used of a ruler several times, especially in the Books of Chronicles. See Isa. 55. 4 ; Dan. 9. 26, and 11. 22.

Pechah (פחה, Ass. *pikhu*), a satrap or pasha, is used for a governor chiefly in the later historical books, also in Hag. 1. 1, 14, 2. 2, 21, and Mal. 1. 8.

Sar (שר, Ass. *sarru*, 'king'), a 'chief captain' in the army, is the title given to the 'captain of the Lord's hosts' in Josh. 5. 14, 15. It is applied to judges or rulers of the tribes (Exod. 18. 21), who are usually called princes in the A. V. in the later books. It is used of government in Ps. **68.** 27 ; Isa. **1.** 23, **32.** 1 ; Jer. **1.** 18 and 52. 10 ; also in Isa. **9.** 6, 7, where the Messiah is called 'the prince of peace,' and 'the government shall be upon his shoulders . . . and of the increase of his government and peace there shall be no end.' The Messiah is also called the prince (**Sar**) in Dan. **8.** 11, **25, 10.** 13, 21, and **12.** 1.

Ba'al (בעל, Ass. *bilu*), to be lord, husband, or master, is used of having dominion in 1 Chron. **4.** 22 and Isa. **26.** 13 ('Other lords beside thee have had dominion over us'). This word is found in the remarkable declaration in Isa. **54.** 5, 'Thy Maker is thy husband.' See Hos. **2.** 16.

Yad (יד, Ass. *idu*), the *hand*, or instrument of *power*, is used of lordship in 1 Chron. **18.** 3 and 2 Chron. **21.** 8. In Gen. **27.** 40 ('When thou shalt have the dominion') a word (רוד) is used the meaning of which is uncertain, but the cognate word **Radah** (רדה, Ass. *radu*) is frequently used for rule. It also occurs in Jer. **2.** 31 and Hos. **11.** 12.

In Job **38.** 33 ('Canst thou set the dominion thereof in the earth ?') the word used is supposed to signify rule or empire, and to be connected with the name of the officer or overseer, **Shoter** (שטר, Ass. *sadhir*, 'writer'), of whom we read in Exod. **5.** 6 ; Deut. **1.** 15, 16. 18 ; 1 Chron. **26.** 29 ; and Prov. **6.** 7.

Nashak (נשק), to kiss, whether as a mark of respect (Ps. **2.** 12) or otherwise, is rendered rule in Gen. **41.** 40, where the margin has 'be armed or kiss' (see R. V.). The word is sometimes applied to armour because it fits closely and is folded together ; it is also applied to the wings of the living creatures which touched one another (Ezek. **3.** 13).

In Prov. **25.** 28 ('He that hath no rule over his own spirit') the word (מעצר) signifies self-restraint. In 2 Kings **25.** 22 and 1 Chron. **26.** 32 we find the word **pakad** (פקד, Ass. *paqadu*), to visit or superintend ; in Deut. **1.** 13, **rosh** (ראש, Ass. *risu*), the head ; in Isa. **1.** 10, **3.** 6, 7, and **22.** 3, **Katsin** (קצין), a captain ; in Jud. **5.** 3, Ps. **2.** 2, and four other passages, the rulers or princes are described by a word which perhaps answers to august (רזן). **Alaph** (אלף), to lead or teach, is used in Zech. **9.** 7, **12.** 5, 6 ; and **Chavash** (חבש), to bind (usually for the purpose of hearing), in Job **34.** 17. **Nachah** (נחה), to lead, occurs in Ps. **67.** 4 ; and **Chakak** (חקק), to decree (lit. to engrave, as in Job **19.** 24, Isa. **22.** 16 and **49.** 16), is rendered governor in Jud. **5.** 9, 14. Compare Gen. **49.** 10 (lawgiver). **Nasi** (נשיא), a captain or prince (lit. one who *bears* responsibility, or who *holds aloft* an ensign), is often used of God's leading His people, and is rendered ruler or governor a few times in the Pentateuch and in 2 Chron. 1. 2.

§ 2. *Judgment and Condemnation.*

The words judgment and condemnation signify two very different things, yet they are sometimes confused by the Bible reader.[1] **Shaphath** (שפט, Ass. *sapadhu*) is the general word for the administration of justice. It is once rendered condemn in the A. V., namely, in Ps. 109. 31, and here the margin points to the true rendering. The usual word for 'condemnation,' as has been shown elsewhere, is **rasha'**, which in the Piel form signifies ' to account or deal with as wicked.' It is used in this sense sixteen times, and is the exact opposite of the Hiphil form of **tsadak,** 'to account or deal with as righteous.' In Ps. 109. 7, 'let him be condemned' is literally 'let him go out as wicked.' In 2 Chron. 36. 3 and Amos 2. 8 the word used (ענש) signifies to be fined or mulcted.

Coming now to the subject of judgment, we have to distinguish the various shades of meaning which the word possesses. When the Psalmist prays, 'Teach me good judgment' (Ps. 119. 66), he uses a word which signifies taste or discrimination (טעם), and asks for a keen moral and spiritual perception, such as is referred to by the writer of the Epistle to the Hebrews when he speaks of those who ' by reason of use have their senses exercised to discern both good and evil' (Heb. 5. 14).

In Gen. 31. 37 Jacob says, 'Set thy goods before my brethren and thy brethren, that they may judge betwixt us both' (יכה), that is, 'that they may decide which of us is right.' On the word **Elohim**, which is rendered judges in Exod. 21. 6, 22. 8, and 1 Sam. 2. 25, see chap. ii. In Jer. 51. 47, 52, 'I will do judgment upon the graven images of Babylon,' the word for visitation (פקד) is used. See chap. xvii. § 4.

Palal (פלל), when used judicially, points to arbitration between two parties. It is rendered judge in 1 Sam. 2. 25, 'If one man sin against another, the judge (**Elohim**) shall judge him (or arbitrate between the one and the other); Ps. 106. 30, ' Then stood up

---

[1] The German language uses *richten* for the administration of justice, and *urtheilen* for the giving a judicial decision ; but many languages are not able to mark this important distinction.

Phinehas and executed **judgment**, and so the plague was stayed.'
The Prayer Book version reads, 'Then stood up Phinehas and
prayed' (*i.e.* sought the arbitration of God). See also Exod. **21.** 22;
Deut. **32.** 31; Job **31.** 11, 28; Isa. **16.** 3, **28.** 7; Ezek. **16.** 52, **28.** 23.

Din (דין, Ass. *danu*), to judge, whence the name *Dan*, implies a
settlement of what is right where there is a charge upon a person,
and so it comes to signify the decision of a cause. It is rendered
judge in more than thirty passages. It is a *judicial* word, while
shaphath is rather *administrative*. The one would mark the act
whereby men's position and destiny are decided; the other would
point to the mode in which men would be governed and their
affairs administered.

Din is first found in the following passages:—Gen. **15.** 14, 'The
nation whom they shall serve will I **judge**.' Gen. **49.** 16, 'Dan
shall **judge** his people.' Deut. **32.** 36, 'The Lord shall **judge** his
people.' Ezra **7.** 25, 26, 'Set *magistrates* (**shaphath**) and **judges**
(**din**), which may **judge** (**din**) all the people that are beyond the
river, all such as know the laws of thy God; and teach ye them that
know not. And whosoever will not do the law of thy God, and
the law of the king, let **judgment** (**din**) be executed speedily upon
him, whether it be unto death, or to banishment, or to confiscation
of goods, or to imprisonment.' Ps. **50.** 4, 'He shall call to the
heavens from above, and to the earth, that he may **judge** his
people.' Ps. **54.** 1, '**Judge** me by thy strength.' Dan. **7.** 10,
'The **judgment** was set and the books opened.' Verse 22, '**Judgment** was given to the saints of the most High, and the time
came that the saints possessed the kingdom.' Verse 26, 'The
judgment shall sit, and they shall take away his dominion.' See
also Gen. **30.** 6; 1 Sam. **2.** 10; Esther **1.** 13; Job **19.** 29, **35.** 14,
36. 17, 31; Ps. **68.** 5, **76.** 8, **96.** 10, **110.** 6, **135.** 14; Prov. **20.** 8;
Isa. **3.** 13, **10.** 2; Jer. **22.** 16; Dan. **4.** 37; Zech. **3.** 7.

Shaphath is the root of the name for the '**judges**' who were
raised up from time to time to be rulers over the land, to defend
the people from enemies, to save them from their oppressors, to
teach them the truth, to uphold them in the right course. It is in
this general meaning that the word is usually found in the O. T.
It is therefore not out of place that it should be rendered **defend**
in Ps. **82.** 3; **deliver** in 1 Sam. **23.** 14; and **rule** in Ruth **1.** 1.
The two words **shaphath** and **din** are found side by side in some
places, *e.g.* 1 Sam. **24.** 15; Ps. **7.** 8, **9.** 8, **72.** 2; and Jer. **5.** 28.
But this by no means proves that their meanings are identical.

Shaphath and **din** are rendered in the LXX κρίνω, διακρίνω, δικάζω, and ἐκδικέω. The word κατακρίνω barely exists in the LXX, but is found several times in the N. T. See, for example, Rom. **8**. 1, 34 ; 1 Cor. **11**. 32. The judge is κριτής or δικαστής; and the judgment is κρίμα, κρίσις, δικαιοσύνη, δικαίωμα.

§ 3. *Judgment in the N. T.*

Turning to the N. T., we may distinguish three kinds of judgment, namely : first, self-judgment, or the discrimination of one's own character ; secondly, the Great Assize, when the destiny of each shall be assigned ; and, thirdly, the administration of the world in righteousness.

It must be noticed, however, that κρίνω is sometimes used of an adverse judgment, as in John **3**. 17, 18, 'God sent not his son into the world to **condemn** (κρίνειν) the world . . . he that believeth is not **condemned** (κρίνεται) . . . he that believeth not is **condemned** already' (ἤδη κέκριται) ; John **16**. 11, 'Now is the ruler of this world **condemned**' (κέκριται) ; 2 Thess. **2**. 12, 'That all might be **condemned**.' In these passages the R. V. uses the word **judge**.

In other passages κρίνω means to *decide* or *form an estimate*, whether favourable or the contrary, as in Matt. **7**. 1, 'Judge not (*i.e.* form no hard estimate of others), that ye be not judged' (*i.e.* that a hard estimate be not formed of you). Compare Rom. **2**. 1 ; Luke **7**. 43, 'Thou hast formed a right estimate ;' Acts **16**. 15, 'If ye have judged me to be faithful ;' Rom. **14**. 5, 'One judgeth one day above another ;' James **4**. 11, 'He that judgeth his brother sets himself up as a judicial interpreter of the law.'

Occasionally there is reference to judicial administration. Thus, in Acts **17**. 31 it is said that God is about to judge the world in righteousness in the person of the Man whom He hath ordained ; Matt. **19**. 28, 'Ye . . . shall sit on twelve thrones, judging the twelve tribes of Israel ;' 1 Cor. **6**. 2, 'The saints shall judge the world ;' 1 Cor. **6**. 3, 'We shall judge angels.'

God is described, under the name κριτής, as the Judge of all (Heb. **12**. 23), as the righteous Judge (2 Tim. **4**. 8), and as the one lawgiver [and judge], who is able to save and to destroy (James **4**. 12) ; whilst the Lord Jesus is called the Judge of quick and dead (Acts **10**. 42).

The word κρίμα occurs nearly thirty times in the N. T., usually in the sense of condemnation. In the wider sense of administrative justice we may refer to the following passages :—John 9. 39, ' For judgment am I come into this world, that they which see not may see, and that they which see may be made blind;' Rom. 11. 33, 'How unsearchable are his judgments;' Rev. 20. 4, I saw thrones, and they sat on them, and judgment was given unto them.'

The word κρίσις is found in about fifty places in the N. T. Sometimes it signifies the formation of a right estimate of another's character and doings, as in Matt. 23. 23, where it is joined with mercy and faith ; Luke 11. 42, where it is coupled with love. Accordingly, our Lord says to the Jews, ' Judge not according to appearance, but judge righteous (or just) judgment' (John 7. 24). He says of His own judgment, or mode of estimating and dealing with others, it is righteous, and just, and true (John 8. 16). An estimate of the character and work of all men is to be formed by Christ; and the period in which this work will be accomplished is described as the Day of Judgment.

The word κρίσις is sometimes used in the sense of condemnation, as in Matt. 23. 33 and John 5. 24 ; whilst in John 5. 29 a contrast is drawn between those that rise to life and those that rise to condemnation. Judgment, however, is the better word.

§ 4. *Punishment and Vengeance.*

The moral relationship between sin and punishment is illustrated by the fact that the latter is expressed by the words **Chattath** and **'Aven** (see chap. vi. §§ 1, 4) in Gen. 4. 13 ; Lev. 26. 41, 43 ; 1 Sam. 28. 10 ; Lam. 3. 39, 4. 6, 22 ; Zech. 14. 19. **Yasar** (יסר), to chastise, is found in Lev. 26. 18, ' If ye will not yet for all this hearken unto me, then I will punish you seven times more for your sins.' **Nacah** (נכה), to smite, is used in Lev. 26. 24 ; **Nakam** (נקם), to avenge, in Exod. 21. 20, 21 ; **Ra'a** (רעע), to bring evil, in Zech. 8. 14 ; **'Anash** (ענש), to amerce or fine, five times in the Book of Proverbs. In the remaining passages, all of which are in the prophetical books, **Pakad** (פקד), to visit, is used, punishment being regarded as a visitation from God.

The avenging or revenging the blood of the slain is referred to under the word **Gaal** in Num. 35. 12, *al.* From the earliest period of human history God is represented as taking the part of the injured, of the oppressed, and even of the slain. Their cries ascend into His ears; their blood calls to Him even from the ground.

Thus the Redeemer is necessarily an avenger, and must exercise retributive justice. **Shaphath**, to judge, is used in this sense in 2 Sam. **18**. 19, 31. For a similar reason, perhaps, **Yasha'**, to save, is rendered to avenge in 1 Sam. **25**. 26, 31, 33. The R. V. offers a marginal correction in the first of these verses.

In Deut. **32**. 42 ('The beginning of revenges upon the enemy'), and in Judges **5**. 2 ('Praise ye the Lord for the avenging of Israel'), a word is used which is derived from **Para'** (פָּרַע), to *strip*.

The most usual word for revenging or avenging is **Nakam** (נָקַם). It first appears in Gen. **4**. 15, 'Vengeance shall be taken on him (or rather *for* him, *i.e.* for Cain) sevenfold.' Compare verse 24, 'If Cain shall be avenged sevenfold, truly Lamech seventy and sevenfold.' The word is used altogether about seventy-five times in the O. T. Personal and private revenge was forbidden to Israel, 'Thou shalt not avenge nor bear any grudge against the children of thy people, but thou shalt love thy neighbour as thyself' (Lev. **19**. 18). The children of Israel were always taught to leave vengeance in God's hand, as He would avenge the blood of His servants, and would take their part against their enemies. See, for example, Deut. **32**. 35, 43 ; Ps. **18**. 47, **94**. 1 ; Jer. **11**. 20 ; Nah. **1**. 2. The Lord's vengeance is regarded as *retribution*, but not as *retaliation ;* it is set forth not as an *evil passion*, but rather as the righteous and unerring *vindication* of His own people and of His own course of action, to the discomfiture of those who had set themselves in opposition to Him. He metes it out with justice, and on such a *day* or at such a time as seems fitting to Him. See Isa. **34**. 8, **61**. 2, **63**. 4 ; Jer. **46**. 10, **51**. 6.

The words ἐκδικεῖν and ἐκδίκησις stand occasionally both for **Shaphath** and also for **Nakam**. They imply the visitation of due penalty upon the criminal, whether by the hand of the human judge (Luke **18**. 3 ; Acts **7**. 24 ; Rom. **13**. 4 ; 1 Pet. **2**. 14), or by the agency of God (Luke **18**. 7, 8, **21**. 22 ; 1 Thess. **4**. 6 ; 2 Thess. **1**. 8 ; Rev. **6**. 10, **19**. 2).

There is no place given in the N. T., any more than there is in the O. T., for the avenging of personal injuries. On the contrary, the feeling of revenge is studiously condemned. Where the magistrate is not called upon to vindicate the sufferer, there God will step in. 'Vengeance belongeth unto me, saith the Lord' (Rom. **12**. 19, Heb. **10**. 30).[1]

---

[1] These words are quoted from Deut. **32**. 35, and are translated from the Hebrew, not from the LXX, which reads ἐν ἡμέρᾳ ἐκδικήσεως instead of ἐμοὶ ἐκδίκησις.

CHAPTER XXII.

NATION, PEOPLE.

§ 1. *Gentile or Heathen.*

THE only word rendered either Gentile or heathen in the O. T. is Goi (גּוֹי); it is generally used in the plural number, and after the time of Moses was generally used of outside nations. Goi is translated nation in all passages where the A. V. has adopted this word, with the exception of about thirty-five. In ten passages it is rendered people. In nineteen out of twenty places in which the word is found, the LXX has adopted ἔθνος as a rendering, and hence is derived the English word heathen. The first passage in which goi appears is Gen. 10. 5, where the historian, writing of the children of Japheth, says, 'By these were the isles of the Gentiles divided in their lands, every one after his tongue, after their families, in their nations.' The word for 'isles' may perhaps be used here in the more extended sense of 'territories.'

The word goim frequently occurs in connection with the promises made to Abraham. His seed was to inherit Canaan, which was at that time possessed by goim; he was to be the father of many goim; and in him and his seed were all the goim of the earth to be blessed.

Where the word has been rendered people it will always be found to be in the singular number, and in these cases it usually refers to Israel; there is, however, one exception, namely, Zech. 12. 3, where we read of all the people (*i.e.* nations) of the earth being 'gathered against Jerusalem.'

Throughout the historical books, the Psalms, and the prophets, the word goim primarily signifies those nations which lived in the immediate neighbourhood of the Jewish people; they were regarded as enemies, as ignorant of the truth, and sometimes as tyrants. Yet gleams of brighter and better days for them appear on the pages of Scripture from time to time. The goim were to seek after the Messiah, the son of Jesse (Isa. 11. 10); God's Chosen One was to minister judgment to them (Isa. 42. 1); He was to be not only a covenant to the *people* (of Israel), but also a light to the **goim** (42. 6), and a salvation to the ends of the earth (49. 6). In Isa. 60. 16, and elsewhere, the **goim** are described as contributing to the glorification of the regenerated Israel; whilst in other places we read of them as agents in punishing Israel (Jer. 4. 7). Their idolatry was fearful, and their abominations were great (2 Kings 16. 3). Their triumph over Israel and their ignorant fury against Israel's king are denounced in strong terms; but, after all, they are to be God's inheritance; they are told to rejoice in His coming to judge the earth, and all nations whom God hath made are to come and worship before Him.

§ 2. *The People.*

If **goi** denotes a nation regarded from without, **'Am** (עַם) signifies a people as viewed by one of themselves. Sometimes it is used in the familiar and domestic way in which we speak of 'folk,' a rendering which it has received in Gen. 33. 15. In the LXX it is generally rendered λαός. It is often brought into direct relationship or contrast with **goi**. Thus Moses, speaking to God concerning Israel, says, 'This nation (goi) is thy people ('am),' Exod. 33. 13. It is used by the later O. T. writers to distinguish Israel as God's people, and to mark them off from the surrounding **goim**. Yet the prophets give a hope that the **goim** who had not been **'ammim** should become the people of God through Divine mercy. Thus in Ps. 18. 43 we read, 'Thou hast made me the head of the heathen **(goim)**: a people ('am) whom I have not known shall serve me.' This will come to pass when God shall be recognised as holding rule as 'King of the **goim**' (see Jer. 10. 7). Compare Hos. 1. 9, 10, and 2. 23.

A word which occupies a less definite position than either **goi** or **'am** is **Lom** (לְאֹם), a race. It is generally found in the plural, and is used frequently in the Psalms and Isaiah, and two or three times in earlier and later books. It first appears in Gen. 25. 23, 'two races shall be separated from thy loins; the one race shall be stronger than the other race. See also Hab. 2. 11, and Jer. 51. 58, which is quoted from it. This word is applied sometimes to Israel, and sometimes to other nations. **Ummah** (אֻמָּה), a tribe or family, literally those sprung of one mother, is rendered people in Num. 25. 15 and Ps. 117. 1, and nations in Gen. 25. 16, Ezra 4. 10, and throughout the Book of Daniel.

R

§ 3. *Nations and People in the N. T.*

The word ἔθνος first occurs in the N. T. in the phrase 'Galilee of the Gentiles' (Matt. **4.** 15). Here the title is brought into close juxtaposition with λαός, which is used in the words which immediately follow, 'The people that sitteth in darkness hath seen a great light.'

Other passages in which the words ἔθνος and λαός are contrasted are:—Luke **2.** 32, 'A light for the purpose of revealing the truth to Gentiles, and a glory of thy people Israel.' Acts **4.** 25, 27, 'Why do the Gentiles rage, and the people (pl.) imagine a vain thing? . . . For verily against thy holy servant[1] Jesus, whom thou hast anointed, both Herod, and Pontius Pilate, with the Gentiles, and the people (pl.) of Israel, were gathered together.' Acts **15.** 14, 'God determined to take from among the Gentiles a people for his name.' Acts **26.** 17, 'Delivering thee from the people, and from the Gentiles, unto whom now I send thee.' Verse 23, 'That Christ should suffer, that he the first should proclaim light to the people and the Gentiles.' Rom. **15.** 10, 'Rejoice, ye Gentiles, with his people.' Verse 11, 'Praise the Lord, all ye Gentiles; and laud him, all ye people' (pl.). 1 Pet. **2.** 9, 'A holy nation and peculiar people.'

The exact interpretation of the phrase 'all nations' or 'all the Gentiles' is sometimes attended with difficulty. We meet with it in the following passages:—Matt. **24.** 9, 'Ye shall be hated by all nations.' Verse 14, 'This gospel of the kingdom shall be preached in all the world, as a witness to all nations' (compare Mark **13.** 10). Matt. **25.** 32, 'All nations shall be gathered before him.' Matt. **28.** 19, 'Make disciples of all nations.' Mark **11.** 17, 'My house shall be called a house of prayer for all nations.' Luke **21.** 24, 'They (the Jews) shall be carried captive to all nations.' Luke **24.** 47, 'That in his name should repentance and remission of sins be proclaimed to all nations.' Acts **14.** 16, 'In past times suffered all the Gentiles to walk in their ways.' Acts **15.** 17, 'That the remnant of men should seek the Lord, and all the Gentiles over whom now my name is called.' Rom. **1.** 5, 'Apostle-ship for the obedience of faith in all nations.' Rom. **15.** 11, 'Praise the Lord, all ye nations.' Rom. **16.** 26, 'Made known unto all the Gentiles.' Gal. **3.** 8, 'In thee all the nations of

---

[1] See chap. i. § 5.

the earth shall be blessed.' Rev. 12. 5, 'To rule or feed all
nations.' Rev. 15. 4, 'All nations shall come and worship
before thee.' Rev. 18. 3, 'She hath called all nations to drink
of her cup.' Verse 23, 'All nations were deceived by thine
enchantment.'

With these passages may be compared Ps. 67. 2, 72. 11, 17, 82.
8, Isa. 2. 2, 25. 7, 61. 11, and 66. 18, which set forth the Divine
promises to all nations of the earth. This expression, however,
cannot always be understood in its full and literal sense, as will be
seen by the examination of 1 Kings 4. 31 ; 1 Chron. 14. 17; Jer.
27. 7; and Zech. 14. 2.

§ 4. *Tribe or Family.*

Two words are rendered tribe, namely, **matteh** (מטה) and
shevet (שבט, Ass. *sibdhu*, 'rod'), both of which originally signify a
rod. The founder of a family was its root, whilst the ancestor of
each subdivision (and so the subdivision itself) was a rod or stem.
Hence the rod was the symbol of the tribe (Num. 17. 2), and
perhaps the heads of the tribes had rods, batons, or sceptres of
office. **Shevet** first appears in Gen. 4. 9, 10 (compare vers. 16, 28).
Matteh is first used of a tribe in Exod. 31. 2. Both words are
used freely in the same sense in the Pentateuch and Joshua.
Shevet is the more favourite word in Judges, Samuel, Kings, and
Psalms, and is found occasionally in Isaiah, Ezekiel, Hosea, and
Zechariah. **Matteh** only occurs twice in Kings, is frequent in
Chronicles, hardly ever in the prophetical books.

The family is a still further subdivision, and is called **Mishpachah** (משפחה) ; the only exceptions were as follows :—In 2 Chron.
35. 5, 12, the word **ab** (אב), the ancestry or house of fathers, is used.
In Jud. 6. 15, **eleph** (אלף, Ass. *alapu*), a 'thousand,' is adopted
(compare its use in the prophecy of Bethlehem, which was so small
among the 'thousands' of Israel, Micah 5. 2). In 1 Chron. 13. 14
and Ps. 68. 6 we find the word **beth** (בית), a house.

In Gen. 47. 12 the Hebrew is **taph** (טף), which is generally
rendered little ones; this rendering, however, has lately been
questioned.

Dr. Payne Smith, late Dean of Canterbury, suggested in his
Bampton Lectures that Israel was divided into three great classes :
—First, there were the nobles, heads, or princes, whose genealogies
are given in the Books of Numbers and Chronicles. Secondly,

there were the retainers, who formed the strength of these noble houses, not necessarily descended in a direct line from Jacob, but forming households or clans under the various nobles. The Hebrew name for these households was **taph** (טף), which the LXX renders οἰκία and συγγένεια.[1] They were circumcised, were sharers of the covenant, and were part of the commonwealth of Israel. Dr. Payne Smith holds the English rendering 'little ones' to be a mistake, because, whilst the **taph** included the children, it also included a great deal more, namely, the whole household or body of retainers. Thirdly, there was the 'mixed multitude' ('ereb), which had gradually united itself with the destinies of Israel, and which included Egyptians, Arabs, and, in course of time, Canaanites. They appear to have had no landed property assigned to them, and were not sharers in the covenant.

Each tribe was divided into *families* (**mishpachah**) which bore the names of the leading descendants of Jacob. Thus the men of the tribe of Reuben formed four families, and these were subdivided into *houses* (Num. 1. 2). Similarly, in Josh. 7. 17, 18, in the history of Achan, we find the tribe of Judah thus divided into families, houses, and individuals. The number in each 'house' must have been large. The chiefs of the 'houses' were important men, and were called 'chief fathers' in Num. 31. 26, and 'heads of the fathers' in Josh. 14. 1.

---

[1] But only once in each case. The usual renderings are παιδίον, τέκνον, ἀποσκευή.

CHAPTER XXIII.

EARTH, WORLD, HEAVEN.

§ 1. *The Soil or Land.*

THREE Hebrew words are rendered land. **Sadeh** (שדה) signifies a field, a plot of land, or an estate; it is rendered 'land' in 1 Sam. 14. 14; 2 Sam. 9. 7, 19. 29; 2 Kings 8. 3, 5; and Neh. 5. 3, &c. **Erets** (ארץ), which is very largely used, signifies a territory, or even the whole earth. It is systematically adopted by Moses and other writers in the expression, 'A land flowing with milk and honey.' **Adamah** (אדמה) properly means the soil, regarded as a productive agent. It is used of the land or ground in the sense in which a farmer would speak of it. This word is used with remarkable consistency of the land of Canaan, of the Jew's own land, and of the fruits of the land. It occurs in Gen. 28. 15, 'I will bring thee again into this land,' where it is in contrast with 'all the families of the earth.' In Gen. 47. 20 we read, 'Joseph bought all the land (*i.e.* soil, **adamah**) of Egypt for Pharaoh . . . so the land (*i.e.* the whole territory, **erets**) became Pharaoh's.' Other instances where the two words occur in juxtaposition are Lev. 20. 24; Deut. 29. 28; 2 Kings 25. 21; Jer. 16. 15, 23. 7, 8; Ezek. 7. 2, 12. 19, 33. 24. In these passages **adamah** is used in a peculiar sense, to mark Israel's 'own land,' whilst **erets** is used more generally of the territory of the Canaanites, or of some other people.

Adamah is used in Deut. 21. 1, 23, with regard to the defilement of the land caused by the presence of a slain body, or of a body that remained unburied. It was regarded as holy or sacred, and death was a defilement because it was the outward and visible sign of sin.

In the passages which relate to the restoration of Israel to their native soil **adamah** is consistently used. See Isa. 14. 1, 2; Jer. 16. 15; Ezek. 11. 17, 34. 13, 27, 36. 24, 37. 12, 14, 21; Amos 9. 15; Zech. 2. 12.

Adamah is rendered earth about fifty times, and always in the sense above designated, as ground or soil. Thus it is used of the beast of the earth (Gen. 1. 25); of Cain being cursed from the earth, so that it should not yield its fruit to him (Gen. 4. 11); of the face of the earth (Gen. 6. 1, 7); of rain falling on the earth (Gen. 7. 4); of the blessing to be given to all the families of the earth (Gen. 12. 3, 28. 14); compare its usage in Exod. 10. 6. In Exod. 20. 24 it is used of the 'altar of earth,' a point interesting to be observed, as making the soil on which man lives and from which he takes his name a participator with the rite of sacrifice. Perhaps it was for an altar that Naaman asked for two mules' burden of soil (2 Kings 5. 17). **Adamah** is also used of the earth which was put on a man's head as a mark of sorrow (1 Sam. 4. 12). It occurs with touching significance in Ps. 146. 4, 'His breath goeth forth, he returneth to his earth, and in that very day his thoughts perish.'

In Isa. 24. 21, where we read, 'The Lord shall punish the host of the high ones that are on high, and the kings of the earth upon the earth,' we should have expected to find **erets**; but **adamah** is used, to enforce the contrast between those that dwell on this soil with the inhabitants of other regions; compare 45. 9, 'Let the potsherds strive with the potsherds of the earth,' and Amos 3. 2, 'You only have I known of all the families of the earth.'

§ 2. *The Earth.*

The great difficulty which has to be dealt with in translating the word **erets** is to determine where it is used with reference only to a special territory, such as Canaan, and where it signifies the whole world. When the earth is spoken of in connection with heaven (as in Gen. 1. 1; Isa. 49. 13, and 65. 17), it must have the larger meaning; the same will usually be the case when we read of the ends of the earth (Isa. 52. 10), or the whole earth (Micah 4. 13); but in a great number of passages there is nothing but the context or the general analogy of Scripture to guide the translator or interpreter.

The distinction between the narrower and wider meaning of the term is important in considering the account of the Deluge, also in the interpretation of many prophetical passages. Thus in Ps. 37. 11 we read, 'The meek shall inherit the earth;' but in verse 29, where **erets** is also used, the A. V. renders, 'The righteous shall inherit the land.' See also verses 22 and 34. In Isa. 11. 9 we

read, 'The earth shall be full of the knowledge of the Lord ;' yet
the earlier part of the verse only speaks of God's 'holy mountain'
In Jer. 22. 29 (' O earth, earth, earth ') is the prophet appealing to
the wide world, or to the land of Canaan? In Isa. 24. 1 we read,
'Behold, the Lord maketh the earth empty ;' verse 3, 'The land
shall be utterly emptied ;' verse 4, 'The earth mourneth ;' verse
13, 'When it shall be thus in the midst of the land,' &c. **Erets** is
used throughout the chapter; but to what does it refer? Ought
it not to be rendered uniformly? The twenty-first verse seems to
imply that it is used in the more extensive sense. In Amos 8. 8 we
read, 'Shall not the land tremble for this?' and in verse 9, 'I will
darken the earth in the clear day.' In Zech. 14. 9, 'The Lord
shall be king over all the earth ;' and in verse 10, 'All the land
shall be turned as a plain.' Our translators seem almost to have
indulged in variety in these passages for the sake of variety, but it
is to the confusion of the English reader.

The Greek rendering for **adamah** is always γῆ. The same word
is the most general rendering for **erets**, but we also find χώρα,
territory, in about fifty passages, and οἰκουμένη, a habitable world,
in nine passages. There are other occasional renderings, but none
which call for special notice.

The word for 'earth,' in the sense of earthen vessels, potsherds, or potter's clay, is always **Cheras** (חרש), except in 2 Sam.
17. 28, where **Yatsar** (יצר) is used, referring to the vessels being
moulded. In Dan. 2. 10, 'There is not a man upon the earth,'
&c., the word used (יבשת) signifies dry land ; whilst **'Aphar** (עפר),
dust, is found in Gen. 26. 15 ; Isa. 2. 19 ; Dan. 12. 2 ; Job 8. 19,
28. 2, 30. 6, and 41. 33—in most of which passages holes or cavities
in the upper surface of the earth are referred to.

In the N. T., it is to be remembered, as in the O. T., that where
the Greek representative of **erets** is found in contrast or juxtaposition with heaven, we know that it must signify the earth as a whole.
This would apply to such passages as the following :—

'Heaven and earth shall pass away' (Matt. 5. 18).

'Thy will be done on earth as it is in heaven ' (Matt. 6. 10).

'Whatsoever ye bind in earth shall be bound in heaven ' (Matt.
18. 18).

In some passages the interpretation admits of a doubt. Thus
Matt. 5. 5, 'Blessed are the meek, for they shall inherit the earth.'
Here our Lord is making use of the LXX rendering of Ps. 37. 11,
in which passage it is natural to suppose that the land of Canaan

would be *primarily* referred to. Here, however, the Hebrew word
is **erets**, as was noticed above, and thus the larger sense of the word
is admissible. In Eph. 6. 3, 'That thou mayest live long in the
earth,' the Hebrew (Exod. 20. 12) is **adamah**, and the land of
Canaan is primarily meant.

The context in these and other cases is the only means whereby
the reader can decide whether by γῆ is signified the soil, the territory,
or the world.

§ 3. *The World.*

The general word translated world in the A. V. is **tevel** (תבל,
Ass. *tabalu*, 'dry land'). There are a few exceptions. Thus in Isa.
38. 11 we read, 'I shall behold man no more with the inhabitants
of the world;' here the word (חדל) may perhaps signify the place
of rest, cessation, forbearance.[1] In Ps. 17. 14, 'From men of the
world,' and 49. 1, 'Inhabitants of the world,' we find a word (חלד)
which may refer to the transitory state of things in this world which
'passeth away.' It is rendered age or time in Job 11. 17, Ps.
39. 5, and 89. 47. In Ps. 22. 27, Isa. 23. 17, 62. 11, and Jer. 25.
26, **erets** is used. 'Olam (עולם) is found in Ps. 73. 12, ' These prosper
in the world;' Eccles. 3. 11, 'He hath set the world in their
heart;' and in Isa. 45. 17, 64. 4.

By **tevel** is signified, first, the solid material on which man
dwells, and which was formed, founded, established, and disposed
by God; and secondly, the inhabitants thereof. It is usually
rendered οἰκουμένη in the LXX, never κόσμος, which was originally used only to denote order and ornament, but had acquired
a new meaning in our Lord's time.

The origin of the word is a little doubtful. A word spelt
similarly, and used in Lev. 18. 23 and other passages, signifies
pollution, confusion, or dispersion (from בלל). It is supposed, however, by Gesenius to be connected with the root **yaval**
(יבל), to flow, and to indicate the stream of people with which the
world is flooded.

In one or two passages only does the word **tevel** or οἰκουμένη
appear to refer to a limited portion of the earth. Perhaps Isa. 24. 4
may be mentioned as an example.

The expression 'round world,' which occurs in the P. B. version
in Ps. 18. 15, 89. 12, 93. 2, 96. 10, and 98. 8, simply stands for **tevel**.

---

[1] We find the root rendered forbear in Ezek. 3. 27 ; frail in Ps. 39. 4 ;
and rejected in Isa. 53. 3.

It is to be found in Coverdale's Bible, and is traceable to the old Latin version, *Orbis terrarum*, the earth being regarded by the ancients as a disk, though not as a globe.

In the N. T. the word οἰκουμένη is certainly used of the Roman Empire in Luke 2. 1, and perhaps in the quotation in Rom. 10. 18, where the larger sense of the word implied in the Psalms could hardly be intended. In other passages we must understand the word as signifying all the earth, *e.g.* in Matt. 24. 14; Acts 17. 31; Heb. 1. 6, 2. 5. Prophetic students have a right to either interpretation in Rev. 3. 10, 12. 9, and 16. 14, but the Roman use of the word is not so likely to be adopted by St. John as the Jewish.

§ 4. *Heaven.*

The Hebrew word generally in use to represent the heaven and also the air is **Shamaim** (שמים, Ass. *samami*). Sometimes it signifies the atmosphere immediately surrounding the earth, in which the fowls of 'the air' fly; sometimes it is used of the space in which the clouds are floating; in other places it refers to the vast expanse through which the stars are moving in their courses. **Shamaim** is also opposed to **Sheol**, the one being regarded as a place of exaltation, the other of degradation; the one being represented as the dwelling-place of the Most High and of the angels of God, the other as the abode of the dead.

In Ps. 77. 18, where we read, 'The voice of thy thunder was in the heaven,' the word **Galgal** (גלגל), which is used, probably signifies a whirlwind. The LXX has ἐν τῷ τροχῷ. In Ps. 68. 4, 'Extol him that rideth upon the heavens,' we find the word **'Arabah** (ערבה, Ass. *erbu*), which generally means a desert; hence clouds of sand, and clouds generally. In Ps. 89. 6 and 37, the word **Shachak** (שחק), rendered heavens, originally signifies a cloud of fine particles; compare our expression 'a cloud of dust.' In Isa. 5. 30, 'The light is darkened in the heavens thereof,' our margin has 'in the destruction thereof;' the Hebrew word (עריפים) used here probably signifies darkness.

In all but these few passages the word **Shamaim** is used where heaven is found in the A. V. It is to be noticed that the form of the word is neither singular nor plural, but dual. This may be only an ancient form of the plural, but it is supposed by some commentators to imply the existence of a lower and an upper heaven, or of a physical and spiritual heaven—'the heaven and the heaven of heavens.' The original idea represented by the root is generally considered to be height, and if this is a right conjecture, the word fairly answers to its Greek equivalent οὐρανός, and to its English translation 'heaven,' that which is *heaved* or *lifted* up. It includes all space that is not occupied by the terrestrial globe, and extends from the air we breathe and the winds which we feel around us to the firmament or expanse which contains the innumerable stars. This it includes, and exceeds; for where our intellect ceases to operate, and fails to find a limit to the extension of space, here faith comes in; and whilst before the eye of the body there is spread out an infinity of space, the possession of a super-material nature brings us into communion with a Being whose nature and condition cannot adequately be described by terms of locality or extension. The heavens and the heaven of heavens cannot contain Him; the countless stars are not only known and numbered by Him, but are called into existence and fixed in their courses by His will and wisdom. Wherever He is, there the true heaven is, and the glories of the firmament faintly shadow forth the ineffable bliss which those must realise who are brought into relationship with Him.

Whilst God is regarded as the God or King of Heaven, we read in the prophecy of Jeremiah of the 'Queen of Heaven' (7. 18, 44. 17, 18, 19, 25). In the margin this title is rendered 'frame of heaven' (מלאכת for מלכת). If the former is the right interpretation, the heathen goddess Astarte or Venus is probably referred to; if otherwise, the prophet is reprobating the worship of the frame, structure, or workmanship of heaven, or, in other words, of the stars, as a substitute for the worship of Him who created all these things.

The usage of the word 'heaven' in the N. T. generally answers to that which is to be traced through the Hebrew Bible, but more stress is laid upon the spiritual heaven, upon the Father who is there, and upon the Son who came from heaven, and who has returned thither to remain hidden from the eye of man until the time of the restitution.

There are, indeed, the same distinct spheres designated by the word οὐρανός in the N. T. as by **Shamaim** in the O. T. There is the air, or dwelling-place of the fowls of the air (Matt. 6. 26); there is also the vast space in which the stars are moving (Acts 2. 19); but in by far the greater number of passages heaven signifies the dwelling-place of the Most High, and the abode of the angelic hosts. The titles 'kingdom of God' and 'kingdom of heaven' are really identical in their signification, though presenting the truth in slightly varied aspects. God is the King of heaven, and His will is done by all its angelic inhabitants. When the kingdom of *God* is spoken of as coming upon earth, we are to understand a state of things in which the subjection of man's will to God is to be completed, and the destruction of all that is contrary to God's will, whether in things physical or in things spiritual, is to be accomplished. When, on the other hand, it is the kingdom of *heaven* that is announced, we are to understand that the organisation of the human race in whole or part, and also perhaps their dwelling-place, will be rendered harmonious with the other portions of the family of that Heavenly Father in whose house are many mansions.

The popular phraseology about 'going to heaven' represents the truth, but certainly not in the form in which it is generally presented in Scripture. We rarely read that the godly will go *to* *heaven*, either at death or after the resurrection. We are rather told of a kingdom being set up *on earth*, of a heavenly city descending from above, and taking up its abode in the new or renewed earth.

§ 5. *The Host of Heaven.*

In Deut. **4. 19** the people of Israel were specially warned lest they should lift up their eyes unto heaven, and when they saw the sun, and the moon, and the stars, all the host of heaven (τὸν κόσμον τοῦ οὐρανοῦ), should be driven to worship them and serve them. Death by stoning was to be the punishment of any such departure from the true God (Deut. **17. 3, 5**). To what an extent the people failed in this matter, and how grievously they suffered in consequence, will be seen by referring to 2 Kings **17. 16, 21. 3, 5** ; 2 Chron. **33. 3, 5** ; Jer. **8. 1–3, 19. 12, 13**. Not only was the host of heaven worshipped, but altars were set up in honour of the stars even in the precincts of the Temple. What a contrast with this impiety is presented by the opening words of the prayer of the Levites recorded in Neh. **9. 6**, 'Thou, even thou, art Lord alone ; thou hast made heaven, the heaven of heavens, with all their host, the earth, and all things that are therein, the seas, and all that is therein, and thou preservest them all; and the host of heaven worshippeth thee.'

The folly of worshipping the host of. heaven is forcibly illustrated by the fact that as the heavenly bodies owe their structure and continuance to God, so will they perish when He withdraws

His hand. 'All the host of heaven shall be dissolved, and the heavens shall be rolled together as a scroll : and all their host shall fall down, as the leaf falleth off from the vine, and as a falling fig from the fig-tree' (Isa. **34. 4**). This passage is taken up and adopted by our Lord, who says that 'After the tribulation the sun shall be darkened, and the moon shall not give her light, and the stars of heaven shall fall, and the powers that are in heaven (*i.e.* the host of heaven) shall be shaken' (Mark **13. 25**). Here the expression powers (δυνάμεις) is the usual rendering adopted by the LXX for host (ἡ δύναμις τοῦ οὐρανοῦ).

In 1 Kings **22. 19** Micaiah says, 'I saw the Lord sitting on his throne, and all the host of heaven (ἡ στρατιὰ τοῦ οὐρανοῦ) standing by him on his right hand and on his left.' The context shows us that the prophet was speaking, not of the physical, but of the spiritual heaven; and that by the host of heaven he meant the intelligent beings who exist in that spiritual sphere in which God dwells, and whose business it is to carry out His purposes of mercy and of wrath. With this passage may be compared the sublime vision contained in Rev. **19. 11–14**, when the heavens are opened, and the seer beholds the Faithful and True One called the Word of God riding on a white horse, 'and the armies which were in heaven (τὰ στρατεύματα τὰ ἐν τῷ οὐρανῷ) followed him upon white horses, clothed in fine linen.'

§ 6. *The Firmament.*

The Hebrew word **rakia'** (רָקִיעַ) stands for firmament, *i.e.* the space in which the stars are set (Gen. **1. 7, 8**). Our interpretation of the word is derived from the Greek στερέωμα, through the Latin *firmamentum*. It means that which is fixed and steadfast, rather than that which is solid. The word once occurs in the N. T., namely, in Col. **2. 5**, 'The steadfastness (στερέωμα) of your faith in Christ;' and other forms of the root are used in the same way. The application of this word to the heavenly bodies is simple and beautiful; they are not fickle and uncertain in their movements, but are regulated by a law which they cannot pass over. 'By the word of the Lord were the heavens made (ἐστερεώθησαν), and all the host of them by the breath of his mouth' (Ps. **33. 6**). 'I have made the earth, and created man upon it: I, even my hands, have stretched out (ἐστερέωσα) the heavens, and all their host have I commanded' (Isa. **45. 12**). 'Mine hand also hath laid the foundation of the earth, and my right hand hath spanned (ἐστερέωσε) the heavens' (Isa. **48**. 13).

The Hebrew word is derived from **raka'**, to spread out. This verb is found in Job **37**. 18, ' Hast thou with him spread out the sky, which is strong, and as a molten looking-glass ? ' Ps. **136**. 6, ' To him that stretched out the earth above (or over) the waters ; ' Isa. **42**. 5, ' He that spread forth the earth ; ' **44**. 24, ' That spreadeth abroad the earth by myself.'

The firmament, then, is that which is spread or stretched out—hence an expanse ; and this is the rendering received by many at the present time. Perhaps, guided partly by this usage of the Hebrew word, and partly by the rendering of the LXX, we may attach two ideas to the term, namely, *extension* and *fixity*, or (to combine them in one) *fixed space*. The interplanetary spaces are measured out by God, and, though the stars are ever moving, they generally 'preserve fixed relative positions ; their movements are not erratic, not in straight lines, but in orbits, and thus, though ever changing, they are always the same.

CHAPTER XXIV.

DESTRUCTION, DEATH, HELL.

§ 1. *Various Words signifying Destruction.*

THE destiny of man after death is the most serious of all questions. If Scripture invariably prophesied smooth things, we should readily accept its verdict. But there are passages in the N. T. which point in another direction. Hence the necessity of studying the O. T. terminology on the subject.

More than fifty Hebrew words have been rendered destroy, destruction, or perish. Some of them need only a brief mention, but others are of greater importance.

Aid (איד) is occasionally so rendered, as in Job **18**. 12 and Prov. **1**. 27. It is usually rendered calamity, and signifies that which oppresses and straitens, the 'tribulation and anguish' of Rom. **2**. 9. **Asaph** (אסף), which occurs in 1 Sam. **15**. 6, means to gather, and we might render the passage, 'lest I include you with them.' Compare Ps. **26**. 9, also Zeph. **1**. 2, 3. **Asham** (אשם) is found in Ps. **5**. 10, 'destroy thou them,' *i.e.* condemn them or deal with them as guilty. In 2 Chron. **22**. 7, the 'destruction' of Ahaziah is literally his treading down; and in Isa. **10**. 25, the destruction of the Assyrians means their being brought to nought or wasted away (so far as this world is concerned). In Prov. **21**. 7, 'The robbery of the wicked shall destroy them,' the verb (גרר) means to saw, sweep away, or drag down. The destruction of the seed royal by Athaliah (2 Chron. **22**. 10) is described by a word which signifies 'to inflict a pestilence' (דבר); compare the use of the word 'pestilent' or 'pestilential' in our own language. **Daca** (דכא, Ass. *daku*), to dash in pieces or crush, is used in Job **6**. 9, **34**. 25; Ps. **90**. 3, 'Thou turnest man to destruction.'

Bala' (בלע, Ass. *balu*), to swallow up, is used several times, *e.g.* in Job **2**. 3, 'To destroy him without a cause;' Ps. **55**. 9, 'Destroy, O Lord, and divide their tongues;' Isa. **25**. 7, 8, 'He will destroy

270

in this mountain the face of the covering cast over all people, and
the vail that is spread over all nations; he will swallow up death
in victory.' Here the same word is rendered 'destroy' in one
verse and 'swallow up' in the other; the last clause might be
rendered, 'He will utterly destroy death.' See R. V.

Damah. (דמה), to be silent, or to cease, is rendered destroy in
Ezek. 27. 32, 'What city is like Tyrus, like the destroyed in the
midst of the sea?' and Hos. 4. 5, 6, 'I will destroy thy mother;
my people are destroyed for lack of knowledge.' We might perhaps give a more literal rendering here, and say, 'My people are
silenced for lack of knowledge.'

In Deut. 7. 23, and in 1 Sam. 5, 9, 11, the word used (הום) is
supposed to signify commotion or confusion; a similar word
(הםם), signifying discomfiture, is found in Exod. 23. 27, Deut.
2. 15, and Ps. 144. 6. **Harag** (הרג), to kill, is used in Ps. 78. 47,
'He destroyed their vines with hail.' **Haras** (הרם), to tear down,
occurs in 1 Chron. 20. 1; of the destruction of Rabbah, in Ps.
11. 3; of the destruction of foundations, in Isa. 14. 17; of the
destruction of cities, in Isa. 19. 18, where we read of 'the city
of destruction,' or, as the margin has it, 'the city of Heres, or
the sun.' It also occurs in Ps. 28. 5, and Isa. 49. 17, 19.

Chaval (חבל), to bind, is used in Ezra 6. 12; Prov. 13. 13;
Eccles. 5. 6; Micah 2. 10; Isa. 10. 27, 'The yoke shall be destroyed
because of the anointing;' 54. 16, 'I have created the waster to
destroy;' Dan. 2. 44, 6. 26, 7. 14, 'In the days of these kings
shall the God of heaven set up a kingdom which shall never be
destroyed;' 4. 23, 'Hew down the tree and destroy it.'

In Prov. 31. 8, the persons described as 'appointed for destruction' are literally 'sons of change or passing away' (חלוף, Ass.
khalafu). **Charav** (חרב), to dry up, occurs in Jud. 16. 24, 'The
destroyer of our country;' and in 2 Kings 19. 17, Ezra 4. 15,
Ps. 9. 6, 'Destructions are come to a perpetual end.' The
exhaustion of a country, city, or individual is evidently referred
to in these passages.

In seven passages in the Proverbs destruction is literally a
'breaking up' (מחתה); in Ps. 74. 8, 'Let us destroy them altogether,' the idea of violent dealing (ינה) is implied; in Exod.
15. 9, the verb signifies to take possession (ירש), and the passage
is rendered in the margin, 'My hand shall repossess them.' In
Job 21. 20, calamity (כיד) is represented; whilst in Job 9. 22, Lev.
26. 44, and 2 Chron. 31. 1, **Calah** (כלה), to finish, to complete,

and so to bring to an end, is used. **Carath** (כרת), to cut off, is
rendered 'destroy' in Exod. 8. 9, Lev. 26. 22, Jud. 4. 24, and
1 Kings 15. 13.   **Mul** (מול), which also signifies to cut off, is found
in Ps. 118. 10, 11, 12 ; **Cathath** (כתת), to beat, in Deut. 1. 44,
2 Chron. 15. 6, and Job 4. 20 ; **Muth** (מות, Ass. *matu*), to die, in
2 Sam. 20. 19 and Job 33. 22 ; and **Machah** (מחה), to blot out, in
Gen. 6. 7, 7. 4, 23, in the history of the Deluge, also in Jud. 21. 17
and Prov. 31. 3.

In Prov. 15. 25, 'The Lord will destroy the house of the proud,'
the word (נסח, Ass. *nasakhu*) signifies to pluck up, and hence to
root out.   In Job 19. 26, 'Though after my skin (worms) destroy
this (body),' the word (נקף) means to cut down.   In Isa. 42. 14,
'I will destroy' is literally 'I will make desolate' (נשם).   In
Ps. 9. 6, 'Thou hast destroyed cities,' **Natha** (נתע), to tear, is used;
and in Exod. 34. 13, Deut. 7. 5, Job 19. 10, Ps. 52. 5, and Ezek.
26. 12, **Nathats** (נתץ), to tear down or beat down, is found.
Tsadah (צדה), to cut down, is the word in Zeph. 3. 6.   **Saphah**
(ספה), to scrape, is found in Gen. 18. 23, 24, 'Wilt thou destroy
the righteous with the wicked ? . . . wilt thou destroy and not
spare the place for the fifty righteous ?' also in 1 Chron. 21. 12
and Ps. 40. 14.

Shavar (שבר, Ass. *sabaru*), to shiver or break in pieces, is
rendered 'destroy' about thirty times, *e.g.* in Prov. 16. 18, 'Pride
goeth before destruction ;' 29. 1, 'He that being often reproved,
hardeneth his neck, shall suddenly be destroyed, and that without
remedy ;' Isa. 1. 28, 'The destruction of the sinners and transgressors shall be together ;' 59. 7, 'Wasting and destruction are
in their paths ;' 60. 18, 'Violence shall no more be heard in thy
land, wasting nor destruction within thy borders.'   **Shiah** (שאיה),
desolation, occurs in Ps. 73. 18 and Isa. 24. 12 ; the word **Shuah**
(שואה) has the same meaning in Ps. 35. 8, 17, and 63. 9 ; **Shamem**
(שמם), to lay waste, or to be astonished, in Eccles. 7. 16 and
Hos. 2. 12 ; **Shasah** (שסה), to spoil, in Jer. 50. 11 ; **Shacol** (שכל),
to bereave, in Deut. 32. 25.   **Shadad** (שדד), to deal violently, is
rendered 'destroy' ten times, *e.g.* in Ps. 137. 8, 'O daughter of
Babylon, who art to be destroyed' (P. B. version, 'wasted with
misery ') ; Hos. 7. 13, 'Destruction unto them ! because they have
trangressed against me ;' Joel 1. 15, 'The day of the Lord is at
hand, and as a destruction from the Almighty shall it come.'

The Chaldean word used of the destruction of the temple by
Nebuchadnezzar in Ezra 5. 12 is **Sathar** (סתר), which in Hebrew

means to hide. In Ps. 17. 4, the word (פריץ) signifies violence; in Job 30. 24, 31. 29, we find **Pid** (פיד), calamity; in Prov. 13. 20, **Rua'** (רוע), evil; in Ezek. 7. 25, **Kaphdah** (קפדה), cutting off; in Jer. 46. 20, the word for destruction is taken from the nipping (קרץ) of the gad-fly. **Kathav** (קטב), contagion, is found in Deut. 32. 24, Ps. 91. 6, and Hos. 13. 14, 'O death, I will be thy destruction.' **Tsamath** (צמת), to cut off, is the word used in 2 Sam. 22. 41; Ps. 18. 40, 69. 4, 73. 27, 101. 8.

In Num. 24. 17 we read, ' A sceptre shall rise out of Israel, and shall smite the corners (or smite through the princes) of Moab, and destroy all the children of Seth.' The word **Karkar** (קרקר), here rendered destroy, is somewhat doubtful. Some take it as meaning dig—hence dig through or spoil; others consider that it is used in a favourable sense of the ' *building up the wall* ' of Seth; but see Isa. 22. 5, where it means to break down a wall.

§ 2. *The Root Avad.*

The words hitherto noticed, though very numerous, are used only in a few passages, and do not play a conspicuous part in Scripture. They point to destruction as a calamity, as a work of breaking down or tearing up, as an act of violence, or as a deed of desolation. They apply to nations, cities, and individuals, and are used in just such senses as we should give them in ordinary history, without at all referring to the destiny of the individual in any state of existence beyond the world. Four words, however, remain to be considered, each of which is used in a great number of passages, and with some important variations of meaning.

Avad (אבד, Ass. *abadu*), to perish, and in its causative form to destroy, is largely used throughout the O. T. This word is rendered 'perish' in about a hundred passages. When used of persons it generally signifies *death*, when used of lands it implies *desolation*. The same is the general state of the case with regard to its Greek equivalent in its various forms of ἀπόλλυμι, ἀπώλεια, ὄλεθρος. The name *Abaddon* (Rev. 9. 11) is rendered *Apollyon*, the destroyer.

It is applied to the case of Korah's company, who 'perished from among the congregation' (Num. 16. 33); to the Amalekite nation, which should 'perish for ever' (Num. 24. 20, see also verse 24); it is held out as a threat to Israel that they should 'utterly perish from off the land' if they became idolatrous (Deut. 4. 26, contrast 30. 18); it is used of the nation's ancestor, 'a Syrian

s

ready to perish' (Deut. **26**. 5); Esther uses it with regard to her apprehension of death as the alternative of success, 'If I perish, I perish' (Esther **4**. 16); it is applied to the memory of the wicked, which dies out of the minds of their survivors (Job **18**. 17); to the disappearance of the wicked man from the earth (**20**. 7); it is used of men perishing for want of clothing (**31**. 19); it is applied to the 'way' or course taken by the wicked in contrast with the way of the righteous (Ps. **1**. 6); it is used of the heathen (as such) perishing out of the land (**10**. 16), of the wicked perishing before the presence of God as wax melteth before the fire (**68**. 2), of the heavens perishing whilst God endures (**102**. 26), of man's thoughts perishing when he dies (**146**. 4).

In Eccles. **7**. 15, **avad** is applied to a just man perishing in his righteousness; and in Isa. **57**. 1, 2, we read, 'The righteous perisheth, and no man layeth it to heart; and merciful men are taken away, none considering that the righteous is taken away from that which is evil. He shall enter into peace.' These passages are important, as showing that the perishing of the outer man in death is perfectly consistent with the entrance into peace.

The passages which have been cited are fair samples of the whole. They show that the word refers to the death of the righteous or the wicked; to the downfall and dissolution of nations; to the desolation of countries; to the withering away of herbage and crops; to the fading away of strength, hope, wisdom, knowledge, and wealth. The word is applied to man with reference to his whole position upon earth; whilst his future destiny is left apparently untouched by it.

A brief examination of the usage of the active voice where it is rendered 'destroy' or 'destruction' will suffice. The word is applied to the destruction of temples, images, and pictures (Num. **33**. 52, Deut. **12**. 33); to defeat (Josh. **7**. 7); to national overthrow (Deut. **28**. 51); and to the taking away of life, whether by the hand of man or by the agency of God (2 Kings **10**. 19; Exod. **10**. 7; Lev. **23**. 30; Deut. **7**. 10, 20; Job **28**. 22).

In Job **26**. 6 we read, 'Hell (**Sheol**) is naked before him, and destruction hath no covering;' and in Prov. **15**. 11, 'Hell (**Sheol**) and destruction are before the Lord.' These words apparently refer to the locality or condition of those who have died or have been destroyed; it is implied that, although so far as this world is concerned they have perished, yet they are still in a state of existence, and are within God's cognisance.

In Ps. **88.** 10, 11, 12, the question is heard, 'Wilt thou shew wonders to the dead? shall the dead arise and praise thee? Shall thy lovingkindness be declared in the grave? or thy faithfulness in destruction? Shall thy wonders be known in the dark? and thy righteousness in the land of forgetfulness?' Here the dead, the grave or sepulchre, the state of destruction, the dark, and the land of forgetfulness, are synonymous; and the Psalmist, in his longing for present help, urges God not to put off His lovingkindness until that time when (so far as this life is concerned) it will be too late.

Avad is frequently rendered lose, *e.g.* in Exod. **22.** 9, Lev. **6.** 3, 4, Deut. **22.** 3, and 1 Sam. **9.** 3, 20, with reference to a lost ox, sheep, or garment. In Ps. **119.** 176 it assumes a moral significance, 'I have gone astray like a lost sheep; seek thy servant, for I do not forget thy commandments;' Jer. **50.** 6, 'My people hath been lost sheep, their shepherds have lured them to go astray;' Ezek. **34.** 4, 'Neither have ye sought that which was lost;' verse 16, 'I will seek that which was lost.'

§ 3. *Destruction as Taught in the N. T.*

The word ὄλεθρος is found four times in the N. T. In 1 Cor. **5.** 5 'the destruction of the flesh' is spoken of. Here reference seems to be made to the special temporal chastisements which were inflicted in the apostolic ages, and a contrast is drawn between the destruction of the flesh now and the salvation of the spirit in the day of Christ. In the other three passages reference is made to the punishment of the ungodly; see 1 Thess. **5.** 3, 2 Thess. **1.** 9, and 1 Tim. **6.** 9.

Ἀπώλεια in the N. T. specially represents the lot of those who go on the broad path (Matt. **7.** 13), who set themselves against the Gospel (Phil. **1.** 28), who live a carnal life (Phil. **3.** 19), who yield to lusts and covetousness (1 Tim. **6.** 9), who draw back from Christ (Heb. **10.** 39), who deny the Lord that bought them (2 Pet. **2.** 1, 3 [1]), and wrest the Scriptures (2 Pet. **3.** 16), and are, in a word, ungodly (2 Pet. **3.** 7).

The infliction of this ἀπώλεια is synchronous with the Day of Judgment and the burning of the heaven and earth that now are (2 Pet. **3.** 7); the whole event being prefigured by the destruction that came upon the earth at the Deluge, when the then world

---

[1] The A. V. has failed to preserve the connection between the *destructive* heresies and the *destruction* which ensues. See R. V.

perished (ἀπώλετο), and also by the destruction of Sodom and Gomorrha. The word also occurs in John 17. 12, of Judas, the son of perdition; of another son of perdition in 2 Thess. 2. 3; in Rev. 17. 8, 11, of the Beast; also in Acts 8. 20 [25. 16] and Rom. 9. 22.

The verb ἀπόλλυμι is applied to the waste of ointment (Matt. 26. 8), to the destruction of physical objects, *e.g.* wine-skins (Matt. 9. 17), gold (1 Pet. 1. 7), food (John 6. 27), and the hair of the head (Luke 21. 18). In these cases it is not annihilation that is spoken of, but such injury as makes the object practically useless for its original purpose. It is applied to the destruction of the world in 2 Pet. 3. 6, in exactly the same sense; for as the world was destroyed at the Deluge, so shall it be hereafter; it will be rendered useless as a habitation for man. Nevertheless, as after the first destruction it was restored, so it may be after the second. Again, the word is applied to the perishing or being destroyed from off the face of the earth in death, when the physical frame which is the temple of life becomes untenanted; and a contrast is drawn between the power of those who can bring about the death of the body, and of Him who can destroy both body and soul in Gehenna. Death is spoken of in this sense in Matt. 2. 13, 8. 25, 12. 14, 21. 41, 22. 7, 26. 52, 27. 20; and probably in Matt. 18. 14, Rom. 2. 12, 14. 15, and 1 Cor. 8. 11. The destruction of the body is compared to the disintegration of the seed which falls into the ground and dies. It is dismemberment and dissolution, and renders the body useless for the time being, so far as its original purpose is concerned, but it is not annihilation. The use of the word in the argument in 1 Cor. 15. 18 is worthy of note; it here implies that, physically speaking, the Christian has perished, if Christ be not risen. There is not a word here about annihilation of the *person* (which would continue in Hades), but simply of the blotting out of *existence in the body.* See Isa. 51. 1, 2, quoted above.

The word is also largely used in a moral sense, with respect to the inner man, as the opposite of salvation. It is applied to those '*lost* sheep' whom the Good Shepherd died to save (Matt. 18. 11; Luke 15. 32; compare Isa. 53. 6). All men are regarded as morally *destroyed*, *i.e.* they have failed to carry out the intention for which the race was called into being. To save them from this condition, God sent His Son, and caused Him to be lifted up like the serpent in the wilderness (John 3. 15, 16), not being willing that any should *perish*, but that all should come to repentance (2 Pet. 3. 9). Those

who reject this salvation have contracted a new responsibility, and
are, in a new sense, in the way of destruction (ἀπολλυμένοι) (1 Cor.
1. 18; 2 Cor. 2. 15, 4. 3; 2 Thess. 2. 10). This final destruction
affects evil spirits as well as men. We cannot comprehend what
will be the nature of this destruction which affects the *spirit* or
person ; but the reading of such words as those uttered by the Lord
in Matt. 10. 28, 39, 16. 25, and Luke 9. 25, impresses the mind with
the idea of the utter rejection and infinite degradation which shall
be the lot of those who judge themselves unworthy of eternal life.
Not only creation, but also redemption, has failed of its purpose
with them.

§ 4. *The Root Shachath.*

Shachath (שׁחת, Ass. *sakhatu*), a word which especially marks
dissolution or corruption, is rendered destroy in about a
hundred places. It first occurs in Gen. 6.13, 17, 9. 11, 15, both with
reference to the moral corruption and also to the physical destruction of all that was living on the earth; and of the earth itself,
which, as St. Peter said, 'perished' (2 Pet. 3. 6). It is next used
of the destruction of Sodom and Gomorrha (Gen. 13. 10, 18. 28. 19.
13, 14, 29), a destruction which is regarded, both in the O. T. and
N. T., as the sample of the punishment of the ungodly. It is used in
connection with the destruction of the first-born in Egypt (Exod. 12.
23), of trees (Deut. 20. 19, 20), of the increase of the earth (Jud.
6. 4, 5), of men in battle (Jud. 20. 21, &c.), of cities (1 Sam. 23. 10),
of nations (2 Kings 8. 19, 13. 23).

In Ps. 55. 23 we read, 'Thou shalt bring them down into the
pit of destruction: bloody and deceitful men shall not live out
half their days.' This is a sample of a large class of passages in
which wickedness is represented as bringing an untimely or violent
death as its consequence. God, on the contrary, redeems the life of
His people from destruction; that is to say, He prolongs their days
(Ps. 103. 4). This word is also used in Dan. 9. 26, 'The people of
the prince that shall come shall destroy the city and the sanctuary;'
and in Hos. 13. 9, 'O Israel, thou hast destroyed thyself, but in me
is thy help.' Lastly, the promise for the restored Jerusalem is,
'They shall not hurt nor destroy in all my holy mountain' (Isa. 11.
9, 65. 25).

The chief LXX rendering of this word is διαφθείρω; we also
find in several passages φθείρω, καταφθείρω, ὀλοθρεύω, ἐξολοθρεύω,
ἐξαλείφω, and ἀπόλλυμι.

The verb διαφθείρω is used of physical corruption in Luke 12. 33, 2 Cor. 4. 16, Rev. 8. 9; of moral corruption in 1 Tim. 6. 5, 'men corrupted in mind,' and Rev. 19. 2; it is used in both senses in Rev. 11. 18, 'To *corrupt* those that are *corrupting* the earth.'

The noun is only used in two passages, namely, in Acts 2. 27, 31, and 13. 34–37, in which Peter and Paul are applying Ps. 16. 10 to the fact that our Lord's body was raised before corruption set in.

§ 5. *The Root Shamad.*

Shamad (שמד), to consume, is rendered 'destroy' in about eighty passages. It is usually rendered ἐξολοθρεύω,[1] but sometimes ἀπόλλυμι. It is applied several times to the destruction of nations, cities, and families by war, especially in the Books of Deuteronomy, Joshua. and Samuel. It is used of the destruction of the wicked in Ps. 37. 38, 92. 7, 'They shall be destroyed for ever;' 145. 20, 'All the wicked will he destroy;' Isa. 13. 9, 'He shall destroy the sinners out of the land.' The word occurs in Isa. 26. 14, 'They are dead, they shall not live; they are deceased, they shall not rise: therefore hast thou visited and destroyed them, and made all their memory to perish.' This is an expression of the security in the mind of the speaker, who feels that there is no fear of the evil rulers rising again to play the tyrant or to mislead, but it is by no means to be taken as deciding the question whether these ungodly men may or may not have a future awaiting them.

Very often a qualifying expression is used, which shows that the destruction spoken of is relative, not absolute. Thus in Ezek. 14. 9, 'I will destroy him from the midst of my people Israel;' Amos 9. 8, 'I will destroy it from off the face of the earth;' Hag. 2. 22, 'I will destroy the strength of the kingdoms of the heathen.' This points to the real meaning in other passages.

§ 6. *The Root Charam.*

Charam (חרם) is a religious word of great importance, as will be seen from its usage. It represents the devotion of some object to destruction or to a sacred use (answering to the double sense of the Latin *sacer*), not for the gratification of any selfish purpose, but as

---

[1] This word only occurs once in the N. T., namely, in Acts 3. 23, which is a quotation from Deut. 18. 19, but not from the LXX.

a religious act. It is rendered devote or dedicate in Lev. 27. 21, with reference to a field; in verses 28 and 29 with reference to man, beast, and land; and the direction is given that the devoted object (if an animal) should not be redeemed, but put to death. With regard to the land, its devotion rendered it the property of the priest (Num. 18. 14; Ezek. 44. 29). This word was applied to the destruction of nations, partly because they were regarded as under the Divine doom, and partly also because the substance of the nations destroyed was dedicated to the Lord. Thus we read in Micah 4. 13, 'Thou shalt beat in pieces many people, and I will consecrate (or devote) their gain unto the Lord, and their substance unto the Lord of the whole earth.' In Ezra 10. 8 it is used of the forfeiture of the substance of those who did not come to the Passover, which was accompanied by the putting them out of the congregation. Also in Dan. 11. 44 it is used of the way in which the king should 'make away' many.

The word is used of the accursed (*i.e.* devoted) city and substance of Jericho in the sixth and seventh chapters of Joshua, and in the reference to Achan's conduct in Josh. 22. 20 and 1 Chron. 2. 7.

The idols and their silver and gold are also described as cursed (*i.e.* devoted) in Deut. 7. 26, 13. 17. In Isa. 34. 5 the Edomites are described as 'the people of God's curse,' *i.e.* devoted to destruction by God; and this accounts for the use of the word in 2 Chron. 20. 23, 'The children of Ammon and Moab stood up against the inhabitants of Mount Seir utterly to slay them' (*i.e.* to devote them to destruction); without knowing it, they were carrying out the Divine purpose. In Isa. 43. 28 God says, 'I have given Jacob to the curse,' *i.e.* I have devoted the people to destruction. This was in consequence of their idolatry and rebellion.

This same word, rendered 'curse,' is the last word in the solemn conclusion of Malachi's prophecy, 'Behold I will send you Elijah the prophet before the coming of the great and dreadful day of the Lord; and he shall turn the heart of the fathers to the children, and the heart of the children to the fathers, lest I come to smite the earth with a curse,' *i.e.* lest I come and devote the land of Israel to destruction. Alas! the warning voice of Elias was not attended to; Jerusalem did not recognise the day of its visitation; and it was smitten with a curse; the country was once more desolated, and the people scattered.

Charam is rendered *destroy* forty times. In almost all of these places reference is made to the destruction of the natives of Canaan and the surrounding country by Israel. The destruction of nations by Nebuchadnezzar is described by the same word in 2 Kings 19. 11 and Isa. 37. 11, perhaps because he was unwittingly carrying out the work of God in his destruction. In Isa. 11. 15 the destruction of the land of Egypt by the Lord is referred to; and in Jer. 25. 9, the destruction of Judah by the King of Babylon. The word is also used in Zech. 14. 11, where the bright promise is given of a time when 'there shall be no more utter-destruction'—a hope that is carried forward in the N. T. in the words, 'There shall be no more curse' (Rev. 22. 3).

With regard to the extermination of the Canaanites, the following points may be noticed. *First*, it was not taken in hand to accomplish personal revenge ; Israel had no grudge against Canaan ; the people had to be almost goaded into the land. *Secondly*, it was not done to gain plunder, for all plunder was regarded as **cherem**, devoted to God, and in that sense accursed. *Thirdly*, it was not done to gratify thirst for military glory; for the Hebrews were the smallest of nations, and were told beforehand that if they conquered it would not be in their own strength, but in God's. *Fourthly*, it was not to be regarded as a reward for merit; they were a rebellious and stiff-necked people, and would have perished in the wilderness had not God remembered His holy covenant. *Fifthly*, the extermination of the Canaanites was to be a security against idolatry and demoralisation on the part of Israel. *Lastly*, these nations had filled up the measure of their iniquity, and the Israelites in destroying them were acting magisterially as God's agents.

The most prominent LXX renderings of this word are ἐξολοθρεύω, ἀναθεματίζω, ἀνάθεμα, ἀνάθημα. The word ἀνάθημα occurs in Luke 21. 5, where we read of the temple being adorned with *gifts*. Ἀναθεματίζω is found four times in the N. T. In Mark 14. 71 it is used of Peter's cursing, which may have been a calling down of imprecation on his own head. So in Acts 23. 12, 14. 21, certain men 'bound themselves with an oath,' *i.e.* invited the curse of God in case they failed to carry out their purpose.

It is not easy to fix the exact sense of ἀνάθεμα in the N. T. With the exception of Acts 23. 14, it only occurs in five passages, which are in St. Paul's Epistles. In Gal. 1. 8, 9, he says, 'If any one preach any other gospel than I have preached unto you, let him be *anathema*.' Again, 1 Cor. 16. 22, 'If any one love not the Lord Jesus Christ, let him be *anathema*.' He does not say, let him be put away from among you, but, let him be regarded with aversion as an object on which the Lord will pour down indignation.

Again, the Apostle says (1 Cor. 12. 3) that whatever spirit calls Jesus *anathema* is not of God.   He is here giving a plain test by which the dullest comprehension could discern spirits.   Whatever spirit prompts a man to speak of Jesus as an accursed object, that spirit cannot be of God.

The only other passage is Rom. 9. 3, where Paul seems to have almost prayed or wished that an *anathema* may have come on him from Christ, for the sake of his brethren.   In Father Simon's translation of the N. T., the passage reads thus :—'I could wish myself to be an anathema, for the sake of Jesus Christ, for my brethren,' &c.   He considered that the Greek ἀπὸ (from) might be rendered 'because of,' or 'for the sake of,' because the Hebrew preposition which answers to it in the O. T. is frequently used in this sense.

§ 7. *Meaning and Use of the Word Sheol or Hades.*

The state which we call death, *i.e.* the condition consequent upon the act of dying, is to be viewed in three aspects :— First, there is the *tomb*, or sepulchre, the local habitation of the physical frame, which is called **Kever** (קבר, Ass. *qabru*), Gen. 50. 5 ; secondly, there is the *corruption* whereby the body itself is dissolved, which is represented by the word **Shachath** (שחת), discussed above ; and thirdly, there is **Sheol** (שאול), which represents the locality or condition of the departed.   The A. V. translates **Sheol** by the words Hell, the grave, the pit; the LXX usually renders it Ἅδης ; the R. V. has unfortunately put **Sheol** in the O. T., and **Hades** in the N. T.   The original meaning of the Hebrew and Greek words is uncertain, but the following passages illustrate its usage :— Gen. 37. 35, 'I shall go down to the grave unto my son mourning' (compare 42. 38, 44. 29, 31).   1 Sam. 2. 6, 'The Lord killeth and maketh alive: he bringeth down to the grave and bringeth up.'   Job 7. 9, 'As the cloud is consumed and vanisheth away, so he that goeth down to the grave shall come up no (more).   He shall return no more to his house, neither shall his place know him any more.'   Job 14. 13, 'O that thou wouldest hide me in the grave, that thou wouldest keep me secret, until thy wrath be past, that thou wouldest appoint me a set time and remember me.'   Ps. 30. 3, 'Thou hast brought up my soul from the

grave: thou hast kept me alive, that I should not go down to the
pit.' Ps. 49. 14, 15, 'Like sheep they are laid in the grave;
death shall feed on them; and the upright shall have dominion
over them in the morning; and their beauty shall consume in the
grave from their dwelling. But God will redeem my soul from
the power of the grave: for he shall receive me.' Isa. 38. 10, 'I
shall go to the gates of the grave.' Hos. 13. 14, 'I will ransom
them from the power (or hand) of the grave; I will redeem them
from death: O death, I will be thy plagues; O grave, I will be
thy destruction.' Num. 16. 30, 33, 'They go down quick (*i.e.* alive)
into the pit.'

The word Hell stands for **Sheol** in the following amongst other
passages:—

Deut. 32. 22, 'A fire is kindled in mine anger, and shall burn
unto the lowest hell.' 2 Sam. 22. 6, Ps. 18. 5, 116. 3, 'The sorrows
of hell compassed me about, the snares of death prevented me.'
Job 11. 8, 'It is high as heaven; what canst thou do? deeper than
hell; what canst thou know?' Job 26. 6, 'Hell is naked before
him, and destruction hath no covering.' Ps. 9. 17, 'The wicked
shall be turned into hell, and all the nations that forget God.'
Ps. 16. 10, 'Thou wilt not leave my soul in hell, neither wilt thou
suffer thine holy one to see corruption.' Ps. 139. 8, 'If I ascend
up into heaven, thou art there: if I make my bed in hell, behold
thou art there.' Prov. 5. 5, 'Her feet go down to death; her steps
take hold on hell.' Prov. 15. 11, 'Hell and destruction are before
the Lord; how much more then the hearts of the children of men?'
Prov. 23. 14, 'Thou shalt beat him with the rod, and shalt deliver
his soul from hell.' Prov. 27. 20, 'Hell and destruction are never
full; so the eyes of man are never satisfied.' Isa. 14. 15, 'Yet thou
shalt be brought down to hell, to the sides of the pit.' Ezek. 31.
16, 17 (see also verse 15, above), 'I made the nations to shake at
the sound of his fall, when I cast him down to hell with them that
descend into the pit: and all the trees of Eden, the choice and best
of Lebanon, all that drink water, shall be comforted in the nether
parts of the earth. They also went down into hell with him unto
them that be slain with the sword.' Amos 9. 2, 'Though they dig
into hell, thence shall mine hand take them; though they climb
up to heaven, thence will I bring them down.' Jonah 2. 2, 'Out of
the belly of hell cried I, and thou heardest my voice.'

These are the most notable passages in which the word **Sheol**
occurs. There is no reason to doubt that what the grave or pit is

to the body, that **Sheol** is to the soul.   It is the *nether-world*, and perhaps this would be the best rendering for the word.   Not in one single passage is it used in the sense of the place of punishment after the resurrection, concerning which little, if anything, is definitely revealed in the O. T.   It is contrasted, as regards its locality, with heaven, the one being regarded as *down*, the other *up*.   It is spoken of as an abode for those who have departed from the way of life and have chosen the path of evil.   Concerning those who live to the Lord, if they enter it, they are to be delivered from its hand by the power of God; death shall not have dominion over them. It is dark and silent, a place where none can praise God.   Its very name possibly signifies a place about which men inquire—an impenetrable hiding-place.   It involves deprivation of the only kind of existence about which we have any definite knowledge, but some passages where it occurs imply a certain companionship.   Though man knows so little about it, **Sheol** is naked and open before God He can find men there; He can hide them there; He can redeem them thence.

It is surprising to notice how few references there are to this region or condition in the N. T., it being only mentioned twelve times altogether.   In Matt. **11. 23**, and Luke **10. 15**, it is used figuratively of the casting down of Capernaum from her exaltation; and in the same way it is said of the Church of Christ, that the gates of Hades shall not prevail against it (Matt. **16. 18**).

In Luke **16. 23** the rich man entered *Hades*, not *Gehenna*.

In Acts **2. 27** St. Peter quotes the sixteenth Psalm, with regard to the interpretation of which there is some difference of opinion. The ordinary rendering is, 'Thou shalt not leave my soul in hell,' but there are critics who consider that the passage, both in the O. T. and N. T., ought to be rendered, 'Thou shalt not consign my soul to Hades;' whilst others are of opinion that it should be translated, 'Thou shalt not leave my dead body in the grave.'   That the word **nephesh**, soul, may sometimes be translated 'dead body' is true (see chap. iv.); and that the word *hades* is often translated *grave* we have also seen to be true.   So far as the usage of the words, therefore, is concerned, there is no objection to this last rendering; but the belief of the early Church as to the meaning of the text was in accordance with the more generally received translation.[1]

In 1 Cor. **15. 55**, the A. V. has adopted the rendering **grave** for Hades.   But, according to many early authorities, the right

[1] See Pearson on the Creed.

reading is *death*, not *Hades*. In Rev. **1**. 18 (and, according to some MSS., in **3**. 7) the Lord is described as possessing the keys of Hades and death, *i.e.* it is He that can open the door of the nether world and call forth the dead into being. In Rev. **6**. 8 Death and Hades are described as the agents of slaughter.; and in chap. **20**. 13, 14, they are said to yield up the dead that had been swallowed up by them, and then to be cast into the lake of fire.

§ 8. *The Word Gehenna.*

The word **Gehenna** means the valley of Hinnom (lit. Gai-Hinnom), immediately outside Jerusalem (see Josh. **15**. 8). In 2 Kings **23**. 10, 2 Chron. **28**. 3, and **33**. 6, it is the scene of degraded idolatrous customs; and in Jer. **19**. it is described as not only a centre of iniquity, but also a place of retribution. In this sense it was used by the Jews in our Lord's time (see *e.g.* Pirke Aboth), and the Lord Himself takes it as the place or condition of punishment. It is only used by Him (Matt. **5**. 22, 29, 30, **10**. 28, **18**. 9, **23**. 15, 33; Mark **9**. 43, 47; Luke **12**. 5) and in James **3**. 6.

§ 9. *Death.*

The general word to represent **dying** is **Moth** (מות, Ass. *mutu*); other words, however, are occasionally used. Thus **Naphal** (נפל, Ass. *napalu*), to fall, occurs in Gen. **25**. 18, 'He died (or *fell*) in the presence of (or *before*) all his brethren.' **Shadad** (שדד, Ass. *sadadu*), to destroy, is found in Jud. **5**. 27, 'There he fell down *dead*' (*i.e.* destroyed). **Gava'** (גוע), to breathe out or expire (ἐκπνέω), is used in Gen. **6**. 17, 'Everything that is in the earth shall die;' **7**. 21; Num. **20**. 3, 'Would God that we had died when our brethren died before the Lord;' verse 29; Job **27**. 5, **29**. 18, **36**. 12; Ps. **88**. 15, **104**. 29; Zech. **13**. 8. This word is only used with reference to the death of our Lord in the N. T.; see Mark **15**. 37, 39; Luke **23**. 46.

Nivlah (נבלה), a carcase, is used in Lev. **7**. 24, 'The fat of the beast *that dieth* (of itself),' lit. 'the fat of a carcase.' So also in Lev. **17**. 15, **22**. 8; Deut. **14**. 8, 21; Ps. **79**. 2; Isa. **26**. 19, 'Thy dead men shall live, together with my dead body shall they arise;' Jer. **26**. 23, **34**. 20, **36**. 30; Ezek. **4**. 14, **44**. 31. Another word, signifying carcase (פגר, Ass. *pagru*), is used in 2 Chron. **20**. 24, 25; Jer. **31**. 40, **33**. 5, **41**. 9.

Rephaim (רפאים, Ass. *rapu*, 'to be weak'), which in other places is rendered **giants**, is used of the dead in Job **26.** 5, 'Dead (things) are formed from under the waters, with the inhabitants thereof;' Ps. **88.** 10, 'Wilt thou shew wonders to the dead? Shall the dead arise and praise thee?' Prov. **2.** 18, 'For her house inclineth unto death (מות), and her paths unto the dead.' See also Prov. **9.** 18, 21. 16; Isa. **14.** 9, 26. 19.

The Hebrew reduplicated form, 'Dying thou shalt die,' or 'Thou shalt surely die,' is found several times in the O. T., and is quoted in the N. T. in Matt. **15.** 4; Mark **7.** 10. It has sometimes been supposed that this expression, being so very emphatic, refers to something more than death, and implies the judgment that follows; but this cannot fairly be inferred from the form in question.

§ 10. *Use of the Word Death in the N. T.*

The word θάνατος (death) answers in the LXX both to **moth** and to **dever** (דבר), pestilence. It has a spiritual signification in the N. T., which calls for a short discussion.

Our Lord said to His disciples (Matt. **16.** 28), 'There are some standing here who shall not taste of death until they see the Son of Man coming in his kingdom.' The words are given in another form by St. Mark (**9.** 1), 'There are some who shall not taste of death until they see the kingdom of God come with power.' See also Luke **9.** 27.

The object of this passage was to prepare the minds of the disciples for the grand truth that death, which had been hitherto the terror of the world, was to lose its *taste* or *sting* in the case of those who united themselves to the Lord by faith. Christ Himself was to die, He was to suffer the pains of death, His soul was to be exceeding sorrowful even unto death, but by death He was to overcome him who had the power of death, and to deliver them who through fear of death had been all their lives subject to bondage. He thus introduced a new view of life and death, telling His disciples that he who would save his life by denying the Lord, should lose it, whilst he who was willing to lose his life for the Lord's sake, the same should save it. The Lord would be ashamed of the one on the Great Day, but would confess the other.

The entrance into a new life which takes place through faith in Christ involves death in another sense. It is a cutting off of human nature from its old modes and principles of existence—in other words, it is death to sin. Just as in physical dissolution the body ceases to feel, the heart to beat, the hands to work, and the feet to walk, so in this mystical death the body and all its members are to be no longer servants to sin; the same breach or gulf is to be made between the Christian and sin as there is between a dead man and the outer world in which he used to live and move and have his being. This death is related to the crucifixion of Christ, who 'died to sin.' The believer is baptized into Christ's death, he dies with Christ, is made conformable to His death, is crucified with Christ (Rom. 6. 5; 2 Cor. 5. 14; Gal. 2. 19, 20; Col. 2. 20, 3. 3). In 1 Pet. 2. 24, the word rendered dead in the A. V. and R. V., and which only occurs here, signifies severance (ἀπογίγνομαι).

The *second death* is mentioned only in the Book of Revelation (2. 11, 20. 6, 14, 21. 8). This is a condition of things which follows after the resurrection. Those that overcome and are faithful unto death shall not suffer injury from it. Those that have part in the first resurrection shall not be subjected to its power. It is thus described in Rev. 20. 14, 15, 'Death and Hades (*i.e.* perhaps, those evil spirits that have the power of death and Hades) were cast into the lake of fire, this (*i.e.* the being cast into the lake of fire) is the second death;' 'Whosoever was not found written in the Book of Life was cast into this lake.' Again, we read (21. 8) that, whilst he who overcometh shall inherit all things, he who does not overcome, but gives way to instability, unbelief, idolatrous abominations, murder, fornication, witchcraft, idolatry, and lies, shall have his part in the lake which burneth with fire and brimstone, which is the second death.

CHAPTER XXV.

SATAN, TEMPTER.

Our knowledge of beings of a less material nature than ourselves, whether good or evil, is chiefly gained from Scripture, though an independent belief in the existence of spirits has been widespread for ages. The intrusion of wild, strange, bold, and blasphemous suggestions into the heart of the Christian in his holiest moments is a phenomenon not easily reconcilable with any other theory. Evil is often breathed into men's hearts, they know not how; their intellects are sharpened whilst their consciences are deadened; they are impelled the wrong way by an evil force which is *in* them but not *of* them; fountains of vileness and sin are opened and almost created in their hearts, and they are in danger of being plunged into every kind of violence. Whence are all these things? Are they to be accounted for by natural causes? Is man the sole originator of his wrong-doing? Has he only himself to blame? Scripture tells us that this is not the case. It unfolds to us the fact that the children of men are beset by tempters who try to make men as much as possible like themselves.

§ 1. *The Words Devil and Satan.*

The word Sa'ir (שָׂעִיר) is translated 'devil' in Lev. 17. 7, 'They shall no more offer their sacrifices unto devils;' and in 2 Chron. 11. 15, 'He ordained him priests for the high places, and for the devils, and for the calves which he had made.' In each of these passages the LXX translates '*vain things*' (μάταια), by which no doubt they meant idols. The first passage evidently refers to a false worship which had become common in Israel during their stay in Egypt; and the second, pointing as it does to the introduction of idolatry by Jeroboam after his return from Egypt, would lead us in the same direction. The word Sa'ir originally signifies 'a goat,' and is usually so rendered; and it is probable that goat-worship is referred to in these passages.

Sa'ir is translated Satyr in Isa. 13. 21, 'Satyrs shall dance there;' see also Isa. 34. 14. In these passages the **Sa'ir** is introduced in company with the owl and the wild beast of the desert as freely taking up its abode among the ruins of ancient cities. There can be little doubt that goats are referred to in these passages, but the LXX adopts the word demon (δαιμόνιον) in the first of them. The idea that evil spirits haunt desolate places and ruins is a very old one.

The word **Shed** (שֵׁד, Ass. *sedu,* 'spirit') is rendered 'devil' twice. In Deut. 32. 17, 'They sacrificed unto devils, not to God;' or, as it is in the margin, 'to devils which were not God;' compare 1 Cor. 10. 20. See also Ps. 106. 37, 'Yea, they sacrificed their sons and their daughters unto devils.'

In each of these cases, and in all places where 'devil' occurs in the plural number in the A. V. of the N. T., the Greek word is demon (δαιμόνιον). The same rendering has been given in Ps. 96. 5, and in Isa. 65. 11, where some form of idolatry is specified in the words 'that prepare a table for that troop,'[1] or, as it is in the margin, 'Gad;' and in Isa. 34. 14, where we read, 'The wild beasts of the desert,' margin 'Ziim.' But little light is thrown by these passages on the real meaning of δαιμόνιον, as understood by the Jewish readers of the LXX in our Lord's time. Its use in the Apocrypha answers to our idea of evil spirits.

Satan (שָׂטָן) is, properly speaking, an adversary or plotter, or one who devises means for opposing another. The word is used either in its verbal or substantival form in the following passages: —Num. 22. 22, 'The angel of the Lord stood in the way for an adversary against him.' 1 Sam. 29. 4, 'Lest in the battle he be an adversary to us.' 2 Sam. 19. 22, 'What have I to do with you, that ye should this day be adversaries unto me?' 1 Kings 5. 4, 'There is neither adversary nor evil occurrent.' 1 Kings 11. 14, 'The Lord stirred up an adversary unto Solomon.' Ps. 38. 20, 'They also that render evil for good are mine adversaries.' Ps. 71. 13, 'Let them be confounded and consumed that are adversaries to my soul.' Ps. 109. 4, 'For my love they are my adversaries.' Verse 6, 'Let Satan (without the article in the Hebrew

---

[1] David Mill has an interesting dissertation on this point. He considers that *Gad* is the god of fortune, answering to *Meni* in the other part of the verse. He hints that there is a connection between the words *Gad*, ater-*gatis*, and *God*, and (possibly) ά-γαθός; he also thinks that there is a reference to Fortune in the use of the name Gad in Gen. 30. 11. He likewise connects **Achad**, which we have naturally translated '*one*' in Isa. 66. 17, with the name of *Hecate*.

and in the Greek) stand at his right hand.' Verse 20, 'Let this be
the reward of mine adversaries from the Lord.' Verse 29, 'Let
mine adversaries be clothed with shame.'

In these passages the LXX renders by the verb διαβάλλω,
ἐπίβουλος, or διάβολος.

In 1 Chron. 21. 1 we read that 'Satan stood up against Israel
and provoked David to number Israel.' There is no article here
in the Hebrew or Greek (διάβολος), therefore the word might be
rendered 'an adversary,' as in other passages. Turning to the
corresponding passage, 2 Sam. 24. 1, we read, 'And again the anger
of the Lord was kindled against Israel, and he moved David against
them to say, Go, number Israel and Judah.' As in 1 Kings 11. 14
we were told plainly that 'The Lord stirred up *a Satan* against
Solomon;' so, putting these two parallel passages together, we may
gather that 'The Lord stirred up *a Satan* against Israel.' The
Bible reminds us more than once that provocations to evil are not
only permitted but ordered by God, to test those who are strong in
faith, and to show those who are depending on themselves how
vain it is for them to trust in any one but the living God. The
instruments that are used for this purpose are in some cases
evil spirits.

Satan is referred to very definitely in Job 1. 6–12, 2. 1–7. In
these passages we have the definite article both in the Hebrew and
in the Greek (ὁ διάβολος), and we have a confirmation of the view
which the previous passages suggested, that human opposition to
what is good is secretly instigated by a being who lives in another
sphere of existence, and who is *the adversary*, or, to use the Greek
translation in its modern English form, *the devil;* that he is permitted by God to put men's faith to the test by the infliction of
various evils, but that he can do nothing without such permission.

In the vision recorded by Zechariah (3. 1, 2) we read thus: 'He
shewed me Joshua the high priest, standing before the angel of the
Lord, and *Satan* (the adversary, not, as in our margin, "*an* adversary") standing at his right hand to *resist* (lit. to *satan*) him.
And the Lord said unto (the) *Satan*, The Lord rebuke thee, *Satan*.'
Here again there is an article in the Hebrew and Greek; and Satan
is brought into conflict with the angels of God, as at the opening of
the Book of Job, where the LXX renders 'sons of God' as 'angels
of God.' The same being is evidently referred to, and he is engaged
in the same work, but is subjected to the rebuke of God.

The word **Satan** is regarded as an equivalent title with *the devil*

T

in the N. T., just as *evil spirit* is often substituted for *demon* in the parallel accounts of the same event in the Gospels. He is regarded as the enemy of souls, leading them into sin, and aiming at their destruction. He appears to have had influence over the bodies of men, and death is regarded as his masterpiece. But the Son of God by dying overcame ' him that had the power of death, that is, the devil ' (Heb. 2. 14).

Where the word διάβολος occurs in the N. T. with the definite article, we may conclude that *the* adversary, Satan, is referred to. The following are instances of its usage :—Our Lord was tempted by the devil (Matt. 4.) ; the enemy who sowed tares is the devil (Matt. 13. 39); the fire is prepared for the devil and his angels (Matt. 25. 41); the devil takes the good seed out of man's heart (Luke 8. 12); the devil put it into the heart of Judas to betray the Lord (John 13. 2). There is no definite article in Acts 13. 10, where Paul addresses Elymas as the son of διάβολος; probably, however, this passage may be classed with the others ; compare St. John's words 'children of the devil ' (1 John 3. 10). The devil is identified by name with Satan in Rev. 20. 2.

The word occurs without the article, and in a more general sense, in 1 Tim. 3. 11 ; 2 Tim. 3. 3 ; Titus 2. 3 ; and also in John 6. 69, where our Lord says, ' One of you is a devil,' *i.e.* an adversary or false accuser.

The verb δαιμονίζεσθαι is only used in the Gospels, and expresses the case of those who are suffering from the agency of demons. These mysterious beings are constantly referred to in the N. T. as being cast out through the Lord's power. In John 10. 20, the being possessed with a demon is regarded as equivalent to madness.

In Acts 17. 18 the Athenian philosophers give the word its more classical usage, and accordingly it is rendered gods, that is to say, *demigods* or *genii*.[1] In this sense it seems to be understood in 1 Cor. 10. 20, 21 ; 1 Tim. 4. 1 ; James 2. 19; and Rev. 9. 20, 16. 14.

§ 2. *Temptation.*

The word 'tempt,' or 'temptation,' occurs sixteen times in the O. T. In Mal. 3. 15 the Hebrew word is **Bachan** (בחן), to *prove* or *test*, as metals are tested in the crucible (see verse 10, where the same Hebrew word is rendered prove. In the remaining passages we find **Nasah** (נסה), literally ' *to test by the smell*,' hence ' *to put to*

[1] See, however, chap. ii.

the proof.' In all these passages (with one exception, namely, Gen.
22. 1, where we are told that God tempted or tested Abraham)
the word is used with reference to the way in which man has put
God's power or forbearance to the test. Thus in Exod. 17. 2, 7, we
are told that Israel 'tempted' God in the wilderness, and the place
was therefore called **Massah**, a name derived from the word **Nasah**.
In Ps. 78. 41 we read, 'They turned back, and tempted God, and
limited the Holy One of Israel.' This *limitation* was the setting
an imaginary boundary to God's power and goodness, and thus
calling Him forth to step over that boundary. The temptations
in the wilderness are referred to several times both in the Pentateuch and Psalms, and usually in the same sense. In three passages,
however, namely, Deut. 4. 34, 7. 19, and 29. 3, reference is made
not to the provocations which God endured when His forbearance
was put to the test in the wilderness, but to the mode in which His
purpose towards Israel and His power of working wonders were
proved and demonstrated by His conduct towards Pharaoh and
his people.

The usage of the two words will be more clearly seen if we
compare other passages where they occur.

Bachan is found in the following passages :—Gen. 42. 15,
16, 'Hereby ye shall be proved . . . that your words may
be proved, whether there be any truth in you.' 1 Chron.
29. 17, 'Thou triest the heart.' Job 23. 10, 'When he hath
tried me, I shall come forth as gold.' Ps. 7. 9, 'The righteous
God trieth the hearts and reins;' so Jer. 11. 20. Ps. 11. 4,
5, 'His eyelids try the children of men. The Lord trieth the
righteous.' Ps. 17. 3, 'Thou hast proved mine heart.' Ps. 81.
7, 'I proved thee at the waters of Meribah.' Ps. 139. 23, 'Try
me, and know my thoughts.' Prov. 17. 3, 'The fining pot is for
silver, and the furnace for gold; but the Lord trieth the hearts.'
Isa. 28. 16, 'Behold, I lay in Zion for a foundation a stone, a tried
stone;' the LXX, as quoted in the N. T., adopts the word elect
(ἐκλεκτός) in this passage. Jer. 17. 10, 'I the Lord search the
heart, I try the reins, even to give every man according to his
ways;' see also chap. 20. 12. Ezek. 21. 13, 'It is a trial.' Zech.
13. 9, 'I will try them as gold is tried.' Mal. 3. 10, 'Prove
me now herewith'—an idea taken up in the fifteenth verse, where
the same word is used in the words, 'They that tempt God are
even delivered.'

Nasah occurs in Exod. 15. 25, 'There he proved them;' Exod.

16. 4, **20.** 20; Deut. **8.** 2, 16, **13.** 3; Jud. **2.** 22, **3.** 1, 4; 2 Chron. **32. 31.** In Deut. **4.** 34 it is rendered 'assay' as well as 'temptation;' and in Deut. **28.** 56, it is rendered 'adventure' in the A. V. In Jud. **6.** 39 Gideon says, 'Let me prove, I pray thee, but this once with the fleece.' 1 Sam. **17.** 39, David girded on his armour and he assayed[1] to go (lit. he was on the verge of starting), but he put the armour off again, 'for he had not proved it.'

1 Kings **10.** 1, the Queen of Sheba came to Solomon 'to prove him with hard words.' Compare 2 Chron. **9.** 1.

It is also used in Job **4.** 2 ('assay'); Job **9.** 23 ('trial'); Eccles. **2.** 1 and **7.** 23; also in Dan. **1.** 12 and 14, where it is rendered 'prove.'

The two words occur together in Ps. **26.** 2, 'Examine (**bachan**) me, O Lord, and prove (**nasah**) me;' and in Ps. **95.** 9, 'When your fathers tempted (**nasah**) me, proved (**bachan**) me, and saw my work.'.

A consideration of these passages leads to the conclusion that the various evils and struggles and difficulties which are prompted from within, or which befall man from without, are ordered by God as part of the great system of probation or testing to which every child of Adam is being subjected. The agency of the Evil One is permitted for the purpose of bringing a man into that sort of contact with evil which will serve to test his real principles.

The LXX translates **Bachan** by ἐτάζω, ἐξετάζω, φαίνομαι, φανερὸς γίνομαι, μανθάνω, κρίνω, διακρίνω, δοκιμάζω (the most usual word), δικαιόω (Ezek. **21.** 13), ἐπιστρέφω, ἀνθίστημι, and ἐκλεκτὸς (Prov. **17.** 3 and Isa. **28.** 6).

Nasah is always translated by πειράζω, or one of its compounds.

§ 3. *Temptation in the N. T.*

The word ἐτάζω does not occur in the N. T., but ἐξετάζω is used three times to represent accurate, scrutinising search (Matt. **2.** 8, **10.** 11; John **21.** 12); φαίνομαι is used to indicate the result of such scrutiny in 2 Cor. **13.** 7; and so φανερὸς γίνεσθαι is found in the sense of being brought to the test in Luke **8.** 17, 'There is nothing hidden which shall not be made manifest;' 1 Cor. **3.** 13, 'His work shall be made manifest;' see also 1 Cor. **11.** 19, **14.** 25; 1 John **3.** 10.

There is some difficulty in giving a consistent rendering to

---

[1] It would have been better to put 'he essayed.'

διακρίνω in the N. T.   It often answers, both in sense as well as etymology, to the word discern, as in Matt. **16**. 3, 'Ye can discern the face of the heavens;' 1 Cor. **11**. 31, 'If we discerned ourselves (*i.e.* our own motives) we should not be judged of the Lord.' In other passages the word is used in a causative sense, as when we read, 'Who maketh thee to differ,' in 1 Cor. **4**. 7; so perhaps we should understand 1 Cor. **11**. 29, 'Not making a distinction between ordinary food and that which represents the body of Christ.'

In Jude 9 we read of Michael contending (διακρινόμενος) with Satan; but in the twenty-second verse, where the same part of the verb occurs, it has been rendered, 'On some have compassion, making a difference;' might it not be rendered 'contending with them,' in accordance with the previous passage?[1] The verb has this sense also in Acts **11**. 2, where we read that they after circumcision contended with Peter.

In the passive voice the word has come to signify doubting, *i.e.* the subjection of the mind and will to fluctuations and contending impulses. Thus we read in Matt. **21**. 21, 'If ye have faith and doubt not;' so Mark **11**. 23; Acts **10**. 20; Rom. **4**. 20 (where the A. V. reads, 'He staggered not at the promise'); Rom. **14**. 23; James **1**. 6, **2**. 4.

The word δοκιμάζειν is also used of the process of scrutiny whereby a man is brought to the test. It is sometimes used as a substitute for διακρίνειν, as in Luke **12**. 56, which may be compared with Matt. **16**. 3, quoted above. So the man says of his yoke of oxen, 'I go to prove them,' Luke **14**. 19; Rom. **2**. 18, 'Thou discernest what is excellent.' Compare Rom. **12**. 2, 'That you may make proof of what is that good, and acceptable, and perfect, will of God;' 1 Cor. **3**. 13, 'The fire shall test every man's work;' 1 Cor. **11**. 28, 'Let a man scrutinise himself;' compare the thirty-first verse, where διακρίνω is used. Compare also 2 Cor. **8**. 8, 22, **13**. 5; Gal. **6**. 4; Eph. **5**. 10; Phil. **1**. 10; 1 Tim. **3**. 10; 1 John **4**. 1.

Sometimes the verb signifies that the scrutiny has been satisfactory; it is then rendered to approve. So we read in 1 Thess. **2**. 4, 'We have been approved of God.' Compare Rom. **1**. 28, 'They did not approve of the retaining God in their knowledge.' In this verse the Apostle carries on the idea contained in the verb δοκιμάζω a little further, for he proceeds, 'Wherefore God gave them up to a reprobate mind' (ἀδόκιμον νοῦν). They rejected Him, so He rejected them.

---

[1] But the text is uncertain. See R. V.

The word ἀδόκιμος has usually been rendered reprobate, as in 2 Cor. **13**. 5, where we have the same connection of words as in the passage last quoted, ' Prove (δοκιμάζετε) your own selves . . . unless ye be reprobate' (ἀδόκιμοι). In one place, however, and that a very remarkable one, our translators have preferred to render ἀδόκιμος by 'castaway,' namely, in 1 Cor. **9**. 27, where St. Paul says, 'I bring my body into subjection, lest, whilst I have preached to others, I myself should be unable to pass the scrutiny (of the last day).'

St. James and St. Peter concur in using the expression 'the trial of your faith.' Here the word is δοκίμιον (James **1**. 3 ; 1 Pet. **1**. 7), and the idea suggested is that the faith which a Christian professes has to be submitted to the test of affliction and temptation, just as gold is put into a crucible and passed through the fire.

The word δόκιμος is used several times by St. Paul, and signifies the condition of him who has stood the test and is approved. See 2 Tim. **2**. 15, and compare James **1**. 12, 'When he is tried,' *i.e.* approved. In accordance with these passages, we can understand Rom. **5**. 4, where we read that 'Patience worketh experience' (δοκίμην). This doubtless means that as tribulation is the occasion whereby endurance or patience is developed, so this endurance becomes a test or proof that our faith is living and true.

When we turn from these various Greek words which stand for the Hebrew word **Bachan** to πειράζειν, which always represents the word **Nasah**, we notice a marked difference of sense. The scrutiny or testing process which we have been considering is exercised by men, aided by the enlightenment of the Holy Spirit, in this life, and will be brought to bear upon the hearts and lives of all men by God hereafter. But πειρασμός is almost always represented in the N. T. as the work of the devil or of those who are following his guidance. Thus Christ during His earthly ministry 'suffered, being tempted,' and those temptations, which were of various kinds, were thrown in His path sometimes by Satan himself, and sometimes by the Pharisees and others, who sought to entangle Him in an offence against God or man. In the Acts we read of Ananias and Sapphira tempting the Spirit of God (Acts **5**. 9), and of Peter asking the brethren why they tempted God by imposing the law of Moses on the Gentile converts (**15**. 10). In James **1**. 13, 14, we have the whole history of temptation, so far as the operations of the human heart are concerned. Satan's operations are implied, but not directly stated. A man is said to be led away when he is baited (δελεα (ζόμενος) by his own passions.   But who is it that uses these things as a bait ?   Not God.   Let no man say, *in this sense*, I am tempted of God.   Not man ; for he cannot bait the hook with which he himself is to be beguiled and destroyed.   It must, then, be the Evil One, who makes use of the inclinations of the heart as a means of dragging him to ruin.

When we ask God not to lead us into temptation, we mean, Lead us not into that position, and put us not into those circumstances, in which we should be in danger of falling an easy prey to the assaults of Satan.   In connection with this prayer, we have the promise that with every temptation in which God permits us to be placed, He provides a way of escape that we may be able to go through without falling.   He allows the way *in*, and He makes the way *out* (τὴν ἔκβασιν), 1 Cor. **10. 13.**

One or two passages only in which the verb occurs are to be interpreted differently.   In 2 Cor. **13.** 5, ' tempt yourselves ' means put yourself to the test, as we see from the context, which shows that the word is used as a parallel to the verb δοκιμάζειν.   In this sense we must understand the use of the word in Heb. **11.** 17, where the writer refers to the temptation of Abraham in the matter of the offering of Isaac.   God put Abraham's faith and obedience to the test, whilst Satan tempted him to disobey.

CHAPTER XXVI.

WITCHCRAFT, DIVINATION, SOOTHSAYING.

SUPERSTITION is the natural complement to materialism. The mind of man, having once become warped in religious matters, does not cling with unerring sagacity to the truth that there is a God, but goes aside into bypaths, sometimes resting in that which is material, and seeking to exclude the idea of spiritual existences altogether from the mind; at other times oscillating in the direction of what is now called *spiritualism*, a system known in earlier days by the ruder name of *witchcraft*. Few things are more fascinating than the thought that the secrets of the hidden world or of the unknown future may be unfolded through dealings with the departed, or that one person may, by going through certain mysterious processes, exercise a powerful influence over the will or destiny of another. Incantations, drugs, vapours, the conjunction of the stars, the voice or flight of birds, the passage of the clouds, mesmerism, animal-magnetism, electro-biology—these and such-like have been used in various ages and countries to take the place of religion, and by their means men have mimicked the supernatural dealings of God. But they are all abominable (Deut. **18**. 10–12), and are to give way before the simple voice of the inspired prophet. Accordingly, the Ephesian converts acted on a true instinct, and in plain harmony with the teaching of the O. T., when they discarded their 'curious arts,' and burnt all their books at a great sacrifice (Acts **19**. 19). How dishonouring to God these practices are the prophet Isaiah plainly shows (Isa. **8**. 19), and how unprofitable to man our Lord teaches when He lays down that if men believe not Moses and the prophets, neither will they be persuaded though one rose from the dead (Luke **16**. 31).

§ 1. *Witchcraft.*

With one exception, which will be referred to under the head of 'divination,' the word for witch and witchcraft throughout the O. T. is **Cashaph** (כשׁף, Ass. *kasipu*). The original meaning of this word is unknown, but if we may judge from the use of cognate forms in Arabic and Syriac, it may be taken to refer to the performance of religious rites, either in the way of prayer or of secret communications with another world.

Witchcraft was adopted in very early days as a method of trading upon the religious instincts and superstitions of mankind. It was largely carried on by the female sex, though not confined to it. Thus **Cashaph** is applied to the 'sorcerers' of Egypt in Exod. **7.** 11, to Israelite sorcerers in Jer. **27.** 9 and Mal. **3.** 5, and to those of Chaldean origin in Dan. **2.** 2. It is also used of sorcery in Isa. **47.** 12. That the Canaanites were well acquainted with the art is evident from the fact that they had a city (**Acshaph**) which must have been specially named from it (Josh. **11.** 1, **12.** 20, **19.** 25).

The word is rendered witch or witchcraft in the following passages:—Exod. **22.** 18; Deut. **18.** 10; 2 Kings **9.** 22; 2 Chron. **33.** 6; Micah **5.** 12; Nahum **3.** 4.

With regard to the exact nature of the art represented by this word, little is known; but the general rendering of the LXX, which is φαρμακεία, leads to the supposition that the use of drugs, probably to produce clouds of vapour, was part of the process. The art, whatever it might be, was denounced as one of the works of the flesh in Gal. **5.** 20, and is referred to in Rev. **9.** 21, **21.** 8, **22.** 15. See also Acts **19.** 19.

§ 2. *Divination.*

The one exception noticed above is 1 Sam. **15.** 23, where we read that 'rebellion is as the sin of witchcraft;' but it would be better to say 'the sin of divination.' The word used is **Kasam** (םסק, LXX μαντεύω). It stands for Joseph's divining cup. The original meaning of the word seems to be 'to divide' or 'partition out.' Its first appearance is where the elders of Moab go to Balaam with 'the rewards of divination in their hand' (Num. **22.** 7), and where the seer announces that 'there is no divination against Israel' (**23.** 23). Balaam is directly called a diviner (A. V. soothsayer) in Josh. **13.** 22. We meet with it among the list of similar practices in Deut. **18.** 10 and 14, where we are given to understand that it was common among the Canaanites.

The Philistines had their diviners (1 Sam. **6.** 2), and the witch of Endor was asked 'to divine by the familiar spirit' (1 Sam. **28.** 8). In Isa. **44.** 25, it is said of God that He 'frustrateth the significant tokens of liars (*i.e.* their false miracles), and maketh diviners mad;' and in Jer. 14. 14, false prophets 'prophesy unto you a false vision and divination, and a thing of nought and the deceit of their heart.' See also Jer. 27. 9, 29. 8; Ezek. 12. 24, 13. 6, 7, 9, 23, 21. 29, 22. 28; Micah 3. 6, 7; Zech. 10. 2.

In Isa. 3. 2 the word is rendered 'prudent;' and in Prov. 16. 10 we read that 'a divine sentence,' *i.e.* a word of divination, 'is in the lips of the king.' The diviners were doubtless shrewd men, well acquainted with the affairs of those whom they had to do with, and able to deliver their prognostications in oracular and enigmatical language.

Three special modes of divination are alluded to in Ezek. 21. 21, 'The king of Babylon stood at the parting of the way, at the head of two ways, to use divination: he made his arrows (or knives) bright, he consulted with his images (or teraphim), he looked in the liver.'

The ordinary word for a diviner in the LXX is μάντις, a seer or soothsayer. This art is only once referred to in the N. T., namely, in Acts 16. 16, where we read of the Philippian damsel that she got for her masters much gains by divining (μαντευομένη).

§ 3. *The Familiar Spirit.*

The familiar spirit is Ob (אוב), literally, 'a bottle' (see Job 32. 19, where the word is used), and hence perhaps the hollow sound which might be produced by the wind or breath in an empty bottle or skin. The LXX renders the word ἐγγαστρίμυθος, ventriloquist; so that the process called Ob must probably have depended in some degree on the power of producing some peculiar sound which might represent the voice of the dead. This point is alluded to in Isa. 8. 19, where we read of 'them that have familiar spirits,' together with 'wizards that peep and that mutter' (lit. that chirp or squeak, see 10. 14, and that utter a low sound or speak indistinctly, see 59. 3). Also in Isa. 29. 4 we read, 'Thou shalt be brought down, and shalt speak out of the ground, and thy speech shall be low out of the dust, and thy voice shall be as of one that hath a familiar spirit, out of the ground, and thy speech shall whisper (or chirp) out of the dust.' The idea that the dead, if they could speak at all, would be represented as speaking out of the ground, is very old and very natural; see Gen. 4. 10, 'The voice of thy brother's blood crieth unto me from the ground.'

In one passage (2 Kings **21.** 6) the LXX renders the word by θελητής, by which was meant perhaps a person with a strong will who could act upon the feelings of others. If this were not a solitary instance, one might be inclined to connect **Ob** with the root **Avah** (אבה), to will, and to class the dealings referred to with those which are now called animal magnetism, and possibly to introduce the ἐθελοθρησκεία or will-worship of the N. T. into the same category. The word **Ob** also occurs in Lev. **19.** 31, **20.** 6, 27 ; Deut. **18.** 11 ; 2 Kings 21. 6, 23. 24 ; 1 Chron. **10.** 13 ; 2 Chron. **33.** 6 ; and Isa. **19.** 3.

The most interesting passage, however, is that in which 'the witch of Endor' is described (1 Sam. **28.** 3, 7, 8, 9). We are first told that Saul had put away these 'familiar spirits' out of the land, then that he charged his servants to seek out a woman who dealt in this forbidden art. Accordingly, they find out for him a 'mistress of **Ob**,' and he visits her in disguise and asks her to divine to him by **Ob**, and to bring up that which he should speak of to her. The woman, under a promise of secrecy, is ready enough to gratify his wishes, and asks whom she shall raise up. Her business then was *necromancy*, the real or pretended dealing with the departed, the 'inquiring of the dead,' which is called necromancy in Deut. **18.** 11. There is no indication from other parts of Scripture where **Ob** is referred to that there was usually any *appearance ;* but generally a voice, which was supposed to be that of the departed person, was heard to proceed, as it were, from the ground, sometimes muttering indistinctly and sometimes 'peeping,' that is to say, piping or chirping like the thin shrill notes of a bird.

Saul says, 'Bring me up Samuel.' No sooner are the words uttered than, to her astonishment, the woman perceives Samuel. She screams with terror, and says to her visitor, 'Why hast thou deceived me ? And thou art Saul.' There was no sham here. God had permitted the prophet to appear, perhaps clad in judicial robes of office, so that she said, 'I saw **gods** (or **judges**[1]) coming up from the earth.'

Did the woman really bring up Samuel ? She professed afterwards that she had done so (verse 21), but the narrative rather implies that it was not so. Certainly there is no encouragement here for Spiritualism or Theosophy, especially when we remember that ' Saul died for his transgression, and *also for asking counsel of a* familiar spirit, instead of inquiring of the Lord ' (1 Chron. **10.** 13, 14).

[1] See chap. ii.

§ 4. *The Wizard and Magician.*

The word for wizard is **Id'oni** (יִדְּעֹנִי), literally, 'a knowing one.' They are always ranked with those who deal in **Ob**, and are to be regarded with equal abhorrence. They are referred to in Lev. 19. 31, 20. 6, 27 ; Deut. 18. 11 ; 1 Sam. 28. 3, 9 ; 2 Kings 21. 6, 23. 24 ; 2 Chron. 33. 6 ; Isa. 8. 19, and 19. 3. These 'knowing' persons were no doubt wise in their generation, 'prudent' like the diviners, and skilled in the art of preying upon the follies and superstitions of those who came into contact with them. The LXX rendering is usually ἐπαοιδός, an enchanter, or γνώστης, a knowing person.

The magicians were **Chartummim** (חרטמים), a name which is supposed to be derived from **Charath**, a graving tool (compare the name Khartoum). The LXX sometimes calls them ἐξηγηταί, explainers. Perhaps they were engravers of hieroglyphics, and possessed of that secret knowledge which these sculptures represented, and which they communicated to the people with considerable reserve. Although at first sight it might be supposed from the facts narrated concerning them in the Book of Exodus that they were possessed of preternatural powers, yet it may well be doubted if they had access to any other secret influences than those which natural science is daily bringing to light, or than those by means of which the Indian juggler astounds his European spectators.

§ 5. *The Soothsayer and Enchanter.*

The Chaldean soothsayer whom we read of in Dan. 2. 27, 4. 7, 5. 7, 11, was no doubt an astrologer, who pretended to do what astrologers in many countries and in various eras have professed to do, namely, to calculate the destinies of man by interpreting the movements and conjunctions of the heavenly bodies. Their name is derived from **Gezar** (גְּזַר), which is literally to cut. Whether this name was applied to them from their marking out the heavens into certain divisions for purposes of observation, or whether they derived it from the fact that they cut off or decided the fate of those who came to them for advice, is a matter which perhaps cannot now be determined.

The astrologer of Dan. 1. 20, &c., is **Ashaph** (אשׁף), for which the Greek rendering is μάγος. Compare Matt. 2. 1, where Wycliffe rightly puts 'astronomers.'

Another mode of attempting to obtain information was by the examination of the clouds. Hence the use of the word **Anan** (עָנַן), κληδονίζομαι, 'to observe the clouds.' These observers are ranked with all the other intruders into unlawful pursuits in Deut. **18.** 10 and 14, under the title of soothsayers. They are mentioned in Isa. **2.** 6, where it is said of Israel that 'they are soothsayers like the Philistines.' See also Micah 5. 12. They are spoken of in Isa. **57.** 3 as the sons of 'the sorceress,' and are classed with the vile, the impure, and the idolater. In Jer. **27.** 9, the A. V. calls them 'enchanters;' and in Lev. **19.** 26, 2 Kings 21. 6, and 2 Chron. **33.** 6, they are described as 'the observers of times,' that is to say, persons who by examining the clouds profess to be able to tell at what exact crisis any event is to be expected to take place, and when a good opportunity arrives for doing a certain work.

The word **Chever** (חֶבֶר), 'binding' or 'fascination,' is rendered enchantment in Isa. **47.** 9, 12, where reference is made to Babylon; and is rendered 'charmer' in Deut. 18. 11, also in Ps. **58.** 5, where the serpent charmer is referred to. In the early part of the same verse, **Lachash** (לחשׁ), to whisper, is used for the art of the serpent charmer, and is also used in the same connection in Jer. **8.** 17, and in Eccles. **10.** 11, where the A. V. has 'enchantment.'

In Isa. **19.** 3, 'charmers' are described as **Ittim** (אטם), those who speak with a soft low voice. These are perhaps serpent charmers. The word itself is used of Ahab going 'softly' (1 Kings 21. 27), as a sign of his humility and repentance.

The 'enchantments' of the Egyptians are **Lahathim** (להטים) in Exod. **7.** 11, and **Lath** (לט) in Exod. 7. 22, 8. 7, 18. Both of these words signify secrecy, and imply that these learned men practised what in the Middle Ages would be called 'the black art,' or perhaps what we call 'sleight of hand.'

Only one other word has to be noticed, namely, **Nachash** (נחשׁ), which is supposed to signify to whisper or hiss, and hence is applied to the serpent. It is rendered 'enchantment' in Lev. 19. 26; Deut. 18. 10; Num. 23. 23, 24. 1 (with reference to Balaam); 2 Kings 17. 17, 21. 6; 2 Chron. 33. 6. These passages imply that it was Canaanitish rather than Egyptian in its origin and connection. The word is used in a modified sense in 1 Kings 20. 33, 'The men did diligently observe whether anything would come from him;' they prognosticated as to Benhadad's fate from Ahab's words. It is also the word used by Joseph's steward in Gen. 44.

5, 15, where the A. V. has 'divine' or 'make trial,' and perhaps was specially used by Joseph's order as a word of Canaanitish origin. The LXX renders it by the word οἰωνισμός, augury, or the interpreting events by the flight of birds; but divination by means of pictures, which were supposed to be formed by liquid in a cup, may be referred to. The verb is used in Gen. 30. 27, where Laban says, 'I have learned by experience that the Lord hath blessed me for thy sake.' Two persons mentioned in the O. T. derive their name from this root, namely, Naasson (Nachshon), the son of Amminadab (Exod. 6. 23), and Nehushta, the mother of Jehoiachin (2 Kings 24. 8).

CHAPTER XXVII.

IDOL, GROVE, HIGH PLACE.

Man is essentially an image-maker. His best works in art and mechanics are imitations of nature. His music is an attempt to present, not indeed to the eye, but to the ear, what may be called a picture of the varied feelings that occupy his heart. This tendency also shows itself in his religious worship, which he is inclined to make as symbolical as possible. Nay, he seeks to make a sensible representation even of God Himself, and gradually to transfer to the work of his own hands that reverence and dependence which properly belongs to the one living and true God. There is a strange fascination in exaggerated religious symbolism; it engrosses and excites the mind, but is by no means of a healthy character. It tends little by little to supplant the simplicity of spiritual worship, and to turn man into an idolater. Idolatry in its first stage is a sort of symbolism; some object is selected to represent the unseen Deity or to set forth one of His attributes; little by little the material image takes the place of the spiritual reality for which it stands, and idolatry ensues, bringing in its train that sensuality which is the sure attendant of every form of materialism; the highest functions of human nature are thus abnegated, and human life is debased. The first chapter of the Epistle to the Romans tells the story of idolatrous degradation with painful vividness, and fully accounts for the oft-repeated admonitions given by Moses on this special point, and for the severe penalties which God inflicted upon the people in order to break through the evil fascination and to deliver them from the snare of materialism.

§ 1. *Idols.*

Twelve different Hebrew words are represented by the English word 'idol.' Some of them point to the fact that an idol is a thing of nought; others are significant of the terror with which the

worshipper of false gods is inspired, or of the aversion with which
the living and true God regards such objects; others, again, refer to
the shape of the idol, to the material of which it is made, or to the
position in which it is placed.

In Isa. **66.** 3 the idol is **Aven** (אָוֶן, Ass. *annu*), iniquity, or a
thing of nought. Compare **Beth-Aven**, *i.e.* the house of idolatry,
which is referred to in Hos. **4.** 15, **5.** 8, and **10.** 5, 8. In Amos **5.** 5
we read, **Beth-El** shall come to **Aven** (A. V. to nought). Here
there is evidently a play on the word. See Josh. **7.** 2.

The word **Alil** (אֱלִיל), which is supposed to have the same meaning, is used in several places, *e.g.* Lev. **19.** 4, 26. 1 ; 1 Chron. **16.**
26 ; Ps. **96.** 5, **97.** 7 ; Isa. **2.** 8, 18, 20, **10.** 10, 11, **19.** 1, 3, **31.** 7 ;
Ezek. **30.** 13 ; Hab. **2.** 18 ; Zech. **11.** 17.

The nothingness of idolatry is brought out by St. Paul, who
reminds the Corinthians that 'an idol is nothing in the world'
(1 Cor. **8.** 4), that the gods of the heathen are 'vanities' (Acts
14. 15), and 'no gods' (Gal. **4.** 8).

In Jer. **50.** 38, where we read, 'They are mad upon their idols,'
the word **Imah** (אֵימָה) is used, which implies that the idol was an
object of terror. The same idea is probably represented by **Miph-
letseth** (מִפְלֶצֶת), the designation of the idol which Maachah made[1]
(1 Kings **15.** 13, also in the corresponding passage, 2 Chron. **15.**
16). In 2 Chron. **15.** 8 idols are called 'abominations,' **Shakuts**
(שִׁקֻּץ), a word which is often used to testify to God's hatred of the
whole system of idolatry, and which answers to the Greek βδέλυγμα.

The connection of abomination (βδέλυγμα) with idolatry is
brought out in Rom. **2.** 22, 'Thou who abominatest idols, dost
thou rob temples?' In Rev. **21.** 8, the 'abominable,' that is, those
who worship idols, are coupled with the fearful[2] and the unbelieving. In Titus **1.** 16, St. Paul speaks of some who profess to know
God, but by their works deny Him, and are abominable, *i.e.*
practically on a level with idolaters. The *falsehood* of idolatry is
brought out in Rev. **21.** 27, where to make an abomination and
to make a lie are put side by side. Probably the cup containing
abominations and whoredom, referred to in Rev. **17.** 4, represents
the various forms of idolatry which 'the woman' shall promote.

---

[1] David Mill considers that this was Pluto, the president of the infernal regions,
whom he also identifies with Beelzebub the prince of flies, of nuisances, and of
the power of the air. He thinks that Ashara or Astarte was Hecate or Luna,
and that Chiun (Amos **5.** 26) was Saturn. But see Sayce, *Hibbert Lectures*.

[2] The word δειλός here rendered *fearful* probably signifies *unstable*, in which
sense it is used in the O. T.

St. Paul tells us that covetousness is idolatry, and in accordance with this truth our Lord tells the covetous Pharisees that what is lifted up among men is regarded as an abomination in the sight of God (Luke 16. 14, 15).

Reference has now been made to all the passages in which the word βδέλυγμα occurs in the N. T., with the exception of our Lord's reference to 'the abomination of desolation spoken of by Daniel the prophet' (Matt. 24. 15; Mark 13. 14; Dan. 9. 27), which signifies that the desolation of Jerusalem was to be caused by an idolatrous power.

There is a word which is found several times in the O. T. which is rather ambiguous, namely, **'Etsev** (עצב). It is supposed to mean *that which causes labour*, either in the making of the idol or in the worshipping it. The Greek rendering is sometimes λύπη, grief, but usually εἴδωλον. Scripture always conveys to us the idea that true worship is not wearisome to the child of God, whereas the worship of idols is hard labour without profit.

This word is used with reference to the false gods of the Philistines in 1 Sam. 31. 9; 1 Chron. 10. 9; 2 Sam. 5. 21; in 2 Chron. 24. 18 and Ps. 106. 36, 38, it refers to the objects of Canaanitish worship by which the Israelites were ensnared, see also Ps. 115. 4 and 135. 15. In Isa. 10. 11, whilst alil is used of Samaria's idols, 'etsev is used of Jerusalem's idols; in Isa. 46. 1 it is applied to Bel and Nebo, which were 'a burden to the weary beast;' see also Jer. 50. 2, where these same idols are described as broken in pieces; in Jer. 22. 28, Coniah is described as 'a despised broken idol' (where some would translate the word 'vase,' but unnecessarily); it is also used of the idols of Israel or Canaan in Isa. 48. 5; Hos. 4. 17, 8. 4, 13. 2, 14. 8; Micah 1. 7; Zech. 13. 2.

Another word for idol is derived from **Galgal** (גלגל), to roll, and signifies a trunk of a tree or a log of wood, or perhaps in some places a round stone. The word only occurs in Leviticus, Deuteronomy, the Kings, and Ezekiel. The LXX usually renders it εἴδωλον, an idol, but sometimes ἐπιτήδευμα, a custom; twice βδέλυγμα, an abomination; and in other passages ἐνθύμημα, ἐπι-θύμημα, διάνοια, and διανόημα, words which would point to the tendency of the heart to idolatry rather than to the object of worship itself. It occurs in the following passages:—Lev. 26. 30 ('the carcases of your idols'); Deut. 29. 17 (margin 'dungy gods'); 1 Kings 15. 12, 21. 26; 2 Kings 17. 12, 21. 11, 21, 23. 24; Ezek. 6. 4, *al.*

U

The word εἴδωλον is the only word used of idols in the N. T., whether these idols are outward and visible objects of worship, or whether they are more subtle influences which attract the heart.

Idolatry is joined with *pharmacy* or witchcraft in Gal. 5. 20; it is identified with covetousness in Eph. 5. 5, and is classed with murder in Rev. 22. 15.

§ 2. *The Image.*

Words referring to the fact that the idol is hewn into a certain shape or image are **Semel** (סמל), 2 Chron. 33. 7, 15 (Manasseh's idol), and Ezek. 8. 3, 5 ('the image of jealousy'); and perhaps **Tsir** (ציר), Isa. 45. 16, 'makers of idols.' **Temunah** (תמונה), 'likeness,' is used in Job 4. 16. It does not, however, refer to an idol, but to some form or outline which presented itself in vision. The same word is used in Exod. 20. 4, in the prohibition from making the 'likeness' of anything; also in Deut. 4. 23, 25, 5. 8, and Ps. 17. 15 ('I shall be satisfied when I awake with thy likeness'). The LXX rendering is generally ὁμοίωμα, similitude.

Tselem (צלם, Ass. *tsalmu*), a representation, answering to the Greek εἰκών, image, is the word used in Gen. 1. 26, 27, 5. 3, and 9. 6, with reference to the fact that man was made in the image of God. In Num. 33. 52 it is used of molten images, and it occurs in the following passages:—1 Sam. 6. 5, 11 (the images of mice and emerods); 2 Kings 11. 18 (the images of Baal); 2 Chron. 23. 17; Ezek. 7. 20, 16. 17, and 23. 14 (images of men); Amos 5. 26 (Moloch and Chiun); Dan. 2. 31, &c., and 3. 1, &c., the image of which Nebuchadnezzar dreamed, and that which he set up in the plain of Dura. The word is also used in Ps. 73. 20, 'When thou awakest, thou shalt despise their image,' that is to say, their form or appearance; and in Ps. 39. 6, 'Man walketh in a vain shadow' (lit. in an image).

In Lev. 26. 1 the 'graven image' is **Mascith** (משכית), which is supposed to refer to hieroglyphics, or to little figures of Thoth and other Egyptian gods. This word also occurs in Ezek. 8. 12, where reference is made to the 'chambers of imagery,' that is to say, chambers with figures painted and carved in relief, such as still exist in Egypt and Assyria. In Num. 33. 52, and Prov. 25. 11, Mascith is rendered *pictures;* and in Ps. 73. 7, and Prov. 18. 11, there is reference to the mental process which we call *picturing up,* or imagination.

§ 3. *N. T. Teaching on Images.*

The word ὁμοίωμα means a resemblance or figure, whether bodily or moral. It is used with reference to idolatry in Rom. 1. 23, where St. Paul speaks of those who changed the glory of the incorruptible God into the resemblance of an image of a corruptible man. When our Lord is said to have been made in the likeness of men, the same word is used, but with what a difference! No lifeless stock or stone shaped by man's hand after the pattern of his fellow-man, but a living Being partaking of all that is essential to human nature, yet absolutely free from stain of sin, and with a body destined to see no corruption, sent into human life, not from nothingness, but from the bosom of the Heavenly Father, and from that glory which He had before the foundation of the world.

The first passage in the N. T. in which the word εἰκών is used gives a good idea of its meaning; it is with reference to the *denarius* of which our Lord asks, ' Whose is this image and superscription?' (Matt. 22. 20). It is curious to observe that whilst idolaters are condemned for changing the glory of God into the similitude of the image of a corruptible man (Rom. 1. 23), we are expressly told that man is 'the image and glory of God' (1 Cor. 11. 7). Christ is said to be the image of God (2 Cor. 4. 4, Col. 1. 15); the Christian is now in a moral and spiritual sense to be changed into the same image from glory to glory (Rom. 8. 29, 2 Cor. 3. 18, Col. 3. 10); and hereafter, so far as his body is concerned, a similar resemblance shall be accomplished (1 Cor. 15. 49).

The word εἰκών is also adopted by St. John when he describes the image of the Beast in Rev. 13. 14, &c.

A hot controversy was called forth shortly after the Reformation in England by the fact that in the English translations of the Scriptures the word εἴδωλον was translated image. Martin, in his controversy with Fulke, laid down that an idol signified a false god; Dr. Fulke, on the contrary, held that it meant an image, and that this was the best word, as it included a representation of the true God. Martin held, and rightly, that **Pesel** (פסל), which is usually translated *a graven image*, only meant a *graven* thing (Lat. *sculptile*), and had no reference to an image; and he made a similar criticism on the word **Massecah** (מסכה), which is rendered *a molten image*. Fulke, however, answered that the object of the engraving in the one case, and of the melting in the other, was to make the

material into an image which was intended to represent the invisible God, or to imitate one of His works, and so to be worshipped. This answer, coupled with the fact that εἴδωλον also
answers to the Hebrew **temunah**, as above noticed, may fairly
justify our translators, and also their predecessors whose work was
being criticised in translating εἴδωλον by the word image.

§ 4. *Other Objects of Worship.*

We now pass to the consideration of words which represent
certain specific objects which were closely connected with old forms
of idolatry. Of these the first to be named is the pillar, statue,
or standing image, the Hebrew name for which is **Matsevah**
(מצבה), derived from the verb **natzav**, to stand, and used of the
object which symbolised Baal in the Canaanitish idolatry. The
LXX usually adopts στήλη, a pillar, as its representative. It
is first referred to in an idolatrous sense in Exod. 23. 24, where
the command is given to break down the 'images' of the
Canaanite gods; so in Exod. 34. 13, where it is connected with
'groves;' it is also found in Lev. 26. 1; Deut. 7. 5, 16. 22;
1 Kings 14. 23; 2 Kings 3. 2 (image of Baal), 10. 26, 27, (images
of Baal), 17. 10, 18. 4, 23. 14; 2 Chron. 14. 3, 31. 1; Jer. 43. 13;
Hos. 3. 4, 10. 1, 2; Micah 5. 13.

Another word used is **Chamonim** (חמנים), sun-images, perhaps
discs, or perhaps pyramidal stones in the shape of a flame. This
last is the idea which Gesenius inclines to, as in accordance with
certain old Phœnician inscriptions which speak of Baal Hanan, the
sun-god. The word occurs in Lev. 26. 30, 'I will cut down (cut off
or smite) your images;' 2 Chron. 14. 5, 34. 4, 7; Isa. 17. 8, 27. 9;
Ezek. 6. 4, 6.

§ 5. *The Grove.*

Closely connected with Baal-statues and sun-images stand the
groves. But before discussing their nature, it is to be observed
that the grove which Abraham is said to have planted, in Gen. 21.
33, was doubtless a *bonâ-fide* grove, or at least a tree. The word
there used is **Ashal** (אישל), which is distinct from the heathen and
idolatrous 'grove,' and may be rendered tamarisk. With this
exception, the general Hebrew word for a grove is **Asherah** (אשרה),
usually rendered ἄλσος (grove) by the LXX; but in two passages,
Isa. 17. 8 and 27. 9, rendered δένδρον (tree). The grove is first

alluded to in connection with Canaanitish worship in Exod. **34**. 13, where it is coupled with the statue or pillar which has already been mentioned. We find it in the same connection in Deut. **7**. 5, **12**. 3, **16**. 21; 1 Kings **14**. 15, 23; 2 Kings **18**. 4; 2 Chron. **31**. 1; Isa. **27**. 9; and Micah **5**. 14. It is introduced in connection with the worship of Baal in Jud. **3**. 7, **6**. 25, 26 (where we are plainly told that it was made of *wood*, and that it used to be set up by the altar of Baal); see also 1 Kings **16**. 33 and **18**. 19. In 2 Kings **17**. 16 the people are described as making a grove, and as worshipping not only Baal, but also 'all the host of heaven;' so in 2 Kings **21**. 3 and **23**. 4, where we read of 'the vessels that were made for Baal, and for the grove, and for all the host of heaven.' See also 2 Chron. **33**. 3.

In 1 Kings **15**. 13 we read that Maachah made 'an idol (or "horrible thing") *in* a grove,' or rather '*for* a grove.' The same change in the rendering is needed in the parallel passage, 2 Chron. **15**. 16, the preposition in each case being la (ל), 'for,' not ba (ב), 'in.'

The question now recurs, What was this Asherah, which we have rendered grove? It was certainly not what we call a grove of trees, nor was it a single tree planted in the earth,[1] but it was an object made of wood, and set up by the side of an altar dedicated to Baal, and in some cases in company with a statue or pillar representing Baal. Gesenius, who is an authority on all matters connected with Phœnician and Canaanite worship, considers that Asherah was a goddess, identical with Ashtoreth (Astarte, or Venus).[2]

It appears not unlikely that grove-worship was a form of that tree-worship which has been found almost all over the world, and which drew its origin from the trees in the garden of Eden. The Asherah was probably, in the first instance, a representation of *the tree of life*, though the traditional idea soon passed away, and was probably superseded by the idea of the reproductive powers of nature. We cannot now say in what form it was, but it may possibly have been in the form of a *cross*, which would be the simplest artificial symbol for a tree, and which appears to have been adopted for this purpose in various countries and in ages long anterior to Christianity.[3] Assyrian sculptures afford elaborate representations of

---

[1] It is hardly ever said to be '*planted*;' usually it is described as '*made*.'

[2] The Tel el-Amarna tablets show that he was right, except in identifying Asherah, the South Canaanite goddess of fertility, with Astarte or Asrati (*Sayce*).

[3] See this subject discussed at length in Fergusson's work on Tree and Serpent Worship; see also the article on 'Pre-Christian Crosses' in the *Edinburgh Review*, October 1869.

this tree of life. Compare 2 Kings 21. 7, where we read of a 'graven image of the grove,' literally, 'the likeness the grove,' evidently a symbolic figure. In 2 Kings 23. 7 we are told of certain women who 'wove hangings for the grove,' and who did the work in 'the houses of the Sodomites.' These 'hangings' are literally 'houses,' and were perhaps shrines or coverings for the symbolical figure.

§ 6. *The High Place.*

Another object connected with idolatrous worship is the High Place. The word used for it is **Bamah** (במה, Ass. *bamahi*). The usual rendering in the LXX is ὑψηλός, high; but we also find οἶκος, a house; ἄλσος, a grove; βοῦνος, a hill; εἴδωλον, an idol; ἁμαρτία, sin (Micah 1. 5); θυσιαστήριον and βωμός, an altar; ἔρημος, a desert; στήλη, a pillar; λίθοι, stones; ἔδαφος, a foundation; τράχηλος, a neck; and ἰσχύς (Deut. 32. 13), strength.

The word appears without reference to idolatry in Deut. 32. 13, 'He made him ride on the high places of the earth,' where it is only used in a general sense. The same, perhaps, may be said of its usage in Deut. 33. 29. In Job 9. 8, the 'waves' of the sea are literally 'High Places.' A high place is spoken of in 1 Sam. 10. 13, where it seems to signify a hill, as also in 2 Sam. 1. 19, 25, 22. 34. See also Num. 21. 28, 22. 41; Ps. 18. 33, 78. 69; Isa. 15. 2, 16. 12; Jer. 48. 35; Amos 4. 13, 7. 9; Micah 1. 3, 5; Hab. 3. 19; with regard to some of these passages, it may be doubtful whether the word is used in its general or special sense.

In the days of Solomon (1 Kings 3. 2, 3), we are told that 'the people sacrificed in high places, because there was no house built;' and when he went to Gibeon, 'where was a great high place,' he offered a thousand burnt offerings upon the altar.[1] Here the Lord appeared to him, but did not rebuke him for what he had done. At that time the permanent temple was not built, and consequently full liberty was allowed. Shortly afterwards, however, Solomon 'built high places for Chemosh and for Molech,' the idols of Moab and Ammon, and then 'the Lord was angry with him' (1 Kings 11. 7). See Lev. 26. 30; Num. 33. 52. Jeroboam also made 'houses of high places' (1 Kings 12. 31), with priests, altars, and golden calves. These priests of the high places burned incense on the altar at Bethel, and were denounced by the man of

---

[1] In the parallel passage (2 Chron. 1. 3) it is stated that the tabernacle of the congregation was at Gibeon, and that the high place was connected with it.

God who came out of Judah. The building and use of high places with statues and groves now became very common in both kingdoms. See 1 Kings 14. 23, 22. 43 ; 2 Kings 12. 3, 16. 4 (Ahaz 'sacrificed and burnt incense in the high places, and on the hills, and under every green tree'), 17. 9, 29, 32. Asa,[1] Jehosaphat, and afterwards Hezekiah, removed them, as far as possible, but Jehoram and Manasseh rebuilt them (2 Kings 21. 3). Josiah again destroyed them, but the passion for these idolatrous rites was not easily to be rooted out. They appear to have been sometimes natural eminences, and sometimes constructed of earth or stones ; occasionally they seem to have been used as altars ; at other times they were surmounted by the **Asherah.** In the discussion on *Pre-Christian crosses* already referred to (see p. 309, note 3), it is stated that the old emblems of the tree of life were constantly placed on hills or mounds. This may throw some light on the origin of the High Place.[2]

§ 7. *The Teraphim.*

The **Teraphim** (תרפים, Ass. *tarpu*, a 'spectre') have now to be noticed. This word, which is only used in the plural number, is not understood by the lexicographer or the antiquarian. The LXX gives various renderings, namely, εἴδωλον, idol; γλυπτόν, carved object ; δῆλα, manifestations ; ἀποφθεγγόμενοι, revealers ; κενοταφία, empty tombs. The **teraphim** appear to be material objects regarded as a sort of 'fetish' or talisman, and consulted in emergencies. They are first met with in Gen. 31. 19, 34, 35. Laban calls them his '*gods*,' but the inspired writer only calls them '**teraphim.**' In Jud. 17. 5, they are connected with the images, with 'a house of gods and an ephod,' but they are evidently distinct objects, see 18. 14, 17, 18, 20. In 1 Sam. 15. 23, teraphim are parallel with divination (compare Zech. 10. 2). In 1 Sam. 19. 13, 16, they are put in the bed to occupy the place of David. In Ezek. 21. 21 they are mentioned as used by the King of Babylon in divining. This fact, coupled with the use of these objects in the house of Laban, would lead us to look for a Chaldean origin for them.

---

[1] Asa removed the high places from *Judah* (2 Chron. 14. 5), but not from *Israel* (15. 17).

[2] When riding through the country of the Ammonites in 1860, the writer was struck with the great number of rude cromlechs which are visible on the hillsides. If these were for religious purposes, as seems most probable, may they not have been of the nature of high places ?

CHAPTER XXVIII.

ETERNAL, AGE TO COME.

§ 1. *Various Words marking Duration.*

THE O. T. words representing *duration*, and their Greek equivalents, call for careful consideration in consequence of the fact that the revelation of man's future destiny must depend to some extent upon their accurate interpretation.

One of the most frequent words used to mark duration is 'A̅d (עַד, Ass. *adu*), which is represented in English by the words eternity, ever, everlasting, evermore, of old, perpetually, world without end. This word is once used where there is a reference to *past* duration of a limited extent, namely, in Job 20. 4, 'Knowest thou not this of old, since man was placed upon earth.' It is used of a state of being which is at once past, present, and future, with regard to God who inhabits eternity (κατοικῶν τὸν αἰῶνα), Isa. 57. 15. It is applied to the endless duration of God's reign, Exod. 15. 18, Ps. 10. 16, where the LXX is very strong (εἰς τὸν αἰῶνα καὶ ἐπ᾽ αἰῶνα καὶ ἔτι); to the throne of God, Ps. 45. 6; to the Messianic kingdom, Ps. 89. 29; to the duration of God's righteousness, praise, and commandments, Ps. 111. 3, 8, 10. It is also used of the duration of national or individual confidence in God, *e.g.* Ps. 48. 14, 'This God is our God for ever and ever (εἰς τὸν αἰῶνα καὶ εἰς τὸν αἰῶνα τοῦ αἰῶνος), he shall be our guide unto death' (εἰς τοὺς αἰῶνας); Ps. 52. 8, 'I will hope in God's mercy for ever;' Ps. 119. 44, 'I will keep thy law continually, even for ever and ever' (διαπαντός, εἰς τὸν αἰῶνα καὶ εἰς τὸν αἰῶνα τοῦ αἰῶνος). The same word occurs in the title of the Messiah, as 'the everlasting Father,' *i.e.* the source of everlasting life, Isa. 9. 6; see also Ps. 148. 6, 104. 5.

Again, the term is applied to the continued existence of the people of God, and to the personal confidence which they may feel in God, whether here or hereafter:—Ps. 9. 18, 'The expectation of the poor shall not perish for ever' (εἰς τὸν αἰῶνα); Ps. 22. 26, 'Your heart shall live for ever' (εἰς αἰῶνα αἰῶνος); Ps. 37. 27–29, 'Depart from evil, and do good; and dwell for evermore (εἰς αἰῶνα αἰῶνος). For the Lord loveth righteousness, and forsaketh not his saints; they are preserved for ever (εἰς τὸν αἰῶνα): but the wicked shall be cut off. The righteous shall inherit the land, and dwell therein for ever' (εἰς αἰῶνα αἰῶνος); Isa. 45. 17, 'Ye shall not be ashamed nor confounded world without end' (ἕως τοῦ αἰῶνος καὶ ἔτι).

Lastly, it is used with reference to the case of evil-doers, whether nations or individuals. Of Assher and Eber it is said that they 'shall perish for ever' (Num. 24. 20, 24). Ps. 9. 5, 'Thou hast put out their names for ever and ever' (εἰς τὸν αἰῶνα καὶ εἰς αἰῶνα αἰῶνος); Ps. 83. 17, 'Let them be confounded and troubled for ever' (εἰς αἰῶνα αἰῶνος); Ps. 92. 7, 'The wicked shall be destroyed for ever' (ἐξολοθρευθῶσιν εἰς τὸν αἰῶνα τοῦ αἰῶνος).

Netsach (נצח), with a preposition (ל), is rendered always, constantly, ever, perpetual, and also in its original meanings of strength and victory. It is usually rendered by the LXX εἰς τέλος, unto completion, but sometimes εἰς νῖκος, unto victory. It signifies completeness, and might usually be translated 'utterly.'

It is used of God not keeping His anger for ever (Ps. 103. 9); and of the pleasures which are at His right hand for evermore (Ps. 16. 11). God is several times appealed to not to forget His people or to be absent from them for ever (Ps. 13. 1, 44. 23, 74. 1, 10, 19, 79. 5, 89. 46).

Netsach occurs in Job several times, either with reference to the utter destruction brought upon man (that is, upon the outer man) by God, or to the final deliverance which is to be obtained by the godly. See Job 4. 20, 14. 20, 20. 7, 23. 7, 36. 7.

No man, says the Psalmist, can cause his fellow-men to live for ever, *i.e.* can ensure him against death (Ps. 49. 9). The destructions of the wicked, that is, their evil machinations against the godly, are described as having 'come to a perpetual end,' or, in other words, as being utterly frustrated (Ps. 9. 6). **Netsach** is also used of the desolation of Edom and Babylon (Amos 1. 11; Jer. 50. 39).

This word occurs in a slightly different form in the Hebrew heading of several Psalms. The LXX uniformly renders it εἰς τὸ τέλος; the A. V. has 'to the chief musician.' Perhaps the real meaning is that the Psalm is one of victory, and to be sung with emphasis.

Three times in the N. T. we read that he that endureth to the end (εἰς τέλος) shall be saved. In 1 Thess. 2. 16 we are reminded of Ps. 9. 6, for we read that 'wrath has come upon them utterly.'

The phrase εἰς νῖκος occurs only twice in the N. T., namely, in Matt. 12. 20, where Isa. 42. 3 is quoted, and in 1 Cor. 15. 54, where the quotation is from Isa. 25. 8. It is curious that in these two places the Hebrew le-netsach is found, but not the phrase εἰς νῖκος in the LXX, the quotation being in each place a new translation from the Hebrew.

Tamid (תמיד) marks continuity or perpetuity. It is usually applied to the permanence of the Mosaic ritual through the history of the Hebrew nation. The LXX generally renders it διαπαντός, but occasionally διὰ τέλους. It is used of the shewbread (Exod. 25. 30), of the lamp (27. 20), of the signet of holiness (28. 38), of the pillar of the cloud and fire (Num. 9. 16), of the 'daily' sacrifice (Dan. 12. 11), of God's eye resting on the land of Israel (Deut. 11. 12), of the sustenance afforded to Mephibosheth (2 Sam. 9. 10), of the constant realisation of the presence of God—'I have set the Lord always before me' (Ps. 16. 8), 'Mine eyes are ever unto the Lord' (Ps. 25. 15); of the constant remembrance of sin—'My sin is ever before me' (Ps. 51. 3); of devotional feelings and conduct (Ps. 34. 1, 38. 17, 71. 6, 119. 44).

God says of Jerusalem, 'I have graven thee upon the palms of my hands, thy walls are continually before me' (Isa. 49. 16); and of the godly man it is said, 'The Lord shall guide thee continually.' Lastly, of the heavenly Jerusalem it is predicted, 'Thy gates shall be open continually, they shall not be shut day nor night' (Isa. 60. 11).

The word διαπαντὸς occurs ten times in the N. T. Two of these passages are quotations from the O. T., namely, Acts 2. 25 and Rom. 11. 10, from Ps. 16. 8 and 69. 23, in which **Tamid** is used. In other passages it is used of the continuous service of God (Luke 24. 53; Acts 10. 2; Heb. 9. 6, 13. 15). It is also used in Matt. 18. 10, where we read of Christ's little ones, that their angels in heaven continually behold the face of God.

Orec (ארך, Ass. *arahu*) denotes length without any reference to limit. It is translated 'for ever' in Ps. 23. 6, 'I will dwell in his house for ever;' and Ps. **93**. 5, 'Holiness becometh thine house for ever.'   In each case the LXX has εἰς μακρότητα ἡμέρων.

Dor (דּור, Ass. *duru*) signifies a generation.   In Ps. **10**. 6, 'I shall never be in adversity,' the words are literally, 'I shall not be in adversity from generation to generation;' and so in Ps. **77**. 8 ('Doth the Lord's promise fail for evermore?').   The word **Dor**, like the Greek γενεὰ and the English generation, is often used in a large and indefinite sense, sometimes perhaps referring to an age or century, as when the Lord promised to Abraham that his seed should be rescued 'in the fourth generation' (Gen. **15**. 16).

Dor is applied to the continuous covenant made between God and Noah (Gen. **9**. 12), εἰς γενεὰς αἰωνίους; to the remembrance of God's name or memorial (Exod. **3**. 15, Ps. **9**. 7, **102**. 12, **135**. 13); to the feeling which was to be kept alive against the Amalekites (Exod. **17**. 16); to the permanence of God's thoughts (Ps. **33**. 11), mercy and truth (**40**. 11), wrath (**85**. 5), existence (**102**. 24), and dominion (**145**. 13, Dan. **4**. 3); to the judgment of Edom (Isa. **34**. 10), and to the desolation of Babylon (Isa. **13**. 20).

A parallel expression is used in Luke **1**. 50 and Eph. **3**. 21, with regard to the continuance of God's mercy and of the glory which is to be ascribed to Him in Christ Jesus.

The word **Tsemithuth** (צְמִיתֻת) is rendered 'for ever' in Lev. **25**. 23, 30, where reference is made to the continuous possession of land; but in the LXX we find εἰς βεβαίωσιν, an expression which is preserved in the N. T. in Heb. **6**. 16, where we read that an oath is 'for confirmation.'   Perhaps there is here a special reference to the continuity of the promise through the oath sworn to Abraham.

Kedem (קֶדֶם, Ass. *qudmu*), which means that which is ancient, is used in Deut. **33**. 27, of the eternal God; in Prov. **8**. 22, of God's 'works of old' (πρὸ τοῦ αἰῶνος); and in Hab. **1**. 12, of God's existence from everlasting (ἀπ' ἀρχῆς).   The Greek rendering adopted in the last passage is often found in the N. T.

Yom (יוֹם, Ass. *yumu*), day, is used in the plural number in a great variety of senses, and is rendered in the A. V. always, continuance, daily, yearly, ever, perpetually.   In almost all passages where duration is implied, the Greek rendering is πάσας τὰς ἡμέρας, which has been adopted in the N. T. in Matt. **28**. 20, 'I am with you always.'

This phrase is applied to periodical or recurrent rites, such as the lament for Jephthah's daughter (Jud. **11**. 40); the feast in

Shiloh (Jud. **21**. 19); the worship in Shiloh (1 Sam. **1**. 3, 21, **2**. 19, **20**. 6); and to the offering of sacrifices (Job **1**. 5, Amos **4**. 4).

It is used of the permanence of man's duty (Deut. **5**. 29); of God's promises (Deut. **6**. 24), and of His threats (Deut. **28**. 33); of the continuance of evil in the heart (Gen. **6**. 5), and of wicked devices (Ps. **52**. 1). It is also used of permanent relations between man and man, or between nation and nation, *e.g.* between Saul and David (1 Sam. **18**. 29), Rehoboam and Jeroboam (2 Chron. **12**. 15), David and Achish (1 Sam. **28**. 2), Hiram and David (1 Kings **5**. 1). See also Jer. **35**. 19, **31**. 36, **32**. 39.

The word 'Eth (עֵת, Ass. *ittu*), which marks a season or opportunity, is used of duration in Job **27**. 10, Ps. **10**. 5, Prov. **6**. 14, **8**. 30, and Eccles. **9**. 8. The LXX renders it ἐν παντὶ καιρῷ, 'on every occasion.' Compare Eph. **6**. 18.

§ 2. *The Word 'Olam.*

No word is so largely used to express duration as **'Olam** (עוֹלָם). It has twice been rendered **long**, namely, in Eccles. **12**. 5, where we read of a man going 'to his **long** home' (εἰς οἶκον αἰῶνος αὐτοῦ); and Isa. **42**. 14, 'Shall I **long** be silent?' (ἀεί). Five times it is rendered '**always**,' namely, Gen. **6**. 3, 'My spirit shall not **always** (εἰς τὸν αἰῶνα) strive with man;' 1 Chron. **16**. 15, 'Let us **always** remember his covenant;' Job **7**. 16, 'I shall not live **always**' (*i.e.* in this world); Ps. **119**. 112, 'I have inclined my heart to perform thy statutes **always**;' also in Jer. **20**. 17.

It is translated '**perpetual**' with reference to the covenant made with Noah (Gen. **9**. 12), to the priesthood of the house of **Levi** (Exod. **29**. 9), to the Sabbath as a sign of God's covenant (Exod. **31**. 16), and to various other religious rites. It is used with a negative in several passages, *e.g.* in 2 Sam. **12**. 10, of the sword **never** departing from David's house; in Ps. **15**. 5, of the godly man **never** falling. See also Ps. **55**. 22; Isa. **14**. 20, **25**. 2; Joel **2**. 26.

In Isa. **60**. 15 '**Olam** is rendered **eternal**, 'I will make of thee an **eternal** joy.' It is rendered **for ever** in a large number of passages, *e.g.* Gen. **13**. 15, of the land being given to Abraham; Exod. **21**. 6, of the slave serving his master **for ever** (εἰς τὸν αἰῶνα). See also Ps. **12**. 7, **29**. 10, **61**. 4, **73**. 26, **81**. 15, **112**. 6, **125**. 2; Eccles. **3**. 14; Isa. **40**. 8, **51**. 6; Dan. **7**. 18, **12**. 3.

Some passages where '**Olam** is rendered αἰώνιος, and used with reference to the wicked, may here be cited :—Ps. **78**. 66, 'He hath given them **perpetual** reproach;' Jer. **18**. 16, 'He hath made their land desolate and a **perpetual** hissing;' **23**. 40, 'Perpetual dishonour;' **51**. 39, 57, 'I will make them drunken, that they may rejoice, and sleep a **perpetual** sleep;' Ezek. **35**. 5, 9, 'Because thou hast had a **perpetual** hatred, . . . I will make thee a per-petual desolation;' compare Zeph. **2**. 9. In Dan. **12**. 2, the word is applied not only to **everlasting** life, but also to **everlasting** contempt, which shall be the lot of some after the resurrection.

In the passages quoted, which are a considerable proportion and a fair specimen of the whole, the LXX rendering is usually αἰώνιος or εἰς τὸν αἰῶνα; these Greek phrases, therefore, when they reappear in the N. T., must be interpreted in accordance with the usage of the word **'Olam**. They give a conception which, though negative, is sufficiently clear. Eternity is **endlessness**; and this idea is only qualified by the nature of the object to which it is applied, or by the direct word of God. When applied to things physical, it is used in accordance with the revealed truth that the heaven and earth shall pass away, and it is limited by this truth. When applied to God, it is used in harmony with the truth that He is essentially and absolutely existent, and that as He is the *causa causarum* and without beginning, so in the very nature of things it must be held that no cause can ever put an end to His existence. When the word is applied to man's future destiny after the resurrection, we naturally give it the sense of *endlessness* without any limitation, except such as the post-resurrection state shall involve; and this is not revealed.

§ 3. *Use of the Word Eternal in the N. T.*

The use of the words αἰών and αἰώνιος in the N. T. deserves careful attention. In a number of passages our Lord speaks of 'this age' (αἰών), of its cares (Matt. **13**. 22), of its end (**13**. 39, 40, 49, **24**. 3, 28. 20), of its children (Luke **20**. 34). So St. Paul speaks of conformity to this age (Rom. **12**. 2), of the seeker of this age (1 Cor. **1**. 20), of its vaunted wisdom (1 Cor. **2**. 6, 3. 18), of its rulers (1 Cor. **2**. 6, 8), of its god (2 Cor. **4**. 4), of its being a present evil age (Gal. **1**. 4), of the age of the world (Eph. **2**. 2), and of those who love it (2 Tim. **4**. 10).

In John **9**. 32 it is said, 'Since the world began,' &c. We here find ἐκ τοῦ αἰῶνος, which points backwards, as εἰς τὸν αἰῶνα

does forwards. We find ἀπ᾽ αἰῶνος in the same sense in Acts
3. 21, 15. 18, Eph. 3. 9, and Col. 1. 26; also πρὸ τῶν αἰώνων in
1 Cor. 2. 7.

There are a few passages which speak in a very special way of
an αἰών or *age to come*, e.g. Mark 10. 30, Luke 18. 30, 20. 35; and
of its powers, Heb. 6. 5. Some interpreters connect these passages
with the Millennium. In Eph. 2. 7 the Apostle speaks in the plural
number of the *ages* to come.

In other passages we have the expressions εἰς τὸν αἰῶνα, εἰς τοὺς
αἰῶνας, ἕως αἰῶνος, εἰς τοὺς αἰῶνας τῶν αἰώνων; see, e.g., Luke 1. 33, 55;
John 12. 34, 13. 8; Rom. 9. 5; Gal. 1. 5; 1 Tim. 1. 17. Some translators have rendered these passages literally, and without respect to
their usage in the LXX (e.g. 'unto *the age*,' 'unto *the ages*,' &c.). In
1 Tim. 1. 17, God is called 'the King of ages' (A. V. King Eternal);
whilst in Heb. 1. 2, 11. 3, He is said to have made 'the ages'
(A. V. the worlds). The rendering of the A. V. is no doubt right
in the first case, and probably in the second also. Ages and worlds
bear the same relation to one another as time and space do, and the
process of creating worlds was the means of bringing ages into
being.[1]

In 1 Cor. 10. 11 we read that even upon those who lived in
apostolic days the ends of the ages had come (A. V. ends of the
world); and in Heb. 9. 26 we are told that Christ has come once in
the completion of the ages (A. V. end of the world) to put away sin.
The word *age* is here thought to answer rather to the sense in
which the word *dispensation* is now used; and a more literal rendering would have been preferable.

In 2 Pet. 3. 18 we meet with the expression εἰς ἡμέραν αἰῶνος,
to the Day of the Age (A. V. for ever), by which we understand the
dawn of eternity.

The adjective αἰώνιος is used more than forty times in the N. T.
with respect to *eternal life*, which is regarded partly as a present
gift, partly as a promise for the future. It is also applied to God's
endless existence in Rom. 16. 26; to the endless efficacy of Christ's
atonement in Heb. 9. 12, 13. 20; and to past ages in Rom. 16. 25,
2 Tim. 1. 9, Titus 1. 2.

---

[1] 'Olam has been occasionally rendered *world* in the A. V., as in Eccles. 3. 11,
where, however, some would render the words, 'He hath put (a conception of)
eternity in their hearts.' It is curious that several translators have rendered the
last verse of the 139th Psalm, 'Lead me in the *way of the world.*' In later Hebrew
'Olam was constantly used in this sense.

This word is used with reference to *eternal fire*, Matt. **18**. 8, **25**. 41, Jude **7** ; *eternal punishment*, Matt. **25**. 46 ; *eternal judgment* or *condemnation*, Mark **3**. 29, Heb. **6**. 2 ; *eternal destruction*, 2 Thess. **1**. 9. The word in these passages implies *finality*, and apparently signifies that when these judgments shall be inflicted, the time of probation, change, or the chance of retrieving one's fortune, will have gone by absolutely and for ever. We understand very little about the future, about the relation of human life to the rest of existence, and about the moral weight of unbelief, as viewed in the light of eternity. If, on the one hand, it is wrong to add to God's word, on the other we must not take away from it ; and if we stagger under the doctrine of eternal punishment as it is set forth in Scripture, we must be content to wait, cleaving to the Gospel of God's love in Christ, while acknowledging that there is a dark background which we are unable to comprehend.

INDEX OF SUBJECTS

INDEX OF HEBREW WORDS

INDEX OF GREEK WORDS

INDEX OF TEXTS

Z

THE END